MONEY
and
POWER

SIR VINCE CABLE was MP for Twickenham for 20 years and is former leader of the Liberal Democrats. He was Secretary of State for Business, Innovation and Skills and President of the Board of Trade in the five years of the Coalition government from 2010 to 2015. Before entering Parliament he had a variety of roles as an economist in government, international organisations, academia and business, latterly as Chief Economist at Shell. He is Visiting Professor in Practice at the London School of Economics and the bestselling author of *The Storm: The World Economic Crisis and What It Means*. He has also published *After the Storm: The World Economy and Britain's Economic Future* and the autobiography *Free Radical*.

MONEY
and
POWER

The 16 World Leaders
Who Changed Economics

VINCE CABLE

Atlantic Books
London

First published in hardback and trade paperback in Great Britain
in 2021 by Atlantic Books, an imprint of Atlantic Books Ltd.

This paperback edition published in 2022.

2 4 6 8 10 9 7 5 3 1

A CIP catalogue record for this book
is available from the British Library.

Paperback ISBN: 978 1 78649 513 6
E-book ISBN: 978 1 78649 512 9

Printed and bound in Great Britain
by Clays Ltd, Elcograf S.p.A.

Atlantic Books
An imprint of Atlantic Books Ltd
Ormond House
26–27 Boswell Street
London
WC1N 3JZ

www.atlantic-books.co.uk

'The ideas of economists and political philosophers are more powerful than is commonly understood. Indeed, the world is ruled by little else. Practical men, who believe themselves quite exempt from any intellectual influences, are usually the slaves of some defunct economist.'

John Maynard Keynes, *The General Theory of Employment, Interest and Money* (1936)

'Almost every political question has an economic aspect and almost every economic question has a political aspect.'

Charles P. Kindleberger, *Power and Money* (1970)

Contents

Introduction: Politicians and the Politics of Economics   1

1   Hamilton: The Economic Founding Father   21

2   Peel: Free Trade   37

3   Bismarck: The Economics of 'Iron and Blood'   51

4   Lenin: From War Communism to State Capitalism   65

5   Roosevelt: The Keynesian Revolution Without Keynes   79

6   Erhard: The Social Market and Ordoliberalism   99

7   Erlander: The Social Democratic Model Made Real   117

8   Perón: Peronism and Economic Populism   135

9   Park: The Development State and Hypergrowth   159

10   Lee: The Eclectic Economics of Lee Kuan Yew   179

11   Thatcher: Thatcherism and Its Cousin, Reaganomics   199

12   Deng: China's Economic Architect   221

13   Manmohan Singh: The Quiet Reformer   245

14   Balcerowicz: Big Bang Theory and Practice   269

15   Abe: Japan Pioneers Abenomics   289

16   Trump: Trumponomics, Economic Nationalism
and Pluto-populism   313

Conclusion: Sixteen Politicians: Sixteen Varieties
of Economics   333

Acknowledgements   349

Notes   351

Index   377

Politicians and the Politics of Economics

Economic policy making is not just a technical matter for economists. Through the actions of political leaders, it has the power to change millions of people's lives for better or worse. It is at the centre of the decision making that every world leader needs to make. And it defines the legacy they leave behind.

Political leadership matters in economic policy. Policy may have its origins in economic theory and analysis of past experience. But it is politicians who put it into practice, who oversee it and who are judged by its results. None of the current leaders of the USA, China, Japan, India or the main European countries are professional economists but they all defined their leadership objectives largely in economic terms. They are now being tested and judged by their performance. This is even more true when the world is reeling from the economic fallout of the biggest pandemic for over a century.

Economic performance may be just one of several claims on political leadership. National survival, physical safety, order, social cohesion, personal freedoms: all matter to various degrees. However, for most of the post-war era, the priority has been the raising of living standards and economic wellbeing.

In practice, a lot of economic policy making is delegated to unelected officials and made on the advice of technical experts, like central bankers, regulators and trade negotiators. Economic outcomes will often depend on market forces rather than political preferences. But it is the politicians who set the framework of public debate and its tone; who set the level of expectations; who pass laws and regulations; and who represent national authority in relation to the wider international system. And their political power goes with responsibility for its success or failure.

Most political leaders complete periods in office having made little more than a few, historically inconsequential tweaks to established policy that was working well enough already – or perhaps riding an economic trend beyond their control. But some have been highly consequential, indeed transformative. These are the individuals on whom I wish to focus.

In recent years, one political figure has emerged – Donald Trump – who could certainly be regarded as transformative, though not necessarily in a positive way. He set out a distinctive approach to economic policy. At its heart has been economic nationalism and trade protection, a fundamental change from the economic leadership role that American Presidents have adopted for a century. The Covid-19 pandemic, in its early stages, reinforced that approach – one which his supporters have dubbed Trumponomics. Now that Trump has been defeated and his agenda rejected by the American voters, it is tempting to regard Trumponomics as an aberration. Time will tell, but there is plenty of evidence that the economic nationalism he has unleashed will endure. Indeed, the Biden administration has continued his 'America First', protectionist trade policy.

Trump isn't the first politician to be credited with a disruptive and personalized approach to economics. Margaret Thatcher gave us Thatcherite economic policy and her US contemporary gave us Reaganomics. The Japanese Prime Minister, Shinzō Abe, who presided over an unorthodox approach to the Japanese economy, gave birth to Abenomics. The affectation of personalized branding probably originates with Rogernomics, used to describe the radical change of direction taken by Roger Douglas when he was Finance Minister for the New Zealand Labour government in the early 1980s.

But even before this recent fashion, the association of a particular approach to economics with political leaders is well established. The economic transformation of modern China is attributed to Deng Xiaoping. Before that, the post-war German *Wirtschaftswunder* – or economic miracle – is credited to the work done by the then Chancellor Ludwig Erhard. F.D. Roosevelt's New Deal represented a decisive break with the economic policies which preceded it even if it was not, as often claimed, an early example of Keynesian economics. The economic tradition in the US of strong federal government intervention to protect domestic industry has long been described as Hamiltonian. The British commitment to free trade has been commonly attributed to Robert Peel and his abolition of the Corn Laws. Populist economic movements can acquire their own 'ism': Peronism has been a dominant theme in Argentine life for most of the last eighty years.

These examples raise a bigger question about the links between economics and politics: between economic policies and the politicians who gave effect to them. The history of economics is commonly treated as the history of economists and their ideas; rarely as the history of their application and the politicians who applied them.[1] Such an approach is limiting at best.

I was prompted to write this book by the experience of having spent over fifty years at the interface between politics and economics: as a British MP, then Cabinet Minister, preceded by years as a candidate, campaigner and pamphleteer; and as an economist carrying out research or teaching economics in universities and think tanks, or advising companies and governments on economic matters. I saw enough of each to want to understand the connections better.

Specifically, I wanted to understand the politicians who brought about some of the big economic transformations in modern history: the adoption in practice of the idea of free trade; the use of government intervention to support industrialization; the attempts to counter mass unemployment; the reconstruction of economies destroyed by war; the creation of new models of capitalism, such as 'social democracy' or 'state capitalism'; the attempts to achieve rapid economic development in poor economies; the attempt to create a communist economic model and latterly the attempts to dismantle communism. I am interested in the key political figures who drove these changes; what motivated them; which economists or schools of economic thought they drew upon and how they found them. But more broadly, I want to highlight a forgotten history: of the exchange and application of ideas which happen at the nexus of politics and economics.

From time immemorial, organized societies have had their politics and have also been concerned with economic questions around trade, monetary exchange and increasing wealth for personal gain or glorification or wider societal benefits. Some embryonic trade theory was recorded in Ancient Greece.[2] Genghis Khan is said to have had an early understanding of globalization and a 'borderless world', though it is difficult to judge this claim in the absence of any written source. Medieval monarchs and Chinese emperors alike had rules and principles governing the issue of coinage, the operation of markets for essential consumer goods and payment for labour. Some of the standard texts of the history of economic thought trace modern thinking about economic matters to seventeenth- and eighteenth-century Britain and pre-revolutionary France.[3] However, in this book, I have decided to begin around the end of the eighteenth century and the start of the nineteenth century when there was a step-change in the sophistication of economies with the emergence of more complex, industrializing societies, and when recognizably modern, democratic institutions became apparent.

Politics and economics converge and sometimes collide when politicians feel that they have to promise and deliver some combination of improved living standards, lower inflation, lower taxes, better public services, fiscal rectitude and sometimes a cocktail of different – and perhaps incompatible – objectives. There are also occasions when the consensus of economists' advice runs directly counter to what is politically attractive, or deliverable: insisting on fiscal and/or monetary discipline when this produces unpopular 'austerity'; opposing controls on rent, wages, prices and foreign exchange transactions; promoting user charges (for example, tuition fees, road charges or payments for health services); applying the 'polluter pays principle' to energy use; insisting that there is no such thing as a fixed supply of employment when politicians wish to 'save jobs'; advocating the superiority of taxes on land (or property) rather than income; expressing a preference for free trade rather than 'protecting' domestic producers. The politician's wish to hold or retain power may well lead to promises which are attractive to voters – like an abundance of free things – but which cannot in reality be delivered without help from the supernatural. Magic money trees grow easily in many soils. 'Good' politics and 'good' economics coexist less frequently.

There has, on the other hand, long been an understanding that the two cannot be separated. Adam Smith wrote *An Inquiry into the Nature and Causes of the Wealth of Nations* but also *The Theory of Moral Sentiments* which explored the ethical – and essentially political – issues behind economic judgements.[4] Karl Marx insisted that the political system and the workings of the economy were interwoven and both subordinate to class interests.[5] Charles Kindleberger was one of the few economists to weave together a narrative of economic history which incorporated the politics of national sovereignty, imperialism and war.[6] There is, now, an emerging economics, or political economy, which tries to incorporate an ethical dimension and incorporates the role of civil society and the role played by 'good citizens'.

But there are also differences of approach. Economists tend to be concerned with 'positive' statements: the description of often complex sets of relationships which explain why 'if x, then y'. Critics will argue that this pretence at scientific method often confuses correlation and causality, though there are quantitative techniques to help distinguish the two. A generation of students has been brought up on various editions of Paul Samuelson's *Foundations of Economic Analysis*, which started by distinguishing positive economics from 'normative' judgements about what ought to be and what is desirable: the language of politics.[7] A classic example of the difference is provided by another economics Nobel Laureate, James Meade, whose textbooks on *The Theory of International Economic Policy* were classics of positive economics, but who also wrote a narrative of what economically literate policy makers should be doing: *The Intelligent Radical's Guide to Economic Policy*.[8]

That is not to say that politics (including a 'normative' approach to economics) is simply a sounding off of likes and dislikes; politics is about how to reconcile different demands and interests, conciliate between opposing views and establish an agreed basis for the distribution of rewards (or hardship). Bernard Crick observes: 'There is no end to the praises that can be sung of politics. In politics, not in economics, is found the creative dialectic of opposites.'[9]

I try to pursue the links between economics and politics through individual politicians. Carlyle once observed that 'history is the study of great men' and I adopt that approach. It can reasonably be argued, however, that the study of 'great men' (and women) is to trivialize economic history: to reduce it to the world of 'good' and 'bad' kings in the manner of *1066 and All That*.[10] It ignores the power of technological change, demographics and migration, nutrition and medicine, changing social mores and popular movements. E.H. Carr's *What is History?* represents that austere approach to history which minimizes the contribution of famous individuals.[11] And much of the critical commentary on the market-based transformations of the last few decades tends to dismiss individual leaders as mere flotsam on a tide of 'neo-liberalism'.

Yet it is possible to overdo the impersonal. When future generations look back on the twentieth century with the same detachment as we currently see the Middle Ages, it will very likely be a tale of three destructive monsters (Stalin, Hitler and Mao) as well as the less memorable and more anonymous people who helped to create unparalleled prosperity and technological advance in Europe and North America and who lifted poor countries out of centuries of destitution.

The heroes of economic progress include, but are not necessarily, politicians. When the definitive history of the 2008 financial crash and its aftermath comes to be written, the individuals who will stand out from the murk are the unelected technocrats in central banks, notably Ben Bernanke of the US Federal Reserve and, later, Mario Draghi of the European Central Bank. The 'rules-based' international system which evolved in the post-Second World War era and underlies its success has depended on the effectiveness of those who led and steered the General Agreement on Tariffs and Trade (GATT; later the World Trade Organization), the Bretton Woods institutions, the European Commission and numerous regulatory bodies.

And I am struck by the fact that the countries which sit at the top of the league table of human welfare and happiness – Denmark, Finland, Sweden, Norway, the Netherlands, Switzerland, Australia, Canada, New Zealand, and, among developing countries, Botswana and Costa Rica – have generally not produced individual leaders who are credited with their economic and social progress. The 'Scandinavian model', a remarkably successful and stable variant of modern capitalism, has largely depended on low-profile political leaders to design and deliver it.

But the cloak of anonymity does not fit for most of the big economic changes achieved through shifts in policy. For very many countries, certainly today, former US President Bill Clinton's dictum 'It's the economy, stupid' defines the priority issues for their government. Politicians get elected or chosen in large part because of expectations that they can deliver better economic outcomes than their predecessors and their competitors. I use the phrase 'economic outcomes' loosely to refer not just to economic growth and improvement in living standards but to low inflation and low unemployment and the quality and abundance of public services. Economic performance is, of course, only one benchmark; issues of national identity, security, corruption, ethnicity and religion can be important too and, in some cases, transcendent. But economic performance matters.

And success or failure accrues very often to individual political leaders, rightly or wrongly. Some of the world's most significant countries have a – powerful – presidential system (the US, Russia, China, France, Brazil, Mexico, Nigeria, South Africa). And while there are constitutional checks and balances provided by independent institutions like central banks or the scrutiny and law-making power of legislatures, presidential leadership can be decisive in economic matters. Not only that, some parliamentary systems are quasi-presidential with personalized leadership (the UK), and the current appetite for 'strong men' leaders has reinforced the trend (Turkey, India). One of the few countries in which political leaders traditionally enjoyed short and inconspicuous periods in office – Japan – has now produced its own brand of personalized economic policy: Abenomics.

So, who are my individual politicians? Those I have identified could be credited with radical or even revolutionary change in the way economic policy was conducted. Some did so with a clear understanding of what was necessary and willed it to happen; others were facilitators of changes that were becoming necessary, perhaps without fully understanding the significance of what they were doing. Some were democrats operating within parliamentary rules; others were autocratic. Some delivered almost unambiguous benefit; others were divisive or did harm as well as good or created economic systems which were not sustainable. Some were team leaders; others were idiosyncratic individuals. Some were, or claimed to be, economists. But, for the most part, the big economic policy reforms and transformations were carried out by political figures who were not economists and lacked any background in economics: soldiers, lawyers, engineers, businessmen, trade union leaders, aristocrats and revolutionary agitators. Yet they got their ideas from somewhere. Keynes referred rather disparagingly to 'practical men, who... are usually the slaves of some defunct economist'. I will seek to establish who the 'defunct economists' were but emphasize the decisive role of the 'practical men' too.

There is an argument for starting in pre-revolutionary France where one of Louis XIV's key ministers, Jean-Baptiste Colbert, established an economic rationale for active state intervention – dirigisme. Similarly, François Quesnay, an influential figure in the court of Louis' successor, developed not just ideas (including the opposing doctrine of laissez-faire) but changed tax policy to reflect those ideas.[12] The leaders of the French Revolution, then Napoleon, introduced economic reforms which helped to shape economic development. Napoleon swept away many of the monopolistic protection rackets and guilds which were a feature of pre-revolutionary France; encouraged training in engineering; established a framework for monetary control through the Banc de France; and introduced standardized rules and systems, like metrication, helpful to business and trade. But economic transformation was very much incidental rather than central to his mission: that of military conquest.

The same could not be said for Alexander Hamilton in the USA, the first leader I discuss. He was a central figure in the creation of the United States, a politician who thought deeply and wrote clearly about economic policy at the end of the eighteenth century in a way that no politician in the modern sense had ever done before (and few have done since). Many of his ideas for the economic modernization of his newly independent country have had lasting relevance and I seek to establish how crucial they were. How did he acquire his subsequent reputation as an advocate of trade protectionism when his main intellectual inspiration was Adam Smith? How far is it legitimate to see Hamilton as a forerunner of Trump's popular economic nationalism or was he instead a pioneer of evidence-based approach to policy, liberal values (like his then unfashionable disdain for slavery) and an enemy of populism? Thanks mainly to the eponymous Broadway musical and his colourful private life, Hamilton has become a well-known historical figure but his contribution to economics is less well recognized.

The British Prime Minister Robert Peel is known for the adoption of free trade in the battle over Corn Law legislation in the 1840s which moved Britain decisively from a protectionist to a free trading orthodoxy which has remained intact, pretty much, for the subsequent 175 years. Unlike Hamilton, he had no pretensions to original economic thinking and was, first and foremost, a practical politician. How far was his big economic policy achievement a result of the political exigencies of the time and how much was owed to the intellectual heritage of Smith and the economist-politician David Ricardo? How was he able to progress from being a member of a government long regarded as the most reactionary in the last two centuries to a hero of working people; from being the founder of the Conservative Party to a rebel who then split it for two decades; and, crucially, what were the steps which took him from defending protectionism to rejecting and fighting it?

My next choice might be said to be an unusual one: Otto von Bismarck. He was primarily concerned with statecraft and diplomacy, including the use of war to further his central objective: the creation of a powerful, unified German Reich out of Prussia and the miscellany of German states. He showed little or no interest in economic policy. So how did he come to be a key player in a customs union (the Zollverein) together with what is now called 'regulatory convergence', providing a model which later became a central feature of economic integration schemes like the Single Market of the EU? How was he persuaded to switch the new Germany from a free trading liberal economic tradition, which he initially espoused, to protectionism, both for agriculture and to promote industrialization (travelling in an opposite direction from Peel)? And how did a man with a well-advertised contempt for socialism, even in its mildest forms, come to establish the first, albeit crude, welfare state based on social insurance, long before such ideas took root in other major countries including Britain? Although not a politician in the conventional sense – he was authoritarian and had an aristocratic disdain for his social inferiors – he was, by necessity, a politician who had to navigate the treacherous waters of an emerging German democracy. The case of Bismarck illustrates a more general question, which is how far a major economic transformation, like the modernization of nineteenth-century Germany and its emergence as a major, and militaristic, state, can sensibly be attributed to an individual?

An entirely different strain of authoritarian politics came from Lenin, who was the first leader to try to put communist economics into practice. His ideological mentors – such as Marx and Engels, and J.A. Hobson – were long on analysis of the failings of capitalism and imperialism but short on economic remedies. In particular, *The Communist Manifesto* is some way short of being a policy manual. Economic policy in the Bolshevik state was largely made on the hoof, often under conditions of war and civil war, by Lenin and his henchmen such as Trotsky and, later, Stalin. So how did Lenin design the command-and-control central planning system, later developed, brutally, by Stalin? Was the ultimately unsuccessful establishment of central planning Lenin's main economic legacy or was it the pragmatic use of markets, especially to incentivize peasant farmers, in the New Economic Policy which became a template for later Soviet reformers, under Perestroika and, more successfully, in the post-Mao Chinese reforms of Deng Xiaoping?

The inter-war period produced several political figures who contributed massively to the way we think about economic policy. Franklin Delano Roosevelt (FDR) has long been lionized as the first political leader to apply Keynesian economics. I look at the evidence around whether the Roosevelt of the New Deal was indeed influenced by Keynes or macroeconomic policies of a more conventional kind. And who converted him to the use of government borrowing to finance public investment – a countercyclical policy which earned him a big place in the history books? Did the New Deal actually achieve all that much in fighting mass unemployment as against other factors (for example, Hitler and war)? Later, how far was the creation of a rules-based international economic system for trade and finance a legacy of Roosevelt in particular?

My first post-1945 politician is Ludwig Erhard. Unlike my previous examples, he was unusual in being both a politician and an economist. He developed his liberal economic ideas in a think tank during the Nazi era and during wartime and applied them during the early post-war years as German Finance Minister and, then, Chancellor. How far can he be credited with the remarkable economic recovery of post-war Germany? What was his role, alongside Konrad Adenauer – the first post-war Chancellor – in the development of the concept of a 'social market' which combined a strong commitment to the competitive disciplines of the market with a strong state? How far is Erhard responsible for the austere 'ordoliberalism' which has dominated German economic thinking until today and has been carried forward into Europe's economic and monetary union?

A post-war politician who created a quite different economic tradition is Juan Perón, the first of a succession of leaders espousing Peronism. Peronism is sometimes described as archetypal economic populism; but what does 'populism' mean in this context? Its policies have frequently led to economic crisis, even chaos. So why do Argentines keep returning to them? How far does Peronism explain the failure of Argentina to maintain its position – of a century ago – as a rich, near-developed country? How far does Peronist Argentina represent the last attempt to salvage an economic model from fascism, neither capitalist nor communist? Or is it – at least in its modern form – an attempt to apply Catholic ideas of 'social justice'?

A contrasting economic model is Swedish social democracy, which for many years was (and even now is) regarded as the most successful attempt to synthesize the best from capitalist and social-ist systems: an open market economy with a generous welfare state. Georges Pompidou's description of paradise as 'Sweden with sun' captures that optimism. The Swedish social democratic model was not launched on the world by one political leader but evolved, effectively, over four generations of long-serving leaders: Hjalmar Branting, Per Albin Hansson, Tage Erlander and Olof Palme. However, of these, Erlander merits individual attention as the longest lasting and the leader who saw the biggest advances in the Swedish welfare state combined with economic success. I seek to establish the role of the prestigious Stockholm School of Economics and some of its leading members – Gunnar Myrdal and Bertil Ohlin – in creating the Swedish model. And I ask how far the subsequent difficulties, and loss of support for the Social Democrats, are a fundamental flaw or a remediable problem.

The post-war era is characterized by the emergence (or re-emergence) of Asia as a major economic powerhouse and the shift of the world's centre of economic gravity eastwards. Asia's economic breakthrough, or 'take-off', occurred in sequence starting with Japan in the 1870s. The reforms associated with the restoration of the Meiji dynasty were one of the main trans-formative economic events of the nineteenth century. But it also appears to have been an achievement of genuinely collective leadership under the figurehead emperor. I shall deal here with

some of the individual Asian leaders who built on the Meiji legacy. The post-war era saw the emergence of the so-called NICs
(the Newly Industrialized Countries: Korea, Taiwan, Singapore
and Hong Kong). Two of these owe their transformation in large
part to individual political leadership. South Korea emerged from
extreme poverty at the end of the Korean War to – what is now
– a developed-country standard of living following the reforms
after a military coup led by General Park. The Park reforms raise
the question of how far his ideas were based on a Japanese model
of industrialization and government support and how far they
reflected Western ideas, including the growth-based development
ideas of the Kennedy administration. Park's experience also challenges Western ideas of liberal democracy. How far can seriously
illiberal and undemocratic regimes act as a – necessary? – midwife
to economically successful development and, ultimately, democracy? I have also looked at the semi-democratic model developed
by Lee Kuan Yew, who led Singapore's modernization for close
to half a century. Unlike South Korea, Singapore is a city state
and has always been open to trade and investment; but (unlike
the Western caricature) the Lee model involves substantial government involvement as a facilitator of growth and guarantor of
(strictly enforced) rules.

Perhaps the political figure who did most in the twentieth century to drive economic transformation was Deng Xiaoping, who
led post-Mao economic reform in China. How far was the subsequent emergence of China as an economic superpower down
to those reforms and to Deng personally? How did an ex-soldier
and communist revolutionary, political commissar and bureaucrat
come to have such an exalted status as an economic reformer?
How did he manage to synthesize the ideas of Lenin and Mao
with those of Milton Friedman and Asian contemporaries like
Lee Kuan Yew? How do we fairly judge someone who is regarded
by many (Chinese and Westerners) as a heroic figure who lifted
hundreds of millions out of poverty, and by others as a brutal

communist dictator who killed many people in cold blood to stifle democracy?

In the West, a major shift in economic paradigm occurred in the 1980s with the emergence of Margaret Thatcher in the UK and Ronald Reagan in the USA. Thatcherism and Reaganomics were about radical deregulation, privatization and tax cutting. I focus here on Mrs Thatcher whose reforms, arguably, were more far reaching. How and when did Mrs Thatcher become converted to the 'free market' economic thought of Friedrich Hayek and Milton Friedman? What were the different elements of Thatcherism in practice and how did they – for a while – attract popular support? Ronald Reagan's approach to economic theory was a little less structured; it is said that he was converted to radical tax cutting when Arthur Laffer showed him the 'Laffer Curve' on a table napkin at dinner, demonstrating that cuts in tax rates may generate more revenue. How did Reaganomics differ from Thatcherism? And what are the legacies of both?

The biggest transformation in recent decades has been the liberalization – and dismantling – of socialist, planned economies. I have chosen two contrasting cases, one revolutionary, the other evolutionary. They both involve leaders who were economists turned politicians. The first is Leszek Balcerowicz, the author – as Finance Minister and Deputy Prime Minister – of the Polish 'big bang' or 'shock therapy' designed to move Poland from a failing (and hyperinflationary) communist economy to a capitalist market economy in a very short period of time. How did he himself migrate within a decade from communist economic orthodoxy to the Solidarity movement to free market convictions? Was his programme a success? The question posed by some critics is how far the Balcerowicz Plan was his and his Solidarity government's and how much was transported from US economists (notably Jeffrey Sachs) and Washington institutions. Why were gentler, slower, more gradual, options disregarded?

The other case was the more modest but still substantial

reform programme in India enacted by Manmohan Singh as Finance Minister and, then, the even more modest reforms which
he enacted as Prime Minister. What influenced his intellectual
journey, which went from Cambridge Keynesian economics and
Nehruvian socialism to market reforms in partnership with the
International Monetary Fund (IMF) and the World Bank? How
much of India's recent impressive economic growth can be explained by those reforms? How do we evaluate the career of
someone who introduced and presided over – apparently successful – reforms but also headed a government steeped in corruption
and scandal (though not his own)?

The 2008 global financial crisis created a new set of challenges
for economists seeking to understand and interpret the post-crisis
world and for politicians offering the public solutions to some
of the legacy problems: slow growth; accumulated private and
public debt; fragile financial institutions; public sector austerity;
historically very low interest rates; and growing public frustration.
Political leadership is coming from an unlikely source: an otherwise insignificant party machine politician in Japan, Shinzō Abe.
Abenomics belatedly reflects the fact that Japan suffered a severe
financial crisis almost two decades before the West and spent
much of that time trying and failing to escape what has come to
be understood as 'balance sheet recession', whereby the outstanding debts of companies inhibit future investment. The question
I address is: has the, now retired, Abe (together with his Finance
Minister, Tarō Asō) found an answer? Who were the economists
who moved beyond conventional thinking to offer the Japanese
political class a new approach? Is Abenomics working, economically and politically? And could it be applied elsewhere?

I complete my biographical selection with a controversial
choice: Donald Trump. This choice is not inspired by admiration.
President Trump did great damage, especially to America's reputation as a democracy. My choice does not seek to imply that he
was a serious economic thinker; his attention span was notoriously

short, and his thoughts were expressed in tweets and pithy sound-bites. He was believed not to read his adviser's briefs or even to listen to challenging ideas.

So how far are his ideas random expressions of his gut instincts or part of a radically different, and consistent, approach to economic policy which appears to be reshaping the world? Has he succeeded in reinstating the nation state as the key economic actor and relegating global and regional economic rules and institutions? Over two and a half centuries after Adam Smith demolished the idea, does 'America First' inevitably lead to 'mercantilist' trade policies where all countries simultaneously try to cut imports and promote exports? How far did he also succeed in upending orthodox monetary and fiscal policy? We do not yet know where Trumponomics will lead but we have to acknowledge its importance and – so far – its political appeal to a substantial base.

These are the stories I want to tell: of men and women who fought their way to positions of political power and used that power to change, in radical and far-reaching ways, the direction of economic policy.

I have omitted some of the technocrats and national or international civil servants who have made a major contribution to economic policy: governors of central banks, heads of international agencies with an economic mission, key economic advisers. A good example of a massively influential technocrat was Jean Monnet who established, after the war, the French Commissariat général du Plan and as much as anyone laid the foundations for France's 'Thirty Glorious Years' of growth, as it was called. He then went on to be a key figure in establishing the European Economic Community. But he was never elected to public office and was the servant of French Presidents and Prime Ministers.

There is no African. It is possible that, as this century evolves, the centre of global economic gravity will shift to Africa following the demographic trends which will, in due course, make

Nigeria and Ethiopia, in particular, major economic powers. Post-Independence Africa is not, however, a great economic success story. But precisely because of its exceptionalism there is a case to be made for Seretse Khama's Botswana: a stable, democratic country which has, apparently successfully, learned to manage its resource wealth competently. But it is yet to be more than a small, isolated, oasis of good practice. In other countries, serious economists achieved political power, like Mwai Kibaki in Kenya, but they did not demonstrably achieve significant change.

The only Latin American, Perón, established a tradition of populist economics associated with failure. Venezuela now vies with Zimbabwe as the textbook example of how political leaders can destroy a potentially wealthy – and successful – economy. Are there happier examples? It seemed plausible to argue five years ago that Luiz Lula and the Brazilian Workers' Party had established a workable social democratic model which combined growth and social welfare, fiscal and monetary discipline and an entrepreneurial approach to state enterprise building on the legacy of Getúlio Vargas from the 1940s and 1950s. But it now appears that the political structure was rotten and has seemingly not survived.

Perhaps the most uncomfortable success story in modern times is that of General Pinochet in Chile. He is reviled for overseeing systematic murder and torture during his dictatorship, after a military coup in 1973. But he also, influenced by the Chicago-based economists Milton Friedman and Arnold Harberger, embarked on a radical programme of fiscal stabilization, welfare reform – particularly pensions – and market liberalization. The economic medicine worked, leading to sustained recovery and poverty reduction and admission to the OECD; democracy was restored; and Chile appeared to have broken free of the dispiriting cycle of failure which has enveloped most of the rest of the continent. But a revolt in 2019 against extreme inequality cast doubt on the stability of the model.

Through my examples, I hope to better understand the links

between good (and bad) politics and economics. Often politicians get things badly wrong. If it were straightforward to convert political power and good economic advice into economic success, there would be more Singapores and Germanies and fewer Venezuelas and Zimbabwes. Nations fail. Many do. And some fail persistently. The authors of *Why Nations Fail*, Daron Acemoglu and James Robinson, observe: 'achieving prosperity depends on solving some basic political problems... Explaining world inequality still needs economics to understand how different types of politics and social arrangements affect economic incentives and behaviour. But it also needs politics.'[13] And, sometimes, politicians emerge who make a big difference. That is my focus here.

1

Hamilton: The Economic Founding Father

The closing decades of the eighteenth century were the first period in which recognizably modern political and economic ideas came to dominate. It witnessed the first stages of what would become the industrial revolution in the UK. The period also spans the American and French revolutions when ideas of 'left' and 'right' and liberalism and nationalism found full expression. It saw the publication of Adam Smith's *Wealth of Nations* (1776) building on the work of John Locke and David Hume. The book's ideas helped to frame the debate around trade – and wider economic policy – for much of the next century and beyond; indeed, its legacy lives on today.

In the new United States, Alexander Hamilton (1755–1804) was at the centre of political and economic life: as a revolutionary soldier; then leading politician; as co-author of the US Constitution; and as economic policy maker and thinker (most prominently as George Washington's Treasury Secretary). According to American economist Douglass North, as Washington's Treasury Secretary, Hamilton was responsible for 'the most important developments for subsequent growth in the economy... as [his policies] formed the monetary and fiscal underpinnings of the new nation. The first established a sound credit basis; the second was an important beginning of an elaborated capital market.'[1] Hamilton set out the framework for America's industrial revolution and private enterprise economy and for a system of trade protection to support manufacturing – widely copied elsewhere in the subsequent two centuries. His approach to economic policy was perhaps best summarized by his biographer Nathan Schachner, who noted that he had read and absorbed Adam Smith but had adapted his ideas to the particular needs of newly independent America.[2] He also anticipated the future needs of a developing market economy for financing business and government. He established the pragmatic formula which has served most successful governments well in the US and beyond: he was an enthusiastic supporter of business and markets but also promoted strong government.

Hamilton attracted much attention for other reasons: his colourful upbringing amid the slave-owning communities of the Caribbean (and his own antipathy to slavery); his brilliant military record as a youthful aide-de-camp to Washington in the War of Independence; his role in framing the new American Constitution and the party system of the fledgling democracy; his contributions as a poet, essayist, lawyer, financier and businessman, educator and political theorist; and his venomous personal feuds and polemics with political opponents, including future Presidents Jefferson, Madison, Adams and Monroe, culminating in an early death aged forty-nine in a duel at the hands of Vice President Aaron Burr. His life and death are sufficiently exotic to have generated a popular musical. He was one of two of the Founding Fathers never to have become President (the other being Benjamin Franklin who was considered too old for office at the time of Independence). However, as the man who established the foundations of American capitalism he is, arguably, as significant a figure as any of those who were.

The Revolutionary

Hamilton has had many biographers[3] – latterly, and most comprehensively, Ron Chernow.[4] But for our purposes, a few details are important to establish the context. He was born on the Caribbean island of Nevis before moving to the Danish colony of St Croix. Both islands' economies were based on enslaved people working the sugar plantations. What are now territories renowned mainly for tourism were then important cogs in the world economy (the British tried to obtain Guadeloupe from France in return for Canada).

His family life would now be described as 'chaotic'. He was illegitimate. His relatives would probably be dismissed today as 'white trash'. He was fortunate, or enterprising, enough to be taken under the wing of a trader who employed him as an apprentice clerk. He also attracted the attention of a wealthy patron who encouraged his love of reading and writing (as a teenage journalist) and paid for the young Hamilton, aged seventeen, to go to North America to study, never to return.

One enduring legacy of his Caribbean upbringing was his fervent opposition to slavery. He was a strong abolitionist, which lay in part behind his subsequent quarrels with Jefferson especially, but also Madison, who held people in slavery. And his approach to economics was based in large part on his insight that economic strength came from innovation, enterprise, education and manufacturing technologies, not from exploiting enslaved people and raw materials. Long before the Civil War he identified the underlying strength of the industrial North as being its industry as against the agrarian, plantation, economy of the South (his crucial work in developing manufacturing was later acknowledged by Abraham Lincoln).

Soon after Hamilton embarked on his college education he was caught up in the colonial uprising against the British crown. He achieved early recognition as a nineteen year old, reportedly making a stirring speech at a mass meeting in support of the Boston Tea Party rebels in 1774. And when military hostilities broke out a year later, Hamilton supported the revolution, albeit initially with a journalistic pen rather than a sword. His writings, alongside his legal studies, did betray a tendency, later held against him by his political enemies, to disdain disorder and the populist politics of the uneducated common man. In the current era, he would perhaps have been marked down as an intellectual elitist and apologist for the 'establishment', despite his humble origins. His speeches at that time also demonstrated his preoccupation with the fact that economic relations with the colonial British authorities were heavily one-sided and needed rebalancing. In one of his pamphlets he foreshadowed the mature Hamilton: 'we have food and clothing in plenty: as for those articles we import from abroad, why not manufacture them ourselves?'[5]

By the following year (1776), however, Hamilton was founding and leading an artillery troop of sixty-five men and within months had come to Washington's attention for his courage under fire and organizational ability. In the early days of the war, when the rebels were mostly in retreat, Hamilton's reputation grew and, aged twenty-two, he was one of Washington's aides-de-camp and a lieutenant-colonel, rising to become, in effect, Chief of Staff. In the years of warfare which followed he would become a heroic soldier despite Washington's instructions to stay away from the battlefield and he greatly improved the logistics of Washington's army. But he also found the time to devour books on classical philosophy (Hobbes, Cicero, Bacon) and history and economics (particularly Adam Smith); to marry into a rich and socially respected family; and to develop a clear philosophy, shared with Washington, for post-revolution America. They envisaged a federal rather than confederal state, with a national army, a strong executive and national unity.

Politics and Policy

In the closing stages of the war against the British colonial authorities and before winning recognition for heroism at the Battle of Yorktown in 1781, Hamilton focused his attention on practical policy issues, especially regarding the economy.

The United States at that time was a small, agrarian country. There were no cities with a population of more than 50,000 in an overall population of 3 million. There was virtually no industry: only one cotton mill in 1791 (there were around 100 by 1808). The economy was badly damaged by the restrictions on exports to Britain (they fell from £1.75 million in 1774 to £750,000 in 1784). And there was double-digit inflation as a result of the demands of the war, greatly reducing the value of the dollar against gold.

In 1781, as the end of the war drew near, Hamilton produced a blueprint for dealing with fiscal crisis involving federal taxation, the creation of a national bank, the use of bond markets and foreign borrowing to raise credit for the government, and a system of public debt management. His contemporaries were also shocked by his open acknowledgement of the useful role of what he called 'moneyed men': the fiscal crisis 'links the interests of the state with those of the rich individuals belonging to it'.[6]

A year later he published the 'Continentalist' essay which advocated higher tariffs – albeit moderate and effective – on a range of goods, mainly for revenue reasons. Protectionism was the norm in Britain. As a result, US exporters faced severe duties on wheat, tobacco, rice and fish. So, Hamilton was reflecting the mercantilist orthodoxy of the day which valued exports over imports and trade surpluses over deficits. Although he had read and been impressed by the arguments of Adam Smith – the 'division of labour' and the 'hidden hand' of the markets –'free trade' had little attraction to him. Indeed, his priority was to restore solvency and pay soldiers. Such a task needed taxes, especially import duties (collected by a strong centralized government machine).

His writing, at this stage, also betrays his contempt for populism and easy solutions, pandering to 'what will *please*, not what will *benefit* the people'.[7] Nonetheless, he opted for the grubby world of politics and became a member of the Confederation Congress (representing New York).

In the aftermath of the War of Independence, Hamilton maintained a polymath existence as lawyer, politician, journalist and campaigner (against slavery). He established a (private) bank for New York, providing the first stock ever to be traded on the New York Stock Exchange. In one of his few lapses of judgement on economic matters he dabbled in real estate speculation in upstate New York rather than Manhattan where he would have made a fortune. He also showed the first signs of the trait that was ultimately to destroy him: an inability to resist being dragged into public arguments of invective and innuendo with political opponents. On this occasion, his opponent was the powerful Governor of New York, George Clinton. Inevitably some of the mud stuck (which included the then controversial suggestion that he was mixed race or, alternatively, the illegitimate son of George Washington).

His major contribution to posterity in these years followed from his participation as one of the fifty-five delegates from twelve states to the Convention which produced the American Constitution. Revered today as having almost religious significance, the Constitution was hammered out over months of often acrimonious argument amid much skulduggery, somewhat removed from Benjamin Franklin's later description of it as 'the most august and respectable assembly he was ever to see in his life'.[8]

The dominant intellectual influence on the Constitution was a series of essays – the Federalist papers – authored by Hamilton and Madison, which appeared in 1787. Though they would later quarrel bitterly, at that stage they were close collaborators and shared a similar view of the necessary balance to be struck between the federal government and the states. Similarly, they broadly agreed on how to achieve the necessary checks and balances between the executive, legislature and judiciary and between order and liberty. Their essays, which Hamilton often had to write in a hurry between his legal cases, are now regarded as seminal works.

Hamilton's distinctive contribution to the papers reflects his antipathy to over-powerful state politicians and to demagogues who claim to speak for the popular will. More positively, he sketched out the commercial benefits of economic union and common monetary policy. And he managed to insert his economic philosophy, which could have come out of the mouth, or pen, of Adam Smith, that monopolistic vested interests are bound to pursue their own interests and so need to be regulated.[9] Hamilton's contribution was not merely to pump out the words; he was able, with Madison, to win – from a minority position initially – the federalist case, and then get the new Constitution approved by the states, most crucially in the recalcitrant state of New York.

The Treasury Secretary

Once the Constitution was agreed, the way was open to choose the first President: at that time, by an electoral college of state representatives, not by party or popular vote. Hamilton was determined that Washington should become President: the only man, he believed, with the stature for the job. Washington, once persuaded to run, was the clear favourite but Hamilton managed, with his characteristic lack of tact, to make a mortal enemy of John Adams, the only other plausible candidate, who became the new Vice President and, in due course, the second President of the USA. Hamilton's reward was to become Washington's first Treasury Secretary in 1789. At that time, it was the most powerful executive position in the new administration (one of only three, the others being Secretary of State – Jefferson – and Secretary of State for War). It was also a highly sensitive post since the new state needed to raise taxes, and taxation was potentially the flash-point for differences between federalists and the states. Yet he was clearly the best-prepared candidate for the job, having spent years reading and drawing up a detailed blueprint for government.

Within hours of being appointed he had raised a large loan for the federal government (from the Bank of New York which he him-self had established) and then another from a new Philadelphia bank. Historians are agreed that he was an administrative genius who combined theory and practice, rapid decision making and careful systems building. To all intents and purposes, he became Washington's Prime Minister, though parallels with government today are somewhat misleading (he had thirty-nine employees, the State Department five and the Department of War only two). He and the other brilliant minds of his generation were deployed cre-ating a new state for just over 3 million people (excluding 700,000 enslaved people) with an administrative apparatus which today would be expected in the lowest tiers of local government. The juxtaposition of greatness and pettiness, visionary constitutional design and small-minded personal jealousies can only be under-stood in that unusual context.

Hamilton's solution to the problem of how to finance the new state was in the form of a fifty-page report. It was typically clear-minded and radical. American governments would need to borrow at affordable interest rates for the foreseeable future; so, debt markets must be efficient and the federal government must always be trusted to honour its debts. He made explicit some-thing we now take for granted: that the national debt will never be repaid. The task of fiscal policy is to be able to service the national debt and to maintain confidence that government can continue to borrow in the markets on good terms. If greater confidence in government securities were then to drive up their price, rewarding speculators, then so be it. By the same token, higher bond prices meant lower interest rates benefiting the economy. Furthermore, confidence in government securities would enhance their status as collateral for private business borrowing and thus for expansion of the money supply, which he saw as essential to maintaining economic activity (his writings on the quantity and velocity of money in circulation show a remarkably modern approach to monetary policy). To uphold confidence that the government would always honour its obligations to creditors, expanding government debt would have to be financed, through a sinking fund, by taxation. For this he proposed luxury taxes on wine and spirits as well as tea and coffee (which had the merit of being foreign-made luxuries). He was, in fact, no stranger to radical tax proposals, having offered a tax plan in 1781 to Governor Clinton of New York which included a flat tax on land, dwellings, servants, lawyers and 'on the privilege of remaining a bachelor' (which was rejected by the state legislature).

For a youthful revolutionary who had so eloquently denounced British taxes on tea to come out in favour of higher taxes on tea was bad enough. His proposed whisky tax threatened to produce a rural revolt against duty enforcement inspectors and an armed force had to be assembled to head it off. His whole approach to taxation and debt management, which was based in part on policies already employed in Britain, suggested to some – implausibly – that he was a British spy. This allegation was fuelled by his defence of Anglo-American trade as it revived after the War of Independence.

But his debt management strategy caused real anger among those who saw themselves as losers. The debt was of three kinds. There was foreign debt which Hamilton insisted should be honoured in full to maintain credit worthiness; few dissented. Then there was the debt of the states which was to be assumed by federal government; this opened up bitter disputes over the fairness of the settlement (as, for example, between Georgia and Massachusetts, fuelling a long-term grievance). For some, this measure was Hamilton's greatest achievement. He effectively put the United into the United States. We can see today in the European Economic and Monetary Union the crucial importance and the difficulty of sharing debt obligations in a union of independent states.

But the main bone of contention was domestic debt, much of it held by relatively poor people – artisans, traders and farmers – many of whom had acquired war debt for patriotic reasons. Creditors were offered the market value or the original issue value – which sounds fine, except that many of the creditors were desperate to sell for cash and were often, also, unsophisticated investors prone to scams. Hamilton's measures inspired confidence in the market, which drove up the price of government stock, enriching those investors who had been smart enough to snap up large holdings. Fortunes were made from speculation, which fed Hamilton's reputation as a friend of 'fat cats', often portrayed as greedy Northerners, and led to accusations against him, and others, of insider trading.

Despite the political backlash, Hamilton got his measures approved by Congress. He then embarked on an even more ambitious project: the establishment of a strong national bank based on the experience of the Bank of England, the Bank of Amsterdam and other European banks. It was to be privately financed (with government backing and a government share in the profits) and its purpose was to stimulate credit to business, which he saw as crucial to the development of the economy. There was strong opposition from those who distrusted banks, who resented 'speculators' or who thought that this was another wheeze to fleece the rural populations and the South. Nonetheless, the bank was approved by Congress and went on to become the Federal Reserve.

Although the debates around the central bank and budget policy were technical and often parochial, there was a bigger purpose in Hamilton's work which marks him out as a giant figure in US history, bigger than some of the more illustrious Founding Fathers. At least on economic matters they – Jefferson and Madison in particular – represented a pre-capitalist vision of America including an agrarian system based on enslavement. One historian describes him, not unjustly, as 'the creator of American Capitalism'.[10] He was unapologetically in favour of enterprise and self-improvement. He consistently supported measures to create the conditions under which business could flourish, including private property rights, patent protection and legally enforceable contracts.

Hamilton was able to maintain the momentum behind his reforms in part because of tangible improvements to the economy. Thanks to America's improved credit standing, long-term interest rates on public debt fell from 6 per cent to 4 per cent, which was a vital improvement when public debt service counted for over half of federal expenditure. The easier availability of credit sparked economic recovery. Although there were no GDP figures, some measure of the state of the economy can be gauged from the tone of a private and confidential note sent by Washington to Hamilton in July 1792. It listed twenty-one grievances Washington had heard about Hamilton's policies but acknowledged that 'the country was prosperous and happy'.[11]

But the grievances were taking a growing toll on Hamilton's reputation. Not least was the impact on public opinion of a speculative boom and bust cycle in the shares of the new Bank of the United States, with allegations that Hamilton (who had impeccable financial integrity and refused a salary) was somehow involved in favouring his friends. To compound these reputational issues, he was caught up in a scandal resulting from an adulterous affair. His many enemies, now led by Jefferson and Madison, had plenty of ammunition.

While Hamilton was fighting these battles, he was also writing – and promoting – a classic paper, *Report on Manufactures*, which helped to define one of the great economic controversies of the nineteenth century, not just in the USA but, later, in Germany and Japan, and indeed to the present day: the circumstances under which the national interest requires the protection of new industries, particularly manufacturing.

Trade Policy, Infant Industries and Economic Nationalism

Hamilton's *Report on Manufactures*, presented to Congress in December 1791, was the product of what would now be called 'evidence-based decision making'. He personally wrote numerous letters to correspondents all over the world to establish the prevailing nature of manufacturing. The state of development of American industry was well behind its competitors and summarized by one correspondent as 'we have no capital. We have no knowledge of the business. We have no skilled workmen. We cannot compete with English goods.'[12] Hamilton argued that he was neutral between manufacturing and agriculture, but he lauded the positives of the former, including the capacity for specialization (he also commented on the use of child labour – and had no problem with it). But the *Report on Manufactures* also led Hamilton into the controversial territory of challenging free trade orthodoxy.

I have noted earlier that while soldiering during the War of Independence, Hamilton read voraciously and he was very familiar with Adam Smith's *An Inquiry into the Nature and Causes of the Wealth of Nations*, published in 1776. Hamilton essentially shared Smith's vision – 'In matters of industry, human enterprise ought, doubtless, to be left free in the main; not fettered by too much regulation'. But it was the politician in him that led him to qualify his agreement: 'practical politicians know that it may be beneficially stimulated by prudent aids and encouragements on the part of the government'.[13]

Smith's defence of free trade emerged essentially from a debate in eighteenth-century France between, on the one hand, the mercantilist orthodoxy that trade was essentially a zero-sum game in which trade needed to balance and, on the other, the free market advocates of laissez-faire, led initially by Boisguilbert and taken forward later by Quesnay and the physiocrats (who favoured agriculture over manufacturing). Smith was not a believer in laissez-faire; he saw a role for government in the provision of public goods and also in the establishment of social and legal structures within which a market economy could operate. But his defence of free trade was trenchant, albeit with two main qualifications: for national defence (a non-economic argument) and to offset tax distortions (where domestic production is taxed but not imports). Smith also saw merit in some instances in using 'reciprocity' as a tactical measure to promote the wider cause of free trade.

Smith was very clear in his writings that free trade was not some vague idea to benefit the world but very much in the national interest of the country liberalizing its trade. Similarly he thought that all the arguments for supporting manufacturing – that is in mid-eighteenth-century Britain – were not national interest arguments at all, but a defence of producers at the expense of consumers by creating monopoly, inflating prices and profits. Smith was neither for nor against manufacturing, believing that the sectoral composition of trade and production should be determined by markets reflecting a country's stage of development and endowment of natural or human resources.

In many ways, Hamilton's quarrel was not with Smith but with the physiocrats who extolled the virtues of agriculture over manufacturing. Where Hamilton differed from Smith was over what became known as the 'infant industry' argument for the protection of manufacturers. Part of his argument was that American manufacturers were having to compete, unfairly, with – British or French – rivals which had become dominant as a result of past (or continuing) 'bounties, premiums and other artificial encouragements with which foreign nations second the exertions of their own citizens in the branches in which they are to be rivalled'.[14] This particular point is partly captured in Smith's understanding of 'reciprocity' and 'retaliation' arguments for protection. And the Britain of that time was hardly a paragon of free trade: there were laws criminalizing the transfer overseas of British technology. Exports of machinery and emigration of mechanics were prohibited. The Navigation Acts governing shipping were fiercely protectionist. Protective Corn Laws were being introduced and would remain for half a century. Any self-respecting American would bridle at the idea of their colonial overlords saying: 'do as we say; not as we do'. And unsurprisingly, Hamilton wanted America to have what the colonial master withheld.

The other part of the infant industry argument represented a more fundamental disagreement with Adam Smith.[15] Hamilton believed that the owners of new – infant – industries, using untried technologies and faced with high risk, would simply not invest without the greater certainty provided, temporarily, by a protected tariff or subsidy. He was not alone. Other Scottish economists of the time, such as James Steuart and John Rae, saw merit in the infant industry argument as, indeed, did an influential German economist, Friedrich List, who began professional life as a businessman in the USA. Smith was, however, not merely critical but contemptuous of the infant industry argument and it is to Hamilton's credit that he studied Smith's arguments carefully and engaged with them. Moreover, he designed government interventions specifically to address the criticism that infant industry protection would raise prices to consumers and enhance monopoly profits: hence a preference for subsidies over tariffs, or for cutting tariffs on imported inputs, and for ensuring that support was temporary and moderate. His approach demonstrated a high degree of economic sophistication – anticipating modern theoretical developments in welfare economics and trade theory – and was in an altogether higher intellectual league than the crude economic nationalists of Trump's America who claim Hamilton as an intellectual forebear.

Unlike his far-reaching work on money, banking and fiscal policy, Hamilton's enthusiasm for promoting indigenous manufacturers did not get far in practice at the time, though it undoubtedly struck an emotional chord (Washington insisted on wearing American-made suits at his inauguration) and was later to have immense influence. Indeed, it was one of the underlying causes of the Civil War. Hamilton did help to set up a Society for Establishing Useful Manufactures and established a prototype cotton mill (stealing British industrial secrets). But, unfortunately for Hamilton, the champions of nascent manufacturing were also the same individuals who were most deeply implicated in the seedier excesses of the financial mania of 1791–2 which tarnished Hamilton's reputation.

By 1794, midway through Washington's second term, Hamilton decided to step down as Treasury Secretary. He had a substantial body of achievement, his last being the enactment of a controversial and unpopular trade treaty with Britain, finally bringing hostilities to an end. Hamilton was now forty and his life's work had largely been accomplished.

The Journey Downhill

Hamilton's outstanding talents and achievements should have led to the presidency. But he was not a serious contender when a successor was sought for Washington, or subsequently. He was very divisive; he had no common touch or inclination to defer to public opinion; and he was dogged by personal scandal. He remained a leading political player and under President Adams was briefly put in charge of the army when it appeared that America would go to war with revolutionary France. But, especially after his enemy Jefferson became President, he was largely confined to his law practice, pamphleteering, family life and pursuing his endless political vendettas and personal feuds. The last of these eventually cost him his life in a duel with a political opponent, Vice President Burr (after Hamilton's son had also died in a duel).

One of the misfortunes of Hamilton's early death is that he was not around to defend himself against the posthumous denigration by Jefferson and his allies. He was rehabilitated by Lincoln for whom the themes of strong federal government, industrialization and the fight against slavery resonated, and then again by Theodore Roosevelt. But Franklin Roosevelt – whose policies were essentially Hamiltonian – took the side of Jefferson. More recently Hamilton's contribution has come to be fully appreciated. And his warnings about demagogic economic populism have acquired a new relevance with Trump.

2

Peel: Free Trade

Arguments about trade are at the heart of the careers of half the politicians I have chosen for their contribution to economic policy: none more so than in the case of Sir Robert Peel (1788–1850). As a conservative and Conservative politician from early Victorian England, Peel would be competing for a place in the history books with the likes of Lord Liverpool or George Canning or his Liberal contemporaries Lords Grey and Melbourne, were it not for his transformative shift in British policy from protectionism to free trade through the abolition of the Corn Laws. Whereas Alexander Hamilton was a force of nature who, in and out of power, influenced the politics and economics of the early USA profoundly and in lots of different ways, Peel's contribution was essentially that of someone who, in power, seized the moment to make a decisive break with the past (and also with a major section of his party). Peel's political interventions transformed the economic orthodoxy of the time about trade, and – with a few intervening wobbles – for the next 170 years.

The Evolution of an Idea

The economic orthodoxy of today – at least pre-Trump – was best summarized by the late Canadian economist Harry Johnson: 'The proposition that freedom of trade is on the whole economically more beneficial than protection is one of the most fundamental propositions economic theory has to offer for the guidance of economic policy.'[1] But that orthodoxy took a long time to arrive and it was certainly not the prevailing view of policy makers in Peel's time. The debate about trade had ebbed and flowed for centuries.

In classical times, international trade expanded under the empires of the period. Plato described the merits of the 'division of labour' two millennia before Adam Smith. But, in general, thinkers of the time, like Aristotle, and then early Christians like St Augustine and Aquinas regarded trade for profit as vulgar, morally questionable and to be avoided in favour of self-sufficiency where possible: to be tolerated only in moderation and where absolutely necessary.[2]

The idea that trade was to be welcomed and promoted rather than tolerated emerged in the late sixteenth and early seventeenth centuries as the voyages of exploration and the activities of merchants made the benefits of trade more apparent.

There evolved a broad set of ideas, which we now call mercantilism, which was prevalent until Smith the economist, Richard Cobden and John Bright the political campaigners, and Peel the practical politician overturned it. In essence, trade was desirable, but the benefits depended on running a favourable balance of trade. Exports were good, especially manufactured goods. Imports were only justified when necessary, especially if they threatened jobs in competing industries. Trade was carefully regulated by government and facilitated through bilateral treaties which were judged by their success in delivering trade surpluses (paid for in gold and silver).

There were serious political skirmishes around free trade once traders started to expand their operations in the emerging British Empire. The East India Company exploited the fashion among the British upper classes for embroidered Indian silks which then developed into calico – cotton – fabrics. Competition impacted

British weavers and there were violent demonstrations in London including (in 1697) an invasion of Parliament by angry workers when it was debating a bill to restrict imports. There was, in fact, little resistance to the clamour for import controls: 'three groups… coalesced into a strange protectionist alliance…: the moralists angered by the social disruption caused by the new finery; the silk and wool weavers made redundant by a cheaper and better foreign product; and the mercantilists angered by the outflow of silver to pay for mere fashion.'[3] The East India Company had insufficient friends and investors to counter protectionism. Parliament fell over itself to legislate to protect British weavers by banning all cotton fabric imports and then, in a later wave of industrial distress and civil unrest (in 1721), criminalizing not just imports of plain cloth, but even the wearing of it.

As has happened throughout modern history – though often not appreciated at the time – trade restrictions were counter-productive since higher prices helped to trigger the technical innovation and investment which created the mechanized British textile industry in Lancashire and the industrial revolution. The British industrial revolution was duly launched – unintentionally – on the back of trade protection. And then there was the additional boost to British industry from cheap, plentiful cotton from the USA picked by enslaved Africans (a point duly noted by Britain's future competitors including Alexander Hamilton in the USA).

The mercantilist doctrine, that trade was beneficial to the extent that it generated surpluses of exports over imports, rather than for its own sake, prevailed for most of the eighteenth century, though there were some dissident voices in Britain, in particular the financier and economist Dudley North.[4] However, the big challenge would come from Adam Smith in his *Wealth of Nations* who demolished the mercantilist case as contrary to the national interest by restricting competition and reinforcing the position of the monopolists in the home market. Free trade, by contrast, would permit the best allocation of a society's resources. Moreover, free trade spreads new methods of production and business practices through an international division of labour.

Smith was, however, very much ahead of his time (as were his French free trading contemporaries like Quesnay). There is little evidence that his ideas were taken seriously by policy makers in the UK. The Napoleonic Wars, which reinforced ideas of natural self-sufficiency, pulled in the opposite direction (ironically, as we saw in the previous chapter, one near-contemporary who did understand and welcome Smith's ideas was Alexander Hamilton who nonetheless did not believe they could be applied to a newly liberated colony). Thus, the context in which Peel entered Parliament in 1809, in wartime, as a precocious twenty-one-year-old Tory, was one where the issue of free trade was very far from the leading issue of the day or the dominant strain of economic thought.

Even so, it was a time bomb ticking in the background because of the particular problems associated with agriculture, in particular food-grains. Since medieval times, grain trade was micromanaged through what became a total of 127 separate 'corn laws' governing all aspects of trade in food stuffs. In medieval times the British economy was largely self-sufficient and so the regulations did not greatly matter. Likewise, for most of the eighteenth century, Britain had big surpluses and was a major exporter. After 1780, however, the UK became a net importer, due mainly to rising demand from an expanding population, especially in the cities. Government and Parliament were exposed to the tricky problem of providing the right balance between the interests of the farming landowners, who wanted higher prices and protection against import competition, and urban consumers, increasingly very poor factory workers, who needed cheap food to survive and to improve their living standards. In the politically fragile and turbulent climate of the turn of the eighteenth century, as food riots occurred, governments capitulated and promoted imports, which in turn enraged landowners. In 1804 the landowners were able to force through a Corn Law involving a 'sliding scale' of import duties on wheat. Again in 1814, wheat prices collapsed and another, this time draconian, Corn Law to support prices was passed, provoking serious riots in London.

The Peterloo Massacre in 1819, when cavalry charged an unarmed crowd in Manchester killing eighteen, was the most extreme manifestation of the unrest at the time and, while the demonstrations which led to it were based on demands for political reform, expensive grain was one of the grievances. Peel was a member of the government which suppressed the protestors and, while he was not directly involved (he became Home Secretary in 1822, three years after the massacre), there is no evidence that he dissented from the harsh response of the authorities.

Peel's Political Rise[5]

For someone who would become a hero to many working people, and champion of one of the great liberal causes of the last two centuries, there was very little in Peel's early life to suggest this late flowering. He was a privileged but clever and hard-working young man – educated at Harrow and Oxford – who entered Parliament, aged twenty-one, in an Irish seat bought for him by his father, a rich Lancashire industrialist who had moved to rural Staffordshire to enjoy the lifestyle of a country squire and served as a Tory MP, a follower of William Pitt.

The young Peel was a thoroughly conservative member of the ruling class in an age when Catholics were seen as a subversive minority deserving few rights; capital punishment was routine for hundreds of non-violent offences; child labour was largely unquestioned; political meetings were outlawed as seditious; political corruption and the buying of office endemic; and slavery was still tolerated in British colonies. Some of these prejudices were challenged in revolutionary France and, in a milder way, by British Whigs, the predecessors to the Liberals. Nevertheless, this was not a society on the edge of liberal democracy.

The parliamentary Tory party Peel joined as an ambitious young man, to the extent that it had any political ideology in the modern sense, was essentially about maintaining order, protecting private property and preserving the status quo. Whenever order was threatened, and the price of food an underlying cause, it was the interests of the landowning, food-growing aristocracy to which the Tories owed primary allegiance.

In the rather shallow talent pool in which the young Tory MP swam, he was quickly spotted as of above-average ability by the then Prime Minister, Lord Liverpool, who took office in 1812 following the assassination of Spencer Perceval. Liverpool was unflatteringly described by a Conservative successor, Disraeli, as an 'arch-mediocrity'. He is now mainly remembered for the period of economic recession and political repression – culminating in Peterloo – following the Napoleonic Wars. Peel progressed in this administration to Secretary of Ireland in 1812 (until 1818) and, after a short period involved in technical work, in Parliament, on the operation of the Gold Standard, he became Home Secretary in 1822.

A more generous assessment of the government in which Peel served would be that, in a profoundly conservative administration by almost any standards, there was a process of gradual, cautious, reform driven by concerns about efficiency rather than justice and reflecting the demands of more meritocratic and ambitious entrepreneurs and middle-class professionals. Peel fitted the bill along with William Huskisson at the Board of Trade (who did push through some tariff cuts) and George Canning at the Foreign Office. In five years as Home Secretary he tidied up the criminal code, greatly reducing the number of capital offences – without greatly reducing the number of hangings – and established what subsequently became the Metropolitan Police (known as 'Peelers').

His biographer Norman Gash defends his subject by concluding of this period: 'It was not surprising that he possessed some of the emotional heritage of the war period and felt himself in a

measure identified with the maintenance of the aristocratic constitution in Church and State against Jacobinism, radical democracy,
Irish Catholic nationalism and the class struggle of an emerging
industrial proletariat. Yet he was never a reactionary.'6

Peel also developed the political skills to steer a course between
the increasingly irresistible demands for political and economic
reform and the implacable 'ultras', as he called them, on the right
wing of his own party. He earned a reputation as a fierce opponent of Catholic Emancipation – that is, Catholics being allowed
to become MPs – but then engineered a U-turn to head off
mounting disaffection in Ireland, alienating the ultras. He forged
a close, longstanding alliance with the Duke of Wellington. The
hero of Waterloo was what we would now call a 'national treasure'
and as a leading figure in the Tory party he combined deeply conservative instincts with a trait, no doubt derived from his military
genius, of knowing when to advance and when to retreat.

This pragmatic streak in the leadership helped it to be rec-
onciled to the 1832 Great Reform Act, launched by a Whig
government which was a little more inclined to reform than the
Tories and more open to ideas from the new class of industrialists
as opposed to the landed gentry. The Act (modestly) expanded the
franchise to small landowners, shopkeepers and other urban property owners while addressing the chronic disparities between the
largely underrepresented, booming cities and the corrupt, rural
'rotten boroughs' which provided the Tories with many of their
MPs. Peel (and Wellington) faced down the Tory ultras and survived, and it was this experience which gave him the confidence
and reputation to relaunch the Tory party as the Conservatives
and then, in due course, to tackle the issue of trade policy.

Peel had become party leader while in opposition to the Whigs
and he faced his first big political test in the 1834 general election.
He chose to rebrand the Tories. His launching of the Conservative Party took place through the 1834 Tamworth Manifesto
which, while it contained a series of bland and familiar promises

– the pursuit of peace abroad; respect for minorities ('Dissenters'); sound economic management – broke new ground by positioning the Conservatives as the party of moderate reform. It sought to attract the new, enlarged electorate of property owners opposed equally to alarming radical reformers and backward-looking Tory ultras.

It took seven years in opposition and a lot of grass roots organization and mobilization but by 1841 Peel had made enough political progress to defeat the Whig government and return to power with a majority of almost eighty. He was now in a position to tackle an issue which had been building up for the previous quarter of a century: the Corn Laws and the wider issue of trade. But we should not exaggerate the extent to which he appreciated the scale of the reforms he would unleash. In parliamentary speeches up to his accession to power he was an advocate of trade protection and resistant to abolishing the Corn Laws even while accepting that they hurt the urban working class.

How the Free Trade Argument Was Won

Peel was a crucial influence in turning Britain unequivocally in the direction of free trade. But, as with most politically significant events in a (semi) democratic country, one man alone was not solely responsible. Essentially four factors were involved: a decisive change in the intellectual climate and fashionable economic ideas; a successful political campaign, led by the Anti-Corn Law League; underlying economic forces shifting power from landowners to urban consumers; as well as Peel's own political influence and skill as Prime Minister and Leader of the Conservatives.

As to the first, there was, under the President of the Board of Trade, William Huskisson, in the 1820s, a gradual move to a more liberal, tariff-cutting approach to imports which Peel supported as part of a modernizing agenda. The views set out by Adam Smith half a century earlier had percolated through, in some part. The main worry was that giving up import duties meant a loss of government revenue (a practical issue which Peel later confronted by using income tax).

The emergence of this liberalizing instinct, albeit not a very radical one, coincided with another major intellectual contribution on the specific issue of trade in grain. David Ricardo was an intellectual – an economist – a successful financier and, briefly, an MP (his seat paid for by his wealth). His magnum opus, *On the Principles of Political Economy and Taxation*, published in 1817, sought to build on the ideas of Adam Smith. It was provoked in part by the protectionist Corn Laws of 1815.

Ricardo took aim at the mercantilist way of thinking, stating that 'we should have no greater value if, by the discovery of a new market, we obtained double the quantity of foreign goods in exchange for a given quantity of ours'.[7] He went on to develop the law of comparative advantage which shows that there is benefit in trade and specialization, even if one country is more efficient in all traded products. In such a case, the less efficient country should specialize in its least inefficient activity and, conversely, the most efficient trade partner, overall, should give up the same activity despite being more efficient (a counterintuitive conclusion which baffles some economics students today).

Ricardo did not have his own way in his free trade arguments and opposition to the Corn Laws. Thomas Malthus, pamphleteering in 1815, argued that the Corn Laws provided stability and security to domestic agriculture and that unilateral liberalization (without reciprocal action elsewhere) was both futile and destabilizing. He also argued that it inflicted unnecessary adjustment costs on agriculture from whence the nation's wealth was primarily derived.

These theoretical arguments in favour of free trade were only of significance once they progressed beyond scholars into the political marketplace. What gave public voice to the theories of Smith and Ricardo was the establishment in 1838 of the Anti-Corn Law

League. The two main spokesmen for the campaign were Richard Cobden, a successful self-made businessman (making printed cottons in Manchester), and John Bright, another textile manufacturer, Quaker and radical, reforming Whig politician. But behind these high-profile orators and campaigners the League developed many of the sophisticated tools used by today's major political parties and special interest groups, such as mass mailings, carefully choreographed travelling campaigns, opinion polling and targeted legal challenge. The rapidly evolving communication system made these techniques feasible just as social media, today, has created a new dimension to campaigning (Cobden was a leading proponent of the 'penny post', which helped disseminate his free trade propaganda).

By 1841 the campaign was well established, with its literature allegedly reaching 800,000 people on a regular basis. Cobden and Bright both entered Parliament in 1841 when Peel formed his Conservative government, albeit on the opposition – Whig or Liberal – benches. Cobden in particular had developed a clear, simple message: that importing foreign food helped raise the real wages of working men directly through lowering the price of bread, but also helped the wider economy since it would be paid for by exporting manufactured goods, which in turn created jobs for workers and profits for industrialists (the last was important since workers were not represented in Parliament, though industrialists were).

The shift in opinion was driven by the realignment of interests arising from the industrial revolution. Industrialists were becoming more important and the landowning aristocracy less so. The electorate after the 1832 Reform Act, while far from granting universal suffrage for men, let alone women, had enfranchised many urban consumers: professionals and craftsmen. The Tory Party was still the party of the landed gentry, but Peel's Tamworth Manifesto had widened its base.

The combination of these forces had already led to some relaxation of imports in 1828 by means of a sliding scale of duties. The crucial new development was that Peel had decided that some reform of the Corn Laws was to be a priority for his administration, though he was still ambiguous on the principle of protectionism and cautious over the scale of reform needed.

What turned an essentially technocratic exercise into something altogether more potent were the economic and social conditions when Peel came to power. There was already in the summer of 1841 a good deal of discontent in the country attributed variously to the Chartists, the Anti-Corn Law League and widespread unemployment. Troops were deployed to quell unrest. Bad harvests also led to more hunger and hardship. Polemicist Thomas Carlyle wrote a widely read paper on the 'Condition of England' which fuelled the demand that 'something must be done'. But the political mood of the times among the Liberals/Whigs – as well as the Tories – was not conducive to dramatic intervention: the state could assist but was not responsible for alleviating poverty and social distress.

Peel's slow conversion to the idea of radical reform – and reforming the Corn Laws – was down to a mixture of pragmatism and Christian conscience: a growing concern for 'the welfare of the people'. He was moved by seeing destitution in Paisley, Scotland, and mobilized charitable relief. His biographer Douglas Hurd argues that while his humanitarian instincts were often expressed in ways that others found 'priggish' and 'self-righteous', he was nonetheless genuine in his compassion, which was by no means the norm in his class and party.

The pragmatism was reflected in the slow and methodical way he went about trying to find practical solutions.

The Battle for Free Trade

Peel approached the problem of tariffs and the Corn Laws by trying to navigate carefully, with a lot of consultation and internal discussion, the narrow path between free traders and landowners.

His initial approach was to cut duties (on the 'sliding scale' devised by his predecessors). Outright abolition was not on the agenda. He criticized both the Conservative ultras and the Anti-Corn Law League as extreme. In parliamentary debates he denied that social distress was mainly due to the Corn Laws and claimed that their abolition would add rural to urban poverty. His aim was to cut tariffs to help consumers, but protectionism was to remain the national system.

The big practical problem was how to recoup the loss of revenue from tariff cuts. There were some who argued (rather along the lines of the Laffer Curve which found such favour with Presidents Reagan and Trump) that such tax cuts would pay for themselves by generating more imports which enter at a lower rate but with a higher volume. Peel did not buy that argument and, moreover, had won the election in 1841 following a Whig administration characterized (and criticized) for budget deficits and heavy borrowing. He was committed to fiscal responsibility and pledged to restore the income tax (introduced by William Pitt to help pay for the Napoleonic Wars but dropped afterwards). The proposed tax was at a rate of 2.5 per cent, which horrified some of Peel's colleagues but which – in his 1842 budget – he was just about able to get through both Houses of Parliament along with the reform of tariffs.

He was helped by the fact that successive poor harvests had fanned the flames of civil unrest and increased destitution, which hardened his commitment to reform. As Norman Gash observed: 'Starting with an enquiry into the best means of balancing the budget, he ended with the broad concept of attacking poverty and restoring social stability.'[8] His determination in turn antagonized the ultras in his own party. His handling of them brought out the political skill which was an essential tool to get legislation through. There was intensive consultation, and patronage was used to flatter and buy off some opponents. Likewise, he mobilized in his support the ancient and venerable Duke of Wellington, who acted as a protector and human shield (rather in the way that Margaret

Thatcher used William Whitelaw and Tony Blair used John Prescott in modern times).

Despite getting the budget and Corn Law reforms through Parliament, the changes were regarded as half-baked by the Anti-Corn Law campaigners and as class betrayal by the landowners. The unstable equilibrium was shattered by climatic events in 1845 which led to poor harvests and an epidemic of plant disease in England and Ireland. The laissez-faire doctrines of the time (which Peel partly shared) and Malthusian determinism – the belief that famine was an inevitable corrective to overpopulation – acted as a drag on the provision of famine relief. Peel nonetheless pushed through emergency measures: the import of American maize and 'poor law' work programmes to give hungry people a source of income to pay for food.

The political dimensions of the crisis came to a head in the latter part of 1845 when the issue arose as to whether to reinstate the duties and import controls which had been temporarily lifted for famine relief purposes. Peel decided at this point to go for broke and abandon the Corn Laws entirely – mindful of the potential backlash on the streets, if he did not, from an angry worker population well mobilized by Cobden and his associates. His party was bitterly divided (the landowners rallying round Disraeli in opposition to the reforms), but he could rely on most of the Whigs under Lord John Russell. The next few months represented one of the most dramatic episodes in parliamentary history. Eventually Peel prevailed over the protectionists, but his party was irretrievably split. The passions of Parliament spilt over into the country and Peel became a public hero while detested by most of his party. As for the Irish, 'The sequence of famine and disease followed its tragic course without regard to the debates and decisions at Westminster.'[9]

The short-term economic legacy of Peel's reforms – now largely forgotten – was disastrous. To pay for cheap grain for the British working man and woman, a large amount of gold flowed out of the banking system. Under the rigid rules of the Gold Standard (which Peel had himself instituted under banking legislation) money supply tightened. Interest rates rose from 2.5 per cent to 10 per cent. Recession and hardship followed, the consequences of which were alleviated by cheaper food but were undoubtedly negative overall.

The longer-term legacy of Peel was, however, altogether more positive and profound. Free trade was irreversible. Moreover, it was unilateral and unconditional; it was based on the benefits to consumers of competition and did not depend on foreign reciprocity or 'trade deals'. When Disraeli eventually rebuilt the Conservatives and returned them to power two decades later he made no effort to reopen the issue. There was a spasm of protectionist thinking in the Conservative Party at the beginning of the twentieth century (with Joseph Chamberlain) but it did not take root; and 'imperial preference' made a brief appearance between the First and Second World Wars. Nevertheless, Britain has remained a largely free trading country for the 170 years since Peel's reform. Even in the recent debates on Brexit, both sides claimed, in different ways, to be the heirs of Peel.

But the free trade doctrine did not take root elsewhere. France only temporarily embraced it under Napoleon III (thanks to the influence of Cobden). The USA has been ambiguous since Hamilton through to Trump. Germany was initially more of a free trading country than Britain but then it took a different path – as we shall now see with Bismarck.

3

Bismarck: The Economics of 'Iron and Blood'

Unlike Hamilton who pioneered a new approach to economic policy in the newly independent USA and Peel who embraced and implemented, against his earlier instincts, a radical shift to free trade, Otto von Bismarck (1815–98) had little interest in economic policy or economic ideas. Yet, by a mixture of accident and design, he oversaw three of the most important economic developments of the nineteenth century.

First, he used a customs union – the Zollverein – to promote closer economic integration. The Zollverein long pre-dated Bismarck's period in power. But he understood how to use it to integrate the many bits and pieces of a divided Germany, economically and politically, while also using it to create tariff barriers to outsiders (in this case, Austria). There are many parallels with today's European Union.

Second, he implemented a policy of protecting Germany's emerging manufacturing and traditional agriculture through tariff protection. He travelled in the opposite direction from Peel – he had been a free trader – and appears to have been going with the flow of political opinion and interest groups. There is no evidence of any interest in, or knowledge of, the underlying economics or that he had even heard of economist Friedrich List, who developed the rationale behind infant industry protection earlier in the century in Germany. List is Keynes's 'defunct economist' on whom Bismarck – however unconsciously – drew.

Third, he introduced social protection for workers, the forerunner of European welfare states and 'social Europe'.[1] This was despite his deep hostility towards organized labour (or, rather, because he was trying to head off 'socialism', which he abhorred): 'better to make a revolution than suffer one', he said.[2]

Bismarckian economic policy making was, therefore, a byproduct of actions pursued for other, political, reasons. It was the result of being a brilliant, skilful politician seeking to maintain the support of his political allies in the embryonic democratic structures which he tried to control. Much of the heavy lifting on economic matters was, in any event, left to a Prussian finance official, Rudolf von Delbrück, whom Bismarck trusted: 'the man of whom I can say that he is completely orientated in every aspect of his office and has an unusual ability to manage affairs and carry them out'.[3] (Between 1867 and 1870 Delbrück introduced a common currency, common standards, a common labour market and free movement in the new, federal, Germany government.) A more deterministic, less flattering view, of Friedrich Engels in his correspondence about Germany with Marx, was that this 'semi Bonapartist' was 'serving the interests of the bourgeoise' through the various political parties which represented the interests of the emerging class of industrialists and bankers.[4] No doubt Bismarck and the various economic interest groups were using each other.

None of Bismarck's biographers suggest that there was anything resembling a grand design through his political life as opposed to a serious of preoccupations – Prussian dominance; then German unification – which were served by the various economic levers he occasionally pulled. He frequently quoted the Latin expression *fert unda nec regitur* – 'one cannot make a wave, only ride it' – and that applies with force to the wave of German economic modernization.

Bismarck's political career was long and very complex with many shifts in alignment and policy position. His career is well chronicled[5] and I have no aspiration to add to the detail but only to extract those elements which explain how he advanced, in a radical way, economic policy in Europe.

The Beginnings

Bismarck was born in Prussia in 1815, the year that British and Prussian armies defeated Napoleon at Waterloo. He was born into a Junker family: a class of aristocratic landlords who owed allegiance to the King of Prussia. Bismarck himself declared: 'I am a Junker and intend to take full advantage of that fact.'[6] He was, in fact, 'the clever, sophisticated son of a clever, sophisticated mother'[7] (but distrusted and disliked intellectuals). He had little patience for the Junker life of a country squire (which he tried in his twenties, mixed with hard-drinking and womanizing), though he was only too happy to use his privileged access to the royal family which his Junker status gave him.

Germany, at the time, was split into thirty-nine, mostly tiny, statelets in a loose confederation dominated by Prussia and Austria. Prussia, with 10 million people, was somewhat overshadowed by Austria and the Habsburg Empire of 30 million. It was, in the early 1800s, predominantly rural and underdeveloped (though it had emerged stronger from the Napoleonic Wars, acquiring Rhineland including the Ruhr from the French).

This was the country into which Bismarck made his political entrance aged thirty-two in 1847. The Prussian parliament was semi-democratic, though Bismarck entered a tier of representatives reserved for Junkers when another member fell ill. At the time, the political mood was dominated by politically 'liberal' ideas – which included greater freedoms, wider suffrage and a yearning for German unity. The mood was encouraged by the King who allowed the press to operate freely. Bismarck was emphatically not of that stripe. After his maiden speech it was said he 'made a reputation for himself as the most extreme reactionary of a reactionary class';[8] but his talent was spotted as a future champion for conservatives and ultra-conservatives.

The conservative world which Bismarck represented was seriously challenged by the 1848 'year of revolutions' which (temporarily) toppled regimes in France and Austria and came close to doing so in Prussia. The rulers had failed to appreciate the social and economic changes coming with the spread of industrialization and a growing middle class (though these forces were well understood by Karl Marx, whose *Communist Manifesto*, with Engels, appeared in the same year). Bismarck's attempt to insert himself into the 1848 crisis as a saviour of the monarchy was rewarded with a job as Prussian representative in the parliament in Frankfurt of the loose confederation which included the German states and Austria.

In this rather unremarkable diplomatic posting he was required to deal with the structures of the Zollverein, the customs union which had been established in 1834 to provide some degree of economic unity, through tariff-free trade, between the many bits and pieces of states and statelets in the 'Confederation'. There is no evidence that Bismarck was particularly interested in the underlying economics. His biographer Edward Crankshaw observed: 'He knew a little about finance, but next to nothing about industry and trade and no idea at all of the tremendous power which the development of railways, of mining and manufactures, above all of coal, steel and chemicals, was in the process of bringing to the Prussian state.'[9]

However, he was able to use the two essential features of a customs union to pursue his main diplomatic objective of strengthening the Prussian cause. The first, the free trading element, bound the lesser states and dynastic rulers closer to Prussia. The second, the common external tariff, provided a mechanism to exclude others, in this case Austria. Complex diplomatic manoeuvring achieved

Bismarck's basic task of denying Austria access to the single market of the Zollverein. He could also see that trade agreements with outsiders could add another tier of discrimination and he cultivated the French Emperor Napoleon III, helping to deliver in 1859 a preferential free trade agreement with France, part of the Cobden-Chevalier network of free trade agreements. This treaty deepened the benefits of belonging to a Prussian-dominated Zollverein and was unattractive to Austria (which wanted higher tariffs to deal with French competition).

Iron and Blood: The Three Wars

In due course, Bismarck manoeuvred his way into the centre of Prussian court politics and in 1862, aged forty-seven, the King appointed him Prime Minister (and also Foreign Minister) of Prussia. He was to retain supreme power for twenty-seven years.

In his first appearance in the Prussian parliament, he made a speech, one sentence of which, for many, defined him: 'The great questions of the day will not be decided by speeches and the resolution of majorities – that was the great mistake from 1848 to 1849 – but by iron and blood.'[10] This statement has been widely characterized as the philosophy of an authoritarian war-monger who brought about the unification of Germany through force, dictatorial control and industrialization. Even those closest to him were not under any illusions. The King is reported to have said of him: 'red reactionary, smells of blood, only to be used when the bayonet rules'.[11]

In fact, Bismarck had to work with a civilian administration and an elected parliament dominated by liberals whose political philosophy he despised. Since he had no settled views on domestic policy he was willing to delegate to expert officials and he tried to build bridges beyond the minority conservatives who were his natural allies. The conservatives 'opposed the constitutional demands of the liberal majority... but they agreed with them on free trade'.[12] There was also an implicit understanding with the liberals, characterized by A.J.P. Taylor: 'Bismarck did not attempt a coup d'état; liberals did not attempt a revolution.'[13] Bismarck was, despite his dominance, resentful of criticism and, without destroying the constitution, created many of the features of a police state: parliamentary critics were fined for attacking the government; independent-minded businessmen lost contracts; and judges were required to be politically 'sound'.

Bismarck's energies were deployed overwhelmingly in diplomacy and foreign affairs. As a consequence of his diplomacy, Prussia embarked on three wars in six years (Denmark, 1864; Austria, 1866; France, 1870), won all of them conclusively (albeit with some heavy casualties) and consolidated Bismarck's control. I do not need to get into the detailed arguments as to whether Bismarck was the instigator of conflict or had, as he claimed, a restraining influence on belligerent generals and aggressive nationalists. Suffice it to say that Bismarck now had the freedom to do pretty much as he chose.

He moved rapidly, after the defeat of Austria, to promote the integration of Germany, economically and politically. He created a Chancellery for the North German Confederation and appointed his faithful supporter to head it – the Prussian finance official Delbrück, who had done the technical work on the Zollverein. Within a short period there was a common currency, a central bank and a common code of commercial law. Bismarck had political backing for the project from the liberal party – the National Liberals – based largely on economic grounds. According to his biographer Edgar Feuchtwanger, 'He was giving economic liberalism its head, but he never believed that political liberalism, which he did not want, would follow.'[14] By embracing free market economics, 'the basis was laid for the rise of Germany into a great industrial powerhouse, which became the one enduring legacy of the whole Bismarckian enterprise'.[15]

Peel, in the same year, was completing his difficult journey to free trade. Bismarck, and his supporters, had no such struggle but the signposts to a journey in the opposite direction were already visible. Creating a customs union, opening up markets, would further consolidate Prussian dominance but it would create strong resistance from those regions which felt themselves overwhelmed by the competition such as the pre-industrial regions of South Germany. Prussian Junkers were still free traders, at this stage, but they would find other aspects of the nationwide market economy a threat to their position.[16]

The End of Economic Liberalism

Although Bismarck never expressed any particular interest in economic policy and ideas, a liberal economic model for a unified Germany based on free markets and free trade took shape under his leadership. The question arises in retrospect as to who was leading whom. Edward Crankshaw notes that 'by the late 1850s it was obvious that the drive towards closer union among the Germans could never be reversed: the cultural, linguistic and military impulses were now powerfully reinforced by the needs of industry and trade, which turned out to be the critical factor... The movement towards closer union, then, was gathering an irreversible momentum... Bismarck, after a false start, found the way to ride that wave.'[17] And he rode it with the economic orthodoxy of his allies and officials. Bismarck may not have made the industrial revolution happen but he created the economic and political conditions in which it could proceed rapidly.

The defeat of France made Bismarck even more of a national hero, and dominant European statesman. But he could not buck the change of the economic weather. There was a major, cyclical, industrial boom in the early 1870s and reckless bank lending fed speculative bubbles. The inevitable collapse and slump followed, with recriminations centring on financial scams and official corruption (Bismarck himself had some difficulty separating his

personal finances from the state).[18] The more profound consequence was a big swing in the political and intellectual mood
against free trade and free market ideas. Industrial and agrarian
interests demanded protection. Groups sprang up – initially in the
cotton textile industry of South Germany which was threatened
by increased competition from the newly annexed Alsace Lorraine; then in the iron and steel industry; then heavy industry at
large – all arguing that national pride and national security, as well
as their own interests, were best served by ditching the prevailing
free trade orthodoxy.

The shift against openness was reinforced by Bismarck's
decision to turn against his longstanding free trading allies, the
National Liberals. Instead, he established a new alliance with the
Conservatives, who had a different – more protectionist – agenda.
Delbrück, the architect of economic integration in Germany,
was ditched. Bismarck's role in this big shift in economic policy is
somewhat obscure; in the words of historian Gordon Craig: 'The
truth of the matter seems to have been that the Chancellor had
no real convictions about the difficult tariff problem… although
he made intermittent attempts to inform himself about it (he read
Wilhelm von Kardorff's *Against the Current…*) he was always dis-
tracted by other matters.'[19] What appears to have converted him
from being 'a free trader by tradition, if not conviction' was the
realization that tariffs could be a valuable source of revenue, making his federal government less dependent on taxes raised in the
states.[20]

The adage of Keynes about 'defunct economists' is difficult to
test in the case of Bismarck whose economic views were somewhat opaque and rarely expressed. He was, however, undoubtedly
influenced by a new pressure group led by industrialists Wilhelm
von Kardorff and Friedrich Stöpel. Kardorff's book was widely
read and secured him an audience with Bismarck, who reportedly
told him: 'I was, myself, a free trader… but I am a complete convert and want to make good my earlier errors.'[21] The philosophy

of the protectionist group was summarized by Stöpel: 'Let us show that Germany is no longer the step-child of foreign interests and that she can stand economically on her own feet, just as she has become independent in political matters.'[22] This thinking attracted the support of a group of German economists called the National School who drew on the theories of American economist Henry Carey, who in turn drew on the thinking of Alexander Hamilton and Friedrich List.

List has often been credited with creating the intellectual framework for German industrialization and the use of protectionist trade policy.[23] He was, in fact, an influential advocate of internal free trade through a Zollverein before one was actually created, but he was also a strong advocate of pan-German nationalism and, as the leader of merchants and industrialists, argued for protection of the Zollverein from overseas competition. His main work in defence of tariffs – *The National System of Political Economy* – was published in 1841. It drew heavily on Hamilton and rejected the free trade ideas of Smith and Ricardo except between countries at the same level of development. At the time it was published, such arguments fell on deaf ears in Germany whose infant industries were flourishing without much tariff protection. A generation later, however, when the infants were already well developed, List's ideas provided academic respectability for what was, in fact, a cruder form of economic nationalism.

Although Bismarck's conversion to protectionism is often portrayed as a mechanism for supporting manufacturing, there was also a powerful agrarian push to protect German farming. And the interests, as they are today, were complex. Even as late as 1877 there was a big drive to cut tariffs on imported iron for iron-using industries including steel until the iron makers fought back (and won). The consequences of Bismarck's conversion to protection were, as Crankshaw describes it, clear: 'Nobody would deny that the abandonment of free trade in favour of protection accelerated the transformation of Germany into the strongest industrial power on the European continent and an active challenger to Britain.'[24]That conclusion has reverberated through economic policy debate to the present time. Free trade worked for Britain and many other, relatively open, economies. But for countries like Germany, the USA and Japan in the nineteenth century, and many others since, protection has been successful in allowing countries to catch up by accelerating their industrialization, including in their development of military capability.

Social Reform Without Socialism

We have seen that Bismarck oversaw and guided two major economic policy revolutions – the German customs union and single market and the adoption of protection – while remaining largely indifferent to the economics and motivated primarily by the politics of the change. That applied even more to his third major transformation: the construction of the world's first welfare state.

Bismarck detested socialism and everyone who advocated variants of it, notably in the Social Democratic Party. Throughout his career he was determined to thwart and repress working-class organizations and constantly manoeuvred to exclude the Social Democrats from power. One of the greatest ironies of his political career was that he delivered a lot of what his socialist enemies were demanding, through regulation, public spending and taxation, in order to head off what he considered to be the live threat of socialist revolution.

The threat of socialism, as Bismarck saw it, had been seen in the 1848 uprisings across Europe. But it did not yet find expression in elections to the Prussian parliament where the complex three-tier voting system favoured the middle classes (and their broadly liberal views) rather than workers. Organized labour made an appearance in 1863 when a charismatic campaigner, Ferdinand Lassalle, established the German Workers' Association together with Karl Marx (who quickly abandoned it). Bismarck sought him out for a series of private conversations,[25] apparently to make common cause against 'bourgeois liberals', while Bismarck continued to denounce everything Lassalle stood for. Lassalle also faced charges of high treason while pursuing his (genuine) friendship with Bismarck but died in a duel before he achieved either revolution or imprisonment.

The threat of socialism became palpable when the Social Democrats made serious progress in elections following the economic downturn of the early 1870s, under the Marxist leadership of Wilhelm Liebknecht and August Bebel.[26] Germany became polarized between the propertied classes and the urban proletariat. Bismarck sought to crush the socialists and he introduced legislation to persecute them. However, it did not achieve its aims. There was, as Crankshaw put it, 'a strain of insanity running through [the anti-Socialist Bill]... Its only effect on the growth of Socialism was to accelerate it, to turn mild idealists into doctrinaire Marxists.'[27]

But in parallel with largely unsuccessful attempts to suppress the new movement, Bismarck sought to address the underlying discontent. He had a record of embracing social welfare, having supported weavers in a strike against employers, and he had long advocated the 'right to work', a key demand of the 1848 revolutionaries. He also honestly set out his approach to unrest as early as 1871: 'The action of the state is the only means of arresting the Socialist movement. We must carry out what seems justified in the socialist programme.'[28] (This somewhat Machiavellian approach also explains an odd episode when a newspaper, which Bismarck controlled, offered Karl Marx an opportunity to write a regular column. Marx declined.[29])

The practical manifestation of Bismarck's social welfare reform was a system of social insurance which protected every German worker against accident and sickness and guaranteed a basic state pension and disability benefits. He also advocated unemployment insurance, though this – very radical – idea was never implemented. Lest anyone be under any illusion that he was really a socialist, he opposed factory inspection and limitation on working hours. Nor did he get his own way on social welfare: the idea of the state contributing to social insurance (as opposed to employers, mainly, and the workers themselves) was struck out by the Reichstag. Moreover, as a political ploy, the social reforms and the repression did not work – the Social Democrats emerged as the largest party in forthcoming elections. But Bismarck had created the architecture for future welfare states across Europe. At their heart was the concept of a social compact in which workers are provided with social insurance and guaranteed employment in exchange for political stability and labour peace.

By 1890, however, Bismarck's political manoeuvring ran out of road and, faced with a hostile set of forces in the Reichstag, he failed to gain the support of the new Emperor, Wilhelm II, and left office.

The Legacy

The unhappy history of Germany in the first half of the twentieth century has led many to blame Bismarck for leaving a poisoned legacy. Even though he was a civilian and his skill was diplomacy, he is accused of legitimizing the militarism which led to the First World War and, indirectly, the Second. The phrase 'iron and blood' has been used to underline this criticism and also the fact that one of his first industrial visits – in 1864 – was to Krupp to support what in the twentieth century has been called the military-industrial complex. A.J.P. Taylor's pithy phrase was that his legacy was 'an excess of militarism and a deficit of liberalism'.[30]

A second and related point is that his attempts to control politics led to his bypassing and undermining the genuine, if flawed, democracy reflected in the Reichstag with its universal male suffrage. And, in the process, he undermined not just liberal democracy but liberal economics in favour of a kind of corporatism, embodied in the *Wirtschaftsrat* – his council of corporate bodies. The habits of cartelization and cosy interest groups dominating policy have persisted until modern times despite the efforts of Ludwig Erhard and others – as we review later – to reform it.[31]

A third criticism is that, on his watch, anti-Semitism grew with the appalling consequences manifest in the Holocaust six decades later. There is a lot of evidence of Bismarck's own casual but selective anti-Semitism.[32] And he undoubtedly made some use politically of the nationalist and socialist demagogue Adolf Stoecker[33] who tried to make anti-Semitism respectable and commonplace in nineteenth-century Germany.

To set alongside these big negatives are the three major economic changes we have discussed: the unification of Germany through economic integration in a customs union; the switch to protectionism which accelerated Germany's industrialization; and the creation of a welfare state, a 'compact' between labour, business and government, which was to provide the social underpinnings of Germany's broadly successful economic model for most of the next century. It would later expand into a wider Social Europe.

How much credit Bismarck should personally claim for Germany's advances is debatable. A.J.P. Taylor is pretty dismissive: 'It never occurred to him that the aggrandisement of Prussia or the unification of Germany might have come naturally by force of economic circumstances.'[34] But, either way, he was a crucial catalyst.

4

Lenin: From War Communism to State Capitalism

Many would question my inclusion of Vladimir Lenin (1870–1924), arguing that the leader of the Bolshevik revolution and the first communist state contributed nothing to the way countries conduct economic policy. They would argue that he created an unambiguously vicious totalitarian tyranny which paved the way for Stalin and made a template for Mao and Pol Pot, who killed millions and created nothing of enduring value. Moreover, the economic model of centralized state control he helped to form simply failed, leading to the eventual collapse of the Soviet Union, its satellites and also its emulators.

There is a more generous view – which I broadly share – which does not gloss over the brutalities and epic mistakes which Lenin perpetrated. But it acknowledges a lasting contribution to our understanding of how economically backward countries can be transformed. Crucially, at the end of his life, he also developed a model of what he called 'state capitalism': the New Economic Policy (NEP), creating market incentives for peasant farmers and utilizing domestic and foreign capitalists on a controlled basis.

The true significance of the NEP is much debated. Lenin launched it in the early months of 1921 and his involvement declined rapidly after the series of strokes which began in December

1921 and which would eventually kill him. We do not really know how much Lenin saw the NEP as more than a short-term, temporary expedient rather than a viable, longer-term strategy for development. We do know that when Mikhail Gorbachev tried to 'reverse engineer' a form of NEP, known as Perestroika, it did not work. That may well have been, however, because the conditions under which the NEP operated in the 1920s were so different from the world of the 1980s in which the USSR was trying, and failing, to assimilate computerization, automated technological systems and creative forms of innovation. We also know that, while the NEP operated, it achieved some impressive economic results. The variants of it which have been adopted elsewhere in developing economies, notably in Deng's China, have been highly successful, at least in economic terms at a certain stage of development.

Lenin also illustrates one of the main themes of this book: the bringing together of practical – albeit revolutionary – politics, economic theory and economic practice. His writings and statements as a leader of revolutionary Russia did not acknowledge disciplinary boundaries. Indeed, he saw politics as an outgrowth of economics; and vice versa. He explicitly acknowledged the intellectual debt to a 'defunct economist', namely Marx, a relationship embedded in Marxist-Leninism, which links economic analysis to revolutionary action.

Formative Ideas

Lenin's biographers, such as Louis Fischer,[1] describe the upbringing of Vladimir Ulyanov (nicknamed Lenin) in an educated, professional family in a provincial town on the Volga. His most important formative experience, aged seventeen, was the hanging of his elder brother, Sasha, for a failed assassination attempt on Tsar Alexander III. It is clear that, as a teenager, he was exposed to the arguments about the role of terrorism in overthrowing the regime. After the execution, he became a committed revolutionary. It is less clear how soon he immersed himself in political theory and Marx's *Das Kapital*; Soviet biographers stress his early theoretically orthodox development; others suggest that he preferred reading novels and was more interested in the practicalities of terrorism.[2] But he was soon, in his early twenties, providing polemical Marxist literature, the first of an estimated 10 million words he would write.

After his overseas exile aged twenty-five (and previous internal exile) he developed his Marxist reading and writing while at the same time engaging in the bitter, intolerant, sectarian feuding which characterized the later revolution and had such disastrous consequences, not least for economic policy. The main schism, of many, was between the Social Democrats, or Marxists, and the Social Revolutionaries, another revolutionary movement which was rooted in the struggle of the Russian peasant. Lenin's Marxism was city based and worker oriented; this reflected the dismissive views of Marx and Engels in *The Communist Manifesto*, referring to the 'idiocy of rural life', welcoming industrial capitalism and the revolutionary potential of the urban proletariat.[3]

In due course Lenin had to modify his views (before the revolution, he promoted a peasant–worker alliance and then embraced the peasantry in the NEP), but this urban–rural dichotomy was to do great damage in the early stages of the revolution (as later in Mao's China). And, within the Marxist Social Democrats, there was another poisonous feud: between the Mensheviks and Bolsheviks who differed essentially on revolutionary tactics (in his famous pamphlet *What is to be Done?*, Lenin attacked 'Economists', like the Mensheviks, who concentrated on what he saw as side issues, like improving conditions for workers rather than revolutionary organization. The Mensheviks were, also, altogether too gradualist and moderate in their approach). There was no indication in his vast output of writing in exile and endless speechmaking at party conferences that Lenin had any interest in the practical problems of how to run a post-revolutionary state beyond the highly

theoretical prescriptions in his *The State and Revolution*: that the pro-
letarian state will 'wither away' into a classless society ('strengthen
the government in order to annihilate it!'). Lenin's aim before the
revolution was simple, but massively ambitious: to seize the Russian state for the Bolshevik party.

The Inheritance and War Communism

The story of the Bolshevik revolution has been told and analysed
many times and does not need repetition.[4] Suffice it to say that
from 7 November 1917, the Bolsheviks took charge of Russia with
the aim of building socialism out of the wreckage of a collapsing society, political demoralization and an economy stretched to
breaking point by war – with a capital city (St Petersburg) populated by hungry, angry people. As the old adage has it: the man
who breaks through a rotting door acquires an unjustified reputation for violence; some credit should be given to the door. The
actions of the Bolsheviks have to be put in the context of a society
which was disintegrating and their approach to economic management reflects the level of development, wartime destruction
and resistance which they inherited.

Although Russia in 1917 was a mess, it would be a mistake to
regard the country as underdeveloped, illiterate and technologically backward. The Russian Empire was, until the First World War,
growing quite rapidly (about 5 per cent per annum over the quarter century before the war) as a consequence of the modernization
programme, infrastructure development and industrialization initiated by the Tsar's reformist ministers, Stolypin and Witte. But,
in 1913, the level of industrial development was still lower than
Spain or Italy and far below the USA and UK in sectors such as
steel making, textile production or electricity generation. Russia
was still overwhelmingly rural and, while improving, the productivity of farming was perhaps half that of the UK or Germany.
There was also an emerging but small middle class (an estimated

36 per cent of men and 1 per cent of women were literate at the turn of the nineteenth century).[5]

War superimposed great strain on an already fragile economy. The mobilization of 15 million men, large numbers of whom perished, led to a decline in agricultural production of around a third. Rail disruption by military demands led to an estimated 60 per cent fall in grain transported and, despite the rising demand, production of coal and steel fell sharply. Industry ran out of spares and food supplies ran short in the cities, despite requisitioning from farmers (a crude and often brutal technique adopted by the Bolsheviks). Disgruntled peasants were paid in a rapidly depreciating currency and there was widespread rural revolt and violence. The provisional government which came to power in March 1917 was not able to stop the rot (not helped by the systematic disruption and strikes organized by the Bolsheviks). Economist Maurice Dobb quotes a contemporary Russian diarist: 'How on earth is Kerensky to cope with the administrative disorganization, the agrarian movement, the financial crisis, the economic debacle, the universal spread of strikes and the progress of separation', and another as saying: 'the situation is so bad that, in everybody's opinion, it could not be made worse'.[6] The way was open to Lenin's seizure of power.

As already noted, the debate around how to implement Marxist economic policy in post-revolutionary Russia had been conducted in high levels of ideological abstraction. There was nothing remotely resembling a policy manual. Marx had not provided much by way of a blueprint. Lenin himself had devoted some thought to economic matters in *Development of Capitalism in Russia*, published in 1899. But as the title implies, it was a work of economic history from a Marxist perspective. Moreover, his years in exile were devoted to thinking about, and organizing, a revolutionary movement; not running the economy of a country in a state of collapse, which will have seemed a wildly improbable scenario until shortly before it happened.

The overall position of the economy, which the optimist quoted earlier believed could not get any worse, did just that. A vast civil war followed the First World War, with the need to direct resources to several fronts. The Brest-Litovsk peace treaty with Germany was costly in territorial terms. There was intervention by Western allies on the side of the anti-Bolshevik rebels in the civil war and a new war – with Poland – was shortly to come.

But it would be unreasonable to say that Lenin was just making it up as he (and his colleagues) went along. On three big, interconnected questions the Bolshevik leadership had a clear view of what it was trying to do.

The first was the use of coercion and state direction as a tool of economic policy. Although they were more ruthless and brutal than their ineffective predecessors, what they were doing was no different, in principle, and many countries, including Western democracies at times of war, have used consumer rationing, direction of labour, production planning and requisitioning. The ruthlessness reflected both their ideology and the exigencies of the time. Amid widespread hunger and hardship, there was crude rationing through state or cooperative outlets; private trade in many consumer goods was banned; hoarding was considered sabotage; and political terror was merged with economic terror, with mass searches and executions of 'speculators'. Lenin's belief in centralized control and direction sometimes led him into conflict with idealistic 'left communists' who believed in workers' control. For example, he removed railways from trade union control to a semi-military control system.

The second was the priority to be given to the urban proletariat (over the peasantry and business and middle-class interests). As summarized above, there had been a long debate on the respective role of agriculture and industry, workers and peasants (of whom there were several sub-categories depending on the size of their holdings). The Bolsheviks, unlike the Social Revolutionaries, placed the emphasis on industry and the industrial proletariat.

However, once the revolution was launched, Lenin saw political advantages in a gesture of appeal to poorer, especially landless, peasants who were involved in numerous uprisings at the time. Land was nationalized and then redistributed by village-level committees. The hiring of labour was banned, and Lenin launched a verbal – and increasingly real – war against the kulaks (better-off peasants). The vicious spirit of the times is captured in a letter from Lenin to a provincial commissar: 'Comrade… Hang (and I mean hang so that the people can see) not less than 100 known kulaks, rich men, bloodsuckers… [the people] are killing and will go on killing the bloodsucking kulaks. Yours, Lenin. PS Find tougher people.'[7] Lenin's theoretical distinction between acceptable middle (and poorer) peasants and unacceptable kulaks made little sense at a village level and was largely ignored by the commissars whose job was to procure grain from the countryside, somehow, to feed the army and the urban workforce. Crude violence and expropriation did not incentivize food production from a sullen farming population, which in turn intensified the brutality of the requisitions and the further alienation of the peasantry.

The third objective was the rapid speed at which it was desirable, and necessary, to socialize the economy in contrast to the more gradualist Mensheviks. There had been a long debate as to the speed with which socialism could be introduced and the degree of accommodation with capitalists and their managers in the early stages of the revolution. The more moderate revolutionaries like the Mensheviks envisaged a mixed economy; the Bolsheviks did not, though they were internally divided on the speed and on such questions as the role devolved to workers' committees as opposed to the state machine. Lenin sought to provide guidance in the few months before the revolution: banks were to be nationalized; the main business groups were to be subject to central control and regulation; independent firms were to be run by the workers (syndicalization); and business practices such as commercial secrecy outlawed. When the revolution came, the banks were, indeed, nationalized and effective centralized control of the wartime economy vested in a body called VSNKh. From June 1918 the tempo of outright nationalization was stepped up.

Lenin led the policy and was fully committed to any measures consistent with his aims. But he was sufficiently pragmatic to desist from the nihilist, murderous attacks on the professional middle class and small businesses associated later with Stalin, Mao and Pol Pot. He was attacked by the utopian 'left communists' (who, confusingly, were later called 'rightists') for making use of 'engineers and economists' in a 'coalition with the bourgoisie'.[8] He wrote scathingly about 'left wing childishness' and demanded realism.

Taken together, however, the revolutionary measures aggravated the problems of a badly damaged economy facing civil war. Hunger was widespread. The Bolsheviks' response was to intensify the use of terror, arbitrary expropriation and requisitions. This 'War Communism' came to be characterized by the banning of private manufacture and the nationalization of all industry; the allocation of all material stocks by the state; a ban on private trade; and seizure of peasant surpluses above subsistence and seed corn level. The effect was the partial elimination of money – what Alec Nove called a 'siege economy with communist ideology. A partly organized chaos.'[9] At a most basic level the militarization of the economy worked militarily. The White Armies, and then Poland, were defeated in what was a remarkable recovery from a position where Russia was totally blockaded (the White Armies had controlled 60 per cent of territory where there were railways).

But the issue of how to reconstruct and run a communist economy in peacetime now became pressing. And this led to a fundamental rethink by Lenin of the economics of Marxist-Leninism.

The Big Rethink

There is a continuing debate as to how far the extreme measures of War Communism represented for Lenin the norm from which the more relaxed, liberal economic policies of the New Economic Policy were an expedient exception, or whether War Communism was itself the exception. Maurice Dobb quotes Lenin very much in terms of the latter interpretation: 'War Communism was thrust upon us by war and ruin… a temporary measure.' And Lenin launched the new policy by proclaiming: 'Some of the things we were compelled to do by necessity… We did much that was simply wrong.'[10]

There were several specific factors which brought about the change in direction. The most important was the breakdown in trade in grain between towns and villages and the alienation of the poorer peasantry, formerly seen as political allies as well as food producers. The argument was not just theoretical. Catastrophic harvests in 1920 and again in 1921 – caused not just by drought but by farmers' reduction in sowing – led to appalling famine. Millions are thought to have died, not just from the decline in food production but from the collapse in transport and trade, hampering relief efforts.

Lenin responded to harshness with more harshness, but his speeches from early 1920 also include references to a new approach, including a recognition that carrots were needed as well as sticks, specifically to replace compulsory requisitioning of grain by a tax in kind. Peasants would have an incentive to grow more food since they would be able to keep the surplus, after the amount taken from them (to feed the army and workers), to buy manufactures or enjoy the freedom to choose how to spend their disposable grain crop. At first sight, it is not clear what was new since both old and new policies involved expropriation of (part of) the food crop; the issue was about quantity rather than principle.

The new policy was, however, as Lenin acknowledged, a compromise which opened the door to bigger changes: farmers who generated a surplus could trade it, initially locally and then in national markets; the middle peasants, who were politically tolerated at this stage, could become richer, relative to their neighbours, and acquire more land, opening up class divides. Once the principle of markets was conceded – allowing the laws of supply and demand to operate – there was to be a fundamental change. As in earlier arguments about the use of experts, Lenin was contemptuous of the 'leftists' who failed to understand the political and economic logic: 'Only by coming to an agreement with the peasants can we save the socialist revolution. We must either satisfy the middle peasant economically and restore free markets or else we shall be unable to maintain the power of the working class. If certain Communists… think it possible in three years to transform the whole economic foundation, to change the very roots of agriculture, they are certainly dreamers.'[11]

Rationing ended and workers were paid in cash. All of this rapid marketization had, however, some unintended and painful consequences: accumulation of a glut of many products with shortages of others; and rising unemployment. And this took place against the background of continued famine and rapid inflation (aggravated in the short run by the lifting of price controls).

One previously unthinkable step was the opening up of the economy to foreign investors in the form of concessions for resource sectors like oil and timber. Foreign investors were, perhaps understandably, nervous and sceptical – but the mere fact of Lenin's personal commitment to reforms of this kind underlined the regime's seriousness.

Lenin was always anxious to justify theoretically what he was driven to do in practice and to define his own concepts. He described the NEP as 'a transitional mixed system' and he used the term 'state capitalism'[12] by which he meant a fusion of socialism – state control over the 'commanding heights' – and capitalism in the form of individualistic small-scale producers (kulaks and NEP-men). What was not clear, and much disputed since, was how long the transition to full socialism was due to last. Alec Nove, analysing Lenin's own contradictory comments, concludes that Lenin was in no hurry and saw the 'transition' lasting for a significant period. Indeed, he said the new policy should be carried through 'seriously and for a long time' – while suggesting that twenty-five years would be a 'pessimistic' timeline to get to a market-less socialism.[13]

The Workings of the New Economic Policy

From the extreme depths of the economic crisis which enveloped the country in 1920–21, there was strong – in some areas, spectacular – recovery. Industrial production doubled from 1920 to 1922 and passed pre-war levels in 1926, as did rail transport; electricity production reached pre-war levels by 1925; harvests recovered strongly from 1922 onwards. Government financial discipline led to a balanced budget in 1923/4 and a surplus in 1924/5 which in turn helped to stop a slide to hyperinflation.

The freeing up of markets, however, generated one major problem: what became known as the 'scissors crisis'. In short, the laws of supply and demand created dramatic and painful consequences in the form of big swings in the terms of trade – that is, relative prices – between urban consumers and peasant farmers.

At the start of the NEP, prices favoured the farmer because of the scarcity of food: a terrible harvest in 1921 followed by a big cut in acreage sown in 1922 led to famine, which caused farm labourers to die and farmers to eat their seed. And this relative price effect was compounded by a surplus of manufactured goods as firms tried to stabilize their finances or increase supply as they quickly recovered their capacity to produce when railways and power supplies improved.

But then there was a sudden and dramatic shift in the opposite direction. Food prices fell sharply as agriculture recovered with a bumper harvest in 1923. The chronic inefficiency of industry caused costs and prices to rise sharply. The surge in industrial prices, peaking in October 1923, then threatened to cause a major glut in manufactured goods as peasants could no longer afford to buy them.

The 'scissors' then corrected themselves with a swing back to higher grain prices and cheaper industrial goods. In an efficiently functioning market economy these fluctuations are partially ironed out through stocks and forward markets, but the Bolshevik state had only very primitive and insecure market mechanisms and there was a constant recourse to interventions, such as price control, to mitigate the impacts. This was nonetheless a period of strong growth and economic recovery, albeit largely in the form of re-establishing pre-war production, rather than creating new capacity.

Having launched the NEP in early 1921 and defended it through its initial difficulties, Lenin ceased to play much of an active role in policy debate after May 1922 when he suffered a series of strokes. Arguments raged around him, with some of his colleagues (led by Nikolai Bukharin) acting as champions of the more economically liberal approach (cautiously supported, at this stage, by Stalin) and others (led by Yevgeni Preobrazhensky, an ally of Trotsky) warning against it. The latter were specifically concerned about the dangers of creating a class of better-off peasants – kulaks and NEPmen – so they set out ideas around 'primitive capital accumulation' – in effect, expropriating the savings of the peasants to finance industrialization – which later became the Stalinist method.

Lenin made no public utterances after March 1923 and died in January 1924 before the decision was to be made of whether or not to retreat from the capitalist elements of the NEP. We do not know which of the factions and their different analyses he would have backed. All we know is what happened when Lenin was alive and functioning. In the words of his biographer Louis Fischer:

'the NEP raised living standards, saved the socialist state, [and] made Lenin the capitalist peasants' hero.'[14]

The Legacy

Lenin established the political apparatus which later was used by Stalin to create a totalitarian state which killed millions. He was also quoted in retrospect in defence of every twist and turn in Soviet ideology and policy. His name was used to justify Stalin and then to condemn Stalin. Then in the 1970s he was used by liberal thinkers to reveal the failures of the Soviet economic and political system. Champions of Gorbachev's Perestroika such as Alexander Yakovlev and Otto Latsis also used Lenin as a role model for how to reform the increasingly sclerotic economy of the Soviet Union, albeit one much more industrialized and technologically advanced than during the NEP.

More important for us today, a young Chinese student and factory worker in France called Deng Xiaoping – the subject of a later chapter – was following events in the Soviet Union and went to study there in 1926 when the NEP was in full cry. Deng's biographer notes that 'Deng believed, as did others at that time, that such an economic structure – whereby private enterprise was allowed, and foreign investment was encouraged, all under Communist Party leadership – promoted faster growth than could be achieved in capitalist economies. The fundamentals of the NEP... were similar to the economic policies that Deng would carry out.'[15]

What Lenin and then Deng both insisted upon was that economic and political liberalization did not go hand in hand. Lenin was reportedly obsessed by the experience of Robespierre, who lost control of the French Revolution. When promoting the NEP, he simultaneously moved to strengthen the Communist Party's monopoly of power to ensure that the beneficiaries of economic liberalization did not become a threat. Deng, in the same spirit, was willing to move decisively and brutally (as in Tiananmen Square) when the Communist Party's grip on power was threatened. The Western belief (shared by Gorbachev's reformers) that economic liberalization must lead to political liberalization and multi-party democracy was never part of the model of state capitalism developed by Lenin and his emulators. It should not surprise us that his ideological descendants in China, Vietnam and Cuba are so tenacious in making market reforms the property of the Communist Party.

5

Roosevelt: The Keynesian Revolution Without Keynes

Franklin Delano Roosevelt (1882–1945) was the first major political figure who came to power almost exclusively to remedy an economic crisis and who was defined largely by the remedies he pursued (before he became a successful War President). Economics and politics were interwoven through his presidency and his New Deal has come to be used as a model, or prototype, for large-scale government interventions in capitalist economies to this day, in the US and more widely. The New Deal experience is especially relevant in the current context in which federal government in the USA and governments more widely are being mobilized to counter economic depression in the wake of the Covid-19 pandemic.

Roosevelt did not need 'defunct economists'; he was surrounded by economic advisers whose mentors were very much alive. His New Deal is frequently and rather loosely described as Keynesian. But the evidence suggests that the direct influence of Keynes was very limited. Roosevelt, certainly in the early years, followed policies which differed from, or directly contradicted, some of the key propositions of Keynesian economics, and his partial conversion to Keynesian economics took place long after the New Deal had run its course. To the extent that economists influenced his thinking, it was through a changing cast of advisers and their influence fluctuated over time. In the early years he appears to have been advised by people who derived their own thinking from the neoclassical economist Irving Fisher and, in particular, the Lehman Brothers' economist Alexander Sachs.[1] Later it was not Keynes himself but the 'American Keynsians' – Alvin Hansen[2] and Lauchlin Currie – who seem to have set the intellectual agenda.

For the most part, the economic policies pursued by Roosevelt have to be considered a success. Except for a recessionary lapse in 1937–8 (for which his administration has been widely, and rightly, criticized), unemployment fell dramatically from 25 per cent in 1932 to under 10 per cent in 1936 (and again in 1940) and the national economy grew by 8–10 per cent per annum as it recovered in the 1930s from a depression which reached its nadir in 1932–3.

But there have been fierce critics.[3] Many are of the 'glass half full/half empty' variety. Problems like mass unemployment were eased but not solved. Some relate to genuine policy errors. Some are essentially ideological rather than technical: a reaction against the highly interventionist, occasionally 'anti-business', style of government. The big dividing line with the Republicans, initially under President Hoover, was over their belief that federal government was not the solution but the problem: a division which continued for decades after.

The Origins of the New Deal

The context of the New Deal was the economic crisis which engulfed the US following the Great Crash – the collapse of the stock market and the ensuing banking failures – from October 1929. In the next three years, industrial production fell by a half; unemployment surged to almost 25 per cent, leaving approximately 15 million without a job and millions of others underemployed. In the absence of a welfare safety net, millions lived in extreme poverty and hunger. An estimated 2 million people were wandering the country looking for work, while towns and cities were surrounded by homeless squatter camps, known as 'Hoovervilles'. In 1932 the United States economy stood at its lowest ebb in modern history. The government was reluctant to intervene, not wishing to get in the way of voluntary self-regulating action by business.

The political consequences were unsurprising. Hoover's Republican administration seemed destined to lose the 1932 presidential election provided the Democrats could choose a credible candidate. They did: Franklin Delano Roosevelt, the Governor of New York, who had built a reputation for 'progressive' politics with a comprehensive system of unemployment relief and measures sympathetic to organized labour.

Marked out from an early stage as a major political figure, FDR had name recognition as a cousin of Theodore Roosevelt, the Republican President (whose closeness was indicated by the fact that Theodore gave away FDR's wife, Eleanor, at their wedding). Wealth and connections got him an excellent educational start at Harvard, the Columbia Law School and then entry to a prestigious law practice (he studied economics as well as law but commented later that he took economics courses for four years and everything he was taught was wrong). He progressed quickly into New York state politics as a Congressman in 1911, aged twenty-nine, and built a reputation for fighting corruption in New York City. Eventually he was brought into the Woodrow Wilson Democratic administration (as Assistant Secretary of the Navy). He was the Democrats' vice-presidential candidate in 1920 against the Harding/Coolidge ticket. He seemed set fair for a shot at the presidency but in 1921 was struck down by polio, which left him wheelchair-bound for life. He staged a comeback and won the New York governorship in 1928. As the economy nose-dived into depression, he took proactive measures in his state to provide economic relief and welfare. These actions established his reputation and made it relatively easy to win the Democratic nomination from an old ally, Al Smith, who suffered the then disadvantage of being a Roman Catholic.

When Roosevelt accepted the Democratic nomination, he pledged himself to 'a New Deal for the American people' coupled with several specific commitments: increasing public works; supporting agricultural prices; creating new mortgage markets; shortening the working day and week; regulating securities; reforestation; and repealing Prohibition. There was a promise of lots of action and government intervention. What was missing was any overriding economic narrative; and what there was ran completely contrary to the later Keynesian interpretation of the New Deal. The Democrats had attacked Hoover for being a profligate spender and Roosevelt echoed the views of the fiscally orthodox:[4] 'I accuse the present Administration of being the greatest spending Administration in peace times in all our history… I regard reduction in federal spending as one of the most important issues of this campaign. In my opinion it is the most direct and effective contribution that government can make to business.'[5] This conservative approach to public finance survived the first five years of FDR's time in office, in marked contrast to the reputation subsequently bestowed on him, by friends and foes alike.

Causes and Cures

The New Deal was a radical programme of reform originating in FDR's election mandate to do something about the economic crisis. What he committed himself to doing, and did once elected, was shaped by popular narratives of what caused the crisis.

Explanations for the crisis were many and various. Some relate to various parts of the period building up to the 1929 'crash'; others focus on mistakes in the policy response. Some involve the search for real villains or imagined scapegoats who can be blamed; others are concerned with underlying impersonal economic and social forces. Some are grounded in overarching economic theory; others in casual observation. Some are self-serving; others dispassionate. Some are linked to practical solutions; others are just theoretical constructs.

Herbert Hoover, on whose watch the economic disaster occurred, searched into the past and events far beyond his control. He blamed the First World War, drawing on Keynes in his *The Economic Consequences of the Peace*: 'the primary cause of the Great Depression was the war of 1914–18' (because it destroyed the pre-war global economic order without creating a new one; together with such problems as unmanageable reparations demanded from Germany).[6] Undoubtedly, one of the contributing factors to the Great Depression was the growth of protectionist sentiment, and the USA led the way with tariff increases (in 1921 and 1922) and tougher immigration restrictions. Hoover made his own contribution by signing into law the Smoot–Hawley Tariff Act in 1930, which did not just provoke retaliation but made it more difficult for European countries to service and repay through exports large outstanding debts to the USA (what is called the 'transfer problem' in economics). An influential movement called the New Nationalists (which included Theodore Roosevelt) played into this 'America First' mood.[7]

However, as the US is a continental economy with a relatively small exposure to trade, the Great Depression could not be blamed primarily on external influences. Another set of explanations was to be found in the build-up of domestic debt, and instability in the supply of credit. The prodigious growth of the USA in the 1920s in production and living standards was driven in significant measure by consumer credit. The 'roaring twenties' featured hedonistic lifestyles underpinned by household debt. The massive expansion in the motor car industry (to 4 million cars produced in 1929) – as well as in radios and refrigerators – drove up demand for raw materials and infrastructure to service it. Demand for these durable goods depended heavily on consumers willing to incur debt to pay for them. Yet credit was not cheap (annualized 30 per cent for cars). And in the absence of social insurance and job security, the mass production of the new manufacturing industries was vulnerable to sudden freezes in consumer spending or a willingness to incur debt.

One of the leading neoclassical economists of that time, Irving Fisher, developed a theory of 'debt deflation', explaining how an accumulation of debt can become a cause of economic collapse (as happened after 1929) because an economic downturn leads to falling prices which increases the real cost of debt, leading in turn to defaults on mortgages and other loans, putting financial institutions at risk.[8] Fisher's influence was somewhat diminished by his having publicly claimed, before the stock market crash, that the market was stable and not at risk. But his emphasis on the need to avoid or reverse deflation was broadly understood by policy makers and, indeed, formed part of Roosevelt's approach to economic matters after he came to office.

There had already been a long history of credit cycles, amplified by a build-up of debt, manic speculation, asset bubbles, and the resultant panic-selling, financial distress and then slump in the real economy. Going back to Adam Smith and John Stuart Mill, there are explanations of this mechanism at work.[9] The experience of the Great Crash followed by the Great Depression followed the historic pattern on a grand scale but there appeared to be little awareness at the time that history was repeating itself yet again – in the United States there were similar cycles of varying degrees of severity in 1857, 1873, 1893, 1907 and 1920–21. The American economist Hyman Minsky would later develop a model based on this experience which was forgotten again in the run-up to the 2008 crisis.

One reaction to the Great Depression was to argue that such crises were inherent in capitalism, leading some to embrace some form of socialism. Roosevelt never went so far but the intellectual climate was influenced by such thinking. FDR and his circle of advisers wanted to reform the system, and a lot of the agenda of the New Deal was addressing the abuses exposed in the mania and panic, leading to large-scale government intervention including around banking and securities market reform.

There was another explanation of the Great Depression in terms of policy failure, and specifically failures in monetary policy. This argument hinged on a strong causal link between changes in the supply of money (variously defined but usually including most forms of credit) and changes in inflation as well as output. The empirical basis of the theory was a classic study by Milton Friedman and Anna Schwartz. They argued that the Depression was made much worse than it need have been by the failure of the Federal Reserve System to counteract a drastic contraction in money supply: 'throughout the contraction, the System had ample powers to cut short the tragic process of monetary deflation and banking collapse. Had it used those powers effectively in late 1930 or even in early or mid-1931... [S]uch action would have eased the severity of the contraction and very likely would have brought it to an end at a much earlier date.'[10]

This interpretation has been strongly challenged subsequently by Keynesians such as Peter Temin, arguing that a collapse of spending caused the contraction in money supply, not the other way around. And that collapse of spending may have been due to the sharp fall in wealth caused by the stock market crash. Alternatively, it may have been due to a restriction in bank credit as banks came under pressure; or a more general retreat into savings from spending as families, with little margin for safety, opted to spend less within a few months of the financial crisis.

Nevertheless, the almost theological debate between the monetarists and the Keynesians occurred long after the event and had little relevance to the political debate raging at the time. FDR scholar William Leuchtenburg said that Roosevelt 'instinctively accepted the under-consumptionist explanation of the cause of the depression',[11] but the influence of those arguing for more

government spending to revive purchasing power were held
to have only 'slight' influence.[12] They were more than counter-
balanced by those in the Democratic Party and in business who
regarded Hoover as a profligate spender. As for Roosevelt, a practical politician seeking to win the presidency for the Democrats for
the first time since Woodrow Wilson, he was on happier ground
attributing responsibility for the crash to where the public thought
it lay: the speculators, the bankers and big corporations. Likewise,
he favoured policies that would reward the coalition he was assem-
bling to cement his base of support: trade unionists, small farmers,
Southern whites and Northern blacks and others in the army of
people who were impoverished by the Depression.

New Deal: Reform – Not Recovery

The New Deal was essentially defined by the rhetoric of economic
warfare and Roosevelt's burst of energy when setting out a programme of action in his first 100 days in office.

His Inaugural Address was a call to arms seeking executive
power to wage war against the emergency; an uncompromising
attack on the bankers (the 'money changers' from the temple); and
a prelude to a rapid programme of legislative and administrative
action. Within those 100 days he had launched a rescue operation
for the banks followed by bank reform legislation and guarantees
for small bank deposits. He also launched an ambitious programme of government–industry cooperation (to be known as the
National Recovery Administration – NRA) and established federal regulation of the securities market. On the other hand, he
embarked upon austerity spending cuts, followed confusingly by
promises to spend large sums on the welfare of the unemployed
and farmers, and to save homes and farms from repossession, as
well as huge public works such as the dam building projects of the
Tennessee Valley Authority (TVA).

Most commentators have been somewhat dismissive of the

contribution of all of this to economic recovery, as opposed to structural reforms of varying merit. Historian David Kennedy concludes: 'the New Deal was not a recovery programme or at any rate not an effective one.'[13] Even such a sympathetic writer as Keynes's biographer Robert Skidelsky describes the New Deal as more about 'reform than recovery' and writes of Keynes's 'genuine but baffled admiration' based on a 'hotchpotch of recovery measures, culled from different strands of America's political tradition, inspired by no coherent plan, certainly not one of Keynesian provenance, but by the conviction that "something had to be done"'.[14] Nonetheless, business and consumer confidence were boosted by the frantic activity; Wall Street started booming again; and there was a surge – a doubling – in industrial production from March to July.

The reform measures were moreover significant in their own right and represented important economic judgements by Roosevelt and his advisers. His first major decision was to extend assistance to private banks to get them to reopen. In effect, he was putting into practice an earlier plan of the Hoover administration to rescue the banking system. There had been some expectation, from Roosevelt's rhetoric, that he planned more radical action, possibly nationalization. But, as a cynical Congressman observed, 'the President drove the money changers out of the Capitol on March 4th – and they were all back on the 9th.'[15] But, more positively, 'capitalism was saved'.[16]

There was additionally a move from Congress to separate investment banking from commercial banking: the Glass–Steagall banking bill, inspired mainly by arguments that the 'casinos' (i.e. investment banks) exposed commercial banks to excessive risks and contributed to the epidemic of bank failures. Critics argued that breaking up the universal banks was unjustified by the evidence and that the main source of bank failures were the thousands of small, specialized, local banks.[17] To protect depositors in big and small banks, Congress legislated to provide deposit protection insurance.

Glass–Steagall was eventually repealed (under President Bill Clinton) but the argument resurfaced in the UK after the 2008 financial crisis when the Vickers Report (with the encouragement of the current author) led to 'ring fencing' of investment banking in universal banks. The New Deal bank reforms taken together – rescue, restructuring and deposit protection – represent a template for how to deal with banking crises which has been used subsequently, notably in the (highly successful) Scandinavian operation in 1991–2 and then in the Asian financial crisis of 1997 and the global (but mainly US and UK) crisis of 2008.[18]

The next big reform initiative was to redefine the executive's relationship with business in general. Given the severity of the economic crisis there were voices around Roosevelt – among his campaign team and policy advisers – arguing for a fundamentally different kind of economic model. According to Leuchtenburg, 'The free market of Adam Smith [laissez-faire], the New Dealers argued, had vanished forever.'[19] But at the same time there was no appetite for socialism; Roosevelt was concerned with saving capitalism, not abolishing it. The key word in New Deal texts was 'balance' – between big business, small business, workers and farmers.[20]

A crucial source of ideas was the work of Adolf Berle and Gardiner Means on the workings of modern corporations which were increasingly dominated by their managers rather than their shareholders.[21] They concluded that monopoly and oligopoly were no longer just exceptions to be tackled through trust-busting in the tradition of Theodore Roosevelt. In other words, a competitive economy could no longer be restored. Instead, they argued that capitalism should be administered from the centre with planned output and prices, preferably in cooperation with business managers. The NRA was to be the vehicle for this planning. Critics of Roosevelt attacked this approach as either anti-business or too soft on business depending on the ideological starting point. Writer and broadcaster Alistair Cooke used the phrase 'ideological innocence' to capture the sense that Roosevelt was not easily pigeon-holed.[22] Admirers like J.K. Galbraith described this synthesis of capitalism and planning as 'liberal', using the word in a very different sense from Europeans.[23] One practical consideration which attracted Roosevelt to this form of government intervention and regulation was that it provided a mechanism to counter deflation. The government could directly drive up wages and prices, especially depressed commodity prices which were causing great hardship to farmers. As noted earlier, Irving Fisher in particular had warned of the dangers of deflation – and its impact on debtors – and the New Dealers were concerned about how to 'create inflation'.

Roosevelt also took another step to stop, and reverse, deflation. His remedy was to take the USA off the Gold Standard. The British had already left it, and since the UK was no longer committed to maintaining the value of the pound in terms of gold, it was effectively devaluing the pound against the value of gold and other currencies still linked to it such as the dollar. The consequent overvaluation of the dollar led to cheaper imports, in terms of dollars, driving down the price level: deflation. By leaving the Gold Standard, the President tried to escape from this deflationary strait-jacket, thereby establishing two important principles. One was to take control over monetary policy. The second was to use that control to counter deflation.

The third, and most important, element in the New Deal was the use of economic policy to promote recovery by boosting purchasing power: demand. Roosevelt's approach was deeply contradictory. On the one hand, he promoted public works and was in favour of extending financial help for the states to provide unemployment relief for the 15 million people out of work. He also launched a programme to convert mortgage debt into government debt, set up the TVA to build dams in the Tennessee Valley, and introduced support schemes for farmers.

However, as already noted, he also had an ascetic and conservative approach to public spending and budget deficits. One of his first acts as President was to cut $400 million from payments to veterans and cut the pay of civil servants by $100 million, saying: 'too often… liberal governments have been wrecked on rocks of loose fiscal policy', and criticizing again the outgoing Hoover administration for 'wild extravagance'.[24] Skidelsky has commented: 'the budget balancers had won a victory for orthodox finance that had not been possible under Hoover.'[25] Roosevelt, despite support for public works in principle, was hesitant about being too ambitious and spending too much money, believing moreover that there were few worthwhile projects.

On the other side of the Atlantic, Keynes's admiration for Roosevelt's dynamism was tempered by frustration over the lack of a coherent recovery programme. He wrote a letter to Roosevelt later published as an 'Open Letter to the President' in the *New York Times*. His criticism was essentially two-fold. First, he was opposed to the corporatist National Recovery Agency. He was a (European) liberal (and Liberal) who believed in markets and competition. He feared that government controls would inhibit private investment. Second, and more important, he believed there should be an accelerated programme of loan-financed public spending together with bond buying to drive down long-term interest rates, which would make investment more attractive to business (which is what Quantitative Easing does today).[26] The first half of his package fell on deaf ears but Keynes is credited with encouraging a quiet but effective US Treasury programme of buying government bonds. In May 1934 Keynes did manage to secure a personal meeting with Roosevelt. He was on a transatlantic tour seeking to explain to US decision makers and economic thinkers Keynesian concepts like the multiplier from public spending and the importance of raising effective demand. All of this bore fruit eventually as influential American economists such as Alvin Hansen shifted their position and Keynesian ideas gradually infiltrated the administration via Roosevelt's advisers.

In actual fact, what first started to shift the administration's thinking was a combination of factional fighting, alarm over a rise in violent strikes around the country and an upsurge of populist politics (from the Democrat Huey Long in Louisiana; and a radio host, Father Coughlin, who combined 'banker bashing' with anti-Semitism and fascist sympathies). Roosevelt held the balance between the various factions in the administration and that balance was crucially disturbed when Lewis Douglas, the Budget Director, resigned over growing deficits in the budget caused mainly by Roosevelt sponsoring a growing volume of public works and relief payments while Congress reversed the earlier cuts. He was replaced by Henry Morganthau who was relatively less austere. Congress was also becoming more radical as mid-term elections loomed, with the threat of violence and populist politics in the background, and legislators became less concerned with spending discipline and rather more with government action. Within the administration, Harry Hopkins, head of the Federal Emergency Relief Administration, prevailed over the much more cautious head of the Public Works Authority, Harold Icke. Politics and personality were pushing Roosevelt to be more ambitious and expansive with public finance.

Roosevelt's first two years of quick-fire legislative action and the stream of new initiatives then ran into serious trouble with the Supreme Court. The Court made a series of rulings which rendered unconstitutional some of the New Deal provisions and threatened to derail it. Roosevelt threatened to pack the Supreme Court with his supporters and succeeded in intimidating some conservative justices while replacing others. He then pushed ahead with major new pieces of legislation. One was the introduction of a social insurance scheme – financed by employers and employees – to guarantee a pension. A second was a bill to strengthen the rights of trade unions. A third took further the earlier banking reforms. A fourth was to strengthen regulation of utilities together with a big rural electrification programme. And finally, there was a 'soak the rich' tax package involving more 'progressive' income tax (with the top rate tax reaching 75 per cent). Similarly, there were higher taxes on estates and high taxes on undistributed profits (the last in particular, penalizing business investment, was strongly criticized at the time for impeding recovery). All of this activity came to be called the 'second 100 days' and created a platform for Roosevelt's re-election campaign in 1936.

The New Deal, for all the criticisms and weaknesses, nonetheless contributed to a strong recovery. National income was 50 per cent up and industrial production doubled from 1933 to 1936. The car industry was back to pre-crash levels of production and electricity generation was at record highs. Despite the regulatory and tax measures of concern to business, business profits had risen sharply while indicators of poverty had fallen. Unemployment was dropping, but was still over 10 per cent going into the 1936 election and there seemed every prospect of millions remaining without work. There was, nonetheless, little risk to Roosevelt's re-election; he remained personally popular and there was sufficient evidence of progress to sustain a real sense of optimism. In the event, he carried every state bar two small states in New England. But the economy flattered to deceive, and no sooner was Roosevelt re-elected than the recovery was hit by a new recession.

Relapse into Recession

The optimism engendered by the New Deal and then by Roosevelt's re-election was suddenly and brutally punctured by a rapid descent into a new recession which none had predicted and appeared unrelated to the normal business cycle (since there was still a large pool of unemployment and a degree of spare capacity). Yet in the summer of 1937 there were reports of unsold stocks and within a few months industrial production fell by a third and durable goods production fell by about 50 per cent. Production in steel fell from 80 per cent of capacity to 20 per cent. About 20 per cent of the workforce lost their jobs and unemployment surged again to over 10 million. The stock market collapsed – from an index of 190 in August to 115 in October.[27]

There were strongly differing views as to what caused this sudden recession and the different viewpoints all found evidence to support their positions. One, monetarist, view is that the Federal Reserve made a serious error in tightening monetary policy in spring 1937. The Treasury Secretary had signalled a wish to curb the growth in bank lending because he feared unwanted inflation caused by the recovery getting out of control. The Federal Reserve then compounded the policy tightening by increasing the reserve requirement of the banks (the proportion of holdings they couldn't loan out). Banks rebuilt their reserves by selling bonds, which drove down bond prices and increased bond yields, i.e. long-term interest rates. Higher interest rates combined with a sharp contraction in money supply ('narrow money', or M1, expanded 12.8 per cent in 1936 but growth fell to 5 per cent in the first half of 1937, 6.5 per cent over the year). The authorities underestimated the fragility of the recovery and the monetary squeeze depressed the economy.

Another, or complementary, explanation is that what we now call the 'supply side' of the economy was damaged by a combination of measures which undermined the willingness of business to invest and to hire labour. These included higher taxes on rich individuals and business (and, specifically, the tax on business-retained profits); new labour laws which pushed up labour costs (there was a big spurt of productivity between 1933 and 1938 as businesses substituted machines for labour); and the extra costs of social security taxes for business. One critical economist, K.D. Roose, argued: 'these taxes... may have contributed to the unwillingness of investors to undertake risky ventures... the level of individual income taxes and capital gains taxes may have assisted in precipitating the recession by limiting profits after tax.'[28]

The key to the recession was the low level of business investment and the fact that most of it was short-term.[29] Threats from

the President and Congress directed at those responsible for holding back long-term investment probably discouraged investment
even further. Joseph Schumpeter endorsed this point of view:
'[Employers] realize that they are on trial before judges who have
the verdict in their pocket beforehand, that an increasing part of
public opinion is impervious to their point of view and that any
particular indictment will, if successful, be replaced by another.'[30]

The Keynesian interpretation was quite different – and ultimately more influential. The recession, they argued, was simply a
product of weak demand which was compounded by an administration decision to tighten both monetary and fiscal policy. The
recession, in fact, was the result of a misguided plan by Treasury Secretary Henry Morganthau to balance the budget by 1938.
Morganthau, as an old and trusted friend of Roosevelt, persuaded
him to go along with this scheme based on the potential political
advantages such as characterizing the Republicans as the party of
profligacy. Morganthau and Roosevelt were concerned that their
own expansionary policies had led to persistent budget deficits.
In 1929/30 the federal budget was balanced (spending $3.4 bil-
lion; tax $4.2 billion) but by 1935/6, expenditure had risen to $8.5
billion with tax revenue unchanged. There was, indeed, a deficit
in every year of the 1930s despite the protestations of Roosevelt
that deficits were unacceptable. He and Morganthau were worried, both that the economy was now threatened by inflation and
that businesses' reluctance to invest was caused by fear of higher
taxes resulting from deficit financing. Since the New Deal, whatever its other successes, had failed to bring the country out of
the Depression they were attracted to the argument that it was
time to try a balanced budget approach, as many businesses were
arguing.[31]

In June 1937 government spending was cut sharply – the job
relief and public works schemes were scaled back – while simultaneously social security taxes were being raised. Keynes himself
made the point that this combination of tax rises and spending

cuts was exactly the wrong policy: 'it should have been obvious that as soon as the government began spending less and as soon as the pace of improvement was somewhat moderated, a set-back was inevitable.'[32] In Keynesian terms an initial stimulus – albeit largely unintended – had worked, and the 'multiplier' had caused modest government spending and investment to generate several times the amount of output and income. But the failure to create an 'accelerator' effect – higher output leading to investment – was because the stimulus had not been big enough. Keynesians like Michael Stewart summarized the wisdom of hindsight: 'looking back today any economist or politician who has assimilated Keynes must feel that the only trouble with the US Administration's deficit spending in the 1930s was that it didn't go nearly far enough', and the lack of investment – the accelerator – was due to an 'excessive amount of idle productive capacity. Until demand was high enough to call existing capital equipment into use there seemed little point in installing more. Only an even greater increase in public spending could have led at all quickly to this.'[33]

Roosevelt's initial reaction to the Keynesian critics was to ignore or repudiate them. He is reported to have told the cabinet: 'Everything will work out if we just sit tight and keep quiet.'[34] The recession continued and deepened. By March 1938, seven months from its start, 4 million had been thrown out of work and the stock market crashed again. Then, at last, the President did a U-turn in response to political pressure and in April asked Congress to embark on a large spending and borrowing programme, reviving the New Deal programmes which had been cut and embarking on large-scale public works. There has long been a scramble to claim credit for the President's late conversion to Keynesian economics. His economy adviser Lauchlin Currie played a key role.[35] But perhaps the crucial influence in shifting the centre of gravity of economic opinion was Alvin Hansen, who had been a long-term sceptic of Keynesian ideas but became a strong and influential convert.

Even then, Roosevelt did not really buy into the new economic thinking; as Leuchtenburg explains: 'he still had not embarked on the kind of massive spending which the Keynesians called for... Roosevelt trusted in common sense... and the Keynesian formula for gaining prosperity by deliberately creating huge deficits year after year seemed to defy common sense. Roosevelt was willing to contemplate limited emergency spending.'[36]

There was a sluggish recovery, with the help of this stimulus – albeit limited and reluctant – and it was reinforced by the build-up of armaments with the approach of war. It was sufficient, with the other New Deal reforms, to provide Roosevelt with a comfortable victory in his bid for a third term in 1940, though unemployment was still standing at 10 per cent until well into 1941 and the Japanese attack on Pearl Harbor, and there was a widespread belief that this was a problem which would never be solved. It was then solved, however, by war, which finally liberated Roosevelt's administration from the constraints of traditional fiscal prudence. Between 1941 and 1945 federal spending rose from $13 billion to $92 billion and budget deficits from $6 billion to $47 billion. Some 3.8 million more jobs were created (to 40 million), near full employment. War became the Third New Deal.

The Legacy

Roosevelt's economic legacy remains a subject of continuing controversy. To some he was 'the saviour of capitalism';[37] others thought he greatly undermined the private enterprise system through high taxation and regulation. To many he saved Western democracy by providing, through active government, a political solution to the economic crisis of the inter-war period, though authoritarian regimes in Europe also admired and copied some New Deal ideas. He is credited with being the first major political figure to understand and utilize Keynesian economics, though, as we have seen, he never fully believed in this approach to economics and frequently pursued policies of an opposite kind. He likewise retained, throughout two big recessions, a belief in balanced budgets.

What he ambiguously did achieve through the Democratic Party was the creation of a powerful and, largely, popular political movement based on strong, active (federal) government, labour rights and social protection: what Americans call 'liberal' or 'progressive'. It remained the – usually – dominant strain in US economic policy making until the era of Reaganomics. At that stage, the words 'liberal' and 'progressive' did not carry the connotations they do today. Roosevelt's political base included not just the trade unions and the ethically diverse cities but Southern segregationists (people such as Governor Bilbo of Mississippi, a Klansman, who was a strong defender of lynching and a promoter of Nazi race theories but a 'liberal' New Dealer[38]). It would be another thirty years before an American President felt able or inclined to tackle these wider social injustices.

One further and crucial legacy was, following the entry of the US into the Second World War, the preparation for the new post-war order. The Bretton Woods Conference in 1944 was initiated by the Roosevelt administration at the prompting of Keynes (and US associates such as Harry Dexter White) to prevent a return to economic nationalism. The New Deal had been an almost entirely national project but there was an understanding in the US that the crisis which led to it was at least partly caused by protectionism, trade blocs and exchange rate competition. White, with the support of Roosevelt, argued that the return of free trade was a necessary condition for world peace. Furthermore, a key element in banishing the destructive economic nationalism of the 1930s was to restore a system of stable exchange rates, linked to gold, avoiding competitive devaluation of currencies. Bretton Woods led to the establishment of the IMF and the World Bank; a system of 'adjustable peg' exchange rates which survived until the 1970s; and (indirectly) to the formation of the General

Agreement on Tariffs and Trade (later the World Trade Organization). Although some of Keynes's more radical proposals were not accepted (the idea of an international clearing union creating a new international currency), he was a central figure in Bretton Woods. And although Roosevelt was, by this time, a sick man who died soon after, he responded more to the Keynesian agenda for multilateral cooperation than he ever did to Keynesian economics.[39] And in doing so, he and his successors, notably President Truman, laid the foundations for over sixty years of economic expansion and rising living standards both in the USA and many parts of the world.

6

Erhard: The Social Market and Ordoliberalism

Among the political figures who made a major contribution to economic policy, there were very few who could reasonably claim to be economists or students of economics. One of the exceptional few is Ludwig Erhard (1897–1977), who was not merely an economist but one who represented a particular school of economic thinking and applied its ideas in office.

His significance is summed up in part of the strapline of one of his own books which was about 'the economics of the German Miracle... by its creator'.[1] He described his own economic model as based on the 'social market', though that term has been subsequently redefined as a kind of social democratic 'middle way', which was not at all what he intended it to mean. He has also been described as representing 'ordoliberalism', which is sometimes used to characterize the thinking of a key group of German economic policy makers, including those influencing the European Monetary Union today, who believe in strict, state-imposed rules to govern a competitive market economy.[2] In reality, 'ordoliberalism', Erhard's 'social market' and the currently fashionable 'neoliberalism' are essentially the same thing.

Unlike some of the German giants of post-war politics – Konrad Adenauer; 'Willy' Brandt; Angela Merkel – or other major figures such as Helmut Kohl and Gerhard Schmidt, Erhard made little contribution to – and was not greatly interested in – the big geopolitical dramas in post-war Germany or the unification of Europe. But by setting West Germany on the course to economic recovery and success – the *Wirtschaftswunder* (economic miracle) – he probably made at least as big an impact as better-remembered German leaders. The systems of economic policy discipline he embedded are being felt even today across Europe in, for example, the handling of the Greek debt crisis. But little is written about him in English, or even in German.[3] His contemporary, Adolf Hitler, who by contrast left nothing positive and an immense legacy of damage and destruction, has generated a vast body of literature.

A Liberal Adrift in National Socialism

Adolf Hitler and Ludwig Erhard were approximate contemporaries; both served in the trenches at the end of the First World War and both were badly injured. After that, their lives diverged: one to seek power, feeding off the hatreds and bitterness following German defeat; the other, to build a career as a professional economist, academic and public intellectual in the tradition of German liberalism.

The German liberal tradition had fragmented after the First World War.[4] The tradition of economic liberalism, which had much in common with Anglo-Saxon 'free market' thinking, based on the ideas of Adam Smith and his intellectual descendants, had shrunk to insignificance. It was represented politically by the Liberal People's Party, led by Eugen Richter and supported by Erhard's father, who ran a small clothing manufacturing firm. Its intellectual and political descendant is today's Free Democrat Party.

The altogether more powerful and influential strand of liberalism was the National Liberal Party, which supported Bismarck and, with Bismarck, evolved a more dirigiste approach, with restrictions on freedom of commerce and rejection of free trade. It supported state-approved cartels, which were anathema to the economic liberals of the Liberal People's Party. After 1918 the National Liberals evolved into the Democratic Party, which subsequently had a somewhat tainted history fraternizing with the Nazis. The tradition of statist, centre-right politics was, however, after several iterations, the basis for today's Christian Democrats.

When Erhard grew up before the First World War, there was no sign of intellectual precocity. He was academically undistinguished and went through a vocational school rather than preparation for an academic education at university. He was on track to enter the textile industry as an apprentice, following his father. The war changed him: a volunteer, he fought in Romania as well as on the Western Front. He had a brush with typhus and was hospitalized for almost a year after suffering serious wounds shortly before the end of the war.

He rebuilt his life – aged twenty-two – by going to a business college, acquiring a close interest in economics. It was here that Erhard developed and clarified the ideas which stayed with him for the rest of his life: economic liberalism; a belief in competitive small business rather than 'cartelized' big business; and hostility to socialism and state intervention in general. At the business school and in a subsequent graduate programme, two economists in particular influenced him. One, Wilhelm Rieger, was a proponent of classical economic liberalism: the importance of the price mechanism and competition, and of rewards for risk, together with a traditional, orthodox belief in 'sound money' to curb inflation. Another, Franz Oppenheim, described himself as a 'liberal socialist' but was primarily influential for his belief in a 'property-owning democracy' with widely distributed land and other assets.[5]

A third influence, and the source of Erhard's first real job, was Wilhelm Vershofen, whose research institute was known, somewhat clumsily, as the Institute of Economic Observation of the German Finished Goods Industry – a mixture of consultancy, market research and industry lobbying. Vershofen's views were very different from Erhard's: he was a supporter of cartels and a critic of competitive markets (as well as a supporter of the National Liberal Party). But despite considerable intellectual tension, Erhard remained at the Institute for over a decade.

The early economic influences on Erhard are summarized by Alfred Mierzejewski, one of his biographers: 'he did not become part of the economic consensus that became increasingly centralist, planning-oriented, and Keynesian. He also did not become part of the German liberal movement, which had abandoned freedom and embraced the state and cartels. He did not flirt with socialism, racism, or other fashionable radical solutions. Instead, he remained loyal to his petty bourgeois, individualist roots.'[6]

Living with the Nazis

Erhard embarked on a career as a professional economist at the time when Hitler was coming to power. Alongside the business consultancy work of the Vershofen Institute (essentially, analysis of consumer goods markets), Erhard started in 1931 to publish serious work on economic policy with the aim of progressing in the academic world. His first piece suggested solutions to the economic depression engulfing Germany (and much of the industrialized world), by reflating consumer demand. Ironically this was a Keynesian remedy, given the antipathy he later developed to Keynesian economics and particularly to deficit financing (he advocated instead breaking up cartels and monopolies, using tax and other incentives to deploy their surplus capital to invest in consumer goods industries).

In his theoretical writings and professional life, Erhard soon had to confront the moral and intellectual challenges posed by the Nazis, a challenge he faced early since his research institute and university were based in Nuremberg, a National Socialist stronghold. Many German professionals and academics were faced with the dilemma of how to develop their careers under a regime which expected their political support but which they privately detested. There were varying degrees of courage or cowardice, active or passive collaboration or resistance. Erhard was neither a hero nor a villain. He refused to join the Nazi Party or any affiliated organization and this is cited as the reason why he failed to achieve a professorship at the University of Nuremberg.

Nonetheless, he flourished, published extensively on essentially technical issues, and rubbed shoulders with some appalling individuals. He was an economic adviser, and apparently a friend, to Josef Bürckel, a high-ranking Nazi in Austria and later the occupied French territory of Lorraine and who was known as a particularly virulent anti-Semite. Erhard was in Austria because his Institute had taken advantage of Hitler's annexation to expand its marketing courses. He also – during the Second World War – had a limited professional relationship with Otto Ohlendorf, a senior official in the Reich Economics Ministry who had commanded one of the Einsatzgruppen which murdered 92,000 Jews during the invasion of the Soviet Union. There is no evidence that Erhard in any way supported their views or activities or, indeed, was aware of their crimes. But these relationships and, indeed, his coexistence with his Nazi-sympathizing boss Vershofen meant that even fastidious anti-Nazis like Erhard could not keep their hands completely clean.

Others walked the same ethical tightrope, wobbling in different places. Walter Hallstein was a brilliant young commercial lawyer when Hitler came to power. He refused to join the Nazi Party but joined some Nazi-affiliated professional bodies: sufficient compliance, at any rate, to secure a coveted professorship. He also volunteered as a Wehrmacht reservist long before the war. Yet his reputation was largely untarnished, and he became the first President of the European Commission and one of the pantheon of European gods.

A striking contrast is with Hjalmar Schacht, Hitler's Economics Minister and the main architect of economic policy under the Nazis. Unlike Erhard who represented uncompromising economic liberalism, Schacht was from that strand in the German liberal tradition which favoured private enterprise but welcomed government intervention in support of private investment.[7]

Schacht established his reputation as a tough and financially orthodox President of the Reichsbank during the Weimar Republic when his monetary policies countered hyperinflation. He gradually shifted his allegiance from the Weimar governments to Hitler and helped to raise funds from big business and banks to assist Hitler's rise to power. Hitler in turn saw the value of his skills and reputation and appointed him Economics Minister in 1935.[8]

His achievement was to introduce economic policies which helped Germany recover rapidly from depression. In 1933 and every year after until the war, there was GDP growth of 6–10 per cent and unemployment fell rapidly to almost zero by 1938. The key to recovery was the portfolio of large public works projects such as the Autobahn network. Schacht made them possible through an ingenious financing arrangement in which capital projects were paid for by five-year promissory notes held by companies involved in the projects. This covert financing arrangement, taking capital borrowing off the balance sheet, worked wonders and ensured that German recovery was well ahead of the USA, where Roosevelt was still struggling with the problem of how to do large-scale public works without resorting to deficit financing.

Schacht's clever plan also facilitated rearmament, Hitler's top priority, since it also concealed the extent of military spending: around six times that of spending on civilian public works.[9] The rapidly escalating national debt – both official and off-balance sheet – was not of great concern to Hitler since he believed that territorial expansion – 'Lebensraum' – would bring in sufficient revenue from conquered territories' raw materials and (enslaved) labour that it would pay off the debts. Schacht's testimony in the

Nuremberg War Crimes Tribunal suggests, rather improbably, he was unaware of, or opposed to, the agenda which he was helping to deliver.[10]

Schacht's essentially pro-business and financially conservative instincts were not shared by leading Nazis and were subservient to a bigger – evil – project to which he claims he did not subscribe. He clashed with Göring and others over the pace of rearmament and treatment of the Jews. He had helped to organize the big privatization programme at the outset of National Socialism and which Hitler had enthusiastically supported (the leading commercial banks, the railways, coal and steel enterprises, shipyards and other companies were sold off). Schacht, however, seemed not to have realized that support for business was merely a means to an end, and that business was expected to be compliant, not competitive. Gradually he was marginalized, though, for appearances' sake, he was kept on as a token member of the government until 1943.

Schacht provided a reference point for Erhard's critique of Nazi economics. Erhard wrote a series of articles attacking Schacht's approach to economic policy. In particular, he rejected the opportunistic 'crony capitalism' of big business, the idea of large capital works sponsored by the state and the autarkic policies of self-sufficiency; he was a liberal free trader. And he was strongly opposed to deficit financing and the dishonest means of concealing it. Erhard's central objection to Nazism appears to have been intellectual rather than moral; Hitler (like Schacht) was not an economic liberal.

Erhard's intellectual detachment from the Nazis, on economic grounds, raises the deeper question of what being a 'good German' meant at that time. Schacht, as described above, was complicit in helping the Nazis come to power and launch their war machine. But he also, if belatedly, argued back; spoke out against anti-Semitism; and from the late 1930s (the mid-1930s on his own account) joined the resistance, actively plotting to overthrow

Hitler. He was eventually implicated in a 1941 bomb plot and sent to concentration camps, including Ravensbrück and Dachau. He survived, was tried at Nuremberg but acquitted, but then sentenced to seven years' hard labour by a West German court (subsequently commuted). When Erhard emerged from the war as an untainted figure, having kept his head down and quietly got on with his work and his economic writings, Schacht was breaking stones in prison. He had chosen the wrong kind of liberalism.

The Right Kind of Liberalism

I have referred earlier to the German economic thinkers who helped to mould Erhard's thinking; and experience of the Nazis in office reinforced his liberal prejudices. The world he inhabited – mainly carrying out pieces of commercial consultancy for an increasingly marginalized private sector and writing academic articles in a style sufficiently abstract as not to attract the attention of the authorities – was something of a bubble. It was detached from the real world of authoritarian government, racial persecution and militarization. During the Battle of Stalingrad, Erhard was preoccupied with office politics and battles over leadership of the Vershofen Institute. But the various 'liberal' economic ideas that fermented at the time provided Erhard with the chemistry to confront Germany's post-war problems (mostly, given logistical issues, communicated via letters or academic journals).

Erhard encountered the work of Wilhelm Röpke, a passionate advocate of free markets, then in exile in Switzerland. His vision was very close to the one Erhard had independently developed, described by Mierzejewski as 'a competitive economy built on private property regulated by a strong government… to prevent market excesses… to relieve suffering caused by economic transitions… to break up monopolies and cartels… and free trade.'[11] Erhard rejected his romantic anti-urban views about agriculture and the countryside but agreed with most of Röpke's analysis.

Then, there was Walter Eucken and his group at the University of Freiburg who also embraced the free market, competition and private enterprise, big and small, but rejected unbridled capitalism, mainly to prevent abuse by powerful private interests. He wanted a government-supervised, competitive, consumer-oriented economy. His group became known as ordoliberals, and their views overlapped with those of Erhard and Röpke.

Another set of influences were Joseph Schumpeter and Friedrich Hayek and the Austrian School of economics, who were to have such an impact in the USA and UK. But their optimistic embrace of laissez-faire capitalism and belief in the minimization of the role of the state was somewhat removed from the German ordoliberals, including Erhard, who wanted a strong state to maintain a framework of stability and to curb private sector monopoly.

In opposition to these, and Erhard's, views were those of the socialists (SPD Party) who had been driven underground and persecuted by the Nazis, but became newly prominent after the war. The SPD had been a powerful force from the days of Bismarck to the end of the Weimar Republic. It represented a powerful strand of opinion which wanted an end to capitalism, a system of planning and the socialization of big business. These ideas were anathema to Erhard and his associates but had great moral authority which owed much to Kurt Schumacher, the SPD leader, who had been imprisoned and tortured in Nazi concentration camps. Early post-war German history was to become a contest between Erhard's intellectually strong, but rather arid, economic liberalism and Schumacher's idealistic and emotionally charged version of socialism.

In addition to this swirl of economic currents, there was another emerging set of ideas seeking to reconcile the free market with Christian ideals of social justice.[12] Erhard was not a religious man and he was not impressed by the heavily diluted version of private enterprise economics which the Church offered: often indistinguishable in his eyes from socialism. Erhard's economic views were as much about what he disliked as what he wanted. He saw three big evils: socialism; market distortion through cartels, controls and other impediments to the market; and anarchic laissez-faire.

In the aftermath of the war and defeat, Christianity and socialism offered more of a comfort blanket for a defeated and hungry people than Erhard's dry, impersonal economic model, as he was to discover when he tried to implement his ideas. Political reality would eventually force him to make the Christian Democrats his political home.

Reform Under Occupation

The economic position of Germany at the end of the war was dire. After a year, the economy produced about a quarter of the pre-war total; food production and availability was insufficient to keep the population above near-starvation levels; transport infrastructure was so damaged that goods could scarcely be moved; 40 per cent of the housing stock was uninhabitable yet the population in West Germany was swollen by 7.5 million refugees, mainly those fleeing a vengeful Soviet army of occupation. There was rampant inflation outside the meagre rationing, and much economic activity took place on the chaotic, criminalized black market. The Allied occupation forces were struggling to manage this economic basket case while repairing their own economies, dealing with denazification in Germany and coming to terms with a new 'cold' war with the USSR. The only positives were a lot of undamaged industrial plants and skilled workers, once servicemen were freed from captivity by the occupying forces.

That was the context in which Erhard volunteered his services, including his market-based solutions to the crisis. He was, as it happens, in the right place at the right time – the US zone. The Americans were more inclined than the British, French and Russians to support ideas for German economic recovery; they were less concerned about securing reparations or about Germany's future war potential. They were also more open to liberal economic ideas than the French or the British whose Labour government was more aligned with the SPD.

Erhard was given a trial by the US authorities: running his town; then his region (northern Bavaria); and, since he seemed to know what he was doing, he was made Economics Minister for Bavaria – six months after the end of the war. He made it clear that he had little interest in administering a system of rationing and economic controls and regarded the appointment as a platform for promoting his more radical, free market ideas, for insisting on the return of decision making to elected Germans, and for reunifying a fragmented Germany. He quickly fell foul of the re-emerging politicians in post-war Bavaria and his role was short-lived. His Bavarian government was defeated in its first post-war, state-level election, and Erhard withdrew temporarily to an academic post in Munich, while building a network of political support initially through the Free Democrats (liberals).

At the end of 1947, Erhard got himself appointed Chair of a panel, a Special Office, giving advice to an Economic Council established by the (Western) Allies as a quasi-parliament to prepare the way for relaunching the German economy on the back of currency reform (to replace the currency in circulation, the Reichsmark, which had become largely worthless). The Council also had participation from the socialists and trade unions who wanted to move to a planned economy and were fearful of a free market. Erhard was, however, quite explicit about where he thought the reforms should head: 'we must do the currency reform in such a way that, if everything goes smoothly, we can go in the basic direction of the free market economy.'[13] He prepared a currency conversion plan which sought to establish a value for the currency which reflected the reality of the economy with massively distorted prices and inflation barely suppressed by rationing and price controls.

The key decision maker administering the reforms was to be the Director of the Administration for Economics and Erhard lobbied for the job. The post was fought over by the three political parties which were to dominate post-war German politics: the conservative Christian Democratic Union (CDU) – then led by Konrad Adenauer; the FDP, whose candidate Erhard was; and the socialist SPD. In the event, the CDU switched its votes behind Erhard, and he was elected by the Council to be Director. In the spring of 1948, Erhard was in a position to implement his plans, which 'depended on linking the currency reform with an equally resolute economic reform, so as to end once and for all the whole complex of State controls of the economy – from production to the final consumer'.[14]

The task was far from straightforward. Consumer goods and food were scarce and available largely through black markets in which market prices were far in excess of controlled prices. Production of consumer goods, like clothing and shoes, was around a quarter of the level of 1936 and all industrial production was 60 per cent less. Productivity was very low as workers were often hungry and spending a lot of time in the black market or queuing or in subsistence activities. There also had to be a formula which shared the burden of adjustment to new prices fairly to give protection to those, such as pensioners, who were heavily dependent on state-controlled prices for staple goods – and to limit windfall gains to those who had a monopoly stranglehold of some markets. Although Erhard made it clear his opposition to laissez-faire and his commitment to eliminating poverty, there was fierce resistance to liberalizing prices from the SPD representatives on the Economic Council. Crucial support came from American General Clay (but not the British or French authorities). Erhard's plan prevailed and was launched.

A new Deutschmark was created. All Germans were given an equal amount, 40DM, to replace the stock of worthless Reichsmarks. All other money – representing the excess of purchasing power artificially created under the Nazis – was destroyed. At the same time, price control was lifted from many items and rationing ended. In fact, some essentials (grain, potatoes, meat), raw materials (iron and steel), rents and transport were held back from price de-control, and basic consumer goods (clothes, shoes, soap) continued to be rationed to some degree. Tough anti-cartel measures were put in place in unregulated markets and – later – wages were freed. And at Erhard's urging, income taxes were cut by the occupation authorities especially for low earners and on business investment.

The impact was rapid and as Erhard had predicted. Some independent observers saw it as akin to a miracle: 'The black market suddenly disappeared. Shop windows were full of goods; factory chimneys were smoking; and the streets swarmed with lorries… In all sectors of economic life, it began as the clocks struck on the day of currency reform.'[15] More sceptical observers pointed to the fact that the German economy had been given a helpful push by Marshall Aid, the reconstruction work of the Allies and the return of industrial plant and skilled workers to more normal patterns of operation. But for consumers, the 'shop window miracle', as it was called, was real.

Not everyone was happy. There were losers and some experienced a good deal of economic pain and resented it. There was a sharp surge in inflation as prices adjusted: by around 20 per cent for food stuffs in the next six months (despite residual controls) and 35 per cent for clothes, as new money chased too few goods (though production increased by a remarkable 50 per cent over this six-month period and inflation soon came under control). Undoubtedly many working families were hurt by the squeeze in real wages. And as firms adjusted to realistic prices and costs, there were many who had to lay off staff or close. Unemployment rose sharply along with inflation, from 500,000 to 1.25 million in the first half of 1949, a figure regarded as horrifying at the time.

Opposition to Erhard and his reforms grew, in the press and in the embryonic German democracy represented by the Economic Council. The SPD and the trade unions called for a General Strike. Schumacher, leader of the SPD, said the Erhard machinery of government was an 'instrument of the class war from above' and 'the poor are being made poorer and the rich richer'.[16] Erhard also clashed with the Allies on the other end of the ideological spectrum, especially the British, who insisted on retaining a strong framework of planning. However, he and the reform programme survived the storm. Residual price controls, tight control of money supply, a campaign of public education on the new free market pricing, and relaxation of wage control – combined with an un-wavering commitment not to back down on the basic principles – saw the reforms survive. And they soon bore fruit: for workers, wages rose by 15 per cent from June to December 1948, after the lifting of wage controls alongside a sharp increase in labour pro-ductivity (from 63 per cent of 1936 levels in June 1948 to 81 per cent in June 1949). Retail prices fell by 11 per cent from the first half of 1949 to the first half of 1950. The new currency strength-ened over six months from 23 Swiss francs per 100DM to 74 in June 1949.

If the Erhard revolution was to continue – and there was still a vast accretion of state economic controls – he would need a stronger political base than the FDP who, for all their clarity of purpose, did not have a large constituency of support. He, there-fore, cultivated the CDU (and its allies, the socially conservative Christian Social Union (CSU) in Bavaria, who were initially hos-tile to Erhard) despite having no sympathy for the interventionist approach of the party or its – largely Roman Catholic – concern for social justice and hostility to free markets. The key figure was Konrad Adenauer, head of the CDU Party and future Chancellor. Adenauer was a successful politician who, as Mayor of Cologne, had demonstrated political courage in the Nazi years and, post-war, had become popular in part from large-scale spending financed by debt. He shared with Erhard a general belief in private property and a market economy, wanted Erhard's reforms to succeed and shrewdly judged that Erhard could be an asset in future elections. For his part, Erhard continued to preach the virtues of his social market – competition and consumer choice – in the face of scepticism and some hostility among his new best friends.

Erhard's philosophy was reflected in the CDU 'social liberalism' manifesto for Bundestag elections in August 1949. The CDU/CSU combined outpolled the SPD, against expectations, and Adenauer's gamble of campaigning on Erhard's economic policies paid off. The SPD had run a campaign which concentrated its attacks on Erhard's policy, which it described as 'the fat balloon of private enterprise filled with the putrid gases of decaying liberalism'.[17] The CDU/CSU was well short of an absolute majority of votes or seats and was obliged to enter a coalition of the 'right' with Erhard's former party, the FPD, and a smaller conservative party, the Democratic Party (DP), establishing a pattern of 'centre-right' coalition that was to be unbroken for two decades during which Erhard was the dominant figure in economic policy.

Consolidating the Social Market Revolution

There is a rather negative view that Erhard was much less effective as an Economics Minister and Chancellor of elected governments than in his essentially technocratic post-war roles during the Allied occupation. For example, Mierzejewski wrote that 'he scored no further breakthroughs [after June 1948]. He did achieve a great deal but nothing on the scale of the liberalization of June 1948.'[18] But that is to minimize the achievements of a man who steered and led German economic recovery over two decades and, as a politician, inspired victory or won five general elections for the CDU/CSU leading to (coalition) government.

He got off to a difficult start. Unemployment rose to 2 million, though Erhard insisted it was not cyclical, requiring a countercyclical demand stimulus, but structural. He argued that it was caused by production bottlenecks, the difficulties of switching labour from one sector to another and lack of investment. Erhard continued to pursue his de-control agenda, dismantling import controls and starting to get rid of his particular bugbear, coal rationing. But his coalition allies were unnerved.

Then came the Korean War and Western rearmament which, because of the boom in demand for raw materials, precipitated more inflation alongside fuel shortages and power cuts. And Germany acquired a large trade deficit, a product of Erhard's import liberalization and the peculiarities of the external payments system introduced by the Americans to facilitate European trade. He came under pressure to go and there was a bitter public disagreement with the CDU's Adenauer.

But he rode the storm and, by the end of 1952, production was growing at an annual rate of almost 9 per cent. Likewise, unemployment fell back to 1 million (5.5 per cent of the labour force), exports were booming, inflation dropped sharply and 430,000 homes were built in a year. All of this provided an excellent backcloth to elections in 1953 which would be highly successful for the CDU and restored Erhard's reputation for competence. The economic miracle – the *Wirtschaftswunder* – was under way.

Thereafter, Erhard's limitations as a politician acted as a serious drag on his effectiveness. He was a loner with no political base beyond his popularity as an economic miracle worker; he was a notoriously poor administrator; he fell out with his colleagues; and his relationship with Adenauer became fractious. As a consequence of these weaknesses, he was unable to win battles which were crucial to the long-term success of the social market. First, his attempts to introduce a strong anti-cartel law were frustrated and diluted by special pleading from industrial lobby groups. Second, there was a clamour to introduce welfare state measures in the Bismarck tradition. Welfare spending was popular across the political spectrum including, crucially, with Adenauer, and Erhard was reluctantly persuaded to support high taxes to pay for it (as well as extensive subsidies to state industries). And third, as the 1950s progressed, there were the early moves to European economic integration along lines which Erhard opposed. He was an enthusiast for free trade but did not like the dirigiste approach of the French – which was later to cause serious conflict with General de Gaulle.

Initially these difficulties did not matter. Explosive growth solved unemployment (and spilled over into large-scale immigration). Germany was the most rapidly growing European economy until 1961. A pattern of export-led growth was established which would endure alongside rising living standards and low inflation.

The Legacy

The most obvious and measurable legacy of Erhard's policies was the long period of strong growth after 1948 until the 1960s. That economic expansion, which helped generate growth throughout Western Europe, made the Federal Republic a crucial economic 'locomotive' for Western recovery alongside the USA.[19]

His critics believe the praise is unjustified and that the recovery would have happened anyway because of the legacy of Allied help combined with Germany's industrial capacity and skill.[20] But his repeated and sustained interventions at crucial points contradict that assessment.

A more serious criticism is that he ran out of steam, contributing to an eventual economic slowdown. To some extent this was inevitable: prosperity naturally weakened the Germans' willingness to make big sacrifices. And he was not helped by Adenauer's approach to politics; after a successful 1957 election (on the back of Erhard's economic policy) Adenauer introduced a 'cake fund' to spend the budget surplus. Erhard won some battles (to revalue the Mark in 1957 against strong industrial opposition) but he was increasingly swimming against the political and intellectual tide.

He also left a mixed legacy of economic policy ideas. His social market suffered the indignity of becoming the slogan of people who had diametrically opposed views. It was co-opted by social democrats in Germany (and eventually by the likes of Tony Blair) to describe a kind of hybrid of capitalism and socialism with expansive and expensive public services, indicative planning and close cooperation between business and government, all of which he deplored. Nonetheless, the original social market was resurrected in the Thatcherite experiment discussed in Chapter 11.

Lastly, he provided a template for the kind of 'shock therapy' which has been employed in rapid liberalization from communist economies. There have been serious failures (in Russia) but successes in Eastern Europe, notably Poland. The reunification of Germany, which also owed something to Erhard's currency reforms and rapid liberalization, must be counted as a success. Erhard never expressed enthusiasm for the project of European unification, beyond the freeing up of trade, but he would have seen some irony in the fact that economic and monetary union, through the Eurozone, is governed primarily through the principles of ordoliberalism or the social market which his German descendants have insisted upon as the price for German participation.

7

Erlander: The Social Democratic Model Made Real

When those of left-of-centre political persuasion are pressed to pick a system that satisfies their politics and works economically they will often cite Sweden. The Swedes have, indeed, evolved a distinctive social democratic model which combines capitalism, in the form of an open market economy, with the promotion of equality and social justice, all within a framework of democratic politics.[1] Variants of that system have been adopted throughout Scandinavia as the 'Nordic model'.[2]

Sweden is a good place to start. It has had Social Democratic majority, minority or coalition governments for all but a decade or so of the last 100 years, enjoying the support of 40–50 per cent of the public in elections over that time, until the last decade. No single individual leader can be said to have delivered such a remarkable political project which depended heavily on collective action within a disciplined and well-organized party.[3] Four Social Democrat Prime Ministers led the party and government for much of that time: Hjalmar Branting, Per Albin Hansson, Tage Erlander and Olof Palme. Of these, Erlander (1901–85) ruled the longest, by far – twenty-three years – and his governments delivered the most substantial building blocks of the Swedish welfare state alongside – and paid for by – a period of strong economic growth.[4] I have, therefore, focused on him and his own distinctive achievements.

Erlander and the Swedish Social Democrats are also excellent examples of Keynes's dictum about politicians deriving their ideas from dead economists, except in this case they were very much alive. The Stockholm School of Economics – inspired originally by Knut Wicksell in the early twentieth century – was at least as influential in Sweden as those of Cambridge and the London School of Economics (LSE) in shaping economic policy in the UK.[5] Several of its prominent members were active in politics. Bertil Ohlin, whose theorem with Eli Heckscher is one of the standard models of trade theory, was leader of the main (Liberal) opposition party for over twenty years facing Erlander's government while agreeing with its main policies. Dag Hammarskjöld is now remembered for his peace-keeping, before his untimely death – probably murder – in the Congo, rather than his economics. He was briefly a minister under Erlander before becoming Secretary General of the United Nations. Gunnar Myrdal, who is said to have developed the main ideas behind Keynesian economics before Keynes, was a Social Democrat MP and also, briefly, a minister under Erlander. There has rarely been a better case of leading economists applying their ideas in a political environment, of true political economy. This is all the more ironic since one of Myrdal's leading early tracts was a critique of economists allowing values to infiltrate pure theory.[6] Indeed, there is a double irony as Myrdal's Nobel Prize was awarded jointly with Hayek whose ideas helped to fuel the economically liberal approach to policy – 'neoliberalism' – which has since been used to attack and partially dismantle the social democratic model in ways that would have horrified Myrdal.

Before the end of his long leadership, Erlander began to acknowledge that Swedish social democracy – and the wider Nordic model – was far from perfect, though he continued to believe in and argue for a larger role for the state in the economy and its benign effects. He promoted his protégé, Olof Palme, to be his successor and Palme in turn pushed the social democratic model in a more radical direction, encountering growing resistance.[7] Subsequent loss of power and the influence of neoliberal ideas have tempered the social democratic model, though it remains substantially intact. And the Nordic model is still the lodestar for parties of the democratic left all over the world. Despite fashionable criticism, and loss of electoral support for social democratic parties, it can scarcely be a coincidence that the World Happiness Index, which purports to measure overall quality of life and contentment, has Nordic countries at the top of the rankings (Finland 1st; Denmark 2nd; Norway 3rd; Sweden 7th – while the UK ranks 15th and the USA 19th).

The Third Generation Social Democrat Leader

Unlike many of the political figures in this volume, Tage Erlander did not break the mould of established thinking to create a new model of economic policy. He grew out of the Social Democratic Party machine and its values. But he was also trained in economics at university. He was familiar with the economic policy thinking of the Stockholm School of Economics and the Keynesian approach which was broadly accepted in Sweden in the 1930s. His main significance lay in what he achieved in his uninterrupted twenty-three years as Prime Minister, both in social and economic policy.

He was the son of a primary school teacher and a farmer's daughter in the rural district of Värmland. His biographer describes his background as steeped in the values of the Swedish lower middle class: ambition, temperance, nonconformism and liberalism.[8] He went to Lund University to study Natural Science and, later, switched to politics and economics. Spending eight years at university, until he was twenty-seven, he was later criticized for having been a 'perpetual student'. But his years of involvement in student politics and intellectual debate helped him rise in a party which increasingly valued the skills of graduates rather than manual workers. He also immersed himself in the theoretical writings of the left, which was good training for future debates within his party and in jousting with Bertil Ohlin, the future leader of the Liberal opposition. He rejected revolutionary Marxism and later interpretations of Marx such as that of Karl Kautsky. He identified more with the gradualist thinking of Eduard Bernstein and with liberal democracy.[9]

As he acknowledged later in his career, in the six volumes of his memoirs, he was preoccupied, like many of his contemporaries, with how to understand the big issue of the day: unemployment.[10] He also wanted an economic narrative that would fit within the beliefs of the Social Democratic Party to which he had attached himself for a mixture of idealistic and career motives. His memoirs refer to the early influence of Keynes who, in 1928, had written a pamphlet for the British Liberal Party, known as the *Yellow Book*.

Erlander welcomed the ideas of Keynesians but in rather condescending terms: '*The Yellow Book* did not contain anything new to us Social Democrats. It reconnected to thoughts which had been present earlier in the workers' movement... Our satisfaction became even greater when during the 1930s the young Swedish economists Gunnar Myrdal and Bertil Ohlin supported the theory of active employment policy.'[11]

Erlander's critics have been sceptical about this self-justifying account of events forty years after they happened but concede that 'what matters is that the longest-serving Swedish prime minister felt that the party's doctrines were supported by scientific economics'.[12] Erlander himself acknowledged his intellectual debt to those who built up the case for active government in the name of Keynesian economics. He often cited the American economist and liberal (in US terminology) J.K. Galbraith whose 1958 book *The Affluent Society* made a powerful case for rebalancing privately affluent societies to address 'public squalor' through stronger public services.

Erlander had mapped out a political career at an early age and became a local councillor shortly following graduation. He became an MP soon after, aged thirty-one. His ministerial experience was modest – six years as a State Secretary (junior minister) in Social Affairs during the Second World War, and then a short period in the Cabinet as Minister for Education. However, the then Prime Minister, Per Albin Hansson, died suddenly, creating a vacancy at the top.

The Swedish Social Democrats had a long history going back to its origins as a revolutionary party aligned to Lenin's Marxism. But its democratic and reformist form dated from 1917 when the left split off to become the Communist Party. After 1917 the Social Democrats were almost permanently in government. Their first leader, Branting, was an idealistic socialist from the upper classes. He led the party from its inception in 1889 to 1925 and defined it as reformist rather than revolutionary. He worked with liberals to campaign to widen the franchise to working people and, when established in – minority – government, his first act was to legislate for universal suffrage alongside an eight-hour working day. There was already, even before this government, a strong sense of Swedish social cohesion, created by: compulsory schooling from 1842; public health services from the 1860s; factory inspection of health and safety; state subsidies for sickness benefit; an old age and disability pension from 1913; and compulsory industrial injury insurance. Branting inherited a welfare system which was already becoming well advanced.

The second Social Democrat leader was Per Albin Hansson, a working-class Swede, who had risen through the ranks of the party. It was the large boots of Hansson which Erlander was to fill. Hansson had been Party Chairman for over forty years and Prime Minister for most of the period since 1932. He had established the basic model of Swedish social democracy which he called the 'People's Home' (*Folkhemmet*). The 'People's Home' was inclusive – the Social Democrats explicitly reached out beyond the industrial working class to farmers, civil servants, professionals and intellectuals. It was also somewhat nationalistic (designed, it is said, to undercut the appeal of fascism).[13] It built on the embryonic welfare state (introducing social insurance for sickness and maternity allowances and free maternity and childbirth services; means-tested benefits for disabled pensioners and widows; some health subsidies as for dental care; and subsidized rents for social housing and families in privately rented property).

Hansson developed a model based on social control of the economy through centralized pay bargaining and labour regulation rather than nationalization. Industrial consensus helped to ensure that there was broad support for Keynesian measures to counter unemployment. He established a way of doing business through compromise and rational argument rather than through confrontation and anger. This world was described, in a popular book at the time (1936) by Marquis Childs, as the Middle Way: 'a happy blend of competing ideologies' or a 'happy union of socialism and capitalism'.[14]

There was an altogether less edifying part of the Hansson legacy, which were the compromises made with Nazi Germany to preserve Swedish neutrality, including facilitation of the invasion of Norway. There was also a wartime policy, in which Erlander was heavily involved, of secret internment camps for communists and ethnic minorities (including the Romany population).

When the governing body of the ruling party met to choose a successor to Hansson there were several strong candidates, much better known and more experienced (and more interesting) than Erlander. The frontrunner was Gustav Möller who had driven the social reform policies with Erlander as his deputy. In the event, Erlander was seen as less risky – a 'safe pair of hands' – and his background as a graduate and intellectual commended itself to a party wanting to move on from the earlier days of class struggle.

Very shortly after Erlander's elevation, through the party, to be Prime Minister the country was plunged into an economic crisis.

The Swedish economy had flourished in wartime because of the demand for its raw materials such as wood and iron ore from both the Allies and Germany (a source of envy and anger among neighbouring Nordic countries which had endured brutal and debilitating occupation by the Nazis or, in the case of Finland, the USSR). The end of war led to a commodity price boom as Swedish raw materials were in even bigger demand. The boom spilled over into inflation and a balance of payments crisis. Wartime rationing and controls were reintroduced and taxes raised to stabilize the economy (income tax, taxes on wealth and inheritance) – while reducing taxes on the low paid. The government was accused of incompetence and the blame was attached in particular to the economist and Commerce Minister Gunnar Myrdal, who – perhaps conveniently – left to work for the United Nations.

The arguments broadened out into a wider debate on economic and social strategy. The liberal-led opposition (under Ohlin) argued that the government, in particular Erlander, Myrdal and the influential Finance Minister, Ernst Wigforss, was pursuing a socialist agenda under cover of the crisis with its highly progressive tax policies. The government's defence was that expansionary and interventionist economic policies were a shield against unemployment. It drew on the Keynesian (or Myrdalian) arguments which had raged in the 1930s in the Stockholm School of Economics. One group of economists led by Myrdal had argued for planning and an interventionist approach to the economy; another group were classical or market liberals like Eli Heckscher and Gustav Cassel.

In an unusually bitter and ideological election in 1948, Erlander enjoyed his baptism of fire. The leader of the opposition Ohlin, head of the Liberal Party, actually agreed with the Social Democrats on economic fundamentals. Ohlin himself, as a leading economist, had been at the forefront of those arguing for a Keynesian approach in the 1930s involving more public investment and deficit financing. And the Social Democrats agreed

with the Liberals on the necessity of a healthy private sector and
the desirability of free trade. Ohlin's criticisms were partly of
incompetence but also of the government's 'socialist' agenda. He
appeared to have the better of the arguments and his opposition
gained some ground in vote share and parliamentary seats. But
the result was sufficiently close that Erlander was able to retain
power in alliance with a farmers' party and a de facto alliance
with the communists. By retaining power Erlander was then able
to embark on what came to be regarded as a 'golden age' of a
strong economy combined with what he called 'strong society'.[15]

Erlander's Golden Age of Social Democracy

After the election of 1948, Erlander fought six general elections
in which the Social Democrats' vote share never fluctuated from
the range of 46–49 per cent apart from his concluding, triumph-
ant result in 1968 (54 per cent). On every occasion the Social
Democrats were returned to office either to share power with the
Agrarian Party (1952–8) or in a 'confidence and supply' arrangement with the Communist Party. Erlander had a sufficiently secure
base from which to take the Swedish social democratic model to
a new level.

The main component of his substantial achievements was
the step-by-step enlargement of the welfare state. More than his
predecessors, Erlander believed, in general, in the principle of
universality rather than means-testing to bind together his 'strong
society' with a shared interest in the welfare system supported by
taxation. He strengthened the pension system by raising the universal pension several times and, later, introduced a supplementary
pension. Child allowances were made universal and raised. There
was also obligatory health insurance providing earnings-related
benefits. And unemployment insurance was boosted to provide
longer benefits through state subsidy. There was paid six-month
leave for new mothers, which was later doubled. Housing allow-

ances were extended to incorporate pensioners as well as young families as part of a regulated housing market that also controlled rents. Erlander's personal involvement was illustrated by a clash with the Bank of Sweden in 1957. The government was trying to introduce a programme of large-scale mortgage lending in the face of credit rationing by the commercial banks. The banks demanded higher interest rates, increasing the cost of mortgages, and they were supported by the central bank. Erlander made the banks back down and forced the programme through over their objections.

The end result was a combination of state-financed benefits, enjoyed by all, and a minimum level of security in case of adversity financed through social insurance. His speeches – and actions – were littered with reference to 'solidarity', 'cooperation' and 'community'. He believed that 'equality' was compatible with Sweden's market economy: 'equality... lay behind our attacks against established privileges and class barriers and behind our attempts to bring about equality, security and justice in the treatment of people.'[16] This concern for equality extended to ensuring equality of opportunity. Erlander established a system of nine-year compulsory, free, comprehensive education replacing parallel, selective, schools. He likewise strengthened adult and further education and introduced student stipends (grants).

These measures did not come cheap. Already by the end of the war there had been an expansion of public spending (from 10 per cent of GDP in 1914 to over 20 per cent in 1948) and social expenditure accounted for half the total. But at least in the earlier stages of Erlander's leadership, the gradual expansion of welfare benefits was carefully orchestrated to ensure that budgets were prudently managed and taxation was kept no higher than the OECD average and lower, even, than in the USA.[17] Erlander saw that the key to the success of the welfare state was economic growth with the public sector expanding broadly in line with the economy.[18] Nonetheless, the public sector share of the economy crept up – doubling to 40 per cent by the end of Erlander's tenure (local and national). Public investment was cut in order to create more fiscal space for spending on the welfare state and welfare payments rose dramatically to make up almost 60 per cent of public spending. Revenue growth was almost entirely in the form of social security contributions, mainly from employers.

To achieve the economic growth to sustain spending growth without severe tax burdens required a healthy, profitable and successful private enterprise sector and the benefits of an open economy and free trade. Erlander vigorously rejected the idea that the public sector and business were in conflict. The right kind of government intervention could, for example, help the labour market to work better – by providing support for retraining and to cover periods of redundancy. The centralized and union-dominated labour bargaining system, leading to high wages, had the effect of driving inefficient firms to the wall; but this was tolerated as a necessary consequence of rising productivity and international specialization through trade. The system was called the Rehn–Meidner model after the two economists from the trade union federation LO who helped to develop it in 1951 under Erlander's political leadership. There was no interest in subsidizing 'lame ducks' (though there was subsidization of high-cost agriculture). And the Social Democrats' definition of socialism did not extend to public ownership. Erlander, according to his biographer Olof Ruin, 'could not understand the value of the state's direct assumption of ownership of companies'.[19]

Relations with business were not always entirely harmonious. Business was, after all, carrying much of the cost of the welfare state. Among the more ideological Social Democrats on the left of the party, there was also suspicion of business which, to them, 'represented everything that the Social Democrat party opposed… such as the capitalist system of production'.[20] As long as the business goose was laying golden eggs and growth was strong, as it was for most of the 1950s and 1960s, there was no problem: a rising tide lifted all boats. But when the tide started to go out, a different dynamic set in: taxes rose and were resented; workers wanted a bigger share of profits. There was also a move to political radicalization among the young in Sweden than in the rest of the developed world – the Vietnam War was a catalyst in the growth of a strong 'new left' movement.

As Erlander's premiership was coming to an end in the late 1960s, politics was becoming more polarized. There had long been personal sparring between Erlander and Ohlin underpinned by bad chemistry, but the disagreements had been about tactics, positioning and power rather than policy. Erlander 'had a great deal of sympathy for many of the reformist positions to be found within the Liberal Party... [whose] positions were quite similar'.[21] The sympathy was not always reciprocated; he was attacked by opposition newspapers as 'unreliable', 'evasive', 'a theorizing leftist', 'a tactician' and 'apparatchik', and this was in a country where respect and deference were more common than elsewhere. The 'social liberalism' of the Liberal Party gradually gave way to a more ideologically differentiated stance as the opposition parties (Liberal, Centre Party and Conservatives) sought to present a more unified front and effective right-wing opposition to the Social Democrats.

For his part, Erlander doubled down on his commitment to expanding and improving public services and, if necessary, raising taxes to pay for them. He refused to set an upper limit to the share of public spending in the economy and continued to argue that public services and welfare spending enhanced personal freedom. The problems which Sweden was experiencing in the 1960s – alienated social groups with alcohol or drug problems; regional imbalances; failures among hitherto successful firms and industries – suggested to Erlander a bigger, not a smaller, role for the state. Having, earlier in his life, carefully distanced himself from the Marxist strand in the Social Democratic tradition, he admitted (in 1969) to a knowledge and admiration for Marxism.[22]

Despite some disillusionment with the Social Democrats as a party, Erlander's personal standing was higher than ever. His greatest triumph was his last: the election of 1968 when he led his party to a stunning victory with 54 per cent of the popular vote, the second highest in twenty elections. According to Olof Ruin: 'It was not until the very last years of his active career, when his popularity achieved its all-time high, that Erlander, like Per Albin Hansson before him, took on the aura of a father figure to his country.'[23] When surveyed, 80 per cent of the public felt he had done a good job. This was a good time to leave. He did, passing on the leadership to his protégé, close colleague and friend Olof Palme.

The Limits of the Swedish Model: Olof Palme

The next period of Swedish Social Democratic government was the eleven years of the premiership of Olof Palme until his assassination in 1986, with an interlude from 1976 to 1982 when the party lost power to a centre-right coalition. Palme has come to be regarded as the man who pushed social democracy on Swedish lines to its limits – and in the process contributed heavily to its decline as a political force and economic model. But he started his political career on the right of the party as fiercely anti-communist (reputedly involved in Swedish intelligence and at one point funded by the CIA[24]). He had been strongly pro-business and even critical of the large universal benefits/high tax model which his mentor Erlander had promoted. But that was all soon to change.

Once in power, Palme – as Erlander had done – cemented his position with a big win in the 1970 election. He had already acquired a reputation as a result of his outspoken comments on racism, 'third world' liberation movements and the Vietnam War (which prompted Nixon's description of him as 'that Swedish asshole'[25]). He used his position as Prime Minister to become an international statesman aligning himself with the developing world and radical, revolutionary movements.

He was seemingly less interested in domestic policy but went along with the move to the left demanded by the union movement and his party. There was a growth in radical feminism and environmentalism which he tried to assimilate. And he accelerated Erlander's push for bigger benefits, adding universal day care and free abortion (the share of overall public spending to GDP – national and local – shot up from around 40 per cent to 60 per cent).

The biggest and most controversial changes related to the so-called Meidner Plan named after the trade union economist who had, earlier, helped to design the system of centralized collective bargaining. Under the Plan it was initially proposed that a share of business profits (what the unions called 'excess' profits) should be transformed every year into union-controlled funds such that, after a generation or so, workers would control most businesses. The policy threatened the whole notion of working within a capitalist framework. Palme did his best to dilute and amend the Meidner Plan but, even in its modified form, a powerful signal was sent to business that the Social Democrats were tearing up the decades-long consensus based on compromise with the private sector.

There was growing dissention among Social Democrats with the Finance Minister in Palme's second government, Kjell-Olof Feldt, denouncing the 'negative inheritance I received from my [Social Democrat] predecessor, which was a strongly progressive system with high marginal taxes. This was supposed to bring about a just and equal society… Progressive taxes created instead a society of wranglers, cheaters… false ambitions and new injustices. It took me at least a decade to get a part of the party to see this.'[26]

Resistance began to grow. In the mid- to late 1970s, in the wake of the first global oil price shock, Sweden was suffering from high inflation, significant unemployment and large budget deficits. A new centre-right coalition entered power. When Palme regained the reins in 1982, he threw his weight behind Feldt and the group of young, liberal economists who wanted to roll back state spending and tax levels, deregulate the economy including the banking sector, apply monetarist methods to reduce inflation and strengthen the role of markets. Palme was killed before he could see where this new shift to neoliberal policies would lead. But the short-term effect of financial discipline was positive: inflation fell to 4.2 per cent in 1986, unemployment was falling from the very un-Swedish heights of 4.8 per cent in 1983 to 3.6 per cent in 1986, and there was brisk growth – around 3 per cent per annum – at the end of the Palme period.

Much as at the beginning of the Erlander premiership, Palme had re-established the Social Democrats as the party of competent and responsible government and sound finance allied to policies of social justice. And the party's political support held up – in the general election of 1988 the Social Democrats polled close to 45 per cent of the total vote and were able to continue in office with a confidence and supply arrangement with the Left Party (communists) much as it had done since the 1950s.

In the three decades which followed, Sweden has passed through a major banking crisis, periods of austerity and public retrenchment alternating with periods of expansion and spending, another spell of non-Social Democrat government and sustained but gradual liberalization of the economy with cuts in the state share of the economy and in marginal tax rates.

Overall, and probably in response to the reforms, Sweden has been one of the better-performing Western economies in terms of growth. But there was a cost to improved economic performance. Low unemployment, which had been Erlander's main benchmark of success, never returned. The Social Democrats also presided over privatization and cuts in the benefit system and never recovered the idealism and sense of a 'strong society' which Erlander had proclaimed and delivered. Strong growth sucked in immigrant labour following the EU's free movement of labour as well as a generous treatment of asylum seekers. Sweden became more cosmopolitan but less cohesive. Immigration became inherent in the model since economic growth was the only way to generate the revenue base for a generous welfare state without ever-rising tax rates. However, it inspired resentment (as in many other countries).

Despite compromises and some retrenchment, much of the Swedish model remains intact today. There is a generous social safety net and universal benefits financed by taxation. Public services are maintained at an enviable standard and this is now reflected in the exceptionally high share of public spending in GDP (well over 50 per cent, the highest in the Western world). The trade union movement also remains strong by Western standards.

Although the Swedish model has survived, the fortunes of the Social Democrats have deteriorated badly and in 2018 overall support in a general election fell below 30 per cent for the first time in over a century. They remained in government in coalition (with the Greens) but dependent on the support of centre-right opposition parties for the first time in their electoral history.

The End of Social Democracy?

The future of social democratic parties and the model they represent is now being seriously questioned.[27] In Germany, the UK and Sweden, the three countries where social democracy took deepest root after the split with revolutionary socialists in the nineteenth century, the parties of the centre left are in deep and possibly terminal decline. There have been major electoral set-backs for the UK's Labour Party and other social democratic parties in Germany, France, Italy, Ireland, Iceland, the Netherlands and Spain, with little traffic in the opposite direction.

There are deep, structural factors involved. The industrial working class has become less important with the shift to service-based economies. Trade unions have become weaker as an organizing force as the labour force has fragmented in response to technological change. Globalization has weakened the power of individual governments to manage their economies around national objectives. Specifically in Germany, Sweden and the UK, all three countries (until Brexit) had subsumed a good deal of policy within EU rules. New issues – notably the environment – have supplanted the combination of idealism and group interest which once fuelled social democratic parties. In Germany, the Greens appear to be replacing the Social Democrats as the main opposition to conservative parties, notably the Christian Democrats. In Greta Thunberg's Sweden they are a major growing force.

Social democratic ruling parties have found themselves having to choose between two options. First, many have embraced part of the neoliberal agenda such as with Palme and his successors in Sweden, with Gerhard Schröder's labour market reforms in Germany, or the Blair–Brown government in the UK. Others have returned to their more radical socialist, and Marxist, roots such as with the Corbyn project. The former has eroded the support base and the idealistic underpinning of social democracy; the latter has led to electoral near-annihilation. The Danish Social Democrats, albeit from a lower level of support than the Swedes, are trying a different approach by embracing some of the ideas of the 'populist' right and appear, for the moment, to have stemmed decline. The Covid-19 pandemic may open up wider divisions within the Nordic group following the Swedish decision to pursue a more permissive approach, avoiding lockdown and relying on self-discipline to curb the spread of the virus.

A positive interpretation of recent trends is that the social democratic model has proved in many respects to be both distinctive and successful even if the parties promoting it are having to seek partnerships with liberal or green parties rather than enjoy the near monopoly of power which existed in the era of Erlander's Sweden. Despite all the difficult cuts made in recent years, the Nordic countries, especially Sweden, have a relatively large public sector (currently 57 per cent of GDP in Sweden; 52 per cent in Denmark), generous benefits; well-funded public services; high levels of labour organization in unions (a union density of 67 per cent in Sweden as against 11 per cent in the US and 8 per cent in France). They are among the least corrupt countries in the world and sit at the top of rankings for human development, happiness, gender equality, post-tax equality, poverty reduction and social mobility. Yet the Nordic countries remain stalwart upholders of free trade, private property rights, ease of doing business and free competition. In all the current soul searching about the future of the social democratic model, the Nordic countries, and Sweden in particular, continue to make it work. There is no longer the hubris captured by the description in the 1930s of 'a functioning Utopia towards which to strive' but the description as a 'happy union of capitalism and socialism' is not too far off the mark.[28] This model was not the creation of one man, but if anyone made a disproportionate contribution it was Tage Erlander.

8

Perón: Peronism and Economic Populism

Many politicians use the language of populism: claiming to speak for 'the people' against the 'elite'. The twenty-first century is proving to be rich in such examples, with Trump perhaps the most high profile. The political figures I have described above as leading major economic transformations occasionally indulged in attacks on the elite even if they were, objectively, part of it, such as Roosevelt and, even, Mrs Thatcher. But their approach to economic policy was usually grounded in a deeper philosophy than taunting and taxing an 'elite' or unpopular minorities and foreigners. Indeed, throughout history, governments based on little more than populism have usually ended badly. Populist economic policy, like fraudulent accounting, at some point fails to add up and is found out, be it in the form of hyperinflation, debt crises or economic decline. The Chávez, later Maduro, revolution in Venezuela is a current example, though not all are based on the political left (for example, Silvio Berlusconi and now the Five Star Movement in Italy; Alberto Fujimori in Peru).

One populist movement which has proved remarkably durable is Peronism in Argentina. Despite repeated economic crises and the continued, relative, decline of the country's economy, Peronist Presidents and parliaments keep being elected and re-elected.

Seventy-five years after Juan Perón himself first came to power in Argentina, a sixth was elected at the end of 2019. Either hope always transcends experience in Argentina or the appeal of *justicialismo* ('social justice') transcends narrower economic considerations.

A century ago, Argentina was one of the world's richest countries but it has been relegated to the status of a middle-income country, overtaken in living standards by numerous others in Europe, Asia and, even, Latin America (Chile). Until 1962, its per capita income was greater than those of Japan, Italy or Spain. Relative decline started long before Perón and has continued under non-Peronist as well as Peronist successors. But it is reasonable to argue that the economic populism of Peronism is a major symptom and probably a serious contributor to an almost uniquely negative national economic trajectory. For that reason, it is worth serious examination as a case study of economic regression and populism.

The Liberal System, the Golden Age and the Great Rift

Before 1930, Argentina was seen as part of the rich, developed world with the world's eighth highest per capita income.[1] Between 1900 and 1930 it outgrew Australia and Canada in income, population and per capita income with successful, diverse (albeit resource based) exports; it was a magnet for European immigration; and it enjoyed large inflows of – mainly British – capital. It seemed inevitable that Argentina would emulate, or better, the performance and living standards of those other countries of European settlement (the indigenous population, like the indigenous peoples of the US and Australia, having been largely eliminated by war, disease and intermarriage).

The prevailing system of organization was called the Liberal System. The term 'liberal' in this context was essentially economic, based on free trade and laissez-faire economics.[2] Argentina's exporters took advantage of the opportunities under the nineteenth-century multilateral trading system: globalization Mark I. Technological advances in refrigeration, meat packing and transport transformed the economy. Exports of beef, hides and grain boomed. Immigration was encouraged to meet the demand for labour (in 1914, 30 per cent of all Argentines were foreign-born, led by Italians, a percentage of immigrants twice as high as ever reached in the US). There was a big influx of capital – two-thirds of it from the UK – mainly in railroads and agriculture-related industry. British influence was enormous (it was said that 40–50 per cent of all British overseas investment before the First World War went to Argentina).[3]

As a consequence, Argentina grew by an estimated 6 per cent per annum. At the time, this was believed to be the fastest growth of any country on the planet. By 1914 per capita income was higher than in France and Germany, 50 per cent higher than Italy's and twice that of Japan. Argentines were four times wealthier on average than Brazilians.[4]

This economic miracle seemed too good to be true, and it was. One economic historian concluded: 'the factors and causes that precipitated the crisis' (i.e. of today) 'have roots in the past… Cracks in the façade accompanied genuine economic promise throughout the late-nineteenth and early-twentieth centuries.'[5] Another noted that 'some strange things happened in that period'[6] as when the (rich and powerful) Province of Buenos Aires effectively seceded, highlighting what was called the Great Rift.

Fiscal and monetary discipline was weak. There was no monetary union until 1890. The easiest way to finance the federal government was to raid the central bank (in one case literally) and print money. The average annual inflation rate was in double figures through much of the 1870s and 1880s; the currency devalued in parallel and interest rates rarely fell below 10 per cent. There were also defaults on bond issues, property rights were repeatedly violated, and Argentina acquired a reputation for corrupt and unreliable 'gaucho banking'. During this apparently successful era Argentina missed the opportunity to design institutions, such as an independent judiciary and central bank, which would support sustainable growth and insulate the society from predatory interest groups and venal politicians.[7]

Moreover, Argentina was unhealthily dependent on the UK. There was a serious recession during the First World War when flows of capital dried up and trade was restricted. The Panama Canal also gave Argentina a much less strategic position on trade routes. Then, in the rush to create protectionist trade barriers in the 1920s, Argentina was badly hit by UK beef restrictions and by trade preferences given to English-speaking Dominions.

The watershed year was 1930 when a long period of civilian rule was interrupted by a military coup which ushered in nearly a century of political instability, numerous coups and economic decline. It is tempting to say that, if only the generals had stayed in the barracks, the country would have flourished. But that is to misunderstand the politics of the time. Beneath the surface, political structures were as fragile as the economy. A presidential system based on elections and civilian governments was compromised by corruption and dominated by an oligarchy of landowners.

By the start of the twentieth century, there was a growing tension between the traditional elite and a rapidly expanding working class whose numbers were being swelled by immigration. There were waves of strikes, a 'state of siege' and other manifestations of deep rifts in society.[8] Politicians started to organize themselves in parties, notably the Radical Party and the Socialist Party, which were competing for the votes of the many – the *gente de pueblo* – as opposed to the few – the *gente decente* – who had ruled the roost until then. The man who did more than any other to exploit this fertile ground and gave the country its first real taste of twentieth-century populism was Hipólito Irigoyen, who first became President in 1916 and who ended his second term in 1930 after the aforementioned coup.

He was a strange man who never spoke in public; never campaigned; was never knowingly photographed or publicized; and drew inspiration from an obscure religious cult. His self-effacing manner and humble lifestyle seemed not to discourage his mass following and he evidently made up for his lack of profile with a talent for plotting. When he reached highest office, however, his effectiveness was undermined by a total unwillingness to delegate and make decisions. This may not have mattered in good times, but it proved disastrous when Argentina was hit by the global Great Depression. Exports fell sharply, imports fell in parallel, and since import duties were a major revenue source there was a budget crisis. Public servants (including the army) went unpaid. This was a bad mistake. The army intervened and seized power. One middle-ranking officer – then a military academic, a professor at the country's war college – was Juan Perón (1895–1974). He played a part in the coup – taking control of the presidential palace – and earned promotion to the rank of major. And a precedent was being created for his own coup, thirteen years later.

Perón: From Soldier to Politician

Perón was born into a middle-class family in provincial Argentina close to the pampas, a low-lying region in the north. The family later moved to Patagonia, in the south, providing a rural upbringing on the periphery of the country around which a compelling political narrative could be created later. He was sent to Buenos Aires for schooling, aged twelve, and then, aged eighteen, he joined the Military College as a cadet. Argentine armies, like most in Latin America, did not expect to face much by way of armed conflict with neighbouring countries. So, Perón became a desk-bound soldier with five years as private secretary to the War Minister. He later became a military attaché to Chile, also building a reputation as a scholar producing textbooks on South American military history.

A crucial, formative, experience was being sent to Europe in 1939 at the age of forty-four when he was attached to the Italian mountain infantry before travelling to Germany and the Soviet Union. His Peronist biographers attest to his enthusiasm for what he saw of fascism in action: 'he saw the success of fascism in overcoming class divisions, mobilising the masses for national reconstruction and achieving national unity through social justice.'[9] He had particular admiration for Mussolini. Perón's thinking was heavily influenced by what he perceived as the good aspects of the fascist model: the sense of political and economic order and discipline combined with the support and engagement of the poor ('the masses'), united by nationalism. He shared the fascist distaste for both international capitalism and communism. He was particularly attracted to the idea of incorporating the main interest groups of society into associations under the state overseen by a powerful leader. Indeed, that is the model he employed when he acquired power.

The Argentina to which he returned had experienced a decade of restored civilian rule after the military had gone back to the barracks in 1932. There had been a substantial growth in industry, mostly behind protective tariffs, as Argentina responded to the closure of overseas markets by building up domestic manufacturing of consumer products, meat packing, textiles and oil refining. The number of industrial workers more than doubled to over 800,000. But in other respects little had changed. Britain still bought 30–40 per cent of Argentine exports and 90 per cent of meat exports. Foreign investment still loomed large and this was largely British-owned (four times greater in value than US investment).[10] The underlying divisions in the country – between modernizing, growing Buenos Aires and the stagnant, poor rural and provincial areas; between rich and poor; the Great Rift – were as deep as ever, or worse. Politics was drifting with rampant corruption and all the major civilian parties seemingly in decline.[11] If there was a dominant theme, it was the growth of nationalism, in economic and political terms, but at this stage it lacked leadership.

In 1943 there was an intense period of plotting in the military and a group of four colonels, one of them Perón, took control through a coup. Although the coup was nominally under the leadership of a respected general, Perón would emerge as *primus inter pares* by building up a non-military political base: a social movement among the poor. He did this by getting himself appointed Minister for Labour and then co-opting trade union leaders into a powerful, unified labour organization while simultaneously appealing over their heads to the millions of poor Argentinians, unionized or not. He communicated through mass rallies and use of the media, especially radio, with a political message of social justice.

An important ingredient in his successful campaigning was his mistress, then wife, Eva Duarte – Evita. He had met her at a gala event to raise money for earthquake victims in 1944 and they promptly embarked on a high-profile love affair. She was from a very poor, single-parent family and carried the stigma of being illegitimate. She had, however, succeeded in making her way as an actress, mainly on radio. Much has been made of their relationship, which followed the early death of his first wife. Apart from the romance it was a very effective political partnership in which, initially at least, Evita played the role of disciple and events organizer.

After two years of manoeuvring and power struggle within the armed forces and on the streets, Perón emerged as the dominant force. His rivals in the military, alarmed by his growing power and popularity, had him arrested in October 1945 but, after mass protests by the trade unions, he was released a few days later. From then on he was firmly in charge. On the back of his new movement, he forced a presidential election in 1946, which he won with 52 per cent of the vote. The election was fought partly on the theme of social justice – with Perón's main offer being a

package of measures, led by 'profit sharing', designed to appeal
to workers. The other issue in the election surrounded allegations
of Perón's complicity in Nazism. That campaign was orchestrated
by the US Ambassador, Spruille Braden, which may have helped
Perón's election campaign, given the rising tide of anti-American
nationalism. The exposé of Nazi activities proved to have weak
foundations as his sympathies were almost certainly with Italian
rather than German fascism and more as an ideology (there was
never any serious suggestion of anti-Semitism, for example).

His wife, Evita's, position in the broadcasting world helped to
secure maximum coverage for his speeches. And after the election,
when she became First Lady, she ran the labour and health ministries, making lavish spending commitments, and started work on
the Evita Perón Foundation which was to accumulate considerable power and resources.

The 'Peronato': Peronism in Practice

Perón's election opened the way to a near-decade in power in
which he was able to give effect to the Peronist model of government and economics.

Perón's first priority was to reinforce his own power base by shifting power and resources to labour and the trade union movement.
He actively encouraged strikes designed to improve workers' pay
and conditions. Union affiliation grew from 22 per cent to 49 per
cent of the non-agricultural labour force. Real wages grew rapidly
– reaching 37 per cent above 1943 levels by 1948 – for unskilled
workers. The labour share of national income (wages and sal-
aries) grew from 37 per cent in 1946 to 50 per cent in 1950, which
boosted consumer demand but squeezed investment. There were
benefit entitlements for workers, better pensions and free medical
treatment and maternity leave – largely financed by employers.
The pro-labour policy, however, stopped short of full syndicalism
– under which organized labour runs business and, indirectly, the

economy. Perón kept power in his own hands, retained a veto over strikes and appointed key union officials.

The second strand in Peronist economics was economic nationalism. There was a wave of nationalization of foreign-owned enterprises, notably the British-owned railways and the American-owned telecoms firm ITT as well as the banks, using foreign reserves accumulated during the war for compensation. He established a state monopoly over foreign trade, the IAPT. A key element of policy was to deepen and strengthen the protectionist trade policies of the 1930s aimed at industrialization through import substitution – replacing foreign-made goods with domestic substitutes. The Argentine economic thinker who inspired these policies was Raúl Prebisch, the 'Keynes of Latin America'. Prebisch was to become – as head of the UN Economic Commission for Latin America (ECLA) and the UN Commission for Trade and Development (UNCTAD) – one of the main influences on post-war development thinking throughout the developing world.[12] The theoretical framework can be summarized in the catchphrase *desarrollo a dentro* (inward-looking development) as opposed to *desarrollo a fuero* (outward-looking development). Prebisch argued that the terms of trade for developing-country commodity exporters were inexorably declining relative to manufactured goods exported from the developed world. Developing countries should, therefore, use trade protection to support domestic manufacturing. In many ways this was a modern version of the ideas of Alexander Hamilton in the USA and, later, Bismarck in Germany and drew on the ideas of the development economist Arthur Lewis and others on the importance of manufacturing industry for post-colonial economies.[13]

In Peronist Argentina, however, this led to the creation of high-cost, inefficient local monopolies, which enjoyed political patronage and absorbed a disproportionate share of credit from the newly nationalized banks. For a while, the spending power of the workers and access to easy credit boosted growth of locally produced consumer goods; but this was growth at the expense of other sectors of the economy, notably agriculture, but also more sophisticated industrial goods. As economist Alan M. Taylor noted, 'Populism required bread and circuses for the working-class constituents, so imports of consumption goods could not be compressed too hard… To maintain external balance [because of export weakness], something had to be squeezed, and unfortunately this turned out to be the goods that form the basis of long-run growth, the capital goods.'[14] Argentina became an extreme example of the broader failure of developing countries – from Brazil to India – which followed this road to development instead of the more outward-looking countries of East Asia which looked to manufactured exports[15] or the developed world which was enjoying a new period of trade liberalization. Argentina diverged from the rest of the world in productivity and, hence, per capita income. Even on its own terms, the policy ran out of steam. Between 1946 and 1948 industry grew by an average of 6.3 per cent, but after 1948 growth slowed to a crawl.

Economic populism manifested itself, in due course, in inflationary budgetary and monetary policies. Under Perón, there was a spectacular surge in public spending which took public expenditure as a share of GDP from 20 per cent to 45 per cent and of the fiscal deficit from 4 per cent to 12 per cent of GDP (though these were corrected later in his administration).[16] The nationalized industries he established lost money and the political appointees who ran them had neither the skill nor the inclination to make the tough decisions to turn them around. Lavish public sector pay awards had to be paid for as did welfare benefits. Cuts in imports caused tariff revenues to shrink. The boundaries between official state spending and unofficial spending by his political allies and his wife became very blurred. Eva Perón's charitable outlays of 'social aid' – gifts of food, clothes, books and toys to poor families – started to get Treasury funding alongside union contributions, betting tax revenues and extortion. It was noted that Evita had no interest in accounting, which she equated with 'heartless capitalism'. Her 'social aid' became a substantial part of public spending.[17]

Budget deficits were financed by printing money.[18] Even before coming to the presidency, Perón had used his ministerial position to remove the independence of the central bank. In 1935 a law had been passed preventing the central bank from lending more than 10 per cent of tax revenues to the government. But Perón rescinded these powers, opening the way to government control of credit and direct monetary financing of the deficit. And since money supply was not tied to the country's reserves but was at the government's discretion, there was rapid expansion (bank credit grew five times between 1945 and 1948). Inflation was an inevitable consequence, jumping from 13 per cent in 1946 to 31 per cent in 1949. It averaged over 20 per cent per annum in the five years from 1946 to 1951, higher than for any administration for a century. There was also serious mismanagement of foreign trade by the IAPT, leading to a serious depletion of foreign reserves followed by devaluation and yet more inflation.

At a deeper level, Perón weakened the independent institutions which stood for the rule of law. Shortly after coming to power he impeached (through his supporters in Congress) four of the five members of the Supreme Court who had given an unhelpful ruling on his labour relations policies. He packed the court with Peronists. Of course, attacks on Supreme Court justices are far from unique to Argentina; the USA has seen attempts to pack the Supreme Court from Roosevelt to Trump. But in general, the political subversion of the judiciary and the rule of law is a key factor in explaining why countries fail.[19]

Perón was a nationalist, but his brand of nationalism was not directed against Argentina's neighbours. On the contrary, he was a strong promoter of Latin American unity, especially with Brazil and Chile: 'Argentina alone,' he said, 'is not an economic unit, nor Brazil or Chile also. Yet these three countries together form currently the most extraordinary economic unit in the world. No doubt that with this union, other South American countries will come into its orbit.'[20] This belief in Latin American unity proved to be more a matter of rhetoric than action but it did motivate decades of work led by Raúl Prebisch and the Economic Commission for Latin America to create common markets or free trade areas in the region.[21] The reasoning was that import-substituting industrialization required economies of scale to be economically efficient, and regional integration among developing economies provided a better route than competitive world markets. This approach proved to be a blind alley but a loose grouping in the 'southern cone' – Mercosur – has survived.

Perón's interaction with his neighbours also helped clarify his thinking about what Peronism was about. He discovered a strong affinity with the Brazilian leader Getúlio Vargas, who first came to power in 1930 through a revolution, was elected President and assumed dictatorial powers from 1931 to 1945 before conceding to a demand for a return to democracy. In his period of office, he styled himself as the 'father of the poor', with a hostility to big business and large landowners – while keeping the fundamentals of a private enterprise system. Like Perón, he endeavoured to define a 'middle way' between communism and the liberal economic system which had failed during the Great Depression of the 1930s. The system he developed, variously described as 'national capitalism' or 'corporatism', drew, like Peronism, on the model of Southern European fascism, as with Salazar in Portugal, Franco in Spain and Mussolini in Italy – with protected industrialization and the incorporation of the union movement into government. Vargas was, for a long period, successful and popular but, like Perón, he antagonized powerful interest groups and, faced with being deposed by the military in 1954, he shot himself.

The Brazilian model, developed under Vargas, was arguably more successful than Perón's in creating a strong industrial base and a more diverse economy. In terms of per capita income, Brazil has also closed the gap to Argentina's level. But, as in Argentina,

Brazil has suffered bouts of hyperinflation due to monetization of budget deficits, debt default, economic volatility and serious institutional corruption.

While Brazil has been a mixed story and the Vargas legacy has some strong positives, it is difficult to be so generous about Peronism. Even relatively sympathetic commentators conclude of his economic policy: 'Though Perón did not destroy the Argentine economy as many of his detractors have claimed, he set the stage for a society that was highly polarized and found itself unable to develop a coherent economic strategy to cope with changes in the world economy and Argentina's place in it over the course of the next two decades.'[22] A less sympathetic verdict would be that the endemic economic instability of the last seventy years owes a great deal to the system he established: the economic nationalism; the power of an unproductive state machine; the reinforcement of powerful sectional interests; the destruction of independent institutions.

By 1951 the economy was in dire straits and it was far from clear that Perón would be re-elected. He did so, however, convincingly. There were many beneficiaries from his policies, notably the trade unions. Perón still had a big following among the *descaminados* ('shirtless ones'). One key electoral asset was Evita. They had planned to run on a joint ticket with her as Vice President and designated successor. This proposal was vetoed by the military establishment and was, in any event, impractical when she was diagnosed with cervical cancer. She stood down but not before a mass outpouring of public support at a rally of an estimated 2 million supporters.

Opinions about Evita were, and are, highly polarized. Her critics have described her as a prostitute, a fascist, profligate, corrupt and a thief.[23] Her more ardent admirers petitioned the Vatican to have her made a saint for performing miracles among the poor and sick. More dispassionate biographers dismiss the accusations of corruption and acknowledge the real achievements of her

Foundation, the impact she made in improving national health care and helping to secure votes for women.[24] Her death in 1952 prompted a massive expression of grief. It may also have triggered a change of heart on economic policy as Perón turned to more conventional advisers.

Unlike some other populists (for example, Nicolás Maduro in today's Venezuela), Perón pulled back when confronted with imminent economic disaster. He imposed an austerity package. Public spending was frozen, having risen 87 per cent from 1945 to 1950. Wages and (after a lag) prices were also frozen; real wages declined by 30 per cent from 1948 to 1953. The government even solicited private investment including foreign capital.

In a symbolically important move, Perón sought (and eventually secured) a profit-sharing agreement with Standard Oil of California, one of the 'seven sisters' of the oil industry and anathema to the economic nationalists in the Peronist movement and the military. This move would do fatal political damage to Perón, but it illustrates the schizophrenic approach to populist versus conventional economics which he passed to his successors. One successor, Carlos Menem, became a poster boy for the IMF and an embodiment of the Washington Consensus; on the other hand, Néstor Kirchner and Cristina Fernández de Kirchner, in their respective terms as President, perpetuated the populism of early Perón.

Decline, Fall and Restoration: Perón II

The dissatisfactions arising from austerity and Perón's adoption of a more pragmatic economic policy coincided with several other damaging developments. Corruption scandals erupted around the late Evita's relatives. Violent anti-government protests, including fatalities, were seen on the streets. Perón himself outraged public opinion, especially the Catholic Church, by taking a fourteen-year-old girl from a poor family as a mistress. After a series of foiled plots, Perón eventually fell to a military coup a decade after his own successful one. He could, perhaps, have held onto power had he mobilized his allies in the labour movement and loyal troops. But he chose to go quietly into exile. He is reported to have said: 'Blood saves time, but it costs a lot', a strangely pacifist message for a military man.[25]

He spent almost twenty years in exile, initially enjoying the hospitality of unsavoury right-wing dictators – Stroessner in Paraguay; Pérez Jiménez in Venezuela; Trujillo in the Dominican Republic – before settling in Franco's Spain. He had little wealth, having been an honest man whatever his other faults, and, apart from maintaining a tenuous link with the decapitated Peronist movement back home, enjoyed quiet domesticity with his third wife, Isabel, who was his PA and a former nightclub dancer he had met in Panama. One of the bizarre features of these domestic arrangements was that the embalmed body of Evita was kept on display in the Peróns' living room, awaiting burial back in Argentina.

What prevented Perón from being totally forgotten in Argentina was the mounting list of failed regimes which followed him: no fewer than six military coups and three elected Presidents in the next eighteen years. Despite an initial attempt to restore Argentina to favour with the IMF and the World Bank, the country continued with a tolerance of double-digit inflation, weak budgeting, state-dominated economic structures and inefficient, protected industries.

Dissatisfaction, when it was allowed expression, mainly took the form of nostalgia for Perón with the formation of Peronist parties claiming allegiance to the former leader in exile, and with Peronist labour unions still having a powerful role in labour markets. 'Peronism' became a portmanteau term for widely disparate organizations from orthodox, traditional trade unions to left-wing guerrilla movements, such as the Montoneros. In the early 1970s Argentina descended into violence caused by a combination of unpopular government policies and fuelled by the radicalization of many young people. In due course, the military government made way for a 'civilian' solution, which meant Perón returning from exile.

The returning Perón was two decades older and not a well man. He had no time to settle into any kind of government beyond resolving a civil war between the right and left Peronists (in favour of the former) and installing his wife Isabel as his successor before he died. Isabel had no talent for politics or administration, despite rather embarrassing attempts to mimic Evita, and she relied heavily on a coterie of advisers of dubious ability and integrity. The brief period of Peronist government under Isabel proved economically disastrous. Any discipline in economic management broke down and inflation soared beyond 600 per cent. The military again moved in, this time with the aim of stamping out the revolutionary left, including Peronists, and using methods similar to General Pinochet in Chile: death squads, torture and an estimated 30,000 'disappearances' of suspected leftists.

There was also, as in Chile, an attempt over the period 1976–83 to destroy the legacy of Peronism and return to the values and policies of the old liberal system. The Finance Minister, Martínez de Hoz, embarked on economic liberalization: lowering tariffs, privatization, cutting subsidies. At the same time strikes were banned, wages frozen and Peronist institutions dismantled. Inflation, however, remained stuck in three digits (on average) over the seven years of military rule. There was no economic growth over the period: the worst sustained period of stagnation since the First World War.

Unlike in Chile, the new regime was not able to force a change of direction; one reason being the fact that the institutions of Peronism, embedded in the trade unions, were too strong and the authority of the military was just not sufficient to force through unpopular – if necessary – reforms. The disastrous Falklands War in 1982 finally broke the military government when it failed at the one thing it was supposed to be good at: fighting. Indeed, the way was now open to a new move back to populism.

The Peronist Dynasty

The brutality, military incompetence and lack of economic success of the generals brought back civilian government under Raúl Alfonsín of the Radical Party who defeated a weak Peronist candidate (the first ever electoral defeat for Peronism). Whatever hopes there may have been of economic improvement were not realized. Financial discipline deteriorated further: government payrolls swelled to boost the government's popularity and government revenues stagnated. Inflation reached four digits – 5,000 per cent per annum – 200 per cent a month in 1989. Government debt reached unprecedented levels (250 per cent of exports, averaged over a five-year period). There was a negative annual growth rate averaging 2 per cent per annum. Living standards inevitably plummeted. Strikes paralysed the country and supermarkets were looted for food. The President gave up, defeated, before the end of his term and power passed once again to a Peronist.

The ten-year Peronist presidency of Carlos Menem – longer than that enjoyed by Perón himself – is one of the strangest episodes in the lengthy history of this particular ideology. Having campaigned as a traditional Peronist (who was imprisoned by the military dictatorship) and having promised big pay rises all around to get the Peronist nomination, in office Menem adopted policies which were the opposite of everything Perón stood for and which he himself had opposed until that point.

The reasons for this Damascene conversion are several. The extremity of the crisis he inherited forced him to look to what seemed to be extreme solutions. And Menem had already demonstrated ideological elasticity in his role as a provincial governor and in his private life (he converted from Islam, a small minority in Argentina, to Catholicism to enhance his appeal).

There were people ready with solutions based on what was called the Washington Consensus. A key individual was Domingo Cavallo who had been incubating a plan at Argentina's National University of Córdoba. He was appointed Economy Minister and given free rein. He brought in sweeping market reforms: far-reaching privatization (involving sale of assets to foreign creditors), the removal of subsidies, cuts in welfare spending, increased taxes to balance the budget and reduced import tariffs on protected industries. External debt was restructured and Argentina was readmitted to the good opinion of the IMF and the World Bank. Cavallo's key demand was that politicians must be prevented from reigniting inflation and his mechanism for doing this was to make the currency – the peso – fully convertible with the dollar.

At first, and for several years, the policy was remarkably successful. Inflation fell to single digits and confidence was restored, stopping capital flight and promoting inward investment. Growth also began to fire – to over 3 per cent per annum in the 1990–95 period. At last, Argentina seemed to have found a formula which worked and, moreover, under a Peronist President who was able to mobilize political and trade union support (or at least that part which did not break off, angry and disillusioned). Menem later disarmingly admitted the cynicism which was at the heart of his project: 'had I said what I was going to do no one would have voted for me'.[26]

Trying to push through a programme of radical liberalization by stealth was never going to work over the long term. After securing re-election in 1995, Menem's administration started to unravel domestically just as it was being lionized internationally as the great success story of neoliberalism. Cavallo claimed that Argentina 'was considered as the best pupil of the IMF, the World Bank and the US Government'.[27]

But the dollar currency peg that had been used to tame inflation was by this stage seriously eroding the competitiveness of exports and industries competing with imports. Unemployment soared to over 20 per cent by 2001 and the manufacturing industry which Perón had built up was decimated. Industry fell to 16 per cent of GDP in 2001, down from 35 per cent in the 1970s, and while much of the manufacturing was highly inefficient there was little to replace it. One reason was that investor confidence was low as doubts crept in about Menem's political durability fuelled by reports of serious corruption. Then, the government's inability to control the budget led to heavy borrowing, much of it overseas.

Things would only get worse. A financial crisis brewed in East Asia and Russia which led to capital flight to the safe haven of the US dollar as investors feared that Menem and the Argentine experiment would not last: a self-fulfilling prophecy. The crisis reached its peak in 2001 with a default on $100 billion of debt, the world's biggest ever sovereign default. The people of Argentina experienced severe hardship with the economy contracting by 20 per cent, wiping out all the gains from the early years of Menem's presidency. Rioting and looting accompanied the disintegration of the regime. A new president, Fernando de la Rúa, fled by helicopter from the roof of the palace. There were five Presidents in two weeks until control passed to another Peronist, Néstor Kirchner, who came to power repudiating neoliberalism and the Washington Consensus.

Kirchner was dealt a difficult hand with an economy that had been in severe recession and a government shut out of credit markets after a massive debt default. The Peronist party, his power base, had fragmented and split after the disillusionment of the Menem years. He also faced expectations on a populist platform which had been shown to fail in government time and time again. In the event, he was lucky and also played his cards well. He was lucky because the early years of the twenty-first century saw a strong boom in commodity prices, fuelled in large part by Chinese demand. The forced devaluation when the currency peg collapsed had also helped to make exports more competitive. The government did not try to re-establish a new fixed exchange rate but moved to a floating rate. It also maintained a roughly balanced budget.

Despite the greater fiscal discipline, the government managed over four years (2003–7) to increase public spending by 30 per cent. Real wages grew by an estimated 70 per cent in the strong recovery from deep recession. Unemployment fell from 20 per cent to under 10 per cent and there was a big drop in poverty levels. But some of Argentina's problems were merely hidden. Inflation, in particular, was artificially suppressed by price controls. There was also some manipulation of statistics and honest statisticians in government were replaced.

The fires of populism were kept alive by an aggressive approach to the renegotiation of debt. Argentina unilaterally cancelled its IMF debt and rescheduled other debt. Kirchner also formed an alliance of convenience with the revolutionary socialist regime of Hugo Chávez in Venezuela to present a common front against the Washington Consensus.

Kirchner died in 2010 but not before he had organized a succession to his wife, Cristina Fernández, who went further than her husband in pursuing populist measures: she reverted to printing money to finance a growing budget deficit arising from generous social welfare programmes. Monetization led to high inflation, only partially suppressed by price controls. The commodity boom which had kept the Argentine economy growing ended, leading to the next serious crisis and recession in 2014.

There had been five Peronist Presidents and an almost predictable cycle of populist measures followed by financial crisis and collapse of the real economy and then a period of painful austerity. But there was to be one more round. A government from the parties opposed to the Peronists was constructed under President Mauricio Macri, who tried to restore stability through monetary and fiscal tightening (again) and to rebuild Argentina's external credit worthiness by reaching an agreement with foreign bond holders and removing capital controls. The IMF was sufficiently reassured to restore credit. The policies were partially successful, but the country was in recession after a period of austerity – in which an estimated two-fifths of Argentines could no longer afford a monthly basket of staple goods. In 2019 inflation was also running at 55 per cent per annum. In the next presidential election, the Peronist Alberto Fernández was returned with Cristina Fernández de Kirchner back as Vice President and the power behind the throne. She has expressed a determination to return to the Peronist traditions of rising government spending, with, inevitably, big deficits and inflation (while fighting numerous corruption charges from her period as President). The cycle continues.

Peronism and Economics

It is tempting to write off Peronist populism, as some economic commentators do, as simply a tale of economically illiterate politicians – starting with Perón – manipulating a gullible public to produce disastrous outcomes in a far-away Latin American country. That would be a mistake.

It would be wrong to ascribe all the damaging economic policies to Perón and Peronism. His predecessors had already gone down the path of inward-looking industrialization and establishing a bias against exports which had been the basis of Argentina's earlier growth and rising if unequal prosperity.[28] Economic nationalism and a belief in strongly statist remedies were well established, though Perón took them to another level.

The Peronist approach to economic matters can be described as populist for the attempts to pin the country's social evils and economic problems on the wealthy elite and on foreign interests, and for promises for a better life without the resources to deliver it. But at its inception Peronism was based on serious ideas.

The first was the fascist model of economics. The descent of Europe into war, the genocidal excesses of Hitler and the repressive dictatorships of Southern Europe have all somewhat obscured how Mussolini's pre-war Italy influenced many other regimes, from Turkey to Brazil. The fascist model had considerable appeal in its state-led industrialization in partnership with business, the primacy of the national economy, full employment, economic planning but without communism, and the incorporation of trade unions and the working class into the heart of government. Of course, there was also the appeal of order and discipline with trains running on time. Naturally, the fascist brand lost its allure after the war, but Perón acknowledged his intellectual debt to it.

A second influence was the school of economics which originated in Argentina with Raúl Prebisch and became the dominant paradigm in Latin America, and throughout much of the developing world in the 1950s and 1960s, based on pessimism about the relative prices of manufactured goods and primary commodities. Argentina was easily portrayed as one of those countries whose dependence on agricultural exports trapped it into a vicious cycle of specialization in products of declining value. The theory went that Argentina and other poor countries should develop their own industries behind tariff walls. There was a more extreme version of these ideas in the 'dependency theory' developed by Andre Gunder Frank, the American-German sociologist.[29] Frank argued that trade with rich countries was positively harmful since it was largely in the hands of multinational companies and rich local landlords and businessmen who all had an interest in sucking profits out of poor countries and transferring wealth to the rich 'core'. Whether in the more moderate or extreme version, the sense of dependence and victimhood in this approach to economics gave substance to the Peronists' economic nationalism.

For completeness, we have to acknowledge a third influence: the reluctant acceptance, under extreme pressure, of market economics. When Perón's populist policies had failed in 1952 he accepted the necessity for a period of austerity even though the backlash was to destroy his presidency. The longest-serving Peronist President,

Carlos Menem, spent almost a decade trying to implement the Washington Consensus following the advice of advisers whose slogan was 'stabilize, privatize and liberalize'.[30] The policies were initially successful in producing growth, improved living standards and low inflation. But the experiment collapsed.

The Menem failure caused the next and current generations of Peronists to reject the Washington Consensus in its entirety. This rejectionism drew intellectual nourishment from, among others, economist Joseph Stiglitz.[31] Stiglitz was, however, careful to argue that the Consensus was 'designed to respond to the very real problems of Latin America and made considerable sense' while criticizing the 'one size fits all' approach of the Washington institutions.[32]

Peronism has shown itself to be nothing if not eclectic, and part of that eclecticism is drawing on the experience of other countries. Perón himself was impressed by the fascist countries of Southern Europe and by Vargas in Brazil. More recently the left has been attracted to Chavismo in Venezuela. Most instructive, and galling, to Argentines has been the experience of being overtaken by Chile, now an OECD country. For some time this could be rationalized as the result of brutal dictatorship followed by harsh, Chicago-school reforms inspired by Arnold Harberger.[33] But Chile has since had thirty years of civilian, often social democratic, governments.[34] Chile has long overtaken Argentina (per capita income $16,000 versus $11,700), though rioting in 2019 exposed some weaknesses.

Peronism has been an abject economic failure which has left Argentina far behind other countries, including its next-door neighbour. We are left with a political question: why do Argentine electors, in a democratic system, keep voting for failure?[35] Part of the answer must be that Peronism has values which are attractive in themselves, especially when there is no consensus on how to improve economic performance. Its underlying ideology from Perón to today has been *justicialismo*: social justice. That idea remains very much alive. It is not entirely a coincidence that Argentina has produced the first Latin American Pope, who has made the Catholic commitment to social justice one of the central tenets of his papacy: 'those who see social rights as outdated advance economic and social policies that lead our peoples to the acceptance of inequality and indignity.'[36] Large numbers of Argentines have been persuaded that greater equality, a sense of national independence and dignity matter more than a track record of competent economic management. So far, the opponents of Peronism have failed to produce a more compelling message.

9

Park: The Development State and Hypergrowth

One of the most remarkable transformations in modern times has been the emergence of South Korea from being one of the world's poorest countries in the wake of the Korean War to an industrialized country with Western living standards (and a functioning, vibrant, democracy).[1] There is a striking contrast with North Korea, which emerged from wartime with a stronger and more industrialized economy but is now (as far as the 'Hermit Kingdom' makes it possible to tell) a desperately poor, albeit well-armed, country subject to periodic famine. Indeed, the contrast is often used as a prime illustration of why economic policy matters.

The differences between the two Koreas is also sometimes made to illustrate the superiority of the capitalist model over the communist system of economic organization. Nevertheless, the capitalism of South Korea has been very different from its forms in Europe and North America, with a much higher level of state direction and state planning. It is perhaps the best example of the 'development state'.

South Korea produced over a sustained period (and at considerable social and political cost) spectacular economic growth rates: 'hypergrowth'. Such performance is not unique. Stalin's industrialization through Five Year Plans achieved it, at immense cost (nor was it sustainable). China's more recent success and hyper-growth have surpassed Korea's and have had far more significant global repercussions. But South Korea stands out (with Taiwan and Singapore) among non-communist countries for having progressed from deep poverty to living standards on a par with rich countries. Likewise, it has become renowned for having developed firms selling world-class technologically advanced industrial products into global markets. Crucially, its emergence was not expected or predicted. A US commentator in 1961 noted that 'the poorer half of one of the poorest countries in the world is trying to exist as a nation with too many people and too few resources... [Korea depends] for the foreseeable future... upon the self-interest and charity of... the USA.'[2] It was also believed to be falling behind North Korea, seemingly growing rapidly under the communist government.

The economic breakthrough of the South owes a lot to long-standing social and economic developments including a strong commitment to investment in education. But the crucial period was the eighteen-year rule of the military leader Park Chung-hee (1917–79) after the 1961 military coup and, within that period, the sixteen years from when he became President in 1963 until his assassination in 1979. There is little doubt that Park, personally, was central to the overall economic strategy and specific policies within it. He defined his ambitions of governing Korea in terms both of economic development, as an end in itself, and also to strengthen the country's military capability.[3] And Park got the credit for the fact that two decades after he took power the economy was ten times bigger. Park is broadly recognized as the author of the 'Miracle on the Han River'[4] (though there was a big downside to this 'miracle' in terms of personal freedoms and working conditions).

The Korean experience raises the question of how a military man with no obvious knowledge or background in economics or business could have formed such clear and definite views on economic policy. Unlike some of my previous subjects he was not shy of acknowledging whence he derived his economic ideas. He frequently referred to Japanese influences in his early life and, in particular, to the inspiration of Japan's reformist and modernizing Meiji dynasty from 1868 onwards.[5] It is said that when, en route to meet President Kennedy to gain acceptance of the 1961 coup, he stopped over in Japan and in speeches (in Japanese) he extolled the Meiji government and asked Japanese friends to send him books on, among other things, Meiji economic policy. This wish to copy all things Japanese was rather brave, given the visceral hatred of the Japanese in large sections of Korean society (which is still very much alive today).

It would be surprising if Western ideas were not also important given the close military ties with the USA and the importance of American aid. As we shall see below, there was strong, not always harmonious, interaction with the US over macroeconomic policy and the role of markets. But US thinking was not simply the conventional (largely Keynesian) views of the time, and of liberal economics, but those of development, growth and planning originating from Paul Rosenstein-Rodan and Arthur Lewis and popularized by the economic historian Walt Rostow, who was a key US adviser at the time.[6]

Some Korean writers are keen to stress how different the Korean model is from the economics of Adam Smith and David Ricardo. Chung-in Moon and Byung-joon Jun, for example, said: 'Park shared the spirit of the Japanese Meiji revolutionaries, Young Turks, and Bismarckian Germans, in which the state commanded the market to expedite the process of development.'[7] There is some suggestion that the young Park was also influenced by the theories of Karl Marx and flirted with communism.[8] And the communist North was then seen as an economic success story, its state-directed industrialization a source of envy for those in the South, like Park, who shared many of the nationalistic instincts of Kim Il-sung's regime. Indeed, the influence of Korean nationalism takes us to the historical context from which Park emerged.

Growing in the Shadow of Giants

Korea's modern history has been moulded by the four economic and military giants which tower over it: China and Russia (which both abut the northern border), Japan and the USA. No other significant modern state, with the possible exceptions of Belgium and Poland, has had quite this degree of external pressure from competing – and more powerful – neighbours.

Korea maintained its independence (as the Chosŏn Kingdom) for five centuries through a combination of self-defence, diplomacy and self-imposed isolation (which first led to the phrase 'Hermit Kingdom'). By the end of the nineteenth century the country started to open up to Western and other influences but the dominant force in the region was Japan, which was emboldened by military victories over China and Russia. Japan annexed Korea in 1910 and turned it into a colony, seeking to eradicate Korean identity, in particular substituting the Japanese language for Korean. There was a campaign of non-violent resistance to the Japanese colonization which, after having been brutally repressed, went underground. Korea was also forced into the Japanese Imperial war machine through conscription.[9]

When war ended, the northern part of the Korean peninsula fell into Russian hands; the south to the Americans. After a failed UN attempt to bring together the two provisional governments and unify Korea under an elected government, war broke out in 1950 between the communist North and the South, which was recognized by the international community. Millions died in fighting across the peninsula (15 per cent of the population); China entered the war on the side of the North; and, eventually, with stalemate in the fighting, a negotiated truce led to de facto partition along the 38th parallel. Kim Il-sung, in the North, inherited what remained of a devastated industrial base and opted for an extreme form of communism based on heavy industry, total collectivization of farming and self-sufficiency. It reflected the prejudices of a particular communist faction – the Manchuria-based guerrillas – which was described as 'militarist, Spartan, anti-intellectual and xenophobic'.[10]

The future leader of the South, Park Chung-hee, was a product of the Japanese occupation and its aftermath. Born in 1917, he was reportedly a very ambitious and intelligent young man from a poor rural family, who graduated from high school, and then taught briefly, before making a crucial move in 1940 to join the Japanese military at a time when China and Japan were at war. The route he chose was through the Military Academy of the Japanese Army in Manchukuo, now Chinese Manchuria, then a puppet state under Japanese occupation. His biographers describe a dedicated and brilliant student fully assimilated into the Japanese system (with a Japanese adopted name). He was a model student (who received an award from the Emperor himself) and he was sufficiently highly thought of to be sent by his Japanese instructors to a military academy in Japan.[11] In the closing stages of the Second World War, he was despatched to fight for the army in Manchuria (against, among others, Korean partisans). Amid the chaotic events – Russian invasion, the collapse of the Japanese forces (and the emergence of Mao's Chinese guerrilla army) – he fled to China and there transferred his allegiance to the Korean resistance army. He returned to Korea to pursue his military career in the new South Korean army.

At this point, Park's fluid allegiances almost cost him his career and his life. The new South Korean army, with American occupying forces, was involved in an increasingly bitter conflict with communist insurgents (and communist cells within the army). It emerged that Park was actually an active but clandestine member of the Workers' Party (i.e. communist); indeed, supplying arms to the rebels.[12] He was sentenced to death, commuted to a

twenty-year jail term, but released shortly after, allegedly for providing intelligence on his communist associates.[13] And just over a
year later at the outbreak of war he was reinstated as a major in
the army having established his loyalty to the South with the backing of some of his former colleagues in the Japanese and, then,
Korean Military Academy.

He progressed rapidly through the ranks to brigadier general
having shown courage in battle, a high level of organizational ability and a talent for using his connections – as well as the shortage
of other qualified officers. Also, a lot of his military work was in
intelligence rather than on the frontline, which was ideal for identifying potential allies and enemies and knowing what was going on.
His miraculous progression continued in peacetime (he became a
major general) despite a succession of scandals in his command,
including the defection of some of his staff to the North and linger-
ing doubts about his communist past.

Meanwhile, the civilian government led by Syngman Rhee was
in serious trouble and increasingly unpopular. Rhee was a veteran
of the anti-Japanese resistance movement (he was already seventy
by the time he had returned as President of South Korea in 1945
after decades in exile in the USA). In his fifteen years of post-war
leadership, he was fervently pro-American and anti-communist,
with a reputation for authoritarian rule (including numerous
extra-judicial killings) and rampant corruption. Despite massive
US aid, the economy and living standards improved only slowly.
Yet some of the building blocks of subsequent development were
laid down at that time, such as heavy investment in education,
rebuilding of infrastructure and a radical land reform programme
which restricted ownership to 7.5 acres, turning tenants into
entrepreneurial peasant farmers and landlords into businessmen
outside agriculture.

The final straw for many Koreans was Rhee's rigged election
in 1960, securing 90 per cent of the vote after his main opponent
mysteriously died. After increasingly angry demonstrations and a

student-led revolution, he was forced into exile again in the USA. There was then a somewhat chaotic period of civilian rule marred by instability, strikes, inflation and allegations of incompetence and corruption until a military coup in 1961.

The coup was the product of five years of plotting, planning and preparation, and was organized by relatively junior officers at colonel level under Kim Jong-pil. They chose Park, a respected general, to lead them. The success of the coup was based in part on the bonding of former classmates as well as Kim and Park's remarkable organizational skills, ruthlessness and capacity for motivation. The South Korean army had 600,000 men under arms, highly trained (by the US), battle hardened (from the Korean War), relatively uncorrupted and driven by nationalist and anti-communist ideology (it also absorbed half the government budget!). For Park (with his close associates) to be able to mobilize this force, neutralizing those parts which were indifferent or hostile to the coup, and co-opting the upper ranks of the forces, was a remarkable achievement. It helps to explain why Park and the military had the confidence and competence to embark on running the country. Their administrative and managerial know-how was arguably ten years ahead of the private sector.[14]

The Junta and Early Economic Mistakes

As with all military coups the first task was to consolidate power; the second was to decide how to use it. As to the first, there was the crucial problem of securing support from the US, the main military ally and aid donor, together with the need to build domestic legitimacy. The business of securing support in Korea itself was closely linked to Park's central objective for the military government: to galvanize economic growth and raise living standards. The coup described one of its declared objectives as being to 'speedily solve the misery of the masses, who are reduced to despair, and concentrate on the construction of an independent national economy'.[15]

To deliver this ambitious objective required a technically competent bureaucratic machine which could assimilate competent army officers into civilian duties, even though not all of them were loyal to the coup. The leaders also had to make use of economic officials of varying quality and loyalty and galvanize the private sector, regarded by the soldiers as corrupt and inefficient. The first step was to establish a Supreme Council for National Reconstruction (SCNR) to drive through a Five Year Plan based on the work of the predecessor regimes, setting up what seemed an implausibly large growth target of 7 per cent per annum. One of the SCNR's early acts was to axe 20,000 civil servants, to be followed by another 20,000 (a cull of roughly 20 per cent), as part of a plan to produce a more efficient cadre of technocrats.

Alongside the SCNR was the Korean CIA (KCIA) which – unlike the US CIA or Britain's SIS, but like the Soviet KGB – was concerned with internal as well as external security. Under Park's co-leader of the coup (and future rival) Kim Jong-pil, the KCIA became the main mechanism for administrative reform and decision making. Within a few months, major reforms were made in banking and credit – the banks were nationalized to establish state control over lending, to pump cheap credit into an expanding economy. There was also a boost to electricity supply, public works for the unemployed, and agricultural, education and welfare reform.

The Junta had to define its relationship with the private sector. Park used the phrase 'guided capitalism', which had echoes of the Meiji approach in which he had been schooled. It was an attempt to reconcile free enterprise ideology and the military instinct for command and control. Although the initial reforms were designed to establish business confidence, the 'guided' aspect of 'guided capitalism' was seen in the arrest and imprisonment of large numbers of 'illicit profiteers' and 'tax evaders'. These included leading businessmen who were released after promising to donate their personal fortunes for 'national reconstruction'. A bitter argument over how much tax and other contributions they should pay led to a standoff in which the companies effectively went on strike and the economy remained stagnant.[16]

This confrontational approach to big business caused serious disquiet in the US government, expressed through its Ambassador, Samuel Berger (who would subsequently become a major source of advice and support to Park).[17] Park's behaviour reinforced the Americans' misgivings about his communist past. More broadly, the Americans had mixed feelings about the coup. They needed a strong South Korean government and army to withstand the communist North – and were reassured by the military competence of the Junta. But they were also concerned about the cost of the US military presence and the aid programme, especially with growing worries about support needed for the weak and corrupt regime in South Vietnam. One complication was the newly elected Kennedy administration which had a more fastidious attitude to military dictatorships and unsavoury regimes in general than its predecessor. Park went to see President Kennedy personally and the Americans were apparently reassured by a pledge to hold free elections and the regime's commitment to rapid development after the predatory, inefficient Syngman Rhee.[18] (Park later endeared himself to the US by sending troops to fight in the Vietnam War.)

Doubts were, however, initially raised by the Junta's handling of the economy. The growth targets seemed implausibly large. There was a surge in inflation. Instead of following conventional (and US) advice on economic stabilization, the regime persisted with expansionary monetary policies to mobilize investment in ambitious development projects. The government also sought to manipulate the stock market, which crashed. The economy initially underperformed (growth was 4 per cent in 1962), and the US withheld some aid funding.

The economic interventions were counterproductive in the short run, but Park managed to ensure that they were blamed on the KCIA and its head, his nephew-in-law and henchman Kim Jong-pil, rather than himself. And the Americans had some common ground with Park. Park's first five-year development plan may have been 'rash and infeasible'[19] with its 7 per cent growth target, but the strong commitment to rapid development chimed with the priorities of the Kennedy administration's economic adviser Walt Rostow whose 'take-off' theory of economic development heavily coloured US foreign priorities. And after the initial stumble, growth did indeed start to take off, averaging 9 per cent in the period 1963–6. Exports – mainly light manufacturers – grew by almost 30 per cent per annum and manufacturing by 15 per cent per annum.

The economy was thriving and it remained only to reassure the Americans on elections. Park duly delivered, in 1963, having put himself forward as presidential candidate for a newly created party: the electoral vehicle for the Junta. The result was sufficiently close to persuade sceptics (and the US) that the election was fair. And the contested election was a powerful signal to Park and the military that they could not rule Korea on a command-and-control basis but had to co-opt civilian allies and mobilize the bureaucracy and business to continue delivering economic results.

President Park, however, now had the executive power to put his views on development into practice (potential rivals like Kim Jong-pil having been marginalized). His vision was clear: to make Korea 'the second Japan'.

The Adoration of the Meiji

Japan, like Korea, sought to shut out the external world for centuries until the forced opening to trade in the mid-nineteenth century set in train a period of turbulence. The culmination was a move in 1868 by a group of reform-minded Samurai to do away with the largely feudal system and embrace and utilize Western technology in order not to be overwhelmed by it. There were several elements.[20] Firstly, there was the spread of mass education, leading to universal literacy for men and women (building on already high education levels in the previous era). Similarly, Japan embraced the rapid expansion of technical schools to disseminate technology. Then there was radical land reform giving production incentives to peasant farmers and a strong tax base to help finance industrialization. Lastly, the Meiji established key institutions – railways, post and telegraph services, banks and insurance companies – based on Western models, and government-led industrial projects – sold in due course to private firms – alongside a strong private textile industry.

The Meiji reformers moved carefully. A minister called Ishikawa organized team visits to the main Western countries to study and understand best practice. It took most of a decade for Japan to assimilate the new institutions, technologies and ideas. There was a lot of trial and error.

Statistics before the 1880s are largely non-existent but after that there is evidence of spectacular growth initially in cotton textiles, then iron and steel, and then chemicals. The industrial growth was translated into military strength which bore fruit with Japan's victory in a war with Imperial Russia in 1905. It was the militarization of industrial strength which most impressed Park and was no doubt emphasized in his Japanese military education.

What was not emphasized were the bumps on the road which, had they been understood better, could have averted the earlier economic errors of the Junta. Conspicuous among them was the Japanese economic crisis of 1881 when there was rampant inflation (caused by printing money to bridge a deficit originating in falling revenues and large government commitments to finance business expansion). Unlike the Korean Junta, the then Finance Minister, Matsukata, accepted that there also had to be painful stabilization: all non-military government aid to industry was stopped; many industries were privatized; money supply was drastically cut and taxes raised. Austerity was severe and caused great pain: the so-called Matsukata Deflation. But Japan was hauled back from hyperinflation, returned to more sustainable but rapid growth and acquired a thoroughly modern regime for financial regulation and the management of money. Matsukata went on to become Prime Minister several times and was feted in the West for his achievements in economic policy.

The tension between the inflationary dangers of hypergrowth and the pain of stabilization would become a recurrent theme of Park's Korea. But there was one particular feature of Meiji Japan which was to prove invaluable when applied in Korea: adapting the Japanese *zaibatsu* model to Korea's equivalent *chaebols* (see below). This constituted a range of sticks and carrots for big firms to produce rapid technological adaptation and economic growth.

The Chaebols: Uncomfortable Partners

Park's model of guided capitalism required capitalists. Korea had numerous small and medium sized companies, but they lacked the economies of scale necessary for a modern industrial economy. Big business was organized in chaebols: essentially family groups (usually under a holding company) of owner-managed firms.[21] This structure is not unusual in economies without the Anglo-Saxon history of developing public limited companies with dispersed shareholdings, separate from management. From Italy to India the big family company still dominates, though they vary from essentially 'vertical' companies (in one industry) – as in Korea and Japan – to conglomerates, such as in India. The Meiji reformers, in whose footsteps Park intended to follow, operated with a Japanese variant of this structure – the zaibatsu – with a holding company – a financial arm – to mobilize and manage capital alongside industrial subsidiaries (initially Mitsui, Mitsubishi,

Sumitomo, Yasuda, and later Nissan, Nomura, Kawasaki and many others). The chaebol – the more famous being Hyundai, Samsung and Lucky-Goldstar (LG) – were similar but usually lacked the financial arm making them more dependent on banks (or the state).

Relations between the chaebol and Park and the Junta had, as noted above, got off to a bad start. The leading businessmen had been arrested for various financial misdemeanours and the public was deeply hostile to them for their involvement in the corruption of the Syngman Rhee era. Korea, then, was a classic example of 'crony capitalism'. The big firms funded Syngman Rhee's political party and he reciprocated with lucrative contracts in uncompetitive markets: 'rent seeking' in economic language. Park had made it clear that he 'loathed' the chaebol, and he explored the alternatives.

One was to use state enterprise. This was tried initially with funds channelled through the state-controlled Korea Industry Development Corporation. But the US, which indirectly funded a large part of the budget, saw the move as 'socialist', reckless and wasteful, and suspended aid.[22] I described above the economic crisis which resulted. The experiment in state capitalism did not last long. An alternative was to turn to multinational companies (as the US would have preferred). But Korea, at that stage, was not an attractive destination for foreign investment and the idea ran totally contrary to the nationalism of Park and his colleagues. He was after all an admirer of the Japanese Meiji restoration that modernized through the nurturing of 'national champions', and he wanted to 'maintain national ownership of production assets'.[23]

So, it had to be the chaebols. Park came to recognize quickly that these companies were not only good businesses but were indispensable to what he wanted to achieve. He settled to the 'task of selecting entrepreneurs that he could trust and work with to devise a new set of rules and norms'.[24] The deal was, essentially, that the chaebols would follow state-formulated policy objectives

and take risks in investing in big, ambitious projects in the knowledge that the state stood behind them with capital and to cover
political risk.

A key step was the nationalization of the banks to control the
supply of capital, providing both a carrot and a stick to ensure that
chaebols followed government priorities: the carrot being large
amounts of funding, loans at subsidized rates, the stick being the
threat to turn off the tap. The balance between stick and carrot
was tricky but crucial. Too much stick and the chaebols would not
cooperate, as we saw with the Junta's clumsy initial tactic of arrest.
Too much carrot and they would revert to being crony capitalists
growing fat and lazy on economic rents. It was helpful that government and chaebols both needed each other – though the balance
of need was constantly shifting. It was also helpful that some of the
business leaders, as at Hyundai, shared Park's visionary approach,
and a serious partnership evolved as trust was built.

Critical to maintaining this balance was competition. There
was competition for cheap loans (including the foreign credit negotiated, for example, as part of the normalization of relations with
Japan, and reparations). Only good projects delivered through
trusted firms had access to the loan finance. Then, chaebols which
failed to deliver were allowed to go bust. Unlike protected industries in other forms of state capitalism, they were not 'too big to
fail'. And, not least, there was international competition. Korea
did protect infant industries by subsidy but only temporarily. They
then had to justify themselves in world markets (Korea was helped
by GATT rules which led to deep tariff cuts in developed country
markets, creating opportunities for Korean exports, and imposed
subsidy discipline on developing countries rather later).

The approach which evolved reflected various economic influences. There was quite an emphasis on competition and markets
which can be attributed to the economically liberal advice and
influence of the USA, which remained a powerful presence. From
Ambassador Berger to numerous advisers in government agencies,

Korea and Park personally were constantly exposed to Western economic thinking. More broadly, the early 1960s were a time of considerable optimism and cooperation in the world economy with a boom in the US reinforced by the post-war recovery of Germany and Japan and a lowering of trade barriers. Park's sympathy for all things Japanese also had one major practical consequence: a normalization of relations opening the way to large-scale Japanese investment and associated technology transfer.

There was a marked acceleration in Korean growth from the mid-1960s on with very high rates of investment (around 30 per cent of GNP) and rapid growth which appeared to vindicate the approach Park was developing. It did not follow the neoclassical orthodoxy of Western economic thought: that low wage Korea should concentrate on labour-intensive manufactured goods for export, its apparent comparative advantage. There were, indeed, successful export-oriented firms in garments and leather goods, plywood and toys, and in the early 1960s this was where growth originated. But priority was then given to capital-intensive heavy industries – iron and steel, chemicals – together with shipbuilding. Later, more sophisticated manufacturing – motor vehicles (Hyundai), electronics (Samsung) – were promoted through the chaebol system. The process was very far from straightforward. The ultimately successful POSCO steel project only got off the ground after a decade of several false starts and with a great deal of Japanese support which owed a lot to politics rather than economics.[25] Similarly, the Hyundai Pony – Korea's first mass-produced car – emerged after numerous different attempts by different firms to develop joint ventures, with many failures, forced restructuring and a lot of government help.

The industrialization and export-based growth of manufacturing through the chaebols were a key part of Park's hypergrowth strategy. But it raised the question of where the capital, the savings, were to come from to finance the government-subsidized investment. Some came from abroad in US foreign aid and foreign loans (Korean chaebols were among the earliest major users of international capital markets). Large capital imports were mirrored in large (current account) balance of payments deficits, which led to periodic crises (and also made the export-based industrial projects so important). But, alongside industrial investment, Park sought to raise domestic savings, and specifically savings channelled (via taxation) into government-led investment. The source was agriculture.

Much of early development economics – as in Lewis and Rosenstein-Rodan – was about the problem of how to transfer the relatively unproductive labour and the savings of the (majority) rural population into industry. Stalin solved this problem but in an exceptionally brutal way. The Japanese Meiji reformers solved the problem through land reform to incentivize peasants while taxing surpluses. Park understood the problem[26] and was fortunate to inherit a reformed, peasant-based, system of agriculture (thanks to his predecessors) rather than the system of absentee landlordism which has blighted many developing countries. But there was also, as industry flourished, a massive exodus from the countryside to the cities: the population of Seoul alone rose from 2.5 million in 1960 (10 per cent of the national total) to 5.5 million in 1970 (17.5 per cent).

The economic task was to squeeze as much as possible from the countryside without undermining peasants' willingness to grow and market food. There was an additional complication in Korea in that Park relied on conservative peasant farmers to support him in elections in the semi-democratic system he developed. As a consequence, policy tended to zig-zag: with a squeeze on agricultural prices to generate surpluses for investment followed by sweeteners for the farmers whenever a presidential election loomed (1963; 1967; 1971). Overall the sweeteners were less generous than the squeeze was painful; so, agriculture performed its economic function.

Bumps in the Road

One of the problems with hypergrowth was that running the economy flat out left little room for error. The economy was vulnerable to bouts of inflation, or balance of payments crises, and was vulnerable to external shocks too. The use of conventional Western macroeconomic stabilization policy, based on interest rate hikes to curb inflation, was particularly dangerous in an environment where the chaebols were heavily dependent on loan finance. By the end of the 1960s, a decade of spectacular, double-digit growth, the World Bank was expressing serious concern about the financial state of some of the chaebols and state banks; by 1972 the chaebols were close to collapse and the South Korean economy was in danger of defaulting on foreign loans.[27]

Park's response was the opposite of orthodox thinking: 'to expand [Korea's] production capacity further with policy loans and realize economies of scale through an aggressive export drive'.[28] He made a calculated gamble that Korea could grow out of the crisis by creating a new round of state subsidised growth. It was even riskier because this was in the middle of the first oil crisis, which was causing serious balance of payments and inflation problems. Park announced the seemingly impractical and inappropriate objective of achieving a six-fold increase in exports and three-fold increase in GDP within eight years – with priority to investing in the heavy and chemicals industries. He moved ministers who were not willing to try to make the impossible possible. And he dealt with growing internal dissention – over wage cuts, for example (resulting in a tight election in 1971) – by making himself effectively 'President for life' under a dictatorial constitution: what he called 'Korean-style democracy'.

The gamble worked. The newly oil-rich countries embarked on a massive spending spree and South Korean exporters were mobilized to take advantage of rapidly expanding opportunities for construction contracts and industrial materials. The chaebols grew out of their financial problems helped by debt write-offs. Spectacular growth targets were exceeded, especially for heavy industry. South Korea grew by 12.3 per cent per annum from 1975 to 1978.

However, the respite was short-lived. The boom and bust cycle returned in earnest, aggravated by another round of OPEC oil price increases. Double-digit inflation returned and attempts at price control did not work. There were big deficits on the balance of payments despite the remarkable export growth.

The prodigious industrial expansion had proved to be not very profitable and many enterprises again found themselves illiquid or insolvent and needing help. The economic crisis in 1979 – inflation together with a marked slowdown – spilled over into the political sphere. There were protests against the oppressiveness of the regime centred on the constitution Park had introduced in 1972 giving him perpetual, dictatorial powers. Strikes paralysed major industrial complexes. Riots erupted in major cities. In the febrile environment there were bitter arguments within Park's inner circle as to how to deal with the unrest. At a banquet within the presidential compound a fight broke out between Park and the director of the KCIA, Kim Jae-gyu. Kim shot and killed the President. The motives have never been clearly established and a committee of inquiry concluded enigmatically: 'the assassination was too careless for a deliberate act and yet too elaborate for an impulsive act.'[29] The most plausible explanation was a bitter jealousy and turf dispute between Kim Jae-gyu and the President's increasingly powerful bodyguard, Cha Ji-chul, who was also killed in the fire-fight (Cha had taken over some years earlier after Park's wife had been assassinated). After Park's death Kim reported what he had done to the army Chief of Staff in the hope of getting army support. But Kim, with four associates, was arrested, tortured and then hanged. After a short period of turbulence within the military, a new military dictator emerged through a coup: Chun Doo-hwan.

The Legacy

It is clear that the decade and a half of spectacular growth – averaging just under 10 per cent per annum – over which Park presided owed much to him personally and the economic ideas which lay behind his policies. Rapid growth was primarily realized through a relentless focus on rapid industrialization supported by capital investment and export growth. Some would say that he was lucky – for example, with the global recovery which helped lift the economy in 1974 – but it was luck he made the best of. Also, some of the fundamentals required for an economic take-off had been laid by his predecessors: land reform and the spread of mass education and literacy. But it was far from clear in 1961 that Korea would emerge as a major economic success story.

The economic model he established based partly on Japanese and partly on Western–US ideas survived him. There were more reforms to the chaebol system by his successors as Korea followed a more orthodox approach to macroeconomic management and trade policy. But the model remained in its essence and was adapted to the more sophisticated requirements of the global automobile and electronics industries. Indeed, the same chaebols which helped Park launch his hypergrowth strategy are global corporations today.

Critics focus on his authoritarian style of government and he remains a deeply divisive figure, especially among those – such as trade unionists – who were repressed, sometimes brutally. But there were elections, which were competitive for the most part: in 1963, 1967 and 1971, Park's opponents in presidential elections gained over 40 per cent of the vote even if the playing field was tilted against them. And the US also acted to limit excesses (less so under the Nixon–Kissinger administration, which turned a blind eye to his attempts in 1972 to install himself permanently in office). In any event, his assassination was followed by a period of instability and violence until a new constitution paved the way to the establishment of a fully democratic system (which in due course elected Park's daughter as President).

Perhaps, most importantly, South Korean economic growth and evolution to become a developed democracy – especially when set against the stagnation and economic failure of the command economy of the communist North – has become a role model for development everywhere. The fact that it has become so successful, while disregarding many of the orthodoxies of liberal economics, has been an important counterpoint to the view of economics which flourished in the 1980s with Thatcher (and Reagan), explored in Chapter 11.

10

Lee: The Eclectic Economics of Lee Kuan Yew

There are few better examples of a country and its economic development being defined by one political figure than Singapore and Lee Kuan Yew (1923–2015). He was Prime Minister for thirty-one years, from 1959 to 1990. He retained considerable influence until his death, aged ninety-one. If that wasn't enough, his successors included his son, Hsien Leong, who succeeded Goh Chok Tong in 2004, giving rise to the Singapore joke that the country was ruled by the Father, the Son and the Holy Goh. The party that he helped to launch, the People's Action Party (PAP), has been in power ever since his premiership, with an overwhelming majority in the legislature. It shows little sign of political mortality.

There is a near-consensus that modern Singapore is a remarkable economic success story. It is regularly close to or at the top of international rankings for growth and living standards, economic competitiveness, freedom from corruption, and education and health standards.[1] The word 'miracle' is frequently attached to Singapore as a statement of fact and it is common to see Lee described as a 'great statesman'.[2] One of Lee's own books is entitled *From Third World to First*, which is a reasonable summation.[3] There have, however, been a fair number of Singapore-sceptics who dispute the miraculous progress, attributing much of it to the colonial inheritance and brilliant public relations. Rodney King, the Australian writer who is perhaps the most trenchant critic of the Singapore model, has written caustically of the Lee years as a 'flawed experiment'[4] and US economist Paul Krugman is another.[5]

But there is little disagreement that Singapore under Lee produced a distinct development model: an overriding commitment to economic growth driven by a powerful public sector (like Korea) but (unlike Korea) also with an open economy, free trade and active soliciting of foreign investment by multinational companies. Sometimes, Singapore is listed as the archetype of a free market, laissez-faire economy (as with the suggestion that it is a good model for a deregulated post-Brexit Britain). Nothing could be further from the truth. It was and remains highly regulated with a strong state machine directing economic priorities. One major economic history of Singapore concludes: 'The Singapore model carries the lesson – perhaps in its most emphatic form – that an extensive role for government can be combined with free trade.'[6]

My primary concern is with Lee's influence on economic strategy and policy as distinct from many other subjects on which he took a view and his role in providing political leadership. There are several apparent paradoxes and inconsistencies which need explaining. He has been lionized by people who would be characterized as neoliberal, from Margaret Thatcher and Ronald Reagan to numerous business leaders. But he was a man of the left, an active supporter of the British Labour Party and a social democrat who led a social democratic party which shared the values of its sister parties in Sweden, Germany and the UK. He believed in socialism, and openly said so. There was undoubtedly some ideological migration as economic growth was prioritized over egalitarian objectives, but he remained firmly wedded to the idea that state planning and big government was a force for good.

A second interesting thing about Lee was that, for an extremely clever man, he showed little interest in intellectual pursuits beyond the strictly utilitarian. His brilliant academic career and that of his family was largely defined by collecting first-class degrees. His own starred first in law at Cambridge was of legendary distinction; his wife, Choo, obtained another first at Cambridge, also in law, as did his son Hsien Leong who achieved a maths starred first in record time. Another son had the same distinction in engineering while a daughter broke the Cambridge tradition by getting a first-class degree in Singapore instead. Education was a matter of winning prizes rather than an exchange of ideas. What was transferrable to politics and economics was a ferocious competitiveness, which was how Lee saw Singapore's survival strategy relative to the rest of the world.

A third issue to explore was from where he derived the economic ideas that he promoted. He was a lawyer not an economist and his writings suggest very little interest in economic ideas and policies. In fact, he largely delegated economic thinking and policy development to his former school tutor and friend Goh Keng Swee. Goh had a first-class degree in economics and a PhD from the LSE and Lee acknowledged that 'Goh was the thinker while I am the executioner'.[7] Even so, Goh shared Lee's preoccupation with practical delivery. His own research was on statistical surveys and suggested no particular approach to economic theory. This operational emphasis which both of them shared was reflected in their choice of economic advisers. The most influential was Albert Winsemius whose background was in Dutch post-war reconstruction and another was E.J. Mayer from Israel who became the first head of the Economic Development Board.[8] Both were experienced in operational roles relevant to Singapore and operated at the applied end of economics. Lee defined what he saw as his own role relative to that of his economists: 'a person recognising that he has some training in the subject [who] uses it to appraise the judgement of fully professional economists and use[s] their advice to check some of his own ideas'.[9]

The Early Lee[10]

Lee's early years as a child and young man, born and bred in Singapore, were spent amid different cultures and influences, which no doubt explains his eclectic approach to building the new, multiracial Singapore. He was brought up in a relatively comfortable family of second generation Chinese immigrants. His mother and grandmother instilled in him from an early age the self-discipline, work ethic and educational aspiration which were to mark him out as a high achiever. Despite his Chinese ancestry, he spoke little Mandarin or Chinese vernacular language and grew up speaking English and Malay. He flourished in an English-language school and progressed as a scholarship boy to the prestigious Raffles Institute which provided a British public school education for colonials. He thrived academically but saw at close quarters the belief in racial superiority demonstrated by the British colonial overlords and the racial tensions between Chinese, Malay and Indian pupils which were to blight Singapore's future.

The Singapore of Lee's youth was Britain's main commercial and naval port in East Asia and had been a flourishing, cosmopolitan city for most of its history under British rule since 1819 (and, indeed, before, as colonial history ignored). Once seen as an extension of the Indian Raj, it was governed as part of the Straits Settlements along with several Malay states.

Then in February 1942 came the Japanese invasion and the fall of Singapore. The Japanese occupation left a deep impression on Lee. He saw the supposedly superior British humiliated and the moral authority of the Empire destroyed by fellow Asians. He also saw the cruelty of the occupying forces and one day he narrowly avoided being rounded up and executed with thousands of young Chinese men in a mass killing. His concern was survival and he did so by making himself useful to the Japanese by learning the language and securing a job in a Japanese news agency which kept him out of harm's way. He retained a respect for

Japanese discipline and competence, notwithstanding the brutality of the occupation.

After the war and the return of the British he set off to the UK to complete his education and train as a barrister. He went initially to the LSE, which he disliked, and managed to transfer to Cambridge where he was befriended by the Master of what is now Fitzwilliam College. He concentrated single-mindedly on obtaining his first-class degree aside from his domestic life in Cambridge, marrying Choo in secret before a traditional wedding could be arranged back home.

He did make some time for politics. He was drawn to the British Labour Party and, with other colonial students, got to know some Labour figures who identified with the quest for self-government. He was greatly attracted to the value of fairness and the ideals of democratic socialism. The Communists' techniques for recruitment and infiltration made him very wary; as he said after hearing the political scientist Harold Laski speak, he had no problem with the Marxism but distrusted the Leninism. He was actively involved in the 1950 general election campaign and spoke at meetings for a British friend who was a Labour candidate, to the bafflement of the Cornish voters. While he had British friends he became somewhat anti-British after encountering racial prejudice and also feeling that Britain was very much in decline. He was pro-independence, but at that stage the notion only had meaning as part of Singapore's hinterland of Malay states (which were developing their own sense of nationhood as Malaya, modern-day Malaysia and Singapore).

When he returned to Singapore in 1950, he established himself at the Singapore bar and started to prepare the ground for a political career. The two activities were intertwined since he concentrated on high-profile cases on behalf of trade unions and political activists in detention or arrested for protesting against the colonial authorities. In 1954 Lee and a few politically like-minded friends set up the People's Action Party. It originally had the modest objective to provide a genuinely multiracial, left-of-centre alternative in a legislature dominated by the colonial authorities. It was specifically targeted at the Chinese-educated who were excluded from political life by their lack of English. Lee was seen by the establishment parties as a dangerous left-wing firebrand. However, for his enemies in Singapore, he was too pro-British.

There were two fundamental problems with politics in Singapore which preoccupied Lee for the next decade. The first was that the Chinese-educated population was heavily infiltrated by communists who owed their allegiance to Mao's China. Lee had no illusions about the communists, whose objective was to take over the colony and seemed well placed to do so. But he also needed to work with them and to win round the moderates. His autobiography tells of dangerous clandestine meetings with the British Special Branch to identify the hard-core communists and then others with underground communist leaders.

The second problem was the relationship with the Malays and in particular with the ethnic Malay leadership in Malaya, led by Tunku Abdul Rahman. Lee made it clear that he wanted independence for Singapore only in federation with Malaya since Singapore could not be viable on its own. But the Malays did not want Singapore. They did not want more communists to add to their own insurgency. And they did not want more Chinese, who they feared would dominate the Malay population because of their business skills and higher level of education. The Chinese were only welcome in a clearly subordinate, non-threatening, role.

The first problem proved more soluble than the second. Lee developed and dominated an effective electoral partnership with communist sympathizers and the PAP grew to be the largest party. He won over the Chinese voters not least by teaching himself Mandarin and then a popular dialect. And, gradually, he out-manoeuvred the communist sympathizers who split off and were defeated at the ballot box. The second problem was intractable. Lee devoted years of diplomatic effort to persuading Malaya and the British (and sceptical Singaporeans) of the merits of a federation; but it lasted only two years. The Malay leadership saw Lee as too powerful and as a potentially destabilizing force. In 1965 they effectively expelled Singapore from Malaysia (as it had become). Lee was heart-broken, and apparently experienced a breakdown, but he had no choice. As Prime Minister, he had to make something of a Singapore Independence he never wanted.

How Miraculous was the Miracle?

There are two versions of the legacy which Lee and the PAP inherited. One, which fits the narrative of the 'miracle', is that the initial position of Singapore was near hopeless, politically and economically. The other stresses the strong foundations which the British had left behind (and which Lee's PAP pre-Independence government had been strengthening for six years).

The miracle narrative, in its most extreme form, has Singapore as a poverty-stricken swamp, alone and defenceless against large and hostile neighbours: 'when Lee took power he found himself governing a mosquito infested swamp dotted with pig and chicken farms, fishing villages and squatter colonies of tin roofed shacks.'[11]

There were certainly reasons to question Singapore's viability. It had lost its economic hinterland in Malaysia. There was in addition 14 per cent unemployment and that was before the British withdrew from the biggest employer: the naval base and shipyard. The Malaysians had resolved to bypass Singapore and use their own ports. Indonesia was threatening 'military confrontation' and Singapore had no army. To add to the pressures, Singapore had no real sense of identity and was racially divided, as manifested in bloody race riots shortly before Independence. The historian Arnold Toynbee, whom Lee often quoted as a source of wisdom, said that Singapore was unlikely to survive as a separate country.[12] Lee himself was on record as saying much the same, though that was usually in the context of making the case for federation.

Looking back dispassionately, it is clear that the political pressures were as described but that the economic problems were exaggerated. The economic baseline was higher than Lee and the PAP acknowledged. The historian John Curtis Perry comments: 'to call the city "Third World" in 1965 [as Lee did in the title of his book] is misleading'.[13] The government's own promotional literature from the time talks of 'streets filled with orderly traffic … modern public buildings… The standard of living is one of the highest in Asia.'[14] W.G. Huff's economic history of Singapore concludes: 'Post-independence economic development in Singapore therefore began from a strong foundation and with very substantial advantages… large accumulated physical infrastructure, substantial human capital, experience of considerable, if not extensive, industrialization, high per capita income and effective government… Singapore exemplifies the "first law of development": "To those who have shall be given".'[15] Huff dismissed as 'unwarranted' the notion, promoted by some PAP ministers, that Singapore was a 'basket case'.[16]

Wherever we place the baseline, it is clear that Singapore made enormous economic progress after Independence. National income statistics do, however, have to be treated with some caution for comparisons between countries and over long periods of time. There is a particular issue for Singapore in that, like Ireland and Luxembourg, it has become a hub for multinational companies which declare profits there for tax reasons or because it is a headquarters. This inflates the country's income without, necessarily, having the same impact on living standards.

Nonetheless, there was spectacular growth. Lee himself claimed that GDP grew fifteen times in real terms between Independence and the end of his period in office.[17] In per capita terms Singapore was around 35 per cent of UK levels in 1960, 70 per cent of UK levels in 1990, and, on IMF data for 2018, is over twice the UK level.[18] Singapore is fourth on the IMF global list ahead of every European country except Luxembourg and just ahead of resource-rich Norway. Singapore set itself at Independence the goal of overtaking Switzerland by the year 2000 and did so ahead of schedule.

While the GDP figures may be flattering, other social indicators suggest that Singapore is not merely a developed country but at the very top. A key indicator is child mortality. In 2017 it was 2.4 per 1,000 live births, slightly higher than Japan (2.0) but still the world's third lowest and well below the UK (4.3) and the USA (5.8).

Critics of Singapore point to an obsession with international league tables and for promoting these metrics as evidence of Singapore's success while belittling others. Rodney King refers to Lee's 'arrogant, conceited and competitive mentality', mocking other nationalities for their lack of hard work and discipline.[19] But, however annoying the self-promotion, the achievements are real. What was behind them?

What Was the Singapore Model?

Even if we take the view that the inheritance of independent Singapore was not as dire as sometimes painted, there were real problems, economic as well as political: capital flight, labour strife and, in the words of a former top civil servant, 'Singapore inherited a stagnant entrepot economy and a crumbling city from a dispirited British colonial administration.'[20] Unemployment was running at around 10 per cent. And the problems were compounded when, in 1967, Harold Wilson's Labour government announced its intention to withdraw from the military base, which accounted for 20 per cent of GDP and employed 70,000 directly or indirectly out of a workforce of 470,000. Singapore was given three years' notice and then handed the naval dockyard and facilities free of charge. But the resulting challenge was huge.

The approach adopted by Lee and his administration was to focus single-mindedly on economic growth as the overriding objective of government; to facilitate growth through a strong government machine; and to keep Singapore open to trade and investment. Within this framework, particular policies and initiatives were to be decided on a pragmatic basis.

This strategy relied heavily on the state being efficient, honest and easy for global business to deal with. So a great deal of effort was made to entice the 'brightest and best' into public service, to be ruthlessly meritocratic in appointments and to remove any incentive to corruption (ministers and top officials are among the best paid in the world). There was never any suggestion that key decisions on the allocation of resources should be left to the market or that state functions should be outsourced to the private sector. The leadership of the PAP showed not the slightest interest in what later was called neoliberal economics. Lee's main economic strategist, Goh Keng Shee, believed in state planning. It was the orthodoxy of the time and coincided with their social democratic politics. It may also have its origin in a disdain for the indigenous Singapore business class at the time whom the PAP leaders saw as merely traders and merchants; some of whom, moreover, had been dabbling in Chinese communist politics.

Huff captures this spirit as follows: 'The leaders of independent Singapore began with a general belief in the effectiveness of planning but with no definite idea of the course it should follow... There was no ideological commitment to free enterprise... [except that it] "can serve as a powerful and versatile instrument of economic growth." '[21] Furthermore the use of state control was not something that would wither away as development progressed. Linda Lim, an expert in South-East Asian business, summarizes as follows: 'the dominant role of the state was maintained and expanded in contrast to the usual ideas of retreat in the course of development.'[22]

This belief in planning and the state was combined with an almost evangelical enthusiasm for free trade. As a small state in a big world it is perhaps not too surprising that Singapore saw the threat posed by protectionist thinking. There was a tradition of free trade, capital flows and immigration going back to the foundation of the colony by the British early in the nineteenth century. The development orthodoxy in Lee's time, however, was inward-looking import substitution. In the early 1960s there was a drive from Lee's government to produce locally assembled cars, fridges, radios and other manufactured goods. But for a state of 2 million people, industrialization could only take place through world markets. Lee therefore became a champion of open markets. He recalls his various encounters with French conservative politicians like Raymond Barre, Eduard Balladur and Jacques Chirac and was genuinely taken aback by their inability to grasp the merits of free trade, describing their French protectionism as 'eccentric and odd for men of intelligence'.[23] (He was more complimentary about François Mitterrand whose subtlety and pragmatic adaptation of socialism to reality perhaps mirrored his own history.)

Where Singapore was so different in its development model from other East Asian countries was its heavy reliance on multi-national companies, especially those from the USA and Japan. From an early stage, Lee and his ministers prioritized the wooing of overseas investors over local business. The reasoning was that these companies would bring the latest technology to Singapore, their management systems and marketing know-how from which local people would learn. Singapore would offer (initially) low-cost labour, a hospitable welcoming environment, pliant unions (once Lee had marginalized the communists), generous tax breaks, strong, well-developed infrastructure with good communications, a strong financial sector and efficient services. Policy was geared to refining this offer.

Lee describes his own role in rejecting 'the accepted wisdom of development economists': 'Third World leaders believed the theory of neo-colonialist exploitation but Keng Swee and I were not impressed. We had a real life problem to solve and could not

afford to be conscripted by any theory or dogma.'[24] Lee devoted
a great deal of time in the early years to cultivating prospec-
tive investors, arm-twisting chief executives and performing at
road-shows to promote Singapore. Some of his own predilections
– for cleanliness, order, discipline and honesty – were allowed
full rein as part of the national marketing. Glowing testimo-
nials followed including regular stellar rankings from bodies like
the World Economic Forum, the Institute for Management and
Transparency International. The country was feted for its 'competitiveness', 'transparency' and freedom from corruption. Critics
like King have claimed that under the surface Singapore's legendary efficiency was much overrated and that government was, and
is, anything but transparent. But in many respects the promotional
success in selling Singapore to the world was self-fulfilling, since
it attracted investors and immigrants committed to delivering the
success story.

Another line of criticism is not to deny Singapore's success but
to point out that with overriding priority given to growth, and a
powerful state to drive it, other important priorities were sacrificed.
Inequality widened (after initially improving following Independence). The Social Democratic ideal gradually disappeared. Labour
and consumer rights and wider human rights were treated as
second-order issues. The prickliness about criticism of government
and Lee personally (leading to libel actions against opposition politicians and the press) may have been understandable when there
was a real threat of violence and communist insurrection but it
became habitual. Strong, single-minded government became
authoritarian. And since a strong, united governing party was the
force behind Singapore's success, the country became a de facto
one party state. As head of government, Lee was responsible just
as much for this as he can legitimately claim credit for the economic progress. Perry summarizes: '[Lee] and the PAP veered
away from any notions of social justice, democracy, and socialism,
heading instead in the direction of authoritarianism. Increasingly

they judged this strategy the best means to the economic development essential to Singapore's survival.'[25]

The irony about the Singapore model is that, after it eschewed the then orthodox ideas about development and embraced an eclectic, pragmatic approach, it stumbled on a new orthodoxy: that development is essentially about 'governance'. Goh Keng Swee summarized the economic philosophy as follows: 'Our experience confirms some of the conventional wisdom of growth theory but refutes much of the rest. The role of government is pivotal.'[26] The old arguments about markets versus the state, big versus small government, have given way to the idea that what matters is effective government: efficient, innovative, honest, responsive public administration. As Singapore undoubtedly has. But it did not get there on its own without advice.

External Influences

Lee and his key economic policy makers, notably Goh Keng Swee, evolved their thinking in response to the responsibilities thrust on them by winning power and then involuntary Independence. Lee, in particular, was not short of intellectual self-confidence. Nonetheless, he and Goh felt the need to seek economic advice, not so much on the principles as on the practical implementation. The economists they turned to were not recognized economic thinkers, let alone theoreticians, but practical, down-to-earth people who shared their preoccupation with delivery.

In many countries it was the IMF and the World Bank which provided a key external influence on policy. In Singapore it was the United Nations through its development programme UNDP. In 1960 it sent a mission to advise on industrialization. The head of it was Albert Winsemius, a Dutch economist whose background was the world of shipping and then, after the war, supervising food price control and leading the Dutch government's recovery programme. He was a former cheese maker and salesman but his experience spearheading the rebuilding of the Netherlands' infrastructure and industry was highly relevant to the task of restructuring and modernizing Singapore. His first report in 1961 was extremely influential and he played a significant role for the next quarter of a century.

He became famous for two recommendations. The first was to stop a campaign by anti-British nationalists to pull down a statue of Sir Stamford Raffles, the founder of the colony. His argument was that embracing the British heritage would send a powerful signal that Singapore was not run by volatile left-wing radicals but was serious about providing a comfortable environment for Westerners and foreign investors. The second was to eliminate the communists who were creating havoc with strikes and other disruption. Lee reportedly laughed at the political naivety of the suggestion but was himself moving more carefully in the same direction.

Winsemius urged Lee and Goh to concentrate on exploiting Singapore's tradition as a shipping centre for the region, to make Singapore attractive to multinational investors and to develop early stage manufacturing destined for world markets. In order to give focus and consistency to the government's interventions he urged the setting up of an Economic Development Board (EDB) with considerable powers and prestige within the administration.

Another key adviser was E.J. Mayer who came to be the first head of the EDB in 1961. Lee had been struck by the parallels between Israel and Singapore, both surrounded by big and hostile neighbours and lacking natural resources, both dependent for survival on the motivation and industry of their peoples (Lee's public love affair with Israel was one of the factors causing friction with Islamic Malaya and Indonesia which supported the Arab cause). Mayer's background was in developing a strategy for Israel's industry ministry. His specific advice for Singapore was to leapfrog its neighbours by developing high tech and knowledge-based industries linked to investors and markets in the West.

The one Asian country which Lee wanted to cultivate was Japan, not just for its investment but to acquire access to its management techniques. The scars of wartime occupation had not yet healed. However, he and Goh visited Japan several times and eventually persuaded a Japanese company with no wartime history to invest in ship repair, leading to shipbuilding and then oil rig fabrication.

Lee's interest was not just in the practical nuts and bolts of policy. He was strongly attracted to the American academic tradition of close involvement in government and took time out from being Prime Minister to take a sabbatical at Harvard, at the Kennedy School of Government. He met the likes of Paul Samuelson and J.K. Galbraith but acknowledges as the greatest influence on his thinking Professor Ray Vernon, whose pioneering work was on trends in multinational company investment and the role developing countries could play in the evolving international division of labour.

The State in Action

The most striking success story was in the interlinked areas of saving and housing.[27] The housing position at Independence was dire, with large amounts of substandard slum housing accompanied by a growing population. The solution adopted by Lee's administration in 1960 was to set up a public body, the Housing Development Board (HDB), to build the good-quality houses needed. Slums were demolished and houses built at a rate of 20,000 a year on government-owned land (almost all of the island). In 1970 30 per cent of residents lived in these government-built houses and by 2010 the figure was around 90 per cent. House building, land assembly and planning were part of an integrated, public sector operation. So was the allocation of housing. In order to prevent racial ghettoes, houses were allocated to ensure integration and when a secondary, resale, market for houses appeared to display a preference for ethnic separation, the government regulated the market to remove the bias.

The crucial step to making the housing policy work was to boost compulsory savings, providing funding for the HDB and a financial mechanism for Singaporeans to buy their own homes, thereby providing reliable demand for the property. In 1968 the savings rate was 20 per cent of GDP and the investment rate was 32 per cent; there was no sustainable way for the government to invest in infrastructure and build houses. It established a Central Provident Fund (CPF) with a rising proportion of employee and employer contributions reaching around 20 per cent of employment income for both. The effect was to boost savings massively. As Krugman put it: 'it was a mobilization of resources that would have done Stalin proud'.[28] Workers were allowed to draw on their accumulated savings in advance of pension age for the sole purpose of financing a deposit on a subsidized mortgage. The government, in effect, decreed owner occupation since renting was discouraged and owner occupation rose from 30 per cent in 1970 to 87 per cent in 2010.

The sheer cleverness of the Singapore arrangements, which owed a lot to Lee personally, was that they successfully achieved several objectives together. And it was all done without the help of Adam Smith's hidden hand. Singapore acquired, as Lee wanted, a nation of house-proud owner-occupiers (albeit with heavily qualified freehold rights). The government was able to tap into the forced savings to finance lots of impressive infrastructure and house building. And the excess of savings enabled Singapore to launch a Sovereign Wealth Fund to generate a future stream of income. The public acquired financial and property assets. And the opaque financial arrangements around the various quasi-state bodies enabled the government to keep most of this activity off the public sector balance sheet, thereby creating for credulous outsiders the impression that Singapore was a model market economy with low public spending and low taxes.

The pivotal role of savings and capital accumulation was a key factor in establishing one of the government's other most successful policies: maintaining financial stability by concentrating on maintaining a stable exchange rate so as to stop domestic inflation. Low inflation was necessary to preserve the value of savings in the CPF. It also sent out a signal to overseas investors that Singapore was a bastion of financial as well as political stability. The new central bank showed great skill in managing monetary policy to preserve exchange rate stability, which contrasted favourably with Britain's disastrous history (as with the collapse of the pound in Nigel Lawson's experience, as Chancellor of the Exchequer, with the fixed exchange rate mechanism) and was also contrary to the orthodoxy of the time favouring floating exchange rates.[29]

The Singapore state was also active in steering the economy. While the EDB played its role in attracting multinational investors (branching out into vocational training and investing in joint ventures), the government became an industrialist in its own right. Unlike many Western governments and contrary to liberal economic orthodoxy, the government had no inhibition in 'picking winners'. Public corporations (GLCs) were set up to invest in strategic sectors such as retail banking, telecommunications, transportation (for example, Singapore Airlines and the airport), shipping, shipbuilding and land. Others were launched to pioneer new technologies, especially defence related, and to take a stake in ventures overseas.[30] Critics of the Singapore model, such as Rodney King, have pointed to many examples of inefficiency in the GLCs and loss making by government entities including bad investment decisions by the state-owned Sovereign Wealth Fund, Temasek. For that reason, and in response to complaints of 'crowding out' by local business, there was privatization in the 1980s. However, the government has often kept a minority stake and controlling interest via Temasek. The Singapore system is in essence a form of state-directed capitalism.

The overriding emphasis on production, export and capital accumulation meant that there was no room for 'welfare' in the Western sense. The state played a major role in housing provision, building up personal savings for retirement through the CPF and in boosting education and basic health standards at all levels. But the emphasis was on 'development welfare' and personal responsibility, not sharing risk through social insurance, and caring for the vulnerable, particularly the elderly. Lee was frank about his priorities: 'watching the ever-increasing costs of the welfare state in Britain and Sweden, we decided to avoid this debilitating system... We thought it best to reinforce the Confucian tradition that a man is responsible for his family: his parents, wife and children.'[31] As a consequence, Singapore's overall rising prosperity masked a minority of working poor in low wages and poor pensioners.[32] And inequality of income widened significantly in the 1960s and 1970s.

The overall story of state-driven development extended to the bedroom. The government was deeply concerned about the declining birth rate and sought to encourage more procreation with the help of cash bonuses and exhortation. The policy was spectacularly unsuccessful and forced to rely on growing immigration to maintain the labour force. Lee also had eugenicist views and made himself deeply unpopular among unmarried women by trying to pair them with partners with high IQs. And as Huff put it: 'the PAP did not question the necessity to direct the lives of Singaporeans... in a host of petty aspects of social behaviour. Over the 70s and 80s as state power increased, so did the interventionist tendency.'[33]

The Legacy

Even with the many necessary qualifications, the Lee legacy was phenomenally successful in its own terms. He set out, as the dominant political figure in the PAP government, to secure Singapore's survival as an independent country and did so. He concentrated single-mindedly on policies which would raise economic growth and succeeded, with spectacular short- and long-term results. The distinctive Singapore formula of a strong directive state with an open economy proved highly effective. It was also often misunderstood: Milton Friedman referred to Lee as the 'benevolent dictator', claiming that he had shown that 'it is possible to combine a free market economic system with a dictatorial political system'.[34] On the contrary, if Lee had a unique role among political figures who transformed economic thinking, it was to demonstrate the crucial role of active and effective government in a capitalist economy.

That said, not everything was rosy. He bequeathed several major problems to his successors, especially Goh Chok Tong who followed him. Goh was not his choice and the PAP leadership chose to override his views. Goh sought to soften some of the more authoritarian features of government, especially the petty intrusions into the personal life of Singaporeans. He annoyed the socially conservative (almost certainly including Lee) by welcoming homosexuals into public positions despite their sexuality being technically illegal. He established 'bohemian' enclaves where creativity could flourish. He realized that if Singapore was to progress as a service-based, high productivity economy it had to succeed in creative industries and that required a less controlling state. A major effort was put into making Singapore a centre for advanced scientific research through its universities. Neither venture has been conspicuously successful, however. Habits of conformity have proved very hard to break.

And the problem remains of making a transition to a much freer society with more diversity of opinion, successful local entrepreneurship and more inclusion. The Covid-19 pandemic has revealed both the strengths and weaknesses of the Singapore model. Like Taiwan and Korea, it was well organized and highly effective in rapidly suppressing the virus and not bashful in advertising its success. And then the forgotten thousands of poorer Asian migrant workers who keep the economy going and live in high density dormitories succumbed to a major second-wave outbreak.

11

Thatcher: Thatcherism and Its Cousin, Reaganomics

In the 1980s and 1990s there was a seismic shift in economic policy in many parts of the world: the transformation of communism into capitalism in the USSR and Eastern Europe; the Washington Consensus in Latin America; the market-based reforms in China and India. The causes and effects differed from place to place but they had many of the same ingredients: the liberalization of markets and deregulation of state controls; the privatization of state-owned assets; the removal of trade barriers; and an emphasis on monetary control to curb inflation. This revolution in policy was widely described as 'Thatcherism', not only in the UK, though it is frequently subsumed under the more generic term 'neoliberalism'.[1]

In some countries, this radical change of direction preceded Margaret Thatcher's period in office in the UK: the reforms of Roger Douglas in the Labour government in New Zealand (earning him the accolade of 'Rogernomics') were overlapping but slightly ahead of hers; the military government of Chile's General Pinochet assisted by the so-called Chicago Boys introduced an extreme version of neoliberal economics in the mid-1970s. Edward Seaga in Jamaica, in the early 1980s, pioneered far-reaching privatization. Much earlier, Erhard in Germany promoted policies which were no less radical and whose ideas were impeccably neoliberal; but his reforms gradually petered out in Germany and gained little traction elsewhere at the time. Nonetheless it is undoubtedly the case that the Thatcher reforms in the UK were an important laboratory for testing policies of economic liberalization. They gave ideological colour to what was otherwise rather technocratic activity and provided practical expertise in subjects like privatization.

It could also be argued that, in terms of their direct impact on the world economy, the parallel reforms of President Reagan (Reaganomics) were more substantial if only because the USA is an economic superpower and has immense influence or 'soft power'. But Margaret Thatcher (1925–2013) could claim to have 'blazed the trail for Reagan'.[2] Reagan inherited the government of a country less obviously in a state of crisis, and did not move the dial so far. Reagan also relied heavily for successful economic management on the Chairman of the independent Federal Reserve.

There is an important distinction to be made between Thatcherism as defined and experienced in the UK, with the distinctive set of problems which Mrs Thatcher inherited as Prime Minister and had to deal with subsequently, and the global brand – the 'ism' – which had its adherents in many countries. The particularly British definition of Thatcherism was best expressed by one of her key ministers, the Chancellor of the Exchequer Nigel Lawson: 'a mixture of free markets, financial discipline, firm control over public expenditure, tax cuts, nationalism, "Victorian values" (of the Samuel Smiles self-help variety), privatization and a dash of populism'.[3] Two of those elements – the nationalism and the populism – were definitely not part of the globally exported version of Thatcherism, though they help to explain her political success in the UK and provide a bridge to understanding the nationalism and populism of today.

Lawson's definition – a fusion of economic ideas and political motives – is a much better guide to Thatcherism in Britain than the condescending verdict of Professor Frank Hahn who judged, as a professional economist, that 'her views on economics were not original' and that Thatcherism, as represented by Mrs Thatcher, is 'intellectually without interest'.[4] Erhard and India's Manmohan Singh might have passed the Hahn test but all the other major political figures who greatly influenced economic policy in modern times could not remotely claim to have been original economic thinkers. That is not why they matter.

No other British Prime Minister has spawned an 'ism' (though Tony Blair acquired a following of Blairites). The importance of Thatcher – and Thatcherism – is that a powerful connection was made between economic forces and underlying moral and political values. One of her biographers captures the ideological dimension to the Thatcherite economic revolution: 'The final decade of the twentieth century was marked by a dramatic, global disenchantment with Marxist theory and experiment... Thatcher's anti-socialist revolution in Britain... contributed to it significantly... She thus prompted observers around the world to ask a crucial question: Why must *we* have socialism? After all Britain got rid of it.'[5]

British 'Decline' and the Origins of Thatcherism

Until Margaret Thatcher, the economics of free markets, or neo-liberalism, did not have much of a political following in the UK, beyond the political fringes. In the 1950s Enoch Powell was almost a lone voice promoting free markets, privatization, strict monetary policy and cuts in public spending. Indeed, the failure of a Tory government to stick to the last of these led to his ministerial resignation in 1958.[6] The Institute of Economic Affairs was established in 1957 as a think tank for free market ideas which were, then, more likely to be absorbed by the much-diminished Liberal Party than the Conservatives. Indeed, the man who was perhaps the most influential economist of that genre – Alan Peacock – was a Liberal, not a Conservative.[7]

The change in national mood which enabled Margaret Thatcher to introduce policies which were hitherto inconceivable emerged from the collapse of the post-war economic policy consensus in the face of slow growth and economic crisis. The mood was captured in the 'declinist' literature of the 1960s and 1970s: from Michael Shanks's *Stagnant Society*[8] to Andrew Gamble's *Britain in Decline*.[9] Successive governments had become unable to deliver the post-war, Keynesian, promise of full employment without triggering inflation: a weakness aggravated by trade unions' control over labour supply. Mrs Thatcher's predecessor, Jim Callaghan, expressed the growing sense of pessimism in a speech to the Labour Party Conference in 1976: 'I tell you in all candour that that option [of countering unemployment with more public spending] no longer exists and that in so far as it ever did exist, it worked by injecting inflation into the economy… Higher inflation, followed by higher unemployment. That is the history of the last twenty years.'[10]

The second element flowed from the first: inflation spilled over into imbalances in trade (since governments attempted to defend a fixed sterling exchange rate which soon became overvalued in relation to the competitiveness of export and import competing industries). Economic crises followed. The devaluation of 1967 was a harbinger of the 1975 crisis which featured soaring inflation and loss of confidence in sterling, culminating in an appeal for help to the IMF. The IMF medicine may have worked temporarily but it represented a national humiliation; the UK was the only developed country to have needed an emergency loan (an experience shared by Greece after the 2008 global crisis). The austerity measures that followed fed the deepening resentment of public sector workers, which found expression in the 1978 'Winter of Discontent' and proved fatal not just for the Labour government but for the post-war economic consensus.

Underlying these two factors was a third: the relatively slow growth of productivity (and of incomes, after allowing for inflation). A variety of explanations were on offer: poor quality, unprofessional British management; uncooperative, unionized workers; poor systems of training; inadequate scale; the 'wrong' products being sold to the 'wrong' (ex-colonial) markets; outdated, poor infrastructure; excessive taxes on individuals and companies leading to inadequate savings, risk taking and investment. Some of these theories may have been true in whole or part, but the crucial factor was a growing lack of conviction that government activism could resolve any of them – and a belief that government was doing too many things, badly. Even if there were serious market failures, the failures of government were seen as bigger and worse.

The failure of the optimistically interventionist Wilson government (1964–70) to harness the 'white hot heat of the technology revolution' and, then, the failure of subsequent Conservative and Labour governments to escape from a succession of crises and sustained underperformance all fed the narrative that government intervention rarely worked and that it was necessary to try something different.[11]

The far left tried to drag the Labour Party towards more radical forms of socialism and to an 'alternative economic strategy' based on economic planning and using import controls.[12] This in turn led to a split on the left making it easier for the right to take and keep power. A crucial turning point for the Conservative Party and the right was the Damascene, and very public, conversion of a leading Conservative, Sir Keith Joseph, to free market economics. He apologized for the past and for the Conservatives' role in creating a bloated state which intervened and spent money to no good effect.[13] He was to have a major influence on Margaret Thatcher, at that point a rather junior Cabinet Minister.

Thatcherism in Action

The history of Thatcher's decade as Prime Minister has been recorded in detail by many friends, critics and more or less objective historians and does not need elaboration here.[14] Much of that analysis relates to her successes and failures as a party politician and to her relationships with her political colleagues. Likewise, many have focused on her role as a national leader during the Falklands War in 1982 and a leader centrally involved in the dramatic events at the end of the Cold War. All these are of only indirect relevance to a discussion of her role in economic policy.

It is tempting in retrospect to depict a grand design, of ideas translated into policy in a systematic way, but that is not the story of Thatcherism. Unlike Erhard, who had an overarching plan, even if he could not deliver much of it, but like Roosevelt, who improvised radical measures in response to political events, Mrs Thatcher was described by one of her greatest admirers, the economist Patrick Minford, as a 'political entrepreneur'. 'Her chosen method has been a step-by-step approach, whereby problems were picked off in order of urgency and solvability.'[15] She was an opportunist (in the good sense of the word). As such, Thatcherism emerged through a sequence of major, high-profile campaigns: the battle against inflation, the curbing of trade unions, privatization, and other major deregulatory measures.

Failure to curb inflation had broken the credibility and morale of the preceding Labour administration. Inflation was running at just over 10 per cent when the Thatcher government took over in May 1979. The aim was to deal with inflation not through the 'socialist' methods of price and pay controls but through a combination of tight control of the money supply and by curbing public expenditure (reducing borrowing to finance budget deficits). The idea behind monetarism, a theory associated with economist Milton Friedman, is that control of the supply of money is what determines changes in the level of prices (inflation).[16]

The new approach, subsequently described as 'Thatcherite monetarism', was not in fact new and the initial combination of policies appeared confused and counterproductive. There was already tight control of money supply at the time and had been since the IMF intervention three years earlier. Despite the government's best efforts, money supply rose during 1980, at twice the target rate and twice the rate under Labour. There were some cuts in public spending, mainly of capital investment, but they were offset by others. In his first budget, Geoffrey Howe cut the basic rate of income tax (from 33 per cent to 30 per cent) and the higher rate (from 83 per cent to 60 per cent). However, he afforded this by virtually doubling the rate of VAT. Combined with the effects of scrapping price controls, this led to retail inflation increasing from 10.3 per cent to 21.9 per cent in the first year. The monetarist anti-inflation strategy was almost discredited and dead in the water before it really began.

What salvaged the strategy (albeit at considerable cost) was an unrelated piece of deregulation: the abolition of exchange controls. The effect was to push up the value of sterling as capital flowed into the UK, further buoyed by growing awareness of the value of North Sea oil (sterling was becoming a 'petrocurrency' in the wake of the – second – oil price shock which followed the outbreak of the Iran–Iraq War). The requirements of strict monetary policy also required that interest rates should remain high (they were increased from 12 per cent to 14 per cent in June 1979). This put further upward pressure on sterling. Sterling rose 16 per cent against the dollar (to $2.40) in just over a year. The effect of this currency appreciation was to squeeze inflation out of the system since industries in the domestic market were competing with cheaper imports; but it also made exports less competitive.

The 'strong' pound appealed to Mrs Thatcher's sense of national pride,[17] but it had a devastating effect on manufacturing exports. Unemployment rose rapidly while industrial output fell 14 per cent in the eighteen months from June 1979 to December

1980. Crucially, inflation also fell rapidly and was back in single figures by spring 1982. Unemployment continued to rise from 5.3 per cent of the labour force in mid-1979 to 12 per cent (3 million) four years later, but by then inflation had fallen to 5 per cent (by the end of 1982). The 'battle against inflation' appeared to have been won, albeit with heavy casualties. The cause was not the successful use of monetary policy – at least in terms of the targets used by the government – but a willingness to break the taboo of permitting unemployment to rise in order to curb inflation. One of the key planks of Thatcherism – monetarism – turns out to be at best a very loose interpretation of what actually happened.

In the event, Mrs Thatcher's continuing belief in – literal – monetarism was later to be a source of one of the biggest crises in her administration. After 1987, the economy boomed with strong growth and rising levels of wages and consumption – and unemployment fell back to under 5 per cent with rapid growth in service sector employment. But the economy became overheated, with inflation of over 10 per cent. The Chancellor, Nigel Lawson, chose not to follow orthodox monetary policy urged by Mrs Thatcher's monetarist adviser, Sir Alan Walters. He decided to put Britain within the disciplines of the European exchange rate mechanism. The effect of trying to stay within a fixed exchange rate system was to provide a sharp brake on inflation but also to make exports uncompetitive. To maintain confidence in the currency required high interest rates. The result was a sharp recession and a spurt of repossessions as high interest rates hit homebuyers who had borrowed heavily against rising housing equity. The reputation for economic competence based on stern monetary policy controlling inflation evaporated. Thatcher's government had been seen to perpetuate the stop–go cycle her policies were supposed to end.

The second plank of Thatcherism is sometimes called 'supply side' economics: the deregulation of markets. In Erhard's liberal economic reforms, the main target of his supply side policies were cartels. In the UK, Thatcher's main target was the trade union movement. There was growing concern, across parties, that one of Britain's underlying weaknesses was lack of flexibility and mobility of a heavily unionized labour force. In economic terms, policy makers worried that powerful trade unions pushed up the rate of unemployment which was necessary to stabilize prices. For Thatcher herself, the trade unions were, simply, too powerful, politically as well as economically. They caused disruption through strikes; pushed up inflation through their wage demands; and they blocked new technology and efficiency. The strikes which characterized the 1970s, culminating in the 'Winter of Discontent' in 1978, had also generated a popular demand that 'something should be done'. The Labour Party had already accepted the need for reform but was unable to deliver major legislative change.

Margaret Thatcher approached the subject with great care and diffidence, no doubt recalling that her Conservative predecessor (Edward Heath) had taken on the unions and been humiliatingly defeated. So, she was content with a few minor legislative changes until, in her second term, the National Union of Mineworkers went on strike over the issue of pit closures. The government eventually won the bloody dispute – the miners abandoned their strike without concessions – opening the way to a much tougher approach, making industrial action much more difficult. Trade union membership fell from 12 million in 1979 to 8.7 million in 1989 (and has since fallen to around 6 million, almost all of the remaining members in the public sector).

The third, perhaps the most significant and recognizable, element in Thatcherism was privatization. The idea was not new: the previous Labour government had sold shares in nationalized industries such as BP. And there is some dispute as to whether, as Thatcher appeared to believe back in 1979, privatization (which she insisted on calling denationalization) was 'all but unworkable' or whether, as Lawson claimed, it was there 'right from the start'.[18] In fact, her first term as Prime Minister involved little outright privatization. She did, however, reverse ongoing nationalization (road haulage, aerospace and shipbuilding) and initiate the sale of bits of bigger public enterprises (railway hotels) and of some other substantial public assets (the oil company BNOC, the National Freight Company).

It was in Thatcher's second term that major sell-offs got under way with British Telecom (after splitting from the Post Office). Privatization had several motives. One was simply her belief that private enterprise was better. Nigel Lawson, who was a driving force behind privatization, echoed her belief that 'no industry should remain under state ownership unless there was a positive and overwhelming case for it so doing'.[19] He said of her: 'Of course she believed that public ownership was an inherently bad thing. But... up to 1983 she was the most cautious among her economic colleagues.'[20]

A second factor was the enthusiasm of the Treasury which was not only able to book a one-off windfall but was able to contemplate an end to open or hidden subsidies to nationalized industries.

An additional factor was the political attraction of making real the slogan of 'a property owning democracy' going beyond housing to making millions of people into shareholders. The idea of popular capitalism took root with the 'right to buy' policy for council housing. By the time of the 1983 election 500,000 council houses had been sold to their tenants. While this may have had a very negative effect on long-term housing policy (since few of the houses were replaced by new social housing at affordable rents) it was undoubtedly very popular with the beneficiaries. Similarly, the BT privatization extended share ownership to 1 million small investors, and then 4.5 million new shareholders were created through the privatization of British Gas. Its poster boy 'Sid' – the term given to the small investor – usually made a quick profit before selling out to institutional investors, and while 'shareholder capitalism' never took root, the easy winnings endeared privatization to millions of people who would otherwise have opposed it.

Privatization remained the one, big, enduring feature of Thatcherism and became its defining characteristic across the world. There have been many criticisms, though usually of the method rather than the principle. Former Conservative Prime Minister Harold Macmillan attacked 'the sale of the family silver' but qualified his criticism to say that assets were being sold not to finance investment for future income but rather to finance current consumption (as, indeed, they were).[21] A bigger issue concerned the utilities (water; gas and electricity generation and distribution), telecommunications and the rail network. These industries were all natural monopolies, or close to it, meaning that there was no plausible competition to keep prices down for these new corporate entities. Complex regulatory structures had to be created and private monopoly profits were being legitimized. In some cases, competition would emerge (mobile telephony; power generators) or was – partially – imposed (train franchising; airports). But, in core infrastructure, competition was simply not feasible because of the importance of economies of scale and network externalities. Today, the regulated privatized monopolies continue to provoke widespread dissatisfaction (National Rail – now effectively re-nationalized; the National Grid; water supply and sewage; BT Open Reach; Heathrow Airport).

As a political leader, Mrs Thatcher had ambiguous views on privatization. She was very cautious initially and worried about private monopolies (BT). She was also partially resistant on nationalistic grounds (the sell-off of BNOC, the state oil company) or for fear of other sensibilities (the Royal Mail, because of the Royal connection). But she eventually threw her considerable political weight behind it, persuaded by a combination of populist appeal ('popular capitalism' – even if the phenomenon never really took off outside home ownership) and a visceral distaste for nationalization.

Deregulation was also a key element in Thatcherism, although, as we have seen, it proved difficult to reconcile with privatization in the case of utilities. Nonetheless, two very big decisions and many small ones had the effect of advancing this aspect of supply side economics. The first, already discussed, was the abolition of exchange controls in the first few weeks in office, exposing the UK economy to global markets – with the effect of strengthening sterling, greatly complicating monetary management and causing great pain to the manufacturing sector. Mrs Thatcher was hesitant, as Geoffrey Howe recalls: 'she certainly believed in the principle, but she was the last to be persuaded that it was prudent to press ahead so quickly' and 'it was the only economic decision of my life that ever caused me to lose a night's sleep. But it was right'[22] (as it undoubtedly was in the long term; or, at least, it was inevitable in a globalizing world).

The other major deregulatory decision was the 'Big Bang' in 1986: opening up the City of London, sweeping away restrictive practices, letting loose new computerized technology and introducing overseas competition and global standards of regulation. Thatcher was reported to be cautious about the political consequences of seeming to favour finance over manufacturing and was, no doubt, privately appalled by the vulgar 'get rich quick' culture it generated and the emergence of easy credit undermining thrift. However, the 'Lawson boom', of which it was part, propelled her back into office in 1987 for a third term and certainly overcame any of her misgivings.

Deregulation took many forms, some of which offended Mrs Thatcher's socially conservative instincts, which pointed in another direction. She introduced state regulation of the video market (after the emergence of video 'nasties'). While insistence on competitive tendering brought deregulation in local government and Urban Development Corporations and cut through a swathe of local bureaucracy, the overall thrust of policy was towards centralized control and micromanagement (or, in London, obliteration) of councils leading to a stifling of local initiative.

The final key element in the supply side revolution of Thatcherism was tax cutting (or, rather, cutting direct and business taxes). The underlying belief was a conviction that tax cuts would sharpen incentives to work and increase investment in business. The initial big switch from direct to indirect (VAT) taxation has been described above. But the overall goal of cutting taxes conflicted, at least initially, with the aim of balancing the budget. Once Nigel Lawson was installed as Chancellor, the priority, from 1983, was tax cutting (cutting corporation tax from 52 per cent to 35 per cent in 1984). But Lawson's enthusiasm for market-based tax simplification clashed with Thatcher's political instincts, which included defending middle-class tax breaks and VAT-free children's clothing.

Nonetheless, once Britain entered the 'virtuous circle' of the 'Lawson boom', higher growth (and privatization) permitted tax cuts alongside reduced borrowing; and this in turn engendered a euphoria which reached its peak in the 1989 budget with the standard income tax rate cut to 25p in the pound as well as a top rate cut from 60p to 40p. The 'Lawson boom' ended ignominiously as Britain fell back into another period of inflation and then economic recession; but the tax cuts mostly remained. In the event, taxation proved to be a major cause of Thatcher's downfall, though it had little to do with supply side economics and incentives. The 'poll tax', to replace local property taxes with a regressive head tax, proved so unpopular that her political authority was seriously weakened.

Policy, Ideology and Belief

The question posed by Keynes about the role played by 'defunct economists' in the moulding of politicians' thinking is, at first sight, not difficult to answer. Thatcher drew on the ideas and advice of intellectuals within her party – Enoch Powell and Keith Joseph – who had championed free market principles. Similarly, both Hayek and Friedman had received their Nobel Prize for economics in the 1970s (1974 and 1976 respectively) and their thinking had a major influence, which she openly acknowledged.[23] There was also, among economic liberals who influenced the Conservative Party, a belief that the influence of powerful interest groups (like trade unions) and voter groups (recipients of welfare) were together making it impossible to run democracy without uncontrollable budget deficits and monetary expansion.[24]

The change in the intellectual climate in favour of economic liberalism was, however, only part of the story. Unlike Erhard, Mrs Thatcher did not have a background in economics and had strong instinctive views on economic matters which she would describe as 'common sense'. She was also a shrewd politician whose reading of the public mood frequently led to her reining back ideologically driven acolytes.

To describe Thatcherism in terms of 'free market economics' is largely to miss the point – or half the point. As her biographer Claire Berlinski observes, there is an additional element: 'a faith in the morally redemptive power of the free market'. She summarized this point as follows: 'free-market economists favour free markets for two reasons: because they believe markets are efficient, and because they are, by definition, free... Thatcher believed both these assertions to be true. But equally importantly, she believed that free markets not only served but *created* robust, self-sufficient and moral citizens.'[25]

The integration of moral philosophy with economics was not new. Hayek's *Road to Serfdom*, which Thatcher read and quoted, was a bible as much as a policy manual. Moral fervour mattered in generating the sustained energy to force through technically complex and unpopular reforms. It provided a common bond with President Reagan in their joint ideological assault on socialism and communism. Berlinski said Thatcher believed that 'Socialism was not a fine idea that had been misapplied; it was an inherently wicked idea'.[26] And it elevated arguments above the technical. Thus, inflation was not just a problem because it distorted prices or squeezed fixed incomes, but it was 'an insidious moral evil to whose defeat everything must be subordinated'.[27]

There were also elements in Thatcherism which contradicted economic liberalism. Thatcherism stood for patriotism and an assertion of national pride. The Falklands War was a high point in her administration and helped to mobilize political support and respect; but it rested on generous defence spending and sentimental attachment to a remote, underpopulated dependency which would defy any economic cost–benefit analysis. Support for a high value in the pound was an appeal to patriotism rather than economics. She enthusiastically promoted British arms exports even though there was a heavy element of subsidy. Similarly, the aid budget was compromised by mercantilist thinking linking overseas aid to export promotion.

The appeal to patriotism is part of what might be more loosely called populism, which was an element in Thatcherism. Some policies – the sale of council houses – were undoubtedly of this ilk. But in general, one of her traits – and an admirable one – was to introduce and persist with measures which she knew to be unpopular but judged to be necessary: the adoption of strong anti-inflation measures at the beginning of her period in office being a prime example; the steel closures and the confrontation with the National Union of Mineworkers over pit closures being others.

One paradox, however, noted by a sympathetic biographer, John Campbell, was that the rampant materialism which her reforms unleashed was 'fundamentally at odds with her own values which were essentially conservative, old fashioned and puritanical. She believed in thrift, yet encouraged record indebtedness. She lauded the family… yet created a cut-throat economy… which tended to break up families.'[28]

A further paradox of Thatcherism was the combination of the freeing up of markets and transfer of ownership from the state, alongside a strong state. In common with German ordoliberalism,

Thatcherism required a powerful central state in order to force through reforms and to police the system. Patrick Minford describes this vision as one of 'a world in which small business could compete for the favours of the individual family consumer; in which the state keeps law and order including the elements of a moral order to protect family decency and provide succour for the genuinely unfortunate who cannot help themselves'.[29] The vision is very different from the libertarian, let alone the wild west (or 'wild east') anarchy which has accompanied Thatcherism in some post-communist states, notably the former USSR. There, privatization became the theft of state assets, and deregulation became an opportunity for gangsterism. Where Thatcherism had a similar trajectory to the UK, however, was in the USA.

Reaganomics: The Transatlantic Cousin

Reaganomics is usually described as having 'four simple principles: lower marginal tax rates, less regulation, restrained government spending and non-inflationary monetary policy'.[30] These objectives (as opposed to the outcomes) were not greatly different from Thatcherism, although privatization did not figure in the list, essentially because the legacy of the New Deal and wartime did not include large-scale public ownership, as with post-war British socialism. Rather, the focus of Reaganomics was on supply side measures centring on tax cuts.

The background to Reaganomics was, as with Thatcherism, a decade of economic troubles under Presidents Nixon, Ford and Carter but without quite the same sense of crisis and national decline, and without the economic and political challenge of very powerful unions. The 1970s saw relatively high inflation and unemployment (respectively 12.5 per cent and 7.5 per cent in Jimmy Carter's last year in office), attributable in significant measure to the two oil price shocks in 1974–5 and 1979–80, but easily blamed on a hapless incumbent administration. In fact, during the

Carter presidency, a programme of contraction of money supply had already begun under Federal Reserve Board Chairman Paul Volcker to combat inflation.

Ronald Reagan (1911–2004) came to the presidency as a standard bearer for conservatism and rejection of the broad consensus of Keynesian economics and interventionist New Deal measures which had existed since the war. He left the Democratic Party in 1962, endorsed Barry Goldwater's maverick bid for the presidency in 1964 and built a reputation for conservatism in economic policy as Governor of California where he turned a fiscal deficit to surplus by cutting spending and raising taxes. His 1980 campaign platform was: lower taxes; less government; state rights; strong defence. Three of the four themes echoed Thatcherism in Britain. Although Reagan showed little personal interest in the intellectual arguments about economic policy, the people around him from the conservative wing of the Republican Party were steeped in the ideas emanating from the Chicago School of economics in particular – led by Milton Friedman – which championed free market economics and monetarist economic management. Like Thatcher, Reagan was inspired by the notion of economic (and political) freedom, rather than drier concerns about economic efficiency.

Trade unions were not a major force in the US, but one of Reagan's early actions was to take on the air traffic controllers who were striking for more pay. He sacked the striking labour force and replaced them, thereby establishing future credibility for making controversial decisions. He moved quickly, as did Thatcher, to deliver promised (direct) tax cuts: the top income tax rate fell from 70 per cent to 50 per cent over five years; the lowest rate from 14 per cent to 11 per cent, together with cuts in corporate and real estate taxes. The economist who encouraged Reagan to cut taxes – Arthur Laffer – was less esteemed than Milton Friedman but offered, in the form of the impressionistic Laffer Curve, the beguiling prospect of lower tax rates and increased revenue.[31] Later in his administration, Reagan was persuaded to keep cutting taxes until the top rate was 28 per cent (the lower earners' rate increased to 15 per cent, though thresholds were raised lifting 6 million out of tax).

Reagan was also committed to big increases in defence spending (40 per cent in real terms from 1981 to 1985). Despite the fact that this was offset by cuts in discretionary government spending, the budget deficit deteriorated. The Laffer Curve did not produce the promised windfall of revenue. Instead, other taxes were increased (eleven times) meaning that the tax take was, overall, at 18 per cent of GDP, no different from before or after Reaganomics. The net effects were large fiscal deficits (4 per cent of GDP in Reagan's presidency as against 2.2 per cent in the previous eight years) which led to a big multiplication of (net) national debt (from $1 trillion to $2.85 trillion). Reagan acknowledged this as the 'greatest disappointment of my presidency'.[32] The conclusion rather vindicated the judgement of Reagan's own Vice President – George H.W. Bush – that Reaganomics, at least in relation to Professor Laffer's curve, was 'voodoo economics'.[33] On the positive side, Reagan and Congress together greatly simplified the tax code.

There is a continuing argument in the US about what Reaganomics actually amounted to.[34] There was extensive deregulation in areas like telephony, energy and banking, though much of this had been initiated before Reagan. It is undoubtedly true that the economic performance of the US improved in the 1980s: real growth averaged 3.5 per cent during Reagan's eight years as against 2.7 per cent in the previous eight years; unemployment peaked at 10.5 per cent in 1982 but then fell to 5.4 per cent in 1988; inflation fell to 4.4 per cent by 1988 when Reagan left office. His supporters claim credit for the improvement, though his critics point out that the policies of the Federal Reserve, the fall in oil prices and cyclical factors were far more relevant – and the rising public debt, falling savings rate and poorer productivity of the Reagan years were storing up trouble to come. And one of the undoubted consequences of the tax and spending policies (combined with a freeze in the minimum wage) was a sharp increase in income inequality, pre- and post-tax. As in the UK.

The Legacy

Would Thatcherism have existed without Thatcher? Certainly, a case can be made that much of what is described as Thatcherism would have happened in any event; possibly in the UK; probably more widely. There were big technological changes afoot which were forcing social change and there were strong anti-collectivist forces building up nationally and globally. Some of the Thatcherite agenda was promoted by the preceding Conservative Heath administration in the early 1970s: the cuts in government subsidies to 'lame ducks' and supply side measures including curbs on trade unions. The fact that Heath's government failed to deliver its objectives was due to a variety of factors including his own political limitations. In any event, five more years of policy failure and crisis helped to create a political environment more conducive to radical departures from the consensus. By the end of the 1970s, even the leadership of the Labour Party had accepted much of the analysis of what was wrong and was already implementing monetarist economic policy and supply side reforms itself.

Yet it is patently clear that Thatcher made a crucial difference. She stuck with controversial and unpopular policies, notably in the period 1980–83, when others would have backed off. She swallowed her own misgivings on privatization, for example, and persisted when there was considerable scepticism and many technical problems. Crucially, she injected ideological zeal into what could otherwise be a rather arid and soulless debate about market efficiency. Opponents – and most economists – would wince at the depiction of state intervention as intrinsically bad, but these simplistic characterizations generated the political energy to push through reforms. She also appointed ministers who had the commitment and competence to push through reforms and she usually (not always) gave them strong backing. Luck of course played a part: Galtieri's invasion of the Falklands created patriotic support for her when she was becoming seriously unpopular. On the other hand, victory in the Falklands War was down to far more than luck.

Even her enthusiastic biographers acknowledge that there were bad mistakes in her decade in office, though all biographers acknowledge that she made major, largely irreversible, innovations in policy that others could not have made. Skidelsky summarizes, very fairly: 'Thatcherism may have been necessary to break out of the corporatist and bureaucratic impasse of the late 1970s, but the analysis was over simple, the means crude and mean.'[35] Even her political opponents acknowledged that the changes were here to stay. As Peter Mandelson put it: 'we are all Thatcherites now'.[36]

The wider international impact is more debatable. What was later called 'Thatcherism' was already being implemented in some countries before she appeared. Reaganomics had a political and economic life of its own, but its sponsors undoubtedly drew strength from the fact that a similar process was happening in a major ally. The same can be said of the Washington Consensus of the IMF and the World Bank, applying a market-based approach to crisis-hit developing countries in the 1980s and 1990s.[37] The Washington Consensus was designed specifically for Latin American countries hit by a serious debt crisis and as promoted by Latin American economists.[38] But it was undoubtedly influenced by the thinking of two of the institution's leading shareholders (the UK and USA) and by the interaction between Latin American, US and UK officials and academics. The 'consensus' broadened out to provide policy prescriptions by the Washington institutions to African and Asian borrowers, and, later, Eastern Europe and the USSR. Experience was very mixed and the intellectual confidence in this set of policies was greatly weakened by the 2008 financial crisis and its legacy of slow growth and fiscal austerity in many countries.

Perhaps the most grievous blow against Thatcherism has come from one of its less highlighted elements – nationalism. Nationalism may have provided temporary, popular political cover for her domestic reforms – and, indeed, formed part of her belief system – but is now proving lethal to the open, liberal international order which sustained it. Her ambiguous attitude to the EU – promoting the EU Single Market and supporting the Channel Tunnel project, but hostile to the EU's 'destruction of nation states' – has lived on as the big dividing line in British politics.[39]

12

Deng: China's Economic Architect

Of all the characters reviewed in this book, Deng Xiaoping (1904–97) contributed the most in terms of his impact: the lifting of hundreds of millions of people out of poverty and transforming a backward peasant economy into a technologically sophisticated country with living standards beginning to approach those of the developed world. When, in 1979, Deng assumed a dominant role in the post-Mao leadership of China, Chinese peasants, the vast majority of the population, had a per capita income of $40 a year – among the world's lowest – and were producing less food grain per head than a generation earlier. Universities had been closed for a decade. And what passed for modern industries were factories using 1950s Soviet technology. When he finally stepped down from decision making after 1992 (aged eighty-eight), China was irreversibly launched, economically, on the path to becoming the country we know today: an economic superpower.

The choice of Deng as the chief economic architect of modern China has to be qualified in various ways. He did not begin the post-Mao reforms; they started under Mao's short-lived successor as party leader, Hua Guofeng. He was also not the leading economic policy maker of modern China; that description better fits Chen Yun, his contemporary and collaborator with whom he ultimately fell out over the pace of China's growth and opening up (Chen was more conservative, though a major contributor to the reforms). His economic impact must also be weighed against wider issues of human rights. Deng's record was far from unblemished: he actively participated in many of Mao's extreme and inhumane policies while tempering others. He is regarded by many Westerners and younger Chinese as directly responsible for the Tiananmen Square massacre and the suppression of political pluralism. But he never claimed to be a democrat. He was always a dedicated communist. What he cared about was his economic legacy, which was more profound and richer than any previous political figure in history could claim. And that legacy was about human rights more widely defined than Western democratic norms: addressing issues of poverty, hunger and the absence of many basic needs.

Deng had no background in economics or business and he never studied at university. Instead, his long and varied experience was as a manual worker, a soldier, a political organizer and commissar, and administrator. He was a graduate of the university of life. And his philosophy and actions were based on what was seen to work – in the words of one of his best-known aphorisms, 'it doesn't matter if a cat is black or white provided it catches mice'.[1] He believed in evidence and experiment: 'crossing the stream by feeling for the stones'. That said, he himself acknowledged several major influences on his thinking: Lenin's experiment with market economics and price incentives in the New Economic Policy which he saw at first hand; the experience of the Asian modernization and technological progress from Japan's Meiji era to the present day; Park's Korea and Lee Kuan Yew's Singapore; and, later, many of the ideas of Western economists, notably in the World Bank, but also including Milton Friedman.

His approach was eclectic, radical and open-minded – and explicitly encompassed market economics and much of what we would regard as capitalism. But he had one consistent, unyielding, principle: that China's economic transformation needed strong, unifying institutions that meant no dilution of the political monopoly of the Communist Party. By the same token, there were some ideas he consistently rejected: 'ultra-leftist' ideology where this conflicted with economic sense; and also the notion that economic and political liberalization must go together (he regarded the Soviet Union's Mikhail Gorbachev as an 'idiot' for confusing the two).[2]

Deng the Man: Model Revolutionary

It is difficult in a short essay to capture the many dimensions and vicissitudes of a political career spanning seven decades with much of it close to, or at, the pinnacle of power in China. Fortunately, there is one brilliant, definitive biography of Deng, by Ezra Vogel, which I draw on heavily. And there are now several fine accounts of Chinese economic reform and its spectacular consequences, with Deng as a central influence.[3] There is also what I regard as one of the truly great biographies of modern times – Jung Chang and Jon Halliday's dissection and demolition of Mao, a monster whom Deng served for the best part of five decades, survived and then substantially reworked his legacy, arguably changing China more than Mao himself.[4]

What is known of Deng's early life is that he was a clever child in a family of high achievers. He was launched on the career of a revolutionary aged fourteen, involved in nationalist riots, and at sixteen (in 1920) was sent to France, the youngest of thousands of Chinese thought to be suitable for a combined study and factory work programme. In 1921 the Chinese Communist Party was formed (initially with fifty members) and it had particular appeal to Chinese students in Europe who were becoming radicalized by their exposure to Western communists and trade unions in factories and colleges in Europe. Deng joined the fledgling party. His Party Secretary in France was Zhou Enlai, later another major figure in Mao's China. Working in factories (he ran out of money for studying) alongside French and foreign workers almost certainly created a mindset which was open to foreign ideas and influences and respectful of Western technology – unlike Mao and many of Deng's later political contemporaries. But almost certainly his most important experience was escaping from France in 1926 (where he was wanted by the police for industrial agitation at the Renault factory near Paris) to the USSR. The Soviet Union was still experiencing Lenin's New Economic Policy shortly before Stalin assumed power. Deng later referred favourably to his impressions of the NEP – particularly the fact that private, including foreign, investment was encouraged under Communist Party leadership. He took it as an illustration of the ideological elasticity of socialism and a model for China's own reform.

In his mid-twenties he was back in China involved in underground revolutionary activity and in the tortuous factional politics of the Communist Party. He aligned himself with Mao – which almost certainly saved his life when he later fell out of favour. As a young communist revolutionary there were numerous adventures and set-backs. But the scale of his responsibilities was immense and helps to explain the confidence with which in later life he was able to press ahead with major policy changes and, also, the high regard in which he was held by his colleagues. In one period – 1939–45 – he was administering a communist-liberated area of Southern China, responsible for feeding and clothing 20 million people, raising taxes to finance its government and keeping the peasant population content and aligned with the communists: disciplines which helped form his pragmatic approach to economic matters. He is quoted as devising a tax system creating generous incentives for hard-working and successful farmers.[5] In the fighting, variously, against the armies of Japan, Chinese warlords and the nationalist Kuomintang he eventually commanded in battle half a million troops (more accurately, he was a commissar rather than a field commander but his biographers – and colleagues – did not doubt his military skills).

When the communist revolution came in 1949, Deng was sufficiently senior in the party hierarchy to be put in charge – as Party Secretary – of one of six regions. In this capacity he had responsibility for 100 million people: pacifying and ruling them and carrying through revolutionary measures. Land reform was a major commitment and it was noted that 'killing those with the largest holdings' was one of Deng's tasks (another was ensuring the conquest of Tibet). His diligence and ruthlessness earned him promotion from the provinces to a national role, as Finance Minister in 1953, his predecessor being 'too soft' (in taxing capitalists) for Mao's tastes. Deng progressed to be Party Secretary General, becoming one of the inner core of the party, under Mao, and was closely involved in the early moves to establish the communist system: collectivization of farms and small firms; nationalization of big enterprises; and the launch of the first Five Year Plan. He further enhanced his reputation for loyalty to Mao and for toughness by being one of the leading protagonists of Mao's 'anti-rightist' thinking in the crackdown on 'bourgeois intellectuals' following the period of 'letting 100 flowers bloom' in 1957 when diversity of thought was briefly encouraged. Those who showed their heads above the parapet in defence of liberal and other unorthodox, critical views were persecuted.

A crucial test of Deng's independence of mind, and rational approach to economic policy, came with the horrors of the Great Leap Forward. Starting in 1959, Mao embarked on a policy of commune-based mass mobilization to generate 'backyard industrialization' at breakneck speed, abandoning a balanced approach incorporating agriculture. Such food as was grown was seized from the farmers to feed urban workers and the army in the form of penal levies. In 1960 alone, according to Chang and Halliday, 'an estimated 22 million people died of hunger. This was the biggest number in any country in the history of the world.'[6] Even Mao's loyal henchman Deng reached a breaking point and he backed efforts by Liu Shaoqi, then effectively Mao's deputy, to change direction: 'Mao had to swallow a policy change. He was forced to abandon the lethal scale of food levies planned... As a result, tens of millions of people were spared death by starvation.'[7] Nonetheless, countless millions died in the famine: 45 million according to some Western sources; 16–17 million on Chinese official estimates.[8] It was this epic disaster which appears to have persuaded Deng (working with like-minded senior leaders) to press for 'adjustments': radical economic changes designed to raise living standards. He promoted the idea of peasants having private plots, opening up freer markets for the produce of the farmers, and encouraged small enterprises.[9] Significant reform, and improved production, took place in the recovery from the abandoned Great Leap Forward.

By 1965 Mao had, however, recovered enough of his authority and revolutionary instincts to launch the Cultural Revolution designed to purge the party and the institutions of government of 'rightest' thinking. Liu and Deng were never forgiven for their earlier defiance. Mao prevented Liu getting life-saving medication, effectively killing him. As the 'second biggest capitalist roader', as Mao called him, Deng nonetheless retained a modicum of respect from Mao, and he survived Mao's revenge, suffering humiliation and hardship instead. After two years of house arrest and criticism, Deng was banished and exiled, doing manual work in a factory in the provinces. His son, Deng Pufang, was less fortunate; he was thrown from a window by Red Guards and crippled for the rest of his life. Deng's relatively lenient treatment, and survival, were almost certainly due to his potential usefulness to Mao, and one area where his usefulness had been demonstrated was in dealings with the leaders of the Soviet Union for whom he shared Mao's hostility and paranoia. We think now of Deng primarily in terms of economic policy but much of his life at the top involved foreign affairs. That expertise provided him with a route back to favour, when Mao wanted – in 1974 – someone who was sufficiently plausible to address the UN General Assembly. Deng's task was to reflect Mao's opposition to the two superpowers and China's unity with the developing world, as well as to speak privately to Western leaders (notably America's Henry Kissinger) making overtures around a common interest in confronting Leonid Brezhnev's USSR.

Returning to Favour and Reform

Years of exile, and being 're-educated' in Mao's thought, had one merit: it gave Deng time to reflect on how to put into practice his ideas for reforming and modernizing China, once he was rehabilitated and in a position to shape policy and once the madness of the Cultural Revolution had abated. It also gave him an opportunity to bond with his wife and three children who had suffered in varying degrees during the Cultural Revolution.

As it happens, internal and external events were moving in a direction which would ultimately lead to more favourable conditions. In China, Mao was, in his mid-seventies and ailing, nearing the end of his period of total dominance. Then Mao's expected successor and longstanding rival, Lin Biao, died in a mysterious, unexplained plane crash. Although the 'leftist' supporters of the Cultural Revolution, notably Mao's wife Jiang Qing, were still very powerful, some pragmatic and moderate influences like Zhou Enlai took a more prominent role (though it was to be short-lived as Zhou was in the later stages of cancer).

Externally, the pivot away from the USSR to the West had not just military implications but raised the question of what a more open approach to the West might mean economically. Vogel suggests that when Deng was in exile he 'would naturally begin to think about how to expand this opening to the West to help modernise China'.[10] One Asian country, Japan, had already benefited from close ties to the West and the selective use of Western technology and ideas. He knew that Japan was completing a decade-long period of double-digit increases in personal income while China, behind closed doors, had fallen only further behind. By the end of the 1960s other Asian countries were also beginning to take off economically; not only Korea but also places with ethnic Chinese populations such as Singapore and Hong Kong. The question naturally arose as to how China could learn from them.

It remained only for Deng to complete his rehabilitation and assume the levers of power to put his ideas into practice. This happened remarkably quickly. Within a few months of Deng's return from exile to deliver the UN speech, Mao publicly acknowledged the need to row back from the eight years of chaos and to re-establish stability. With Zhou fatally ill, Deng was effectively put in charge of government albeit with the crucial qualification of needing to retain Mao's support. The challenges were immense: a stagnant economy; insufficient food supply; a broken transport system; a chronic lack of technical expertise because of the disruption in education and training; officials traumatized and unwilling to make decisions; armed forces bloated in numbers but incapable of military activity.

In a remarkable, intense period of activity, under Deng's leadership, the transport system and then coal mining and steel production were brought back to life. He started the process of rebuilding scientific research, reopening universities and strongly defended experts who had been persecuted during the Cultural Revolution. And to signal future intentions to open up China to foreign technology and ideas, in 1975 Deng made a high-profile visit to France, inspecting and admiring factories using the latest technology and management systems.

But he overreached himself in the eyes of Mao. By the end of 1975 there was a build-up in criticism – and he fell from favour as quickly as it had earlier been restored. A crucial step was a demand from Mao that he should explicitly endorse the

Cultural Revolution, which he declined to do. He was frozen out of decision-making roles; denounced by Mao's wife as a 'fascist' and 'counter-revolutionary'; and more generally subjected to sustained verbal attacks, albeit not as extreme as when he was sent into exile. Mao sought to reconcile the conflicting pressures – to preserve the ideological priority of the Cultural Revolution, while countering the destructive economic consequences – by making as his heir-apparent the more pliable Hua Guofeng in April 1976. Deng was stripped of all his posts within the party.

This time it was less than a year before Deng returned to work, albeit initially in a subordinate role. The critical change was the death of Mao himself in September 1976 and the move of Hua and leading military officials to arrest the infamous 'Gang of Four' including Mao's widow. There then followed – under Hua's leadership – the first major moves to open China and press ahead with modernization, post-Mao, with Deng sitting on the side-lines at first. A decisive step was to send out large numbers of Chinese ministers and officials around the world to establish how far behind China had fallen and what needed to be done about it. The model adopted was Deng's visit to France and also the Iwakura Mission from Japan a century earlier when the Meiji reformers set out to discover what they could learn from the West. There were visits to study reformed communism in Yugoslavia; another to Hong Kong, which led to the first steps to establish an export processing zone, later to become the Shenzhen Special Economic Zone (SEZ); to Japan; and, crucially, a team led by Gu Mu to France, Germany and several smaller European countries. The visits were reported to have made a major impression on the party leadership, and plans were developed for the large-scale importation of foreign technology; for foreign borrowing in order to pay for the technology transfer; and for beginning the process of liberalizing markets. Deng followed these developments from a distance. But the preconditions now existed for him to return for the last, and most important, period of influence, two years after his demotion.

The Spark of Economic Revolution

Deng used one of Mao's revolutionary metaphors of how 'a single spark can start a prairie fire' to rationalize his own interventions to galvanize the reform movement in 1977–9.[11] He used speeches to ridicule official dogma: 'if a farmer has three ducks, he is socialist but if he has five ducks, he is a capitalist'.[12] Deng was aware that he would need to fight the more cautious reformers like Hua. The confrontation took the form of a theoretical debate couched in the following terms: 'practice versus the two whatevers'. 'Practice' referred to Deng's belief that if something works in practice, it doesn't matter what it is called (the pragmatic 'two cats' theory). The 'two whatevers' was the doctrine set out by Hua that whatever policies Mao supported and whatever instructions Mao gave should be followed.[13] Deng developed his points by arguing that the best way to stay faithful to Mao's thoughts was to follow their spirit, which meant adapting Marxist-Leninism to the conditions of the time.[14] In practice, to those in the party familiar with the dog whistles hidden in official speeches, Deng was arguing that Hua was not being bold enough, or quick enough. A seminal event was a party congress in December 1978 (the Third Plenum) when Deng effectively usurped Hua and then gradually pushed him aside along with others resistant to reform. It was a succession without coronation in that Deng emerged as de facto leader without the formal trappings. He was known informally as the 'paramount leader' but confined his formal roles to chairing key committees necessary to wield power, such as the Military Commission overseeing the armed forces.

There were several major dampeners on the spread of the 'prairie fire'. Deng's own temperament, experience and political judgement led him to be bold but not reckless: to proceed on the basis of experiment and 'feeling the stones in the river'. He also needed to maintain political support in the party, at the centre and in the regions. This meant treating his – soon to be side-lined –

predecessor Hua with respect. It also meant accepting a sharing of status and authority, in particular with Chen Yun, officially his equal and with a major say on economic matters. Chen Yun was of Deng's generation; he had done much of the spadework in establishing a system of economic planning after the revolution and had also fallen foul of Mao, by criticizing the Great Leap Forward, and, later, the Red Guards. He and Deng had long been allies but, after 1978, Chen Yun was the restraining voice of economic conservatism, of moving more gradually.

Chen's thought was essentially a rational conservatism worrying about inflation, the public finances and the balance of payments rather than Maoist doctrine. His emphasis on stability was a useful counterpoint to Deng's ambition for unconstrained economic growth. They and the rest of the party leadership team were also fully united around the hegemonic role of the Communist Party: 'if anything was sacred for Deng it was the Chinese Communist Party... [he] emphasised that public criticism of the Party would not be tolerated.'[15] Neither would Deng tolerate criticism of 'the dictatorship of the proletariat'; but he, unlike Mao, was not a dictator – rather, the leading figure within a collective leadership.

Deng was further constrained by external geopolitical events and in particular being encircled by hostile powers, especially the USSR and its ally, the newly reunified Vietnam. One of Deng's earliest priorities was to prevent Vietnam from expanding its influence in South-East Asia and to this end he decided on a punitive military offensive (similar to Mao's humiliation of India in the brief border war of 1962).[16] Unfortunately, the short war was something of a fiasco for China: the Vietnamese were better organized, better equipped and battle hardened. Nonetheless, the attack appeared to have deterred the Vietnamese from further expansion in Indochina and Deng used the military failures to rub in the message about the need for modernization (and to reform the military).

The main initial push towards economic modernization came through deepening ties with leading developed countries. The

first target was Japan and Deng organized an official visit. Deng
and other Chinese leaders were already aware of Japan's extraordinary economic success, under capitalism, in the nineteenth
century and then again after the Second World War. Now they
could see that Japanese workers worked hard, apparently without
coercion, and enjoyed such luxuries as cars and TVs. On his visit
Deng saw the latest technology – including an automated Nissan production line. He appreciated that technology could not
just be bought 'off the peg' but required an understanding of the
management systems which lay behind efficient production. That
in turn opened the door to direct foreign investment in China by
Japanese companies as well as a determination to spread modern
(i.e. Japanese and Western) management practices throughout
China.

Despite historic animosities, dating from wartime atrocities,
it proved easier to cement closer relations with Japan than it did
with the USA, where there were geopolitical complications and
the touchy issue of Taiwan. Deng sought nonetheless to overcome
those barriers by promoting student exchanges and then through
a well-publicized visit to the USA which introduced the Chinese
people, through TV coverage, to a different and very attractive
way of life.

Having established a direction of travel and successfully broken earlier taboos on collaboration with former enemies and
'imperialists', Deng launched a series of experiments designed to
encourage and incentivize initiatives where officials were eager
to try new methods, and also to try out new policies on a small
scale. The most far-reaching experiments were the special zones
in Guangdong and Fujian provinces.[17] There had long been processing zones in these coastal areas designed to simplify import
and export procedures, but Deng envisaged something far more
radical: 'The zones would be given the flexibility to experiment
with different ways of doing things. The SEZs will be regulated
primarily by the market.'[18] Foreign companies were free to use

their own labour and management systems (which in practice often meant lower labour standards and wages than were permitted in the home country).

For most Chinese, in a predominantly rural economy, what mattered rather more were freedoms for farmers to produce more food and generate income. Deng seized on an experiment in the poor, mountainous province of Anhui where peasants were literally faced with starvation until radical decentralization of decision making produced a spurt of food production. These departures from Mao's insistence on the collectivization model spread rapidly with Deng's endorsement and within five years peasant income had doubled, and grain consumption per head had risen by over 25 per cent with a rapid growth in consumption of pork, beef, poultry and eggs. Deng 'had no ideological commitment to household farming' but he allowed it (decollectivization) because it worked. He was carried along by the popular enthusiasm for the rural reforms, both among peasants who enjoyed more freedom and income and among urban consumers who enjoyed more varied food supplies.[19]

Deng's willingness to let experiment- and market-based solutions evolve spontaneously led to one of the biggest, and completely unexpected, successes: the township and village enterprises (TVEs). The abolition of communes created a vacuum of governance which was filled by villages and townships assuming control over assets like workshops and stores. These became enterprises free to use local resources and sell their products if they could find the markets. As long as the number of workers was no more than seven, they were still accepted as 'collectives' free of control from above (and free from social obligations). As household enterprises expanded to become, in effect, entrepreneurial firms the limitation of seven employees was quietly ignored. Employment in TVEs surged from 28.3 million in 1978 to 105.8 million in 1992 when Deng stepped down, producing 9 per cent of industrial output initially, growing to around 30 per cent.

Success Breeds Success – and Hubris

The combination of reform initiatives had an early and spectacular impact. Recorded growth in 1978 was almost 12 per cent and just short of 8 per cent in 1979 and 1980. Even bearing in mind the primitive, and often politicized, statistical recording of the time, these results were in sharp contrast to the stagnation of earlier years. Moreover, the sense that rapid growth was happening and officially promoted meant that new investment was attracted from overseas Chinese or foreign investors who received a warm welcome.

Momentum was sustained by Deng's appointment of reform-minded allies into key decision-making roles. They in turn gave promotion to party officials at provincial level who were willing to force the pace of change. Two crucial appointments were Zhao Ziyang, elevated from a provincial role where he advocated decentralization to the premiership and a seat in the Politburo in 1980, and Hu Yaobang who became Party Chairman in the same year, then General Secretary. Both carried the load of pushing through controversial changes on Deng's behalf. But, in due course, both were to cross the red lines which defined permissible reform and fell from grace.

The economic reforms had to proceed alongside very sensitive issues including the public evaluation of Mao's legacy, rehabilitation of victims of the Cultural Revolution, and the easing out of Hua and his supporters. It required immense skill by Deng to maintain the unity of the party, consensus within the leadership, the support of the military and a favourable response from the public. There was also one major economic controversy which emerged at an early stage concerning the speed with which the economy should expand. Concern was expressed by Chen Yun, whose importance I have already noted and who was more involved with day-to-day economic policy than Deng, that the rapid growth being unleashed, and encouraged by Deng, was well in excess of the targets set in the Five Year Plan.

This might seem a somewhat pedantic, bureaucratic, objection but reflected a genuine concern among planners and finance officials that 'excessive' growth would generate shortages of key resources and spill over into inflation, fiscal and balance of payments deficits and external debt burdens. I have noted, in the chapter on Park in Korea, that similar concerns about the consequences of hypergrowth were a recurrent theme. Deng, like Park, was – in principle – for maximizing growth, but in the early stages of reform he backed Chen Yun who was, in most respects, a reformer who supported the growth of TVEs and household, decollectivized, farming. The controversy was expressed in terms of 'builders or balancers'. Deng was a 'builder'; Chen Yun was a 'balancer'. Chen Yun's idea of balance was not simply financial; he noted that twenty years of Mao's emphasis on heavy industry had led to 57 per cent of industrial production being 'heavy' in 1958 and only 43 per cent being 'light' consumer goods. TVEs and Deng's liberalization, more broadly, were a powerful force rebalancing the economy (light industry grew by 18.4 per cent and 14 per cent in 1980 and 1981). The reformers deferred to Chen Yun's common-sense caution. As he trenchantly put it: 'We need balanced development... some people make fun of cautious people making it seem as if cautious people believe that the less steel we produce, the better. Ridiculous... local industries are competing with our big national projects for materials. Five people want to eat when there is only food for three... I can only do my best.'[20]

Deng considered the balancers necessary but annoying and recognized that the public finances were in danger of spinning out of control, with the biggest budget deficits since the revolution (attributed in varying degrees to the brief war with Vietnam, higher procurement prices paid to farmers, cuts in agricultural taxes, and higher retention of funds by TVEs and provinces).[21] He was able to blame his predecessor Hua and also sought technical advice from the World Bank on what would be realistic growth targets. The World Bank is often, rather lazily, dismissed as a purveyor of the Washington Consensus, reflecting the prejudices of the Reagan/Thatcher era. But its longstanding deep collaboration with the Chinese reformers (and, in parallel, with reformers in India) was one of its most productive activities.[22]

The gulf between the 'builders' and the 'balancers' widened with the publication of a Five Year Plan (1981–5) which had planned annual growth of 4.5 per cent, half of what was actually being achieved. Deng had set a long-term strategic objective of quadrupling GNP by the year 2000, which implied growth of 7.2 per cent. Chen Yun responded with a speech incorporating the metaphor of 'birdcage economics'. Chen Yun explained that the birdcage could be economy-wide, permitting local experiment, and that he was merely, sensibly, arguing for macroeconomic controls – but the caricature of a negative, excessively cautious bureaucrat stuck and, this time, Deng supported his main reformers Zhao and Hu Yaobang with the call: 'Don't argue, just push ahead.'[23]

'Pushing ahead' happened. Deng coined the phrase 'socialism with Chinese characteristics' to provide an ideological framework for further reform. Cloth rationing was ended after the textile industry had grown to be able to meet demand. The scope for state enterprises to use market prices was enlarged to provide incentives to seek profitable activity. A decision was made to expand the rapidly growing SEZs into a further fourteen coastal areas, where foreign investment would be welcome (in the meantime, a negotiated settlement of the future of Hong Kong reinforced the links with overseas Chinese willing to invest in China). There were still major gaps in the reform programme – how to integrate the interior with the rapidly expanding coastal areas; how to attract advanced technology rather than investors seeking cheap labour. But the cork had been removed from the bottle and reform was increasingly difficult to reverse.

Nevertheless, the balancers versus builders controversy represented an underlying tension in policy and resurfaced at the end of

1984, a year when GNP growth reached 15 per cent, capital investment in construction grew 33 per cent and inflation was just short
of 10 per cent. Chen Yun's criticism widened to include reports
from the SEZs of corruption: money laundering, smuggling and
pornography. He argued that serious energy, transport and other
bottlenecks would emerge, as well as inflation, unless growth was
held below 7 per cent. There was a consensus around the need for
credit (and wage) controls. The economy continued to boom, with
15 per cent growth again in 1985, but the retrenchment policies
prevented the economy from spinning out of control.

One reason for the failure to realize the dire consequences
predicted by the 'balancers' was that the market economy was
beginning to work: rapidly increasing supply was feeding rapidly
increasing demand and this demand was feeding more supply.
The success of incentives in producing more food and consumer
goods meant that what could have been rampant inflation was
dampened by the increased availability of goods. And the migration of a vast supply of labour from the rural interior was a
natural check on labour market inflation (the human dimension
of this massive process was captured in the book *Factory Girls* and
other accounts[24]). China was also benefiting from advice from the
World Bank and a group of economists including James Tobin on
how to manage monetary and fiscal policy in more sophisticated
ways.

Confidence, however, soon tipped over into hubris. In early
1988 Deng encouraged the idea of lifting the remaining price controls. Price controls created an incentive for black markets, which
were not just used by entrepreneurial factory managers to by-pass
official controls but led to personal corruption. Moreover, price
controls inhibited supply and aggravated inflation, albeit hidden.
What the reformers failed to anticipate was that in a capitalist
market economy (which China was becoming) there are more
complex and less positive responses to sudden, proposed, policy
changes – like speculation and panic. Inflation surged in the short

term – to an officially (and conservatively) estimated 26 per cent in 1988. Deng and Zhao, the main architects of de-controlling prices, badly misjudged the public mood and the degree of nervousness of their colleagues. The experiment was stopped (to be attempted again, much more successfully, in the mid-1990s by the next generation of reformers). Chen Yun's battery of 'readjustment policies' was wheeled out again and aimed at the problem of inflation: higher interest rates; cuts in government-approved investment; reinforced price controls. The dragon of inflation was slayed (it was reduced to 3 per cent in 1990) but at the cost of sharply reduced growth (4.1 per cent in 1989; 4 per cent in 1990). The consequences were harsh: an estimated 20 million industrial workers lost their jobs due to the 'austerity' drive.

The Problem of Democracy

Deng was concerned with the big picture, which he defined in terms of economic progress and rising living standards. This was to be accompanied and reinforced by more secure external relationships: the opening up to Japan and the West; business-like relations with Taiwan and Hong Kong; and reducing threats from the USSR and its allies, notably Vietnam. Western ideas of political change – 'bourgeois liberalization' – were of no interest to him whatsoever and unwelcome to the extent that they might lead to disorder and the weakening of the Communist Party.

Deng's ability, however, to separate the economic from the political would fly in the face of some underlying changes in public attitudes over which he had no control. Overseas travel by students, scientists and others, which he strongly encouraged, broadened the mind. The rapid spread of TV (from 3 million in 1978 to over 40 million in 1985) was opening a window on the world (and the rest of China). In 1986 demonstrations spontaneously broke out across China led by students who, instead of being placated by the re-establishment of 'normal' university education,

wanted to air a variety of grievances over living conditions, suffo-
cating authority (they were allocated jobs on graduation and had
no choice) and lack of democracy. The liberalizing Party General Secretary, Hu Yaobang, failed to curb the demonstrations
and was sacked, having recanted his 'errors': that is, in being too
permissive. His dismissal cost Deng a key reformer, though the
consequences were not immediately apparent.

The protests died away but returned with a vengeance in April
1989, triggered initially by the sudden death of Hu, who had
acquired the status of a hero among the students. Demonstrations
grew in volume and the accumulation of popular grievances –
notably over inflation and de-control of prices – added to the scale
of the protests. The authorities became increasingly nervous and
were aware of the dangers from contagion: they only had to look
at the disintegrating Soviet Empire (visibly reinforced by a visit to
China by Gorbachev). Martial law was imposed to restore order,
but initially it failed to stop increasingly violent demonstrations.
The climax of the crisis was the military opening fire on demonstrators in Tiananmen Square. Order was restored by the army.

There is little doubt that Deng had personal responsibility for
ordering the crackdown and he never expressed any regret.[25] The
massacre was the logical consequence of his approach to party
authority. In the context of the many brutal and bloody episodes
he had experienced, and sometimes been complicit in, it was a
minor episode. But China had changed and its failings, as well as
its achievements, were no longer hidden. Deng's reputation was
badly damaged, not least with the Western governments which he
had mobilized in support of reform and growth.[26] His Premier,
Zhao, the head of government and leading reformer, was made
the scapegoat for Tiananmen Square and removed from all his
posts. Deng, now eighty-four, in failing health and largely deaf,
seemed destined to end his long career with a tarnished reputation
outside the hard-line core of the party leadership, who appreciated his tough, uncompromising defence of authority. He stepped

down from his role as 'paramount leader' in late 1989, retaining only a titular position as head of the Chinese bridge-playing association.

But, yet again, he had not played his last card. He had used the few months between Tiananmen Square and his formal resignation to engineer a hand-picked succession to Jiang Zemin, the Party Secretary of Shanghai. Jiang was untainted by the suppression of the demonstrators (he had defused demonstrations in his city without violence). He likewise commanded broad political support as a party disciplinarian and had a track record as a reformer in Shanghai and as a minister (for the electronics industry).

Deng no longer had any power, having abdicated all his various official roles, but he still had potentially great influence and respect, which he sought to exploit in reigniting the 'prairie fire' of reform. He agitated for greater freedom for Shanghai to be allowed to experiment with the visionary redevelopment project at Pudong which had hitherto failed to get approval. This was designed to appeal to Jiang Zemin and Jiang's successor in Shanghai, Zhu Rongji, one of Deng's protégés who later in the 1990s, when Deng was dead, drove the reform agenda.

Finally, Deng embarked upon a southern tour to visit Guangdong, to defend the SEZs in Shenzhen and Zhuhai against criticism and to advertise their progress. The publicity around the visit and Deng's provocative comments on the need for resurrecting the reform agenda had the desired effect: Jiang publicly endorsed his comments using the phrase 'socialist market economy' to define future policy. Even the more conservative Chen Yun signed up to the need for accelerated reform. Jiang adopted a 9–10 per cent growth objective just as Deng wanted. And the growth was delivered, with double-digit figures for the rest of the decade and beyond. There were problems of overheating and inflation but, from now on, they would be managed. The battle for reform had been won.

The Legacy

When Deng finally stepped aside in 1992 he had achieved his mission: the economic transformation of China. Nothing on this scale, lifting hundreds of millions from poverty in such a short period, had ever been achieved in human history. Moreover, he left an enduring legacy which profoundly influences the way we think about economics, development and politics today.

He established a model of development – a socialist market economy or, as Lenin called it earlier in the century, state capitalism – which worked. A combination of markets, privately and socially owned businesses and farms together with a powerful state, and a system of planning, proved to be a viable – indeed, very effective – system. Although Korea and Singapore (and on a bigger scale, India) have evolved their economic structure from a very different starting point, the end product is not markedly different. Deng's successor Jiang reiterated his view that it was simply irrelevant to discuss if something was called 'capitalism' or 'socialism'; they could be mixed interchangeably. Indeed, Jiang went further, establishing the basis for markets for capital, labour and property, as well as goods and services; and also introducing private shareholding.

In the twenty-five years since Deng ceased to play a role, the Chinese model has developed greatly under his successors. China now has a predominantly urban, high tech, society. It is much more integrated with the global economy; but, despite that, was able to counter the global recession that began in 2008 with a massive countercyclical infrastructure investment programme in the best Dengist 'builder' tradition (allegedly pouring more concrete in three years than the US did in the previous century).

There are still enormous development challenges to overcome. Firstly, with an authoritarian political system it may be difficult to establish clearly defined property rights and the rule of law. The same applies to regulating for financial stability in debt markets and taming some of the wilder business practices and corruption. Likewise, China now increasingly faces the challenges of a developed economy, such as ageing, advanced urbanization, managing climate change and new technologies like AI and robotics. The Dengist model is still, however, recognizable and going strong.

Secondly, the element of modernization which is still wholly missing is democracy in the Western sense. Unlike Korea and also Taiwan, China has not sought to liberalize its politics. Deng's belief that dominant – single – Communist Party government was (and is) necessary to maintain order in such a big, complex country with a history of internal conflict and civil war remains as strongly entrenched as ever. Successive Chinese governments have been, apparently, vindicated by the chaotic collapse of communism in the USSR and Yugoslavia, and latterly by the emergence of populism in the USA, the UK and elsewhere. There are examples of big, complex societies combining rapid growth and pluralistic democracies (notably India and Indonesia). And there are good reasons to believe that, as countries become richer and rely more heavily on brain rather than brawn, the educated population expects to exchange new ideas in a way that is only possible in a politically open society. However, it will take at least a generation to come to a more definitive conclusion on whether economic and political liberalization are linked or independent or antagonistic.

Deng also established within his model an important element of institutional, long-term stability and continuity: a leadership transition. He made a successful handover of power to Jiang Zemin who, like him, was *primus inter pares* within a collective leadership but not a dictator and who handed over power in turn to a new generation of leadership. Jiang managed a smooth transition to Hu Jintao who in turn handed over power to Xi Jinping. At present it is not clear if Xi will respect that tradition or what his alternative would look like. Perhaps out of underlying insecurity, the Xi regime is becoming more authoritarian with no political challenge permitted at any level: a personalized dictatorship in the mould of Mao rather than Deng.

Another aspect of the Deng legacy is also now in doubt. While fiercely patriotic, Deng was not an inward-looking nationalist. He welcomed foreign technologies and investment and believed China was resilient enough to withstand exposure to foreign ideas and information. That has changed with the attempt to create a firewall around the internet and more generally, under Xi, to promote a more nationalistic ideology. Faced with a hostile and belligerent, if erratic, American President determined to pin responsibility for the massive loss of life in the Covid-19 pandemic on China and painting China as an economic and security threat, Xi's regime has reacted angrily and aggressively, appealing to Chinese wounded pride.

We simply do not know how Deng would have wanted China to behave as a superpower, now faced with hostility rather than offers of positive engagement. His challenge was one of helping to make China a superpower. We do know that he attached great value to China's involvement in global institutions like the IMF, World Bank and GATT (now the World Trade Organization – WTO). That is a tradition his successors (including Xi) have maintained so far despite the distraction, and provocation, of a 'trade war' and war of words with Trump's US. So far.

13

Manmohan Singh: The Quiet Reformer

As the world's largest democracy, by far, India is not short of politicians; and in the seventy-plus years since Independence a succession of prime ministers and economic ministers have made the relief of India's vast poverty, and economic development, central to their mission.

The glass is half empty; but also half full. Economic growth (and specifically per capita growth), which is a necessary if not a sufficient condition for eliminating poverty, has gradually improved from the period when it was dismissed as 'the Hindu rate of growth' (a term attributed to the economist Raj Krishna in 1978). In the last two decades, India has been among the world's most rapidly growing economies, and consistently so. Hundreds of millions of people have been lifted out of absolute poverty (i.e. bare survival) and similar numbers have risen into what in India is called the middle class.

No single individual in government can claim too large a share of credit for the acceleration in the tempo of development. It could plausibly be argued that India often grew faster in spite of, rather than because of, government ministers of whatever stripe. As an Indian joke has it: 'the economy grows at night when the government is asleep'.[1] And much of the political dynamism has come from below: proactive state governments rather than the distant (federal) government in Delhi.

Manmohan the Man

However, if any individual stands out as having liberated India's growth potential it is Manmohan Singh (1932–), Finance Minister from 1991 to 1996 and Prime Minister from 2004 to 2014. He has been eulogized by his allies as 'India's Deng Xiaoping' and his admirers as the 'Father of Indian Reform'.[2] But even a detached observer such as the BBC's Mark Tully described him as the 'architect of the new India'.[3] These compliments were bestowed before his decade as Prime Minister about which one of the less hostile observations was *Time* magazine's description of him as an 'underachiever'.[4] The pattern is, however, not unique to Manmohan Singh; Erhard's work was largely done before he became, and achieved little as, Chancellor.

As with Erhard, Manmohan Singh is one of the very few economists to have reached the top of the political greasy pole and to have had an opportunity to apply economic principles to the government of their country. Unlike Erhard he was not a classic economic liberal but was immersed in 'left Keynesian' economics at Cambridge and then the development economics of the 1960s, at the United Nation's UNCTAD under Raúl Prebisch focusing on the trade barriers facing developing country exporters.

He left little economic writing setting out his own views beyond a book on trends in Indian exports based on his DPhil thesis at Oxford.[5] He was a practitioner rather than an academic. He spent around twenty years as a public servant: economic adviser, top official in the Finance Ministry, Governor of the Reserve Bank and head of the Planning Commission. He became accustomed to working with politicians of different parties and prejudices and it was his job to operate within the framework of a planned social-ist economy and then later the more market-oriented approach favoured by the World Bank and the IMF which lay behind his own reforms. Since he was always a model of tact and discretion there is no trace of his personal preferences beyond a longstanding commitment to alleviating rural poverty, which may owe something to his upbringing in a Punjab village without electricity, studying under the dim light of a kerosene lamp.

He could have spent his twilight years in the comfortable world populated by his fellow former public servants on international expert groups, in Delhi think tanks, writing books and in university sinecures. But he chose to go into politics as Finance and then Prime Minister. There is no suggestion that he was a frustrated politician and every indication that he acted out of a sense of duty when asked to serve by people who valued his expertise and reputation for wise judgement and personal integrity.

He joined the Congress Party and became a member of the (indirectly elected) Indian upper house of parliament. By the 1990s Congress had lost its ideological and idealistic appeal and had acquired an unsavoury reputation for corruption while standing for little more than the dynastic rule of the descendants of Jawaharlal Nehru, India's first post-Independence Prime Minister. After the assassination of Rajiv Gandhi, however, there was an interlude under P.V. Narasimha Rao, who asked Manmohan Singh to join the government. There was in the party a vestigial belief in inclusive political secularism which would have attracted Manmohan Singh as the rather conspicuous, turban-wearing member of a religious minority: the Sikhs.

Indian politics is only partly about economics and the 'left–right' issues which have dominated European politics until recently. There is a powerful strand of 'identity politics' based on caste, language and, above all, religion. Manmohan Singh's personal life had been scarred by the sectarian hatreds which have been incubated in the politics of identity. He was born in what is now Pakistan and, when he was a teenager, his family was uprooted and moved to the Indian side of partitioned Punjab.

Then, he could hardly not have been affected by the massacres of thousands of Sikhs, especially in Delhi, following the assassination of Indira Gandhi in 1984. At the time of writing, in his eighties, he is a Congress Party grandee and elder statesman. He is a strong spokesman for religious tolerance after the scapegoating of Muslims under Narendra Modi's Bharatiya Janata Party (BJP), the government which succeeded his own administration. Economics has now taken a back seat.

The Heritage of Economic Ideas

Manmohan Singh was a teenager at the time of Independence and as a student of economics in the Punjab and then in Delhi was caught up in the arguments about the legacy of the British Empire and the opportunities presented by Independence. India's approach to economic policy has been shaped by the different strands of the Independence movement, which was in turn shaped by India's experience as part of the British Empire. Economic historians are agreed that, for most of the colonial era, most Indians lived on the edge of starvation.[6] If the monsoon fell, there was just enough to eat; if the rains failed, many died of hunger. In the century from the mid-1800s to Independence, for which there are reasonable statistical records, per capita incomes remained roughly flat, despite some development based around improved physical infrastructure: notably the railways. British economist Angus Deaton concludes brutally: 'It is possible that the deprivation in childhood of Indians born around midcentury was as severe as that of any large group in history, all the way back to the Neolithic revolution and the hunter-gatherers that preceded them... death and deprivation kept the population in check, but even for the survivors, conditions of life were terrible.'[7] And, while there was significant progress before Independence in the development of Indian business there was a degree of dependency – on Britain – in trade and investment, which heavily influenced those working on post-Independence economic policy towards more self-reliance.

The dominant element in the economic thinking of the first generation of post-Independence leaders was the belief that India should progress by developing – especially its industry – through a system of central planning rather than a market economy. Nehru was a democrat and had no truck with communism (because it was not rooted in national traditions) but he had a somewhat rose-tinted view of Stalin's USSR and saw much in that model to emulate: 'the practical achievements of the Soviet Union were... tremendously impressive', he wrote.[8]

Successive Five Year Plans in the Soviet manner were launched aiming to double per capita incomes over twenty-seven years built on rising levels of investment and a push to industrialize.[9] The notion of a centrally planned development strategy with the state playing a major role did not just come out of nowhere at Independence. A ten-year plan had been drawn up by one M. Visvesvaraya – one of the first Indian civil engineers – as early as 1936. The development of the Indian planning system, under Nehru's political leadership, was largely the work of an internationally renowned mathematician and statistician, P.C. Mahalanobis – the originator of the Mahalanobis Distance, a statistical construct. As a member of the First Planning Commission he developed a mathematical model for the Indian economy which underpinned the first and subsequent Five Year Plans.

There was another, strong but different, tradition in post-Independence economic thinking emanating from Mahatma Gandhi. Gandhi was not primarily interested in economic policy as such and more concerned with broader spiritual values and the deployment of his philosophy of non-violent resistance to the political struggle for Indian Independence. But in the course of his teaching and campaigning he evolved what might be called a Gandhian approach to economics, quite different from Nehru's ideas around socialist planning. One of Gandhi's themes was *swadeshi* – meaning 'of one's own country'. One of his campaigns was to stop the import of (mainly) British manufactured textiles which, he argued, were destroying Indian village-based handicrafts. Swadeshi has since become a slogan of economic nationalists and protectionists, divorced from the context of village industries and the struggle for Independence.

The main element in Gandhi's thinking was the importance of the Indian village: building up agriculture and village industries, rather than heavy industry, to provide employment (and rural development more generally – emphasizing health and education). Nehru did not so much attack this approach as to damn it with faint praise and to ignore its economic significance: 'It is true, I think, that there is a fundamental difference between [Gandhi's] outlook on life generally and what might be called the modern outlook. He is not enamoured of ever-increasing standards of living and the growth of luxury at the cost of spiritual and moral values.'[10] There is, however, a legacy of Gandhian economics in the continuing attempts to develop alternative technologies suitable for small-scale operation in villages. S.N. Agarwal drew up a Plan based on Gandhi's economic ideas in 1944 and, more generally, Indian reformers have tried to rebalance the economy towards village India, in recent years.

A final strand was provided by another, top, Congress leader, Sardar Patel, who was revered as one of the most committed and effective leaders of the pro-Independence, civil disobedience campaign of Gandhi, his fellow Gujarati. He is credited with many of the achievements of India at Independence, from rapidly unifying numerous semi-independent statelets to establishing an all-India civil service, the 'Steel Frame' as he called it. He would also go on to lead India's armed forces in the war with Pakistan which followed Independence. Economic policy was not one of his areas of responsibility, or interest, but contemporary accounts suggest that he was well disposed to business, including the big industrial groups – Birla and Tata – and had little time for ideological and idealistic socialism. A group of industrialists, close to Patel, drew up a 'Bombay Plan' in the 1940s in which business and the government operated in partnership. That pragmatic pro-business approach was adopted by an important faction within Congress and has re-emerged in recent years in both Congress and the Hindu nationalist BJP. The BJP leader, Narendra Modi, also from Gujarat, has erected a massive statue in honour of Patel.

The first decade and a half after Independence were dominated by Nehru's vision of a planned socialist economy and the creation of a strong industrial base. Then, in a brief interlude, Lal Bahadur Shastri sought to shift the balance towards Gandhi's preference for rural development and small-scale industry. Nehru's daughter, Indira Gandhi, in the early 1970s – when Manmohan Singh became the government's Chief Economic Adviser – strengthened her father's socialist model with a wave of nationalization and also, briefly, abandoned democracy in the 'Emergency'. She in turn was succeeded by Congress defectors led by Morarji Desai who tried to shift the emphasis more to private enterprise; and then came Charan Singh who represented and favoured the – better-off – peasant farmers (Jats). The emphasis shifted as rapidly as the frequent changes of government but the Nehru model, and the complex system of controls built around it, remained essentially intact.

The Planning Model and the Permit Raj

The framework of economic policy based on planning and industrialization established at Independence reflected a consensus at the time. Indian policies were consistent with the mainstream of economic and political thought that then predominated. There was a high degree of openness to foreign economists who could add prestige and technical knowledge to the planning process.[11] Bimal Jalan, former Governor of the Bank of India, notes that a long list of leading Western economists were involved in policy thinking at that time including Paul Rosenstein-Rodan, J.K. Galbraith, Ian Little and James Mirrlees.[12] Sometimes the impact was embarrassing. Nicholas Kaldor – Manmohan Singh's professor at Cambridge – was unable to persuade British ministers to adopt his theoretically sound but complex proposal for an Expenditure Tax, to boost savings; but he did persuade the Indians. However, the tax was a costly failure, soon to be abandoned. But some external influences were more durable. Ian Little, who was Manmohan Singh's DPhil supervisor at Oxford, was important in steering Indian economic thinking in a more liberal direction.

The initial belief in economic planning was derived not just from the apparent success of the Soviet Union but was also fashionable in post-war UK, France and Scandinavia. The USA was still intellectually dominated by New Deal economics after experience of wartime mobilization and controls, popularized by the likes of Galbraith (who became Ambassador to India). The belief in the essentially benign nature of government and the usefulness of planning was widely held among economists and transmitted through the new World Bank, whose biggest customer quickly became India. The emerging discipline of development economics emphasized planning, and mainstream economists like Alec Cairncross and Arthur Lewis wrote books explaining how to do it.[13]

New techniques – like the Input–Output analysis developed by Wassily Leontief, quantifying the interconnections across the economy[14] – added detail to the modelling, building on the statistician P.C. Mahalanobis's mathematically sophisticated design. An MIT project, in particular, involved close working relationships with Indian planners. The Indian Planning Commission was soon staffed by the 'brightest and the best': Indian economists who had learned their trade at the LSE or Cambridge and were very familiar with emerging theory. In addition, there was a widespread belief in industrialization following the path of other – developed – countries which had achieved 'take-off' and a belief that this could be achieved within India's potentially large economy without much recourse to exports: modernization together with self-reliance.[15] Manmohan Singh was steeped in this tradition.

Planning operated directly through state enterprises and indirectly through private companies which were subject to state control and direction through a system of permits (the 'permit raj'). Planning performed the function of aggregating the different elements of India's – already by 1947 – complex economy. It identified the scale of investment to be financed by the government and the gap between investment and savings to be filled – hopefully – by foreign aid. And it assembled lists of projects designed to fulfil the Plan objectives, and to put forward to aid donors for financing. Since the aim of the planning system was to use scarce capital effectively, to generate growth, permits were required for private investment and for access to scarce commodities.

Initially the new system seemed to work well. The first Five Year Plan (1951–6) targeted 11 per cent growth over five years and actually achieved 18 per cent, while investment rose from 5 per cent of national income to 7.5 per cent. Compared to the colonial times, these were exceptional figures which reinforced the conviction that India was on the right track. The Second Plan period (1956–61) was even better, with a target of 21 per cent growth over five years, which was almost achieved. Nevertheless, one problem was already becoming apparent: per capita income growth (2.1 per cent per annum) was way below the target (3.3 per cent) because population growth was eating up material improvements. By the end of the Third Plan (1961–6) it was clear that something was wrong – growth at 2.5 per cent per annum was less than half the target of 5.6 per cent per annum, and in per capita terms there was no improvement at all. Also, in 1965 there was a famine when the monsoon and crops failed. It was not as bad as in the worst of colonial times but a serious set-back. The Fourth Plan (1969–74) was little better: a target of 5.7 per cent per annum of which 3.4 per cent was realized with per capita income growth of 1.1 per cent per annum, as against a target of 3.4 per cent. The Indian economy seemed trapped in slow growth while population growth swallowed it up without leading to higher living standards.

The failure of the economy relative to expectations created an unfavourable contrast with some of the industrializing countries of East Asia, notably post-war Japan and Korea (and, until the disastrous Great Leap Forward, China). It became fashionable to despair and to predict revolution, in what was called India's 'quiet crisis'.[16] Foreign commentators such as Swedish economist Gunnar Myrdal were reluctant to admit to a failure of socialist planning and thought that there must be some failing in Indian (or Asian) culture.[17]

Under Indira Gandhi, economic policy took a left turn in response to this 'quiet crisis'. The private sector was subject to tighter control, foreign investment more severely restricted and banks nationalized along with insurance companies, the coal industry and some loss-making textile companies. As in much of the developing world from Sukarno's Indonesia to Tito's Yugoslavia, Nasser's Egypt, Nkrumah's Ghana and revolutionary Cuba, Indian economic policy was conducted in terms of 'socialism' and 'self-reliance'.

Things did not improve. By the mid-1970s Indira Gandhi still faced economy in crisis (aggravated by the first oil shock) and plummeting popularity. She doubled down, intensifying populist economics – nationalizing more companies – and then blamed the cumbersome workings of democracy, declaring a State of Emergency. Her elder son, Sanjay, was obsessed by the then fashionable idea that India suffered a Malthusian problem – poor people had more children than they could care for – and embarked on a brutal mass sterilization programme. The Emergency was mercifully short-lived and Mrs Gandhi was ejected from power in an election, ending three decades of Congress rule.

In the meantime, Indian agriculture saw real progress in food production following the application of 'miracle' hybrid seeds in the mid-1960s and the rapid spread of scientific farming. There had been a 'Green Revolution' in those parts of India, notably the north-western states of Punjab, Haryana and western Uttar Pradesh, where there was irrigation. A combination of seeds, fertilizers, water, effective government advisory services and generous prices for the procurement of grain (all boosted by effective political lobbying by the newly affluent peasant farmers) transformed India's food supply situation so that, for the first time in known history, there was enough rice and wheat for India to be comfortably self-sufficient.

The beginning of the 1980s marked something of a turning point. The economy (thanks to the farmers) had stabilized as had politics. Mrs Gandhi and Congress returned to power, chastened, with a large majority. There was a growing recognition within government and among commentators that India was underperforming and that after over three decades and five completed Five Year Plans there was a need for a fresh approach. The head of the Planning Commission, Manmohan Singh, previously government Chief Economic Adviser, was at the centre of the reappraisal and growing appetite for reform.

Looking at the thirty-year post-Independence period as a whole, there was average annual per capita income growth of 1.4 per cent, which translated into 50 per cent improvement overall. There is, however, some dispute as to how far this growth translated into poverty reduction. Over a twenty-year period from 1970, the proportion below the poverty line – based on very basic food needs – fell from 56 per cent to 46 per cent, though absolute numbers of poor people rose.[18] Political rhetoric reflected the need to be seen fighting poverty. But the levels of poverty remained painfully high after three decades of heavy industrial investment. There was a growing understanding that population growth – a major factor in low per capita growth – could better be reduced by educating women and through health care to reduce child mortality rather than through compulsory sterilization.

While these things happened, for example in Kerala, education and health remained a state-level matter, not amenable to centralized planning.

The first three decades of planning did achieve some of its objectives, however. Domestic savings rose from 7 per cent of GNP in 1950/51 to 20 per cent in 1979/80, which (together with 2 per cent of GDP investment from overseas – mainly aid) bolstered investment. Industry grew from 12 per cent of the economy over this period to 21 per cent (manufactures grew by 5.2 per cent per annum; agriculture 2.2 per cent per annum). But by the end of this period there was clear evidence of slowing growth and unproductive use of the savings. Why?

Vijay Joshi, one of the academics arguing for economic liberalization, explains: 'Indian policymakers acted with a mistaken conception of the role of the state. Convoluted regulation of economic activity created large inefficiencies and stifled business drive. At the same time, the state neglected to attend to areas where it should have been active. In particular, it failed to ensure that poor people could gain access to primary health care and education.'[19]

At the heart of the criticism of controls on private business was a changing reality: a system devised when the private sector accounted for 90 per cent of corporate assets was less relevant when the public sector accounted for 70 per cent. A complex system (designed originally to regulate a few rich industrialists) had expanded into a vast bureaucratic apparatus of licences involving numerous agencies and ministries and covering nearly all aspects of the economy. Private business required permits before it could legally undertake a wide variety of activities: new investment branch closures and redundancies, change in location, capital goods, imports, foreign investment and technical collaborations, capital market borrowing, credit, takeovers, registration, plus – at state level – environmental and labour laws, electricity connection and much else.[20]

The effect of these restrictions was to suppress investment and innovation, to create a high level of inefficiency and numerous opportunities for corruption. Many businesses were comfortable with arrangements which protected them from competition, passing on their inefficiency to consumers. Corruption became commonplace at all levels and rarely prosecuted. The time was ripe for reform. Who would do what was politically necessary to make it happen?

A Decade of Partial and Halting Reform

The 1980s, before the big reformist push under Manmohan Singh, were a frustrating period in which there was a broad intellectual consensus about the need to liberalize the system, but action was slow to follow. That is not surprising. India was – and is – a huge, complex democracy with a multiplicity of interests in every sector and every state, let alone at an all-India level. To build up support for a big change of policy, and legislative change, is a major political challenge. Political economists such as Mancur Olson have described more generally the difficulty of taking collective action in large and complex entities: a classic 'prisoner's dilemma' game with many prisoners.[21] In essence, individual decision makers have little incentive to change, unless others do so first. But then no one does: a Catch-22.

There was, however, an emerging consensus among the top civil servants in key departments (Prime Minister's Office; Finance Ministry; Reserve Bank; Planning Commission). The economic advisers, like Manmohan Singh, were a key influence though there was far from unanimity and powerful support for traditional 'socialist planning'.

The Indian economic decision makers were also influenced by the World Bank, which had particular clout as India's largest aid donor (with around 55 per cent of gross aid in the Sixth Plan period and as Convener of the All India Consortium which supplied 85 per cent of aid). The World Bank had moved on from the intellectual fashions of the 1960s when there was genuine enthusiasm for 'planning' to, by 1980, a much more market-based approach reflected in the Washington Consensus.

The IMF was also able to make an important intervention when the new government of Mrs Gandhi, in 1980, faced the combination of a drought, an oil price shock and a balance of payments crisis. The IMF stepped in with a large loan (5 billion Special Drawing Rights), subject not only to the usual macroeconomic conditions but pushing strongly, in the IMF Memorandum attached to the Letter of Intent, for liberalizing imports, allowing more foreign technology and ending policies which discriminated against exports. Manmohan Singh was then the top civil servant in the Finance Ministry who negotiated the agreement with the Fund, and the detailed trade policy agenda was a subject on which he had written his DPhil and arguably knew more about than anyone else.

There was, in general, support for reform from business, especially from a new generation of executives familiar with computers and Western or Japanese management systems. Likewise the emerging middle class – roughly the top two deciles of the income pyramid – was beginning to enjoy consumer durables and better clothing and was impatient with services from poor state-run infrastructure. But there were powerful vested interests from protected monopoly positions and other rent-seeking activities. The message to government from them was 'liberalize but not here'. The big companies were skilled at protecting their specific privileges and small companies were vocal in demanding protection from big companies. The commercial farmers had large subsidies to protect – for fertilizers, water and seeds. If these vested interests could be dressed up in the language of Indian nationalism or socialist principle or Gandhian spiritual values, so much the better. As the economist Pranab Bardhan observed: 'The Indian public economy has thus become an elaborate network of patronage and subsidies... The reflexive and blanket protectionism encouraged in this political culture has resulted in sheltering the oligopolistic profits and chronic inefficiencies in many industries, apart from lining many pockets in the corridors of power.'[22]

Translating the growing consensus on the need for reform into action required political heft and that meant mobilizing the Congress Party and the Nehru family – led by Indira Gandhi. She was a skilled and pragmatic politician. She accepted the advice of her officials to go along with the terms of an IMF loan and to pursue cautious liberalization. But she was also not about to trash her father's legacy of socialist planning.

She was assassinated in 1984 and her remaining son, Rajiv (Sanjay had died in a plane crash), won an extraordinarily big majority in an election which gave him the mandate for radical change. He started with good intentions and a commitment to press ahead with reform and was surrounded by young, enthusiastic, Western-educated businessmen and technocrats. But he lacked his mother's political skills, alienated senior Congressmen and allowed himself to be tarnished by a major corruption scandal over an arms contract. Unhelpfully, liberalization became associated in the public mind with conspicuous consumption (and corruption) by a new elite. Rajiv Gandhi was then ousted in 1989 by a weak coalition which depended on the support of communists and the Hindu nationalist BJP.

In the nine years that the Gandhi family had been continually in office with a reform agenda, quite a long list of modest steps had been taken to make the 'permit raj' more flexible: licensing was lifted from some industries and there was an easing of the controls on the 'big houses' – the giant Indian conglomerates. Similarly, the number of items reserved for production by small firms was cut, high tech industries were freed from some controls and public enterprises lost their privileged status. Lastly, corporate and income taxes were cut, import restrictions were eased and exports supported.

There was also a marked increase in applications to launch businesses and make investments in the form of letters of interest. After the slowdown of the 1970s industrial growth in the 1980s went back up to 7.7 per cent per annum, much as in the 1950s. Overall economic growth went up from 3.0 per cent to 5.6 per cent (3.4 per cent per capita), by some way the most rapid period of growth in Indian history.[23] In part it represented a recovery from the lows of the 1970s when India had been badly hit by oil price shocks. In part it reflected a better investment climate with higher and more stable investment (public and private). And, there was some improvement in efficiency from the limited reforms. But the main reason was 'rampantly expansionary macroeconomic policies'[24] leading to a financial crisis in 1991 – with inflation at 12 per cent, a current account deficit of 3.5 per cent of GDP, a fiscal deficit (capital and current) of 10 per cent of GDP and foreign reserves down to two weeks' supply of imports. India again had to turn to the IMF.

The Politics and Economics of Reform

During an election to decide who should manage the economic crisis, the Congress leader, Rajiv Gandhi, was assassinated (seven years after the assassination of his mother). Congress won the 1991 election albeit without an overall majority and relied on the support of smaller parties to form a government. P.V. Narasimha Rao became Prime Minister and he invited Manmohan Singh to become Finance Minister.

Paradoxically, the politically weak government which emerged proved to be the most radically reforming in practice of any government in post-war India (or since). Prime Minister Rao gave Manmohan Singh as Finance Minister a mandate to press ahead with stabilization and liberalization as part of a fresh programme agreed on the back of an IMF credit. Manmohan Singh's appointment was in part a reflection of his authority and credibility as the leading economist in the government, and his reputation as a totally honest, incorruptible public servant was an antidote to the public perception of endemic corruption. He was also no threat to the Congress hierarchy since he had no power base of his own. Further, his economics were, and were seen as, mainstream and practical; he was not one of the free market ideologues who (often from academic berths in London or Washington) were seeking revolutionary rather than evolutionary reform. He had some allies in the Congress Party such as Palaniappan Chidambaram (later to succeed him as Congress Finance Minister) but the socialist grass roots of the party were not keen on reform and accepted it only because there was an economic crisis.

His own views on the link between economics and politics were captured in an interview with the journalist Mark Tully: 'I first became conscious of the creative role of politics in shaping human affairs and I owe that mostly to my teachers, Joan Robinson and Nicholas Kaldor [at Cambridge]… [Robinson] propounded the left-wing interpretation of Keynes maintaining that the state has to play more of a role if you really want to combine development with social equity… Kaldor influenced me even more… he used the Keynesian analysis to demonstrate that capitalism could be made to work.'[25] He had also studied at Oxford under the economist Ian Little who later became an effective critic of inward-looking, protectionist, development. And he had some outstanding younger colleagues in India such as Montek Singh Ahluwalia and Shankar Acharya who were close to the thinking of the World Bank and the international consensus behind market-based reform.[26]

The government was not strong and prone to splits and scandal. One apocryphal tale was that the English- and Telugu-speaking Prime Minister was not able to communicate with his Hindi-speaking Defence Minister who was in office as leader of a party representing a group of low caste voters in the biggest state. And stories soon emerged of suitcases of rupees being smuggled in and out of the Prime Minister's house for some nefarious purpose or other.

Despite the distractions, Manmohan Singh embarked on far-reaching and controversial changes from Day 1. The budget was subject to painful retrenchment and the rupee was devalued, contributing to a year of recession and then a rapid recovery in both growth and financial balance (fiscal and current account). There was more extensive deregulation of trade and industry than had been attempted hitherto: quotas on imports of capital goods and raw materials were scrapped and tariffs slashed; investment licensing was largely abandoned; foreign investment was welcomed in many more sectors of the economy. The most sensitive issues – like privatization of state assets or freeing up the highly regulated labour market or the land market – were largely left for another day. But, by Indian standards, these were big changes[27] and sufficient to excite business into launching a wave of start-ups – in new high tech, information-based industries and pharmaceuticals. They also precipitated a process of investment rationalization and productivity improvement in established firms. Although cause and effect are difficult to disentangle, the reforms were almost certainly a key factor in pushing up the growth rate for the next decade to around 6 per cent per annum.

The inherent tensions in the Congress-led coalition led to the reform programme running out of steam and eventually to defeat at the next general election due in no small part to corruption scandals, notably in the securities market (for which Manmohan Singh held himself responsible, though he was not personally implicated). There followed a period of mostly short and unstable governments, and then a period under the Hindu nationalist BJP. However, crucially, economic policy did not change and there was no rolling back of reform. The BJP positioned itself as the voice of a resurgent India trumpeting the success of its business and its technology. Manmohan Singh went into opposition. But then in 2004 the Congress Party staged a partial and unexpected comeback as part of an uncomfortable coalition – the United Progressive Alliance (UPA) – with various leftist parties and relying on parliamentary support from the two communist parties. The Congress Party leader was Sonia Gandhi, the Italian-born widow of Rajiv whom she had met when he was studying in Cambridge. She was realistic enough to recognize that she would not be acceptable as Prime Minister of India so she handed the role to Manmohan Singh.

There followed a decade in which very little happened in policy terms – the communists and the BJP opposition blocked any reforms – but in which the economy surged ahead, driven in part by the dynamism of the private sector generated by reforms a decade earlier. Between 2003 and 2011 India achieved the remarkable growth of 8.5 per cent per annum (7 per cent per head). It was not quite as dramatic as the double-digit growth of South Korea or China in their phase of hypergrowth but remarkable for a vast and democratic country with a host of obstacles to progress at national and state level.[28] It was at that stage the second fastest growing economy in the world. As Prime Minister and architect of the earlier reforms, Manmohan Singh attracted international recognition; his face appeared on the front of *Time* and *Forbes* magazines. He was honoured with the 2010 World Statesman Award.

The aggregate figures masked more modest improvements in living standards and poverty reduction. The numbers in absolute – extreme – poverty on one of the main and rather frugal Indian definitions fell to 270 million in 2011 (around a quarter of the population) from 404 million in 1993 before Manmohan Singh's reforms took effect.[29] Other definitions suggest that the numbers are higher but that there was a clear reduction. There were also big regional and caste differences. On social indicators, India made significant progress over this period in life expectancy (to sixty-five years), infant mortality (to 38 per 1,000 live births) and adult literacy (63 per cent) but these levels were, and are, much worse than in – say – China. The evidence also suggests that inequality of income increased after the reforms from a broadly flat Gini coefficient of around 30 per cent in the period 1960–90 to over 35 per cent in 2011–12. Inequality between the richest states (like Punjab) and the poorest (Bihar) also widened.

Manmohan Singh himself was well aware of these deficiencies in Indian development but also of the inherent difficulties of trying to change the economic and social structures of hundreds of thousands of villages. Likewise all attempts at reform required navigating through or round state governments of varying competence, venality and political alignment. He launched a unique identification scheme which led to ID cards enabling poor people to access (rather meagre) benefits and subsidized food without dependency on hostile or corrupt intermediaries. He promoted a Rural Employment Guarantee Scheme which proved in some states to be an invaluable safety net for the destitute. Education became free and compulsory between six and fourteen years (at least in theory).

The economic success story over which Manmohan Singh presided started to sour when the UPA Congress-led coalition government was comfortably re-elected in 2009. Consumer inflation, which had been well under 5 per cent in the booming early years of the new century, surged to double digits after 2008. The fiscal deficit, which had been curbed in the post-1991 period and again after a relapse in the 2001–3 period, went back to levels of over 5 per cent of GDP. The current account deficit widened to 4.5 per cent GDP in 2011–12. The high levels of corporate savings, investment and productivity growth came to an end in 2011–12 as heavy corporate borrowing reached its limits and companies retrenched to deal with non-performing loans.

Non-performing loans, particularly in state-owned banks, were approaching 20 per cent of assets and any write-down supported by public funds incited accusations of cronyism in India's open but corrupt system. Beneath the bad numbers was a whole set of interconnected government failures: an inability to control spending on subsidies mainly for food and fuel, and ballooning public sector pay.

Despite the reforms of the 1990s, the 'commanding heights' of the economy were still run by government bureaucrats with a predisposition to avoid risk and bold initiatives, to defer to political pressure to hold down prices and indulge in patronage and corruption. Thus, the mainly state-owned electricity generators and transmission networks, coal supplies and the railway system remained in a perpetual state of mutually reinforcing crisis. Manmohan Singh's government repeatedly tried to wade through the political treacle which was needed to reform Indian institutions, but the political viscosity was too high. He tried also to establish a national indirect tax – the GST, a version of VAT – which would have strengthened the revenue base (India raises only 10 per cent of GDP in central government tax as against 21 per cent in China, 18 per cent in the USA and 45 per cent in the EU) and also unified India into a single market. The vested interests of states blocked his proposed reform.

Although Manmohan Singh was personally incorruptible, his ministers were not and there was a succession of scandals around the auctioning of 2G spectrum, the allocation of licences to mine coal and the 2010 Commonwealth Games – all of which he was held responsible for. As the second UPA government petered out amid disillusionment and corruption scandals, his reputation fell at home and abroad. *Time* described him as an 'underachiever'; the opposition denounced him as 'weak'.[30] In reality, the crisis exposed his political weakness rather than his weakness as an individual. He had no power base of his own. He was dependent on the support of the Congress Party chief, Sonia Gandhi, whose own authority was weakened by her tenuous dynastic link to Nehru and Indira Gandhi and her own unsavoury reputation for tolerating corruption in her political associates and her family.

Unlike Narasimha Rao, who had the self-confidence and authority to let Manmohan Singh apply economic disciplines,

Sonia Gandhi's preoccupations had been with bolstering her own, and her son Rahul's, position and maintaining a fractious coalition with powerful regional political bosses like Mamata Banerjee in West Bengal, a fierce opponent of unpopular reforms. Even modest changes like the admission of foreign-owned supermarkets or insurance companies were blocked, let alone more controversial changes like land reform, freeing up labour laws or large-scale subsidy reduction. Paralysis led to failure and the replacement of Congress by a BJP government in 2014 and a strongman leader, Narendra Modi.

The Legacy and a New Broom

Manmohan Singh's achievements and legacy can be measured against the performance of his successor, Modi. Modi had a strong electoral mandate; enthusiastic support from the business and trading community; and a record as Chief Minister of Gujarat presiding over one of the most successful, efficiently run, business-friendly and honest administrations in India.[31] The doubts centred not on his competence or lack of economic reforming commitment but on the sectarian agenda of his party: Hindu nationalist with a record of hostility to Muslims (and allegations of complicity in pogroms). That reputation has been reinforced by new citizenship legislation treating Muslim immigrants less favourably than those of other religions, by sectarian riots in early 2020 killing mainly Muslims, and by attempts to blame the Covid-19 pandemic on gatherings of Muslims.

The economic record of the BJP is mixed. Growth has averaged around 7 per cent per annum (until the Covid lockdown), one of the world's fastest among major countries – but a little less than in the Manmohan Singh era and some way off the 8–10 per cent hoped for. The fiscal deficit (of central and state governments) has remained consistently above 6 per cent of GDP and growth has been driven by rising public rather than private investment.

No progress has been made with privatization (an attempt to float Air India was abandoned). The government also quickly backed off from reforming labour markets and land acquisition laws (the latter after protests from farmers). More positively it passed a new bankruptcy law and simplified taxes. While the Central Bank Governor, Raghuram Rajan, cut inflation to 5 per cent and strengthened monetary policy, the government squandered the benefits of the latter by failing to back Rajan, who resigned. The Prime Minister also launched a highly idiosyncratic ban on high denomination notes, supposedly to stop criminal money laundering but achieving only large-scale disruption and economic damage. The new, all-India, VAT-type GST tax was at last introduced but riddled with exemptions designed to appeal to vested interests.

The BJP government has now been re-elected. It remains to be seen if it can do better and tackle the issues Manmohan Singh could not. So far, the quiet economist-turned-politician has proved to be the most effective economic policy maker India has produced. The negative interpretation of his role was that he was merely the conduit for externally imposed conditions in an economic crisis. But selling and then delivering and embedding the reforms in an essentially hostile party and country was no mean feat. Manmohan Singh was not the Deng of India; but, then, democratic India is not communist China. And it is certainly possible in the long run that the political and economic freedoms of India will be of more enduring value than China's centrally powerful but brittle system of government.

14

Balcerowicz: Big Bang Theory and Practice

The biggest economic and political transformation in modern times has been the collapse of communism in the Soviet bloc: the former Soviet Union and its Eastern European satellites. Those who were part of the process of liberating Eastern Europe from 1989 onwards were broadly united by an appetite for liberal democracy which historian Timothy Garton Ash described as 'a Western European, liberal, democratic system with a market economy based on property rights, a freely elected parliament and an independent judiciary. Something between Switzerland and Sweden.'[1]

Three decades later almost the whole of Eastern Europe has seen the adoption of a market – capitalist – economy, mostly as part of the EU or progression towards membership, though the transformation occurred at different speeds and with somewhat different outcomes in terms of living standards, quality of life and the distribution of income, wealth and opportunity. The accompanying democratization has occurred also, albeit producing political parties and government with a wide range of ideologies and commitment to political pluralism.

Poland stands out for several reasons. It is the most populous country in Eastern Europe, outside Russia, with the biggest

economy. The economic consequences of communism were especially dire and culminated in hyperinflation. In 1989–90 inflation
hit 600 per cent and the country was on its knees. Something
needed to be done. Poland adopted a 'big bang' approach to
economic transformation in 1990 and was a testing ground for
a similar strategy followed shortly afterwards by Boris Yeltsin's
Russia. And while there is still bitter argument as to whether 'economic shock therapy' is preferable to more gradual adjustment,
and over when and how it can be applied,[2] the long-term outcome was undeniably very positive in Poland's case. The country's
economy has grown without interruption – even during the global
economic crisis – for twenty-five years; faster than other countries
in Central and Eastern Europe. There have been accompanying
big improvements in living standards.

The Balcerowicz Plan was launched by a Solidarity government under Prime Minister Tadeusz Mazowiecki, but economic
direction was given by Leszek Balcerowicz (1947–) over a two-year
period as Deputy Prime Minister and Finance Minister. Balcerowicz attributed the radicalism and overall success of the programme not only to the principles of economics which he sought
to apply but also to 'extraordinary politics' which made revolutionary change possible.[3] He returned to the same offices later in the
decade to manage the economy six years on from the 'big bang'.
He owns the policy, its positive and negative impacts. I return later
to the criticisms from Naomi Klein and others that the Plan was
not authored by Balcerowicz but by Americans acting for the IMF.[4]
Klein specifically mentions Jeffrey Sachs, who vigorously denies
the claim.[5]

I proceed on the, broadly accepted, basis that Balcerowicz was
indeed the author of the eponymous Plan and likewise that he
implemented it and sold it politically. He created a political party
and an intellectual infrastructure to explain, justify and propa-
gate his ideas. He became one of the most respected practitioners
and analysts of the transition from communism with a particular

emphasis on rapid change and maintaining fiscal discipline. Lastly, his own journey – from communist to Solidarity activist to free market economist – captured the experience of his country and his contemporaries.

The Historic Legacy

It is difficult to understand the development of modern Poland and its political and economic transformation outside the context of Polish nationalism (and its link with Catholicism). For most of the 150 years until 1945 Poland did not exist as a state.[6] There was a twenty-year period of genuine independence between the world wars until Poland was dismembered by Nazi Germany and the USSR. 1945 was – at least initially – a turning point. A largely homogeneous Polish population had undivided control of a territory called Poland, albeit after the German population was expelled and new territories with a surviving Polish population added, mainly from Ukraine. Stalin's USSR was effectively in control and three years later Poland acquired a communist government. Poland became the 'Polish People's Republic' with an official Marxist-Leninist ideology.

The economic consequences of communism are best seen in three distinct phases: Stalinism; national communism; and reform communism or market socialism. Until 1956, Poland saw the imposition of a fully Stalinist model of centralized state planning with priority given to heavy industry and collectivized agriculture. But in 1956, with Nikita Khrushchev in power in the USSR, a faction within the Polish Communist Party led by Władysław Gomułka succeeded in achieving greater national autonomy and pursued a strategy of national communism which allowed decollectivization of agriculture and more trade with the West. However, attempts at partial reform based loosely on the semi-liberalized model adopted in Hungary under János Kádár after the 1956 uprising did not work.

An attempt by the party leader, Edward Gierek, to boost Polish productivity and living standards by importing, on credit, large amounts of Western machinery led to unsustainable levels of hard currency debt and no discernible improvements in the economy. Then, an attempt to achieve more realistic food prices led to widespread strikes and protests coordinated by Solidarity, based initially among workers in the shipyards but becoming a national movement for greater freedom backed by the Catholic Church. After a brief period in which Solidarity was effectively the main source of political authority, the Communist Party, through the army under General Jaruzelski, imposed martial law.

The party sought to reimpose its will, faced with a deteriorating economy as the government sought to counteract the failures of the communist system with market socialism. But it failed to stop the rot, which culminated in hyperinflation. With the Soviet Union collapsing and Gorbachev's Perestroika unable to resuscitate the failing Soviet economy, Poland also reached its terminal crisis in 1989.

The economic legacy of communism in Poland was structurally similar to that of the rest of Eastern Europe. At the end of the 1980s state ownership predominated: over 80 per cent of production (as against 95 per cent in East Germany, 65 per cent in Hungary, but only 10–15 per cent in Western Europe). The service sector was relatively small and industry much bigger than in the West (60 per cent of GDP, twice the OECD average at that time). Poland, unusually, had a relatively large peasant sector. The average firm was very big – over 1,000 employees – and the economy dominated by 3,000 state-owned firms with very few small or medium sized firms, reflecting a belief in economies of scale and lack of specialization. Living standards were low by Western standards and on a par with Argentina. This was reflected in the paucity of consumer durables and shortages of some essentials like toilet paper (though it could be argued that Poland's relative poverty long pre-dated communism and reflected low productivity in agriculture as well as the devastation of war and inter-war economic failure). But levels of income (and wealth) inequality were low and universal standards of welfare had ensured Western levels of low infant mortality and high life expectancy. There was also low unemployment, albeit with low wages and low productivity.

Apologists for the communist economic system (which included Leszek Balcerowicz, until he left the Communist Party and joined the Solidarity movement) argued that, apart from the social benefits of adequate social services for all and job security, communist planning was good at mobilizing investment resources for rapid growth and industrialization. But it became increasingly apparent that the investment was not used efficiently, dragging down productivity and living standards. Likewise, there was little or no innovation since neither workers nor managers benefited from it. Planning failed since there was every incentive to cheat by diluting quality to achieve quantity with a growing disconnect between plan and results. Lastly, heavy industry and mining had damaging environmental side effects not captured in the planning system. The public experienced these failures in shortages, which grew worse as the economy became more complex, exposing failures of coordination and lack of incentive for producers to meet the population's expectations. These problems had long dogged the communist system elsewhere and Poland was no exception.

Superimposed on the structural problems of communist economics were the failures of market socialism and reform communism to allow any escape from economic stagnation and consumer shortages.[7] Support for the radical Balcerowicz Plan was based in large part on a broad public acceptance that the system was broken and required fundamental change rather than tinkering. One of the lessons from the 1980s and earlier reforms had been that merely removing the command from the command economy and decentralizing decision making to state-owned firms was counterproductive. Managers no longer feared the consequences of non-delivery. They also had no incentive to expose themselves to painful competition and the risks of contraction and closure.

There was large-scale 'spontaneous privatization' with the theft of public assets. Corruption became endemic. Workers wanted more pay and managers had no motivation to resist since they could either pass on higher costs to consumers or rely on state subsidies to fill any deficit. Moreover, there was no incentive for workers or the management to improve productivity so there was no increase in supply to meet the increased demand generated by the higher wages. Excess demand led to both inflation and shortages. With the government funding subsidies by printing money, the ingredients were in place for runaway inflation. Inflation fed on itself to reach hyperinflationary levels defined as over 50 per cent per month, 15,000 per cent per annum.

External creditors could no longer finance an increasingly chaotic Poland and so imports dried up, aggravating consumer shortages and raw material shortages for businesses. Debt service on outstanding loans did not dry up and escalated from $25 billion in 1978 to $45 billion in 1991 without any further borrowing. Poland was in default externally, and internally inflation was out of control. The communist regime lost all credibility and when it called a referendum to impose a painful package of economic stabilization measures, including cutting subsidies, it lost. It pushed ahead anyway, which led to a sharp rise in prices, in turn fuelling unrest. The government sought accommodation with the Solidarity-based worker organizations and offered almost 100 per cent indexation of wages, which caused inflation to spiral further but did not save the government; it suffered a massive defeat in the 1989 elections.

Solidarity assumed power in coalition with two smaller parties hitherto aligned with the communists and was left to face the problems of hyperinflation, which reached 54 per cent per month (17,000 per cent per annum) in October.

'Extraordinary Politics'

A point had been reached where the deterioration in public confidence in the communist government after its repeated tries at reform fed the growth in popular support for the alternative offered by the Solidarity-led opposition.[8] It was critical to what happened next that there was broad acceptance that there was no alternative. As the Swedish economist Anders Åslund put it: 'there was no middle course… [which was] theoretically desirable, unworkable in practice'.[9] It was common ground outside the dwindling ranks of Communist Party loyalists that communism was a failure from every point of view. The economic model had survived for so long only because of repression (and previous failed uprisings). Longstanding critics of the communist system were vindicated in their view that a command economy is inherently incapable of working without political repression.[10] That realization in the period of 'extraordinary politics' in Poland brought together on a common platform those who were primarily fighting for democratic freedoms and those whose priority was a functioning economy.

Events in mid-1989 were moving very fast. The economy was in a state of collapse and the Soviet Empire was disintegrating. The Solidarity-led government was installed on 24 August and had to move quickly. This was not straightforward as the movement reflected a wide variety of opinions. The industrial workers who led it were simultaneously concerned with how to ensure that their wages were indexed against hyperinflation while giving direction and support to a new, inexperienced government. The scale of the economic challenges was without precedent: not merely the massive step of moving from a planned socialist to a market capitalist economy but against the background of hyperinflation and loss of external credit.

Comparisons have been drawn with the protected economies of Spain and Portugal before EU membership, but these were already semi-capitalist economies and they had time to prepare. Similarly, South American countries which had faced extreme inflation and debt crises in IMF-supported programmes usually had a business sector and commercial exports to build upon. China, under Deng's leadership, was moving towards a more capitalist model but gradually under Communist Party control and with the fallback position of using force to deal with dissent (as, indeed, occurred later in the year at Tiananmen Square). Perhaps the closest parallel was the emergence of West Germany from its Nazi past and the ruins of war and, indeed, Erhard was, if anyone, the role model to follow – though post-war Germany still had an efficient industrial base and a capitalist class which could be used to fuel the economy.

The Solidarity-led government needed a plan of action. Mazowiecki, the Prime Minister, was editor of the Solidarity newspaper and immersed in the politics of the movement but he had no pretensions to economic expertise. There were two economic plans on offer, both recommending a 'big bang' approach. One came from a group of economists under the leadership of Balcerowicz who had been advising Solidarity for some time. He had been a graduate and postgraduate of what is now the Warsaw School of Economics in the late 1960s and early 1970s when it was a repository of orthodox Marxist-Leninist teaching. He later moved to the Institute of Marxist-Leninism and was a member of the Communist Party throughout this period, advising the government. He participated in the main economic preoccupation of the time, which was how to make the planned economy work better by grafting on Western techniques, equipment and management systems (he spent a year at a US business school).

But after the imposition of martial law he abandoned the Communist Party, like many idealistic, educated young Poles, and became an economic expert for the pro-democracy movement based around independent trade unions. He established sufficient trust that he was asked to take on the Finance Minister role in the new government. His decade with Solidarity, liberated from the ideological constraints of communism, and interacting with Western economists, had exposed him to the main currents of Western economic thought. Much has been made, by critics, of his public acknowledgement of the influence of Milton Friedman: 'I live in a Poland that is now free and I consider Milton Friedman to be one of the main intellectual architects of my country's liberty.'[11] Friedman's belief in free markets, a monetarist approach to economic management and his insistence that economic and political freedoms go together had also been a major influence on Margaret Thatcher, on the school of economists in Chicago and represented much of the prevailing economic orthodoxy of the 1980s.

The other related plan was sketched out (in a hurry) by American economist Jeffrey Sachs who had been advising Solidarity. Sachs had built a reputation for his work in developing economies and was said to have been a key influence on the design of the 'shock therapy' programme to stabilize the hyperinflation and debt crisis in Bolivia.[12] Naomi Klein's description of the subsequent events has Sachs rather than Balcerowicz calling the shots: it was his plan (drawn up jointly with David Lipton of the IMF) which carried the day; and it was his debates with the Solidarity leadership which overcame their resistance to dramatic change and their preference for operating through workers' cooperatives towards a Scandinavian middle way.[13]

The Sachs (and Balcerowicz) interpretation of events was quite different. Their plans were essentially the same since that was what the economic situation demanded. There was no conspiracy involving investor and philanthropist George Soros, the IMF, the US government, private interests and the 'shock therapy' economists, as Klein alleged. Solidarity was not divided and bullied into abandoning its social democratic principles. Sachs argued: 'The notion of moving radically, rapidly, and decisively was strongly held by the political leadership of Solidarity.' Indeed, he argued that Solidarity forced the pace because of their determination to overcome the resistance of factory managers and communist officials in government: 'It was here that economic logic and political logic combined… radical reform was not just an economic strategy, but also a political strategy to overcome Solidarity's lack of personnel and control in the ministries.'[14] The market would make obstructive and corrupt communist apparatchiks redundant. Moreover, Solidarity had been persuaded by the experience of the 1980s that tinkering did not work; that hyperinflation had to be dealt with; and that there was a unique, unmissable opportunity to change the system, whatever the ultimate destination (be it Sweden, the US or some other variant of liberal democracy).

The government had to consider the wider public mood, not just Solidarity activists. Surveys of public opinion conducted at the time suggested a big appetite for reform because of the economic costs and instability of the crumbling communist system.[15] The government was also acutely aware that the transition would lead to anger and disillusionment and it had a limited honeymoon period – probably two years – until the next parliamentary elections – to demonstrate overall success and hope for the future. Balcerowicz himself acknowledged that he had a small window of opportunity in which 'normal politics' (consultation, discussion, debate) would not apply.[16] And he did not know how long was needed; he was strongly resistant to 'the fallacy of misplaced concreteness': predicting the end of the painful transition.[17]

On that basis, the Solidarity government empowered Balcerowicz to proceed with the Balcerowicz/Sachs Plan. It was to be launched on 1 January 1990. Events in Poland were overshadowed by the euphoria following the pulling down of the Berlin Wall (and the reaction to Tiananmen Square). But in economic policy terms, this was just as important.

The Balcerowicz Plan

There were several elements to the Plan which depended on each other, though they varied in the immediacy of introduction and impact. The immediate priority was stabilization to stop hyper-inflation, which required firstly drastically reducing the subsidies which underlay the large budget deficit, and secondly tightening the money supply, a key element of which was credit to keep industry afloat. These measures interacted strongly with the second imme-diate step, which was to lift most price controls, a consequence of cuts in subsidies, and also providing the main mechanism for a mar-ket economy to operate. There were some exceptions, such as rents and temporary wage controls under an incomes policy designed to break the cycle of 'wage push' inflation, whereby increasing wages led to increased prices and ever higher wages, etc.

To ensure that prices were meaningful and reflected genuine costs and efficiency rather than domestic monopoly positions, trade was rapidly liberalized to establish competition based on a benchmark of international prices. Sachs claims that this was a crucial, distinctive step making Polish transformation quite dif-ferent from the gradual trade liberalization experienced under market reform in developing economies ('the importance of rapid trade liberalization in the Polish reforms cannot be under-stated'[18]). To complete this list of Day 1 measures, the currency was devalued to enable the newly liberalized Polish enterprises to compete internationally and the currency was made fully convert-ible. There was to be no more 'soft currency' trade with the rest of Eastern Europe based on artificial exchange rates that bore no relation to their underlying value alongside 'hard currency' trade with the West.

Along with these immediate 'shock' measures there were to be longer-term, deeper reforms. Privatization was a key objective but there were 3,000 large state-owned firms (as against fifty in Mrs Thatcher's Britain). To ease the transition Poland needed external help and set about negotiating an IMF loan and the cancellation of around half the outstanding official debt. And to reduce the impact on workers affected by the inevitable painful restructuring there was a new system of unemployment compensation and a redirection of some of the money saved by cutting subsidies to the most vulnerable. There were the beginnings of the inevitably long and complex process of establishing a new legal system based on commercial contracts and property rights with reliable institutions affecting all economic behaviour: in the words of Hungarian economist János Kornai, 'under Communism allocation is by political criteria… [under capitalism] by market relations'.[19]

The short-term impact was both positive and negative. Shops were promptly full of a wide variety of goods. Overnight, shortages, queues and rationing disappeared. But the price levels surged by 80 per cent in two weeks, though they then stabilized with monthly inflation of 77 per cent in January, 16 per cent in February and 4.5 per cent in March. Farmers initially hoarded stocks of food but then started to sell in the cities, improving availability and reducing inflation.

The budget turned rapidly from deficit (7 per cent) in 1989 to surplus (3 per cent) in 1990 as subsidies were cut and tax revenues rose. Exports boomed (45 per cent in 1990) and there was large-scale registration of private firms (71,000 in just over two years). But austerity cut deep not just into industrial subsidies but also into health and education spending.

Who bore the pain? The figures suggest that a combination of rapidly rising prices and wage controls cut real incomes of workers by a third between 1989 and 1990 (though only 7 per cent below 1987 levels). The much-increased availability and quality of goods, and the absence of queuing, suggest, however, a much smaller negative impact. Industrial production fell by between 35 per cent to 40 per cent but a lot of this was unsustainable heavy industry and ignores the rapid growth in services, which had been previously undersupplied. And, most conspicuously, recorded unemployment rose to 13 per cent in 1991 (and again to 16.4 per cent in 1993) as firms were forced into productivity improvements to survive (it was already around 6 per cent before the 'shock' and, before the Plan, pessimists had predicted a rise in unemployment to 25 or 40 per cent[20]). Overall the economy declined by 20 per cent over two years (12 per cent in 1990; 8 per cent in 1991) before starting to recover.

For a while, Balcerowicz became cordially hated by the millions who opposed and/or suffered from his Plan. There was a popular clamour that 'Balcerowicz must go' orchestrated by one of the many opposition parties which had mushroomed in the new democracy. And his – initial – political career did not last long. He lost his patron, Prime Minister Mazowiecki, after he was defeated by Lech Wałęsa in a presidential election in 1990. Balcerowicz left his posts – Finance Minister and Deputy Prime Minister – after just over two years in office. But, by then, the major objectives of the 'big bang' had already been achieved.

How Successful was the Big Bang?

Some Polish critics of Balcerowicz's economic policy denounced it as 'unduly cruel'[21] and Naomi Klein treats it as a brutal example of 'disaster capitalism'.[22] But 'unduly' relative to what? 'Brutal' relative to what alternative? In 1989 there was no portfolio of attractive alternative options to choose from. There was, among economic policy makers, a deference to Mrs Thatcher's friend TINA (There Is No Alternative). The collapse of communism was a unique event and Poland made the big jump from communism before the rest of the Soviet bloc and so became the testing ground for policies tried elsewhere.

Any evaluation of the 'big bang' also has to take into account the time frame of the comparison. After two years, when Balcerowicz was personally directing the 'big bang', there were spectacular gains from the emergence of a free market economy but also big

negatives in lost incomes, unemployment and their social consequences. But, after two years, privatization of state enterprises
had scarcely begun, capitalism had only just started to take root
and there were deep problems around structural unemployment
and distribution yet to address. Now, we have the benefit of thirty
years of hindsight.

Comparisons with the rest of the post-communist Soviet bloc
are not straightforward since each country had a different history
and economic structure. Anders Åslund concludes his comparative review by noting that the biggest initial shocks and costs were
experienced where the initial conditions were worst, 'in terms of
macroeconomic imbalance, foreign indebtedness, structural distortions, level of economic development'.[23] The smallest impact
was felt in Hungary and the Czech Republic (16–18 per cent drop
in GDP from peak to trough) – though in Slovakia, the other part
of the former Czechoslovakia, the experience was more severe
– Poland next (20 per cent), then Romania (30 per cent) and Bulgaria (40 per cent).

Comparative experience also tells us something about the
relative merits of 'shock therapy' versus gradualism in the form
of Polish/Czech radicalism versus Balkan gradualism. The key
argument for gradualism is that restructuring, involving large
job losses, is less traumatic for the workforce when there is time
to retrain and develop new skills. More generally, even economist
Joseph Schumpeter – the proponent of creative destruction –
agreed that 'economic institutions must develop organically and
cannot be transplanted'.[24] That lesson has been demonstrated by
the failure of many structural adjustment programmes in Latin
America and Africa (or Russia) where the legal and trust basis of
a market economy has been slow to take root. French economist
Olivier Blanchard explains the importance of what he calls a state
of 'disorganization' when the collapse of central planning under
'shock therapy' destroys the trust which had been built up between
suppliers on a bilateral basis; a sudden collapse often leads not

to stable market relationships but to opportunistic 'rent seeking' including a lot of outright corruption. Blanchard concludes, carefully, that he has not 'come up with a simple judgement as to whether big-bang policies are better than gradualism'.[25]

The counterargument, the basis of the Balcerowicz Plan and variants of it adopted by Yegor Gaidar in Yeltsin's Russia and Václav Klaus in the Czech Republic, rested on two simple, intuitively sensible propositions: first, there may not be the luxury of time in a major crisis with a collapsing communist economy; second, if there is to be pain, it is better to get it over with quickly to avoid losing the patience of the public. This conclusion is reinforced by more sophisticated economic arguments. When there is extreme inflation it is necessary to break expectation of further inflation. To achieve this entrepreneurs have to face a 'hard' budget constraint without reliance on continued subsidies and unsustainable government deficits.[26] And the parallel liberalization of prices has to be seen as 'one-off'. So, a combination of severe monetary and fiscal discipline alongside price liberalization is required. And politically this is easier to sustain if the public is prepared and if there is a real sense of urgency. A further point, based on the Polish experience, is that the swift establishment of a market economy is easier if there is simultaneous trade liberalization to establish real competition and to break supply bottlenecks. All of this argues for a consistent set of market-based policies which is seen as having momentum and being irreversible.

On the balance of the evidence, Richard Layard, a social democrat, concludes: 'It does seem that the worst place to be is in-between capitalism and communism, and the best policy is to hasten through that phase as rapidly as possible.'[27] An interagency study of transition concedes that 'ideally, a path of gradual reform could be laid out which would minimize economic disturbance and lead to an early harvesting of the fruits of increased economic efficiency. But we know of no such path.'[28]

The success of the 'big bang' cannot simply be judged in terms of economists' judgements but through the eyes of the public on whose behalf the reforms were conducted. The arrival of democracy meant that there was recourse to the ballot box and frequent, well-publicized, opinion surveys. The latter showed that 'Poles greeted the Balcerowicz Plan with a high degree of support and acceptance... acceptance lay not so much in public acceptance of how market mechanisms work but rather in the belief that the market economy was the opposite of "real socialism".'[29]

In 1991, two years after the launch of the iconic Plan, Solidarity leaders retained overall approval. Mazowiecki had a 59 per cent favourability rating. There was less enthusiasm for Balcerowicz – with 46 per cent favourable and 44 per cent unfavourable – but, still, there was a small net positive. The public expressed a strong preference for gradual reform (75 per cent) rather than radical change (12 per cent) and this no doubt accounts for slippage in support for Solidarity in parliamentary elections. However, the Solidarity coalition retained power (under a new Prime Minister and Finance Minister).

Two years later, in 1993, there was a second year of strong growth but unemployment peaked at 16.4 per cent and real wages were still declining (albeit with better quality and more abundant goods and services). The public was running out of patience. Although 37 per cent thought life was 'better in general', the majority did not. Elections in that year swept out the Solidarity government and there was a period of unstable coalitions dominated by the 'social democrats' (SLD) who were mainly drawn from ex-communists. But even four years is too short a time to judge the overall success of the reform project.

Longer-Term Success

In economic terms, Poland has gone from strength to strength. Over the thirty-year period from 1989 to 2019, Poland grew at an average rate of over 3 per cent, much the fastest of any post-

Soviet era economy. Even during the global financial crisis of 2008, then the Eurozone crisis, Poland continued to grow. The consequent improvement in living standards has led to Poland being reclassified by the World Bank as a high-income country.

One reason for this success was that the momentum of the radical reforms was sustained despite more sceptical politicians being elected. Having external support helped. The IMF extended two big loans despite Poland being in default on its debts. Creditors, notably Germany, reacted calmly to Poland's unilateral refusal to service its debt and half the debt was written off. Then, Poland joined the European Union in 2004, which provided market opportunities for Polish businesses (and Poles who wanted to seek work abroad), access to structural funds and support for hitherto disadvantaged agriculture.

In order for success to be embedded and for Poland to flourish in the competitive European Single Market it was necessary for a generation of entrepreneurs to emerge. There was a rapid growth of new Polish small firms (building on the entrepreneurial base of privatized agriculture). But the process of restructuring large-scale enterprises took place, initially, in state-owned firms, many of which adapted very quickly under pressure of competition.[30] Some became successful exporters (by 1991 only 20 per cent of Poland's trade was with Eastern Europe and the USSR). Many of these firms had oversight from workers' councils, which helped to obtain cooperation but made agreement on ownership more difficult. Much time and money were wasted on British-style privatizations which enriched consultants but made painfully slow progress. Eventually a lot of privatization occurred through investment funds, with shares owned in varying degrees by workers and the general public. Enterprises based on this kind of mixed ownership are now well established in domestic and international markets.

The main political and social problem has been unemployment especially among older, less mobile workers. The post-shock unemployment rose to a peak of 16.4 per cent in 1993 and then fell back to 10.6 per cent in 1998. There was a big push to help the long-term unemployed. By 1999 only about a third of the un-employed had been out of work for over a year. But slowing growth at the turn of the millennium took unemployment up again to just under 20 per cent in 2002. It declined to single figures in 2007 and eventually to 3.8 per cent in 2018, below the EU average. The earlier figures understate the seriousness of the problem since it was concentrated in some depressed regions. Moreover, many young Poles moved overseas, especially to the UK, looking for work. By 2018 about 2.5 million were working abroad. Since then, the process has gone into reverse. For the first time, in 2018, almost 100,000 (net) returned to Poland attracted by growing labour shortages and much-improved pay (and Brexit in the UK). Furthermore, Poland itself was attracting immigration, notably from Ukraine. The unemployment problem has now largely gone but for almost twenty years a generation was scarred by it.

Critics of reform also point to other groups of losers. Farm-ers appeared to fare relatively badly with the opening of markets. Pensioners had their pensions indexed at great cost to the budget (and were, therefore, better protected than workers) but other groups dependent on benefits were hit. Surveys conducted in 1999, almost a decade after the reforms, showed that 52 per cent felt that the economic situation was better off, 40 per cent felt it was worse off. With regards to the political system 59 per cent said things had improved and 40 per cent thought the opposite. There were roughly equal numbers who thought 'life in general' was bet-ter or worse.[31] But the mere fact that democracy was thriving and popular suggests that one of the main arguments against 'shock therapy' – that it destabilizes democracy – had no force.

These public attitudes, optimistic on balance only by the end of the millennium and with many negatives, influenced politics. By 1995 the political backlash led to Lech Wałęsa being ousted in presidential elections by the former communist Aleksander

Kwaśniewski. As the economy recovered, the ex-communists' SLD – then in power – claimed the credit. In 1997 only 28 per cent of the public credited the Solidarity parties with recovery; 22 per cent credited the SLD; 27 per cent gave both sets of parties equal credit for recovery. The SLD built a political platform based on acceptance of the market reforms (while denouncing Balcerowicz for the speed and cruelty of his Plan), pressing ahead with negotiations on EU membership and shifting the emphasis of privatization towards more state involvement: essentially, a social democratic programme.

But the arguments between political parties were not primarily between proponents and opponents of the market economy. There is little opposition to the idea of a market economy modelled on the advanced systems of the West. Rather, the core of the debate has been over the distribution of losses and gains from market reforms and increasingly on the role of the state in the economy.[32]

The SLD in turn succumbed to centre-right parties drawing on social conservatism linked to the Catholic Church. A big political gap has opened up not between the old left and right but between the more liberal (and European) cities and the socially conservative and nationalistic countryside and small towns. In the jostling between competing philosophies, Balcerowicz founded his own liberal, free market, party, the Freedom Union, and, as part of a governing coalition, returned as Deputy Prime Minister and Finance Minister from 1997 to 2000 before moving to head up the central bank where he oversaw economic management through the period of global financial crisis (and a surge in Polish unemployment).

In summarizing Balcerowicz's contribution, he was an economist trying to apply economic principles in a uniquely difficult political and economic context. His Plan moving Poland from a planned to a market economy must be judged a considerable success overall, though historians and economists will continue to argue as to whether the process could have been managed better to minimize the costs and casualties. His success hinged on his engaging with the politics, understanding that, in Layard's words, 'the problem of reform is mostly political rather than social or even economic'.[33] And as Sachs added: 'Any meaningful strategy and set of tactics for reform must take into account the political minefield, not just as an aside but as the very centrepiece of thinking about change.'[34]

15

Abe: Japan Pioneers Abenomics

The usual, somewhat condescending, economic cliché about Japan was that it was a country catching up with the West. It did so with spectacular effect in the nineteenth century when the architects of the Meiji restoration ushered in a remarkable period of economic transformation from a large feudal society to a modern industrial state in a little more than a generation.[1] It did so again after the Second World War, initially under US occupation and then as a democratic state, when it progressed from being a defeated and physically destroyed country to the status of 'the emerging Japanese superstate',[2] the world's second biggest economy, again in just over a generation. It was widely predicted at the time that Japan would overtake the US and became 'number one'.[3]

Then, dramatically, a major financial crisis in 1989 brought the economy to a shuddering halt and threatened depression, let alone recession. The party seemed to be over. There was a 'lost decade' – in fact, over two – of economic stagnation. The world forgot about Japan and discovered China, the Eurozone and the newly liberated Soviet bloc (and India). But some Japanese policy makers came to understand sooner than anyone else the nature of the crisis which had derailed their economy and which would hit the rest of the world almost two decades later.[4]

Financial crises are not unusual; one author estimates there have been 147 between 1980 and 2011 alone, starting with the East Asian crisis and the milder banking crisis in Scandinavia, leading to the global crisis in 2008.[5] The Japanese crisis was unduly severe and the three decades since have provided a laboratory for policy experiment. There has been a prolonged post-bubble malaise in Japan. But by accident and design, trial and error, Japan evolved policies to deal with balance sheet recession ahead of the rest of the world and managed to survive the global crisis and its aftermath with little by way of falling living standards and unemployment.

The Japanese also, by necessity, had to find a solution to a problem which is creeping up on Europe, China and other countries: the demographic challenge of ageing, causing a declining population and workforce. Japan is leading the world in finding creative answers to the economic and social impacts of an ageing population.[6]

Political leadership has been supplied by the Prime Minister, Shinzō Abe (1954–). But the nature of Japanese decision making in the political world tends towards consensus and the collective. Tall poppies invite decapitation. Leading political figures usually have limited power and reflect the balance of power between factions in the ruling party – usually the Liberal Democratic Party (LDP) – or wider coalition.[7] Mr Abe's ownership of Abenomics is perhaps flattering to him and unfair to his Finance Minister, and a predecessor, Tarō Asō, who got to the same policy ideas rather sooner; or indeed to the anonymous huddle of post-crisis ministers and advisers who – perhaps for the wrong reasons or by chance – alighted on a policy formula which has saved Japan from economic collapse, declining living standards and high unemployment.

Abenomics is the public face and personalization of an economic strategy summarized in the imagery of 'three arrows': monetary and fiscal expansion together with structural reform.

The most striking feature of it is the acceptance of further fiscal, alongside monetary, expansion for a country whose public debt levels (debt to GDP) are already – at over 200 per cent of GDP – the highest by far in the developed world.

Now, Japan has been hit, like the rest of the world, by the Covid-19 pandemic. Japan appears to have managed the health impacts far better than most Western countries, despite the demands of the Olympics – and has tried to minimize the economic consequences. Nonetheless, there has been an economic recession and a need for stimulus. Public debt has risen to even more extreme levels and this will seriously test Japan's willingness to push the boundaries of unorthodox fiscal and monetary policy even further. The crisis will test severely the skills of Mr Abe's successors and the durability of Abenomics.

The Build-up to the Financial Crisis

Abenomics emerged from the financial crisis which hit Japan in 1989. It arose from a massive speculative bubble which in turn was a result of attempts to liberalize the post-war economy. The rapid post-war recovery of Japan took place in parallel with that of Germany, but it happened in a totally different way. The German *Wirtschaftswunder* was launched on the back of Erhard's liberal economic reforms. The economics of National Socialism was ditched along with almost every other aspect of Nazi rule. By contrast, in Japan, the economy remained on a war footing albeit with American agreement. The rough Japanese equivalent of Albert Speer, the Minister of Armaments and War Production in Nazi Germany, Ichirō Hatoyama, led the LDP into its first post-war election and, despite being barred from office by the Americans for complicity in war crimes, later became Prime Minister.

The economy of post-war Japan resembled, in many ways, wartime Japan and was overseen by many of the same officials. Likewise, business was dominated by the same companies.

Together they perpetuated a highly regulated system with strong cartels and an absence of takeovers, preserving the profitability and freedom from competition of the leading companies. There were credit controls targeting resources on particular companies or sectors, job security providing lifetime employment, and a system of top-down planning (but without micromanagement). Companies concentrated on growth rather than profitability. Households were encouraged to save, and their savings provided the capital for business investment on a large scale.

This model proved highly successful in peacetime. Large companies, the zaibatsu, motivated by a search for growth and market share, and largely protected by cartels from competitive domestic rivals, became formidably competitive in international markets. The key government departments – Finance, Trade and Industry, and the Bank of Japan – stood behind the industrial economy and ensured that exports received maximum help and imports were minimized: a classic mercantilist economy. Successive waves of export-based industrial expansion took place featuring steel and shipbuilding, cars, consumer electronics, and then higher technology. In each case, Japanese competition was sufficiently powerful to displace Western rivals in what was still a largely open trading system (except in Japan itself).

This was the system of organization popularly known as Japan Inc. Some Western observers sought to interpret the system in terms of cultural stereotypes and the 'Japanese mind',[8] though others have pointed out that Japan in the pre-war era had been much closer to the model of Anglo-Saxon free market capitalism.[9] Whatever it was, it was spectacularly successful; there was annual double-digit growth throughout the 1950s and 1960s. The strategy was not only successful but became a model for others – Korea, Taiwan and in due course China. Finance professor Michael Pettis summed up the model as: systematically undervalued currencies, relatively low wage growth and financial repression in which the state allocates credit and forces interest rates below equilibrium level.[10]

The extraordinary success of Japanese export-led industrialization began to have an impact on the world economy. By 1970 Japan's economy had overtaken West Germany's to become the world's second biggest economy and GDP had almost tripled in size in the preceding decade. There was full employment and a high level of equality. But there were also growing external imbalances: of OECD's overall trade surpluses in 1971 of $7.4 billion, $5.8 billion was accounted for by Japan and had its counterpart in deficits elsewhere as in the USA and UK. The more forward-looking Japanese officials, who appreciated that the 'war economy' model was not sustainable and acceptable to Japan's allies, especially the USA, started to consider remedies including revaluation of the yen.[11]

In the event, revaluation was effectively forced on Japan by the collapse of the fixed exchange rate system in 1971. There was, however, strong resistance by exporters, whose sponsors in government persuaded the Bank of Japan to boost money supply, driving down market interest rates and limiting the degree of currency revaluation (essentially, by increasing the supply of yen relative to dollars). As a result, the Japanese model survived largely unchanged. But monetary stimulus from the Bank of Japan – to keep the yen from appreciating too far and to provide domestic demand to replace export demand – went too far and the results gave some indication of what was to happen later on a much bigger scale.

There was a boost to land prices – by 50 per cent between 1972 and 1974 – and to the stock market (almost doubling in value in a year) since firms were fully invested and instead used low interest bank loans to buy shares for speculative purposes, pushing up asset prices. Asset inflation spilled over into wider inflation and the oil shock of 1974 pushed up prices further. Wholesale inflation reached 37 per cent in 1974 and consumer inflation was just over 25 per cent. The Bank of Japan slammed on the brakes and precipitated a recession; industrial production fell 20 per cent between late 1973 and early 1975. Unemployment rose rapidly. Asset prices tumbled. The economy recovered, however, in response to a fiscal stimulus and low interest rates: sufficient to prevent any fundamental rethinking of the 'war economy' and the mobilization of resources behind industrial exports.

The 1980s entailed more of the same: exporters had responded to the currency revaluation and rising domestic costs by upgrading the quality and sophistication of their products; imports remained tightly controlled except for raw materials. Japan continued to run large trade surpluses. The 'miracle' continued, now sustained by productivity improvements as well as sheer volume. Moreover, the freeing up of global capital movements, including in and out of Japan, meant that the large excess of Japanese savings was free to find more profitable outlets overseas. Since capital outflows are balanced by current account surpluses, there was an apparently stable model in which Japan exported both its goods and savings to the rest of the world (as China was to do later).

The underlying characteristic of Japan's economy has been a very high propensity to save (rather than spend), a frugality which is deep rooted and perhaps has its origins both in war psychology and in a need to save for old age. There was an average 16 per cent personal savings rate over 1961–90 (in 1990 the savings rate was 15 per cent, 6 per cent in the USA). Gross savings including of the corporate variety were around double that level. Much of this saving was (and is) channelled into productive investment, which has led to strong productivity growth in industry, enhancing competitiveness. The savings surplus over domestic investment was exported and took the form of overseas acquisitions and also greenfield investment by Japanese companies which enabled them to maintain their market share overseas without the need to export from Japan (the Japanese car plants and consumer electronics factories which appeared in the UK and USA in the 1980s were a manifestation of this phenomenon). Net outflow of capital grew from $10 billion in 1981 to $137 billion in 1987, though much of this was portfolio investment in overseas shares and purchase of bonds – buying US government securities, helping to finance the US deficit under Reagan. The remainder of the current account surplus was absorbed in the accumulation of foreign exchange reserves (that is, dollar and other leading currencies and gold).

Japan's big current account surplus had several consequences for the way the economy was managed. Foreigners regarded the yen as a strong currency and bought yen, pushing up the exchange rate, which appreciated from ¥240 to the dollar in 1985 to ¥130 in 1988. Appreciation undermined export competitiveness and also cut domestic inflation (since imports were now cheaper in terms of yen) and the central bank worried that Japan was under-shooting its inflation target, requiring lower interest rates and monetary expansion. Also, the US and other Western countries were seriously concerned about Japanese surpluses, which they equated with job losses at home, and pressed for Japan to open up to imports by deregulating its economy, including the controls on lending, which they also believed underpinned the export machine of the 'war economy'. The cumulative effect of these pressures was to greatly increase the availability of bank loans. Credit was cheap and abundant.

What were Japanese business and financial institutions to do with access to all this cheap credit? One option was to borrow to invest in real estate and shares which had already generated spectacular returns. The index of real estate prices in the six biggest cities had risen from 100 in 1955 to 4,100 in the mid-1970s to 5,800 in 1980. The main Tokyo share index had appreciated from 100 in 1949 to 6,000 by the early 1980s to 40,000 by 1989. So, companies used their access to credit to speculate. Specialist companies doing little else flourished on the stock market. As long as the prices of these assets rose faster than the interest on the loans there was money to be made. Values became ridiculous. Land (which inflated with real estate) in central Tokyo was worth a million times more than the average land price in California. The grounds surrounding the royal palace were (in theory) valued at more than the whole of California.[12]

Japan was in the grip of a speculative mania in which investors came to believe that asset prices, and the value of their investments, could only go up. From tulip bulbs in seventeenth-century Holland and the South Sea Bubble in eighteenth-century Britain to mining in South America in the 1820s and the Wall Street Crash in 1929, economic history has a long record of speculative bubbles followed by crashes.[13] In this case the problem was exacerbated by the fact that the speculative bubble was fed not so much by individuals gambling with their savings but by companies and financial institutions investing money which was often borrowed. A balance sheet crisis was looming since the liabilities would remain whatever happened, but the value of assets rested precariously on markets continuing to rise in value.

The obvious question, posed after every crash but rarely before it, is why no one saw it coming. The Japanese economy had already experienced a boom and bust cycle fifteen years earlier with a very painful recession hangover. Surely someone should have seen that something was wrong? Why was credit allowed to expand at 15 per cent per annum in the 1980s when the economy was growing at 6 per cent per annum? That is easy to say in hindsight but most bubbles (including the build-up of house prices in the Western world in the run-up to 2008) are not seen as such at the time. In Japan, the senior economic officials and ministers were still – as described above – preoccupied by the problem of how to prevent the yen from rising to the point of creating serious pain for exporters.[14] The same people were seeking to steer Japan away from the war economy model and towards a more market-based system (and subject to strong peer group pressure from their opposite numbers in the USA, the OECD, the IMF and the G7). And who was to say that the markets for land and shares were 'wrong' when the prevailing intellectual orthodoxy – this was the time of Thatcher and Reagan – was that markets were 'efficient' and better at allocating resources than governments?

Some economic indicators were genuinely confusing. There was full employment, labour shortage and, apparently, a booming economy while inflation was close to zero and tending to deflation. Neither Keynesian nor monetarist economists could easily explain the fact that Japan seemed to have produced a 'miracle economy' without unemployment or inflation (rapid productivity growth is part of the explanation; also, the combination of a strong currency and falling raw material prices). As the economist Robert Shiller would later point out: 'Japan had troubled economists for a while. It seemed to defeat the cherished tenet of classical economics that only free markets can lead to economic success. Japan was obviously full of regulations, cartels and the obstacles to trade and competition... It should have been an economic disaster zone... Economists could not make head or tail of Japan's strange economy.'[15] Japanese politicians from the ruling LDP, basking in public approval and the envy and admiration of foreigners, saw no problem either. They left economic management to the 'experts'. But there was a problem, as there was on the *Titanic*: an iceberg ahead.

The iceberg was the bubble in asset prices, fed by speculation. Although there is a well-chronicled history of economic bubbles and crashes, there was not, until recently, a well-developed exploration of how and why they occur and how to manage them. There certainly does not seem to have been much by way of discussion of the issue in Japan – before the crash.

Robert Shiller received a Nobel Prize for explaining how stock markets are not necessarily 'efficient' markets, which incorporate all available information, but are driven by emotion and fashion rather than economic logic. As with fashion, people buy stocks in part because they see other people buying them and do not want to miss out on a new craze. Then the market bursts because fashion changes. A comprehensive explanation of boom and bust came from Hyman Minsky, whose work was only acknowledged after the 2008 global crisis and was largely ignored before.[16] Minsky explained how capitalist economies progress from cautious to daring to reckless behaviour through banks lending against property based on a bet that house prices will continue to rise and that interest rates will remain low enough to service the loans. When the boom in housing prices takes off it is possible to make capital gains and others want to join in and not miss the opportunity to make money. The more is lent out, the more prices rise, creating a self-fulfilling boom in prices. Minsky called this lending 'Ponzi finance' after the infamous financier who made a fortune from swindling innocent investors in pyramid calling schemes. When the market stops rising, investors want their money back and the sale of houses drives down the price. Investors panic and more sell. Eventually the panic affects the real economy and stops new investment, leading to recession.

This is essentially what happened in Japan. The bubble burst. Japanese officials and politicians knew nothing of Shiller and Minsky. But what is extraordinary about the Japanese story is how they then improvised a response which, while it did not avert recession and stagnation, did avert what could have been the mother of all crashes. They then developed a new way of thinking about post-crash economics ahead of the rest of the world – what we now call Abenomics.

Boom and Bust

The peak of the Japanese asset bubble, centring on real estate and land prices, was in 1989. Banks had reached the stage of aggressively pursuing customers, with offers of loans. Property was seen as good collateral even though prices, especially the underlying price of land, were unrealistically inflated in value. More lending pushed up the price of property and land prices further and banks started lending against expected increases in price which they themselves were creating. Then, in the middle of 1989, the Bank of Japan under a new governor, Yasushi Mieno, called a halt. Credit was tightened. Speculators, who could see that the peak had been reached, sold to realize their gains, starting a stampede to quit the market. Share prices fell 32 per cent in 1990 alone, 30 per cent again in 1991. Land prices collapsed much more in some areas. Some speculators went bust creating bad loans for the banks, which responded by curbing lending, aggravating the fall in asset prices. Banks also cut their lending to small and medium sized firms – a credit crunch – which led to closures, unemployment, a fall in consumption, and recession. Households tightened their belts to offset the loss of (paper) wealth. Companies switched their attention to exports again, setting off a new round of current account surpluses and currency appreciation.

The impact of the crash, however, was not as dramatic as it could have been. The plunge in asset wealth was the biggest in history: 300 per cent of Japanese GDP. In the US in the 1929 crash it was a mere 100 per cent of US GDP. The US crash led to a catastrophic fall in the real economy – by almost 30 per cent from peak to trough and cumulatively by around 120 per cent of GDP over eight years – and the Japanese crash would have been, on a proportional basis, three times bigger.[17] The scale of unemployment and impoverishment would have been so savage as to be barely comprehensible. Nevertheless, it did not happen and was far less dramatic than the 1930s in the USA (or, even, in the aftermath of the most recent banking crisis).

Monetary policy helped as official interest rates were slashed to zero – in what would be a forerunner to the response to the 2008 financial crisis. But the key was an aggressive fiscal policy with big deficits and rising government debt, which helped to stimulate and stabilize the economy. The sponsors of this policy were unlikely heroes. Richard Koo, the economist who has done most to explain Abenomics to the rest of the world, observed that these heroes were vote-seeking politicians of the ruling Liberal Democratic Party who recommended that government stimulate the economy by repairing and building infrastructure.[18] Government spending rose from ¥40 trillion in 1980 to ¥70 trillion in 1990 and then to ¥90 trillion in 2000; government revenues rose from ¥27 trillion in 1980 to ¥60 trillion in 1990 but fell after that so a big gap opened up between spending and revenue. Koo observed that 'it was a miracle made possible by government spending'[19] and 'one of the most successful fiscal policies in human history'.[20] Effectively the government 'bought' ¥2,250 trillion of production with a ¥460 trillion stimulus (i.e. the cumulative totals of government deficits). Japan appeared to have recovered on the back of an (unplanned) fiscal stimulus and a drive to export more.

The Lingering Sickness

By the mid-1990s, the Japanese economy was still far from normal, however. Interest rates were still very low and a lot of non-performing loans still sat on the balance sheets of banks and corporates. But what worried the policy makers, and attracted criticism of the OECD and IMF among others, was the vast amount of public debt which had been accumulated. The ratio of public debt to GDP had risen from 20 per cent to 70 per cent after the 1970s crisis but increased to 220 per cent after the 1989–90 bubble burst and the fiscal stimulus (financed by government borrowing) of the early 1990s. Such levels of debt are common after wars (when survival takes precedence over budget constraints) but are very unusual in peacetime.

In fact, there was no particular need to worry, let alone panic. With very low interest rates on government bonds the debt could be serviced. And, unlike the Latin Americans in the early 1980s and Southern Europeans in the post-2008 Eurozone crisis, the Japanese government did not depend on the 'kindness of strangers' for marketing its debt, but on its own citizens. It could borrow in its own currency. There was no risk of a 'bond strike' by the markets or a run on the currency. Nonetheless, public debt was seen as a problem. It has to be serviced and eventually repaid. Moreover, the Japanese public were concerned about reports that the government was wasting their money. 'Bridges to nowhere' and road projects, built at the request of (sometimes corrupt) politicians in the ruling party, became a scandal. The big spenders in government were not seen by the public as economic heroes but as sleazy and incompetent, not helped by known links between gangsters (*yakuza*) and the ruling party.

The ruling party was thrown out for the first time since the Second World War but, after a brief period in opposition, it returned chastened and committed to more puritanical habits. The government raised taxes and cut spending in 1997. The economy was plunged into another severe recession which aggravated rather than improved the public finances. The recession prompted another banking crisis as asset prices fell (land prices dropped by over 50 per cent), damaging further the balance sheets of many companies and leading to many bankruptcies. The explanation subsequently given by Koo and others was that Japan was still in balance sheet recession in 1997. Companies were still overwhelmingly concerned with paying down debt out of their profits. They depended on government to expand demand to boost the value of their assets and to help generate profits to restore their solvency. Yet, now, the government was doing the opposite. Japan staggered through a double-dip recession.

The Bank of Japan had another idea: to stimulate the economy without aggravating the public debt problem using monetary policy. Interest rates were already at zero; so, something else was needed. In 2001 Quantitative Easing (QE) was launched in Japan. QE – the purchase of government bonds – by the central bank solved two problems at once. It forced down long-term interest rates (the reverse of higher bond prices) increasing the attractiveness of business investment. And it expanded money supply (since banks received cash in return for bonds and could lend out the cash).

Although Japan initiated what was to become the main policy instrument for stimulating Western economies, it did not, in the event, do much to help Japan. Companies were not tempted by the low cost of capital to invest since investment had lower priority than paying down debt. As long as liabilities (from the days of the crash) exceeded the value of assets there was a reluctance to invest. And so, the Japanese economy limped along with low growth and with no obvious escape from the trap of having, seemingly, reached the limit of monetary and fiscal policy. Various 'structural' reforms were attempted to make markets work better, but without obvious result.

Then came the global financial crisis and with it the realization that the problems which Japan had been struggling with for a decade and a half now affected all Western economies. Cometh the hour, cometh the man (or men). Japan's rather colourless political class, which had hitherto largely left economic policy to the experts, produced a couple of leading political figures who were willing to learn from the past and try something different: Asō and Abe.

The Politicians Take the Stage

Japan is a democracy with a competitive party system but, until recently, political leadership has been less important than policy consensus among the officials in key government economic departments. For most of the post-war era, Japanese government has been dominated by the Liberal Democratic Party and its allies, loosely characterized as 'centre right' with occasional interludes for a socialist-led government in the mid-1990s and another 'centre-left' government from 2009 to 2012 (in both cases following the onset of a financial crisis). Japanese Prime Ministers generally have very short periods in office – there have been twenty-nine since the war and only three – Nakasone in the early 1980s, Koizumi in the early 2000s, and then Abe – have lasted more than a couple of years. Factional power struggles as well as frequent elections have prevented the development of stable political leadership (in contrast to the 'long termism' which characterizes much of Japanese business). Until Abe, none had the time or, apparently, the inclination to develop an economic vision for the country since, despite the episodes of boom and bust, Japan was doing well enough.

An economic vision had to be anchored in Japanese politics. The Japanese electorate clearly does value and reward economic competence and punishes apparent incompetence. The Liberal Democratic government enjoyed forty-five years of uninterrupted rule on the back of the 'miracle' economy. Then, after the collapse of the bubble, the opposition parties came to power (in 1993) but after three years of floundering, unable to put together a stable coalition let alone an economic policy, the LDP and its own coalition returned for another thirteen years. They were in turn unseated after the 2008 crisis and economic collapse for another three-year interlude until Abe was able to form a stable LDP government around his economic package. In Japan, politicians have learned the force of the Clinton slogan 'It's the economy, stupid'.

Shinzō Abe, the creator of Abenomics, and his Finance Minister and predecessor Tarō Asō have the biographies of typical LDP politicians. Abe came from a political family with a great-uncle who was one of the early post-war Prime Ministers (Eisaku Satō), a grandfather who was a Class A war criminal suspect and a mother who was the daughter of another leading wartime and post-war politician. Apart from short periods in the US and in business, he progressed rapidly through government and parliamentary roles to lead his faction in the party. He progressed to Prime Minister (twice) where he became Japan's longest serving leader, winning three elections with a landslide. Until the beginning of his second term in 2012 he had demonstrated no serious interest in economic matters but was identified with socially conservative views and was associated with a revival of more nationalistic politics.

Tarō Asō has a rather greater claim to be the serious economic thinker of the government. Like Abe, he is from a political – LDP – family with a mother who was the daughter of a Prime Minister and a wife who is the daughter of another. His background is more cosmopolitan than Abe's, having had a stint at the LSE and living and working for the family mining company in Africa and Latin America (and, unusually, he is a Roman Catholic). He progressed, like Abe, through one of the factions of the LDP to become Prime Minister on the threshold of the global financial crisis in 2008 when he warned the world of the economic dangers based on Japan's own experience. But he was unpopular at home and was blamed for the sudden rise in unemployment when the new crisis hit Japan. He led his party to the worst electoral defeat in its history. When the LDP returned to power three years later, Abe brought him on board as his deputy and Finance Minister where he applied Abenomics, perhaps more accurately known as Asonomics.

What caused Asō, then Abe, to emerge from the ruck of Japanese politicians was by making a very public break with the orthodoxy of their Japanese predecessors and most Western governments. Previous LDP leaders, Hashimoto in 1996 and Koizumi in 2001, had acted on advice to curb the fiscal deficit and debt, in both cases leading to recession and even bigger deficits as government revenue fell. Asō argued that regardless of the level of public debt, the overriding priority was to keep the economy going through a fiscal stimulus. According to Koo: 'Asō was one of the few Japanese politicians who understood from the beginning that Japan was in a balance sheet recession.'[21] As Koo goes on to explain, when Asō and the UK Prime Minister Gordon Brown were removed from office by the electorate the G20 lost the only two people able to explain the need for fiscal stimulus to avoid a slump.[22]

That judgement proved unduly gloomy since Asō's approach was taken up by Abe when the LDP returned to office in 2012 while Asō was given the job of implementing it. Abe was a skilful politician who realized that counterintuitive ideas – running fiscal deficits to improve the public finances; increasing government debt in order to reduce it – have to be carefully packaged. He also needed a narrative. He developed the theme of helping Japan to compete economically with China, appealing to an undercurrent of nationalism and deep fears of being dominated by a bigger and apparently more successful neighbour with historic scores to settle. He also hit on the idea of a comprehensive package with a visually striking image – of 'three arrows' combining monetary as well as fiscal stimulus and structural reforms – which would work if all three arrows hit the target. There was also a fourth arrow which was disguised to avoid upsetting Japan's trading partners: devaluation.

Three – or Four – Arrows in Flight

The global crisis of 2008 hit the Japanese economy very hard, predominantly through its impact on exports. Exports fell in 2009 by 27 per cent in dollar terms. The fall in real GDP was 5.2 per cent (about the same as in the UK, but for different reasons). Unemployment rose above 5 per cent, which was deeply troubling in a country where lifetime, secure, employment was the expected norm for 'salarymen' (in fact the small companies which made up the supply chains of big companies had long offered less secure work). Asset markets – for shares and property – crashed again, impacting those institutions which had spent the previous two decades repairing their balance sheets.

Fortunately, lessons had been learned. Ben Bernanke at the US Federal Reserve had studied the Japanese experience as well as the US economy after 1929 and had been persuaded of the need for very aggressive monetary policy including Quantitative Easing. And, at least initially, there was a willingness in several key countries – the US, the UK, Japan (with Asō) and China – to deploy fiscal deficits to fight off the risk of depression. So, by the time Abe returned to office in 2012, the global outlook was less desperate. Nonetheless, Japan was still stuck in seemingly perpetual stagnation. The three, or rather four, arrows were fired.

The first was a series of four spending commitments spread over two years and worth around $430 billion – for infrastructure projects: bridges, tunnels and earthquake-resistant roads. The importance of the fiscal stimulus (around 2 per cent of GDP) was partly that it provided a direct injection of spending power into the economy. But the fiscal deficit also provided an outlet for excessive private savings which would otherwise contribute to a balance of payments surplus, driving up the exchange rate.

The second 'arrow' was pumping vast amounts of money into the economy through QE with the aim of stimulating more lending and creating inflation (but not too much; the target was 2 per cent). As noted above, Japan had pioneered QE after the 1989 crash. Abe and Asō recognized that while QE was not sufficient, it was still necessary. And alongside this, some interest rates were made negative so as to penalize savings and encourage spending. One reason why the inflation target matters is that, without it, Japan would slide into deflation with falling price levels. Monetary policy would then no longer work effectively since even if official interest rates can be reduced to zero, deflation has the effect of keeping interest rates positive in real terms (the so-called liquidity trap). Also, if GDP in real terms stagnates and prices fall, nominal GDP falls by definition. When that happens, the real 'burden' of public debt (debt to GDP) rises. A key part of the 'inflation' strategy is to push up wages, leading to more spending and investment.

The third 'arrow' was a series of supply side measures increasing competition, reforming labour markets and liberalizing trade with Japan's neighbours.

The fourth (hidden) 'arrow' was to devalue the currency to revive Japanese exports and, therefore, growth. Martin Wolf argues that this is probably the main motive behind Abenomics which cannot be declared for fear of triggering beggar-my-neighbour reactions from competitors, notably the USA.[23]

The package attracted support from economists including Joseph Stiglitz: 'Abenomics can only help the country's recovery. Abe is doing what many economists have been calling for in the US and Europe: a comprehensive programme entailing monetary, fiscal and structural policies.'[24] For the first five years of Abe's rule, the policy appeared to work. There was sustained, uninterrupted, real growth based on business investment and exports. Unemployment halved (to 2.7 per cent). Wages and household income rose more than for years. The currency devalued 30 per cent in dollar terms. Prices rose (but did not meet the 2 per cent inflation target). The ratio of debt to GDP levelled off despite the rush of public spending. Stock market prices rose (by 150 per cent over five years), diminishing balance sheet recession.

Critics of Abenomics, however, became increasingly vocal as the initial impetus appeared to dissipate. Fiscal policy was seen as confused and lacking in conviction because the government simultaneously planned to raise the VAT rate from 5 to 8 per cent, hitting consumption. The hike was justified as necessary to curb government debt, which contradicted the aim of the fiscal stimulus. Nevertheless, the tax hike had the effect of pushing the economy back into negative growth – though that was temporary. Economists Paul Krugman and Larry Summers, who had become strong advocates of Abenomics, were highly critical of the move.[25] The government responded by postponing a further rise in VAT. And it stuck by its determination to use public investment and deficit financing to maintain demand and economic growth as long as balance sheet recession is a problem. Then, in the autumn of 2019, the government again lost its nerve and accepted the advice of those who were worried about high debt levels; it pushed ahead with an increase to 10 per cent in the rate of consumption tax, precipitating a sharp fall in demand and production, leading to recession.

Devaluation is problematic in a different way. The Abe devaluation may have worked for Japan in the short run but with Trump, an economic nationalist, in the White House, there was a real danger of retaliatory currency warfare which, alongside trade protectionism, would not only destroy any semblance of a rules-based international order but specifically Japan's role within it. Japan is also torn between deepening the Transpacific Partnership, which liberalizes trade among most of the Asia-Pacific countries except China, and Trump's preference for a bilateral deal.

The monetary 'arrow' has attracted criticism for other reasons. Some argue, simply, that it has failed in its own terms by the failure to hit the inflation target. Others say that it is bound to fail on its own because it is irrelevant to balance sheet recession – unless it is used, by bond purchases (QE), to help the government finance budget deficits. And there is the issue of how to unwind QE in due course: selling bonds, thereby raising bond yields and long-term interest rates, risks killing off recovery. Still the government, or rather the Bank of Japan, continues to encourage expansionary monetary, alongside fiscal, policies and there have been reports that the Bank of Japan may now be directly financing the government deficit: in effect, printing money.

The 'structural' reforms are designed to improve long-term growth potential by creating new opportunities for investment. Critics have argued that the fashionable policy of liberalizing labour markets or deregulation of service industries – for example – may make matters worse by increasing insecurity and reducing demand in the form of final consumption. Rather, the priority is to extend labour rights to temporary workers (as Abe is doing).

There is, however, one 'structural' problem with major implications for Japan's future economic health that is difficult to avoid: the declining population, a problem likely to affect other Western and some developing economies before long. The problem is sufficiently serious that Abe made the reversal of demographic decline a focus of what is called Abenomics 2.0.

The Disappearing Population

Japan's population has declined from a peak of 128 million in 2010 to 126 million in 2019 and it is projected to decline further. The share of the population who are over sixty-five increased from 5 per cent in 1950 to 28 per cent in 2019 and it is projected to be 37 per cent by 2050. At first sight this may have some advantages. After all, if the size of the economy stagnates and the population declines then per capita income will rise. It is indeed the case that living standards have not declined in Japan as one would otherwise expect from its twenty years of economic troubles. Japan has combined negative population growth (mortality exceeds birth rates) with low immigration (only 1.3 per cent of the population – 1.7 million – are immigrants and that figure includes overseas students). Many Japanese would claim, moreover, that low immigration creates a greater sense of cohesion and identity (and there are strong racial undercurrents in the debate).

But the costs of an ageing population are becoming more apparent. The labour force is contracting rapidly: by 3 million between 2005 and 2010, ten times the rate of immigration. There are fewer people of working age to support an older population and to pay taxes to fund pensions, health and care. Some sectors, especially physically onerous ones like construction, are unable to meet the demand because they are short of workers. Some economists have argued that the challenge of demography is one of the main reasons why demand is structurally so weak.[26] The main argument is that the elderly, who live off their savings, are particularly hit by low interest rates and respond by cutting consumption. The response of Abe has been to invest heavily in policies designed to get more women to join the labour force; to provide incentives to raise fertility; and to press ahead with robotics and other labour-saving technologies. So far there is no evidence of much impact; but this is a long-term project. Japan is spontaneously producing numerous product innovations for its elderly population and social innovations like multi-generational 'shared houses' where the elderly care for the children of working parents and the young run errands for the old and ease their isolation. The oldest district in Japan – Akita – has become, in the words of an author studying 'extreme economics', 'the backwater that leads the world'.[27]

One consequence of Japan's apparent success in adapting to ageing is the confident way in which Japan has approached the Covid-19 pandemic. Unlike most Western countries with vulnerable, ageing, populations, such as Italy, Japan has not been forced down the route of lockdown but allows continued social intercourse, adopting fierce restrictions only when it identifies a serious local cluster.

The economic response to the pandemic has, however, produced a more extreme version of Abenomics. In the early stages of the pandemic, to June 2020, Japan had introduced a stimulus package supported by public borrowing of 40 per cent of GDP, four times the scale of most developed countries. Moreover, the expansion was directly financed by the Bank of Japan buying up bonds. While this does not amount to outright monetization of the deficit (there remains a theoretical repayment obligation), Japan has come closer to that point than other developed economies. Since there is no inflation risk at present, a carefully controlled programme of financing the massive deficits through the central bank has been perfectly sensible. Other major countries did the same.

The Legacy

The Japanese economic experience has anticipated many of the problems of the Western world as a whole and Japanese policy makers have accumulated a wealth of understanding of what works, and what doesn't. Japan has become a laboratory for economic experiments with the breakdown of conventional thinking.

As Martin Wolf has pointed out, 'This orthodoxy... broke down, first in Japan in the 1990s, and then in the West after 2007, because of what both Keynes and Friedman had ignored: the tendency of the credit system to run riot.'[28]

Japan has given succour to those like Krugman and Stiglitz who argue, at a global level, that in a world with a glut of savings (be it from Japan, China, Germany or the Gulf States) there is a role, indeed a need, for active fiscal policy.[29] Koo concludes: 'Japan demonstrated that no matter how large the bubble and how extensive the damage to private balance sheets, the continuous administration of fiscal stimulus from the beginning in sufficient quantities can sustain incomes.'[30] In 2019 Abe launched a new round of big projects – rail, road, other infrastructure – which has attracted a wave of criticism of wasteful investment, much like the 'bridges to nowhere' of the 1990s. But he was using fiscal stimulus, based on borrowing at ultra-low interest rates, as the best way to keep the economy afloat.[31] Then, later in the year, the government reversed its expansionary policies and raised consumption tax, leading to another sharp downturn. But the pandemic has taken Japan back to extreme levels of public borrowing and public debt. It has also taken Abenomics into the uncharted waters of direct financing of the government's deficit by the central bank.

The implications of Abenomics go far wider than Japan. As Greg Ip has commented in the *Wall Street Journal*, 'Almost the entire rich world is stuck in a zero-interest-rate liquidity trap situation, and I think everyone is haunted by the possibility that there is no way out of it. If Japan shows a way out of that, it will be very encouraging.'[32] It is, however, yet to be seen whether Abenomics, with Abe retiring on health grounds, has been able to manage the bigger economic challenge of the economic depression following the Covid outbreak. So far the government has shown a willingness to be as radical as is necessary with fiscal and monetary expansion. There are indications, however, that political support is ebbing.

Messrs Abe and Asō may not have had the back-story, the cha-
risma and the political authority of a Roosevelt or a Thatcher.
But a willingness to try unconventional new approaches to economic policy and to engage with the big economic challenges of
the future – like ageing – puts them among the more interesting
political figures of today. They have seemingly created a model
which, so far, has sustained an enviable combination of success
factors not found elsewhere among developed countries: high living standards; relatively low inequality of income and wealth; a
wide range of successful, advanced technology companies able to
compete internationally; high levels of educational attainment;
and stable politics without populism.

Abe himself has now retired having served as prime minister longer than any other modern Japanese leader. He has left
behind not just an 'ism' but a serious legacy in economic policy.
Faced with the challenges of a post-industrial society, and now the
Covid depression, Japan offers an interesting model for the rest of
the world.

Trump: Trumponomics, Economic Nationalism and Pluto-populism

We do not know if the presidency of Donald Trump (1946–) will have major long-term consequences. He may come to be defined by his eccentricities, the daily tweeting and his highly personalized style of administration. He will certainly be defined in part by his response to the Covid-19 pandemic and its humanitarian and economic consequences. But our particular concern is how successful he has been in redefining American economic policy. The fact that he has been defeated may reduce his significance. But he has a large number of followers who will continue to influence politics and policy. And he has set in train a series of actions, domestically and internationally, which will not be quickly or easily reversed. Nor does the Biden administration seem inclined to.

The economics of Trump and his administration defy simple classification. He appears to have identified with no recognized school of economic thinking other than his own. Attempts have been made to describe a new economic philosophy dubbed Trumponomics.[1] On closer inspection, it is hard to discern an overarching theory; instead there is a collection of prejudices from the different elements of his political base and his own personality. The traditional Republican concerns with small government –

Reaganomics – are one element. But his own economic nationalism and the 'America First' appeal to a large section of his supporters have been a bigger part of it – in relation to trade and immigration and the rejection of global, multilateral, commitments. Some at least of his thinking will continue within the Republican Party and trade protectionism has been embraced by Democrats.

Critics call Trump's approach to economics 'populist'. He has called it 'popularist' – making the obvious riposte that politicians who want to be elected or re-elected usually try to be popular. But there is a serious point that Trump's politics – from which the economics derives – is based on identifying with 'the people' against a national or international 'elite'. Populism in this sense is a phenomenon of our times, from Brexit in the UK to the 'nativist' and 'anti-globalist' movements of Eastern and Western Europe.[2] It unites an otherwise improbable collection of leaders from the US, the UK, Russia, India, Hungary, the Philippines, Turkey and Brazil, contrasting with leaders from France, Germany, Canada, Japan and Sweden. The Populist International may not have much in common and is not easily pigeon-holed as right or left but is united by its disrespect for agreed norms and rules – nationally and internationally.

Describing Trump as populist does not, however, take us very far. He has little or nothing in common with leaders of populist movements in Venezuela – from the Chávez/Maduro regimes – or, as described earlier, the Peronist movement in Argentina. Their declared intention was to serve the poor and dispossess the rich. By contrast Trump is a billionaire and proud of it. His brand of populism sees no inconsistency between appealing to the 'left behind' and rewarding fellow billionaires – hence the phrase coined by Martin Wolf: 'pluto-populism'.[3] There have been other 'pluto-populists': Berlusconi in Italy, for example. Andrej Babiš, Prime Minister of the Czech Republic, has been described as a 'technocratic populist',[4] less flamboyant than Trump but offering the same political proposition: that plutocrats can run a country because they can run a big company and, moreover, are incorruptible since they do not need the money. And then there are populists appealing to native sentiment on grounds of race or religion, like the various Le Pens in France, who are not, in any obvious sense, 'pluto'. Trump's Democratic successor has embraced the populist economic nationalism but certainly not the 'pluto' bit.

The Origins of Trump's Economics

Trump was an unusual US President in having had no political experience in government or legislatures. His predecessors were Vice Presidents (Nixon, Truman, Ford, Bush Snr), state governors (Reagan, Roosevelt, Carter, Clinton, Bush Jnr) or senators (Kennedy, Johnson, Obama). Only Eisenhower, as a military commander, came from outside politics but he was a consensual figure, not, like Trump, an anti-politician committed to 'clearing the swamp'. Andrew Jackson, the seventh President, with his championing of the 'common man' against the 'corrupt aristocracy', perhaps bears some comparison. However, he was a military man and also founder of the Democratic Party.

Trump uniquely, claimed that his experience in business qualified him for the highest office, particularly on economic policy. He was also unique in having graduated with an economics degree (from the Wharton School of the University of Pennsylvania), though he made little of this particular qualification. His business career – in property development, hotels, casinos and golf courses – has been shrouded in some controversy in respect of how much he inherited or borrowed from his father, a successful property developer. Likewise, he has faced criticism for the use of corporate bankruptcy as a technique for minimizing debt and tax obligations. But, despite all this, he made much of his business prowess and is still one of the richest men in the USA (the exact figure is a matter of dispute but it's probably around $3 billion[5]). He was accused of numerous breaches of business ethics and conflicts of interest, not least, in 2018, by the head of the federal United States Office of Government Ethics, but he stayed, with legal help, on the right side of the criminal law and, to be fair, never sought or claimed to be a reincarnation of Mother Teresa.

His approach to business, and economics, is summarized in his autobiography *Trump: The Art of the Deal* (though his collaborator, Tony Schwartz, claims to have actually written it). His ideas are much mocked. But, in his defence, the skills required to navigate the New York commercial property market are not trivial. As he says in *The Art of the Deal*, 'in New York real estate… you are dealing with some of the sharpest, toughest, and most vicious people in the world'.[6] The same could be said of Presidents. The ability to bargain matters in face-to-face negotiations over life and death issues and also over trade and other international agreements, in bartering with Congress over the budget or in dealings with big corporate lobbyists and other vested interests.

He also understood, from personal experience, the workings of financial capitalism and business cycles. Hyman Minsky, who understood financial crises ahead of most economists and economic policy makers, said of Trump, long before he became President, that he was 'the epitome of a Ponzi-scheme capitalist living hand to mouth by borrowing against the expected appreciation of his assets'.[7] Trumponomics is, in significant part, about ways of doing business and negotiating: far removed from corporate smoothness and reputation management. His popular TV show *The Apprentice*, moreover, captured honestly the rough world of 'hire and fire' and uninhibited financial ambition. Trump's allies will claim, and may prove to have been right, that as with President Lyndon B. Johnson, half a century ago, crudity and cynicism go along with considerable effectiveness.

Trumponomics does not just incorporate his personal business experience and style. It also reflects the very tribal, polarized nature of US politics and his reliance on the Republican Party and it on him. While he was a fulsome supporter of Barack Obama's prompt, interventionist response to the financial crisis of 2008, he soon reverted to the Republican Party's negative orthodoxy. The party has been dominated, since the era of Reagan, by an obsession with small government, tax and spending cuts. Trump's politics may have been fluid, but since his election as President he became committed to delivering tax cuts for his affluent Republican base, and big business, while enlisting his new political constituency of workers and their families exercised by the loss of manufacturing and mining, 'unfair' foreign competition and 'illegal' migrant labour.

Another important influence on him, as on all US Presidents, was the interplay of arguments between advisers within the White House and the wider administration, particularly in a technically complex area like economic policy and, specifically, trade policy where it was clear that Trump had strong gut instincts but little expertise. In the Trump White House there was clearly a lot of tension between those like Gary Cohn, the former President of Goldman Sachs – for a while, the Director of the National Economic Council – and the President and staffers who shared Trump's instincts. There were striking, and sometimes hilarious, exchanges recorded in journalist Bob Woodward's fly-on-the-wall account in *Fear: Trump in the White House*.[8] For example:

> [Trump in response to the fact that interest rates are low:] We should just go borrow a lot of money…
>
> [Cohn explained:] If you as the federal government borrow money through issuing bonds, you are increasing the US deficit.
>
> What do you mean? Trump asked. Just run the presses – print money.

Apologists might say that Trump had an early grasp of New Monetary Theory, which describes the way a government like the USA can create money directly via the central bank. But Cohn was making the point that Trump did not understand the difference between a firm and the government.

A unifying thread in Trump's thought was an understanding of the force of Clinton's slogan 'It's the economy, stupid'. Trump conducted his presidency on the basis that his re-electability and reputation depended on economic success measured in rising living standards: wage growth, job growth and low unemployment. His favourite metric was the price of stocks, which may be a poor measure of economic welfare but is a useful forward indicator and measure of business optimism. The Covid-19 pandemic knocked the strategy sideways. But Trump's initial reluctance to suppress the pandemic and wavering commitment as it continued had an economic – and political – motive.

My question is whether Trump has changed economic policy in a way that is truly distinctive and transformational. There are three areas where that claim can be made.

First, there was a bellicose 'America First' economic nationalism which has been manifest in trade policy generally and more specifically in regional trade agreements, the functioning of the WTO (and other attempts at multilateral cooperation as with climate change), bilateral relations with China in particular and immigration policy.

Second, there was his aggressive 'pro-growth' strategy, perhaps fanciful in terms of desired growth numbers, but significant in terms of policy: tax cuts (at the expense of inequality); deregulation (at the expense of financial stability and of health and safety); promotion of domestic energy production (at the expense of agreements on carbon emissions); and infrastructure spending. His approach was in many ways a continuation of Reaganomics. The growth strategy has given way to the post-Covid imperative of averting a slump but it still includes a big dose of what was called 'supply side reform' in the Reagan years.

Third, there was a shift in macroeconomic policy away from monetary policy anchored in strong, independent central banks and a retreat from earlier commitments to balanced budgets and debt reduction. The pandemic reinforced those trends.

Of these the first is the closest to being transformative though he had a personal preoccupation – even an obsession – with bilateral deficits with US trade partners: a product of a belief that trade is a zero-sum game and that trade deficits have arisen because the US has been weak and taken advantage of. Bob Woodward describes Trump's determination to tear up a bilateral trade agreement with South Korea because of an $18 billion bilateral trade deficit despite advice that to do so would seriously damage wider security cooperation with that country.[9] Eventually his staff hid the document authorizing termination and he forgot about the issue. But deficits rankled with him and he was egged on by his Commerce Secretary (Wilbur Ross), his Trade Representative (Robert Lighthizer) and, above all, his trade adviser (Peter Navarro).

However, it is not yet clear that there was a totally different agenda as opposed to a cruder, more aggressive, less diplomatic style of doing business designed to appeal to a domestic audience. His trade policy initiatives were broadly supported by Democrats in Congress and much of the anti-globalization rhetoric was shared on the left of US politics and had been for a long time. Successive US administrations have been less than enthusiastic promoters of multilateral trade liberalization, a process which was already moribund before Trump came along. The preoccupation with bilateral deficits and 'currency manipulation' may be questionable economics but was directed by Trump's predecessors at Japan before China became a target. And complaints about Chinese trade priorities, its discriminatory state capitalism and theft of intellectual property long pre-dated Trump.

A generation ago, liberal economists fretted about 'the new mercantilism'[10] and the spread of bilateral arrangements.[11] The United States was one of the key obstacles to a multilateral trade agreement under the WTO's Doha round of negotiations, before Trump. On a wider definition of economic nationalism, while

President Obama may not have built a wall to keep out Mexican immigrants, his administration expelled millions of 'illegals'. To a degree, 'America First' is simply a statement of what political leaders are elected to do in a world where technology, finance and business may be global but politics is national. The question in practice is whether Trump's rhetoric actually meant something radically new and different from a world in which, despite grumbles and frustrations, US leaders bought into the idea that the sum was bigger than the parts, that international economic integration and a 'rules-based system' was, on balance, good for America. The answer is that Trump turned this worldview on its head.

Trump's Economic Nationalism

According to Trump, America has been a victim of globalization. The free(ish) movement of goods, finance, capital investment and people are against US interests, although they may be favoured by an elite of business executives and bankers and their allies in government, international organizations and the media. Trump's final TV slot in his 2016 presidential campaign said: 'it's the global power structure that is responsible for the economic decisions that have robbed our working class, stripped our country of its wealth, and put that money into the pockets of a handful of large corporations and political entities.'[12] A virtually identical statement could have been made by someone from the socialist left (Bernie Sanders in the USA; Jeremy Corbyn in the UK) or the far right (Marine Le Pen in France).

Like them, there is a big element of nostalgia for the loss of manufacturing industry. There is a long history of American preference for the manufacturing sector (over farming and services) going back over 200 years to Alexander Hamilton. And there are entirely legitimate economic arguments for wanting to capture the relatively high productivity and capacity for innovation of some industries. But in the Trump White House the motivation was in part a sense of obligation to Rust Belt states which voted for him, but also, rather more, a sentimental attachment to the industrial past. As Bob Woodward observed, the President 'clung to an out-dated view of America – locomotives, factories with huge smoke stacks, workers busy on assembly lines'.[13] Trump's own business had never gone near manufacturing and relied on service-based users of his properties; but he refused to accept that over 80 per cent of US GDP was made up of services.[14]

In practice most of the arguments about economic nationalism have concerned trade and stemmed from Trump's conviction that trade is a zero-sum game in which there is little overall benefit and countries lose out if they import more than they export. This is by no means a new idea; mercantilism was the dominant way of thinking about trade before Adam Smith. But Trump refreshed those old ideas in colourful language: foreigners are 'eating our lunch'; Americans have been 'played like suckers'; supporters of trade are 'bloodsuckers'.[15] His starting point has been that a bilat-eral trade deficit is evidence that foreigners are getting the better of the USA.

Despite his rhetoric, some of Trump's comments (and tweets) suggested a more sophisticated approach and an eagerness to distance himself from the inter-war history in which the Smoot–Hawley tariffs, signed into law by Republican President Hoover, contributed to the Great Depression. Stephen Moore and Arthur Laffer, who were strong supporters of Trump but also free traders in the Republican conservative tradition, describe a conversation with Trump in which he insisted: 'We need to make the point that I'm not an isolationist or a protectionist… I am a businessman. Of course I understand the value of international trade.'[16] Rather, he saw himself as a skilled negotiator who could negotiate much better deals for American companies and American workers. He intended to use the threat of tariffs against China, Canada, Mex-ico and the EU among others as leverage to get them to lower their tariffs on US products. He claimed (at least to this audience, which was anxious to be reassured) that he wanted to reduce global tariffs and trade barriers, albeit in ways that create more jobs in the USA. His hostility to the World Trade Organization was not based, he claimed, on hostility to trade but because as a master negotiator he could do better in one-to-one bilateral trade deals than complicated multilateral trade deals. This is a generous interpretation – that tariff barriers are a tactic rather than an end in themselves. How has it been borne out in practice?

Protectionism in Practice

A useful place to test out Trump's motives and effectiveness is in relation to the trade agreements which he tried to renegotiate. He claimed many times that the North American Free Trade Agreement (NAFTA), agreed between the USA, Mexico and Canada after being initiated by President Reagan, 'is the worst trade deal in the history of the world' and that he was 'ready and psyched to terminate it'.[17] There had long been arguments around Mexican adherence to labour standards and access to Canadian agriculture markets but, equally, there were benefits for US agricultural exporters, manufacturers and financial services as well as consumer benefits from cheaper food and gas. At the core of the political discomfort about NAFTA was the agreement to open the US market to Mexico, a low wage economy, which stirred up longstanding fears among US workers of being undercut by cheap labour. These arguments have long been swatted aside by economists as economically nonsensical,[18] but they have been, and are, politically potent not just in the US (as in the EU's reluctance to embrace Turkey as a member). NAFTA was justified politically on the basis that a more prosperous Mexico would mean less pressure to export its population as illegal immigrants. But Trump had a more direct answer to that problem: build a wall. In the event, Canada and Mexico coordinated skilfully, made some concessions to Trump (cars imported from Mexico to the USA must have

75 per cent US components) and were able to negotiate a new agreement twenty-five years after the old one. Ultimately no great harm was done, and all three countries could claim a 'win'.

That cannot be said of the Trans-Pacific Partnership (TPP) which was agreed between the US, Australia, Japan, several other Asian and several Latin American countries just before the end of the Obama presidency. The purpose was to liberalize trade (and investment) between the signatories but there was also a more powerful political motive for the US: to weaken the spreading dependence of the region on China and to draw the Pacific region within US influence and standards. One of Trump's first acts, which appeared to be motivated by a wish to negate Obama's achievements rather than by trade policy considerations, was to refuse US ratification. The other parties have, however, pressed ahead without the US; China is expressing interest in participating (as, improbably, is the UK). In contrast to NAFTA, damage appears to have been done to US interests, alienating and embarrassing governments otherwise well disposed to the USA and anxious to reduce their dependence on China. With the movement in China under President Xi to a more belligerent, nationalistic, approach to its neighbours – Taiwan, Australia and India in particular – the undermining of Pacific cooperation has been particularly crass.

Another set of negotiations which Trump discontinued has been with the EU: the Transatlantic Trade and Investment Partnership (TTIP). The negotiations were making little progress in any event. The EU was refusing to accommodate US demands for market access for agricultural products subject to different food and animal welfare standards and had also declared that access for US companies as suppliers of public services was off limits. For its part, Trump has been exercised by a bilateral deficit with the EU (especially with Germany; and particularly in cars and car components), even though these imbalances are very small in relation to the overall value of bilateral trade.

The end of TTIP and the lack of interest in reviving it illustrate the problem with Trump's approach. Faced with a counterparty whose economy and bargaining power are as strong as the US, or stronger, it is difficult to demonstrate a 'win'. Disagreements escalate to economic war with tit-for-tat retaliation leading to 'mutually assured destruction' by undermining business confidence, investment and growth. This may be what happened after Trump sought to exploit a legal ruling in the WTO in favour of Boeing, which had complained about EU subsidies to Airbus. The US proposed $7 billion of tariffs on EU exports and the EU threatened retaliation in kind. A similar contretemps over US steel tariffs was diffused with difficulty in 2018. The incoming Biden administration was eager to reduce friction with the EU without losing popular protectionist policies – and so made concessions on Airbus. China, not the EU, was to be the main target of its trade protectionism.

The China Trade War

In the case of China, Trump's hostilities led to the US imposing a wide range of tariffs on Chinese goods, which may be either dropped or escalated depending on negotiations which are suspended at the time of writing. Trump was preoccupied with the bilateral deficit on trade (and current account) which he described in one of his many tweets as 'the greatest theft in the history of the world', though it is reduced from its peak and somewhat smaller than the bilateral deficit with Germany. The bilateral trade in goods deficit with China has been just under 2 per cent of US GDP for a decade and a half.

There is a much bigger, and widely shared, grievance that China has benefited unfairly from membership of the WTO. It has gained access, with few trade barriers, to Western markets while hiding behind its status as a developing country to block access to its own markets. Similarly, it has failed to act against

theft of intellectual property and allowed its own state industries
to benefit from subsidies and the absence of competitive procurement. The EU and China's other Western trade partners wanted
a coordinated approach to tackle such issues, using the processes
of the WTO, and strengthening agreements from which China is
excluded (such as TPP). But those routes were anathema to Trump
for other reasons. So the US was on its own.

Trump was also encouraged to escalate the conflict by those
who saw – and see – China as a wider threat. The 'threat' is partly
seen in security terms: that as China develops parity or suprem-
acy in new technologies from 5G to Artificial Intelligence,[19] the
US is in danger of becoming dependent on China and vulnerable
to 'attack' through its supply chains and corporate collaborations.
That is what lies behind the decision to isolate the Chinese technology firm Huawei (which is also being made unwelcome in the
UK, Australia and Japan, among others). There is also a wider
strategic concern, which has little to do with economics, that
China will 'overtake' the US in technological (and ultimately military) capacity; so, it should be confronted now.[20] That somewhat
apocalyptic view culminates in what is described as inevitable conflict between a rising power and a ruling power – the Thucydides
Trap. Nevertheless, it contradicts decades of American conventional wisdom – from Nixon and Kissinger to Condoleezza Rice
and George W. Bush and Obama and Clinton – that engagement
and cooperation are greatly preferable (and hopefully would lead
to convergence in economic and political systems). There is little
evidence that Trump shared these wider philosophical and strategic concerns, as opposed to his own, which were narrower and
more transactional. The Covid-19 pandemic, however, provided a
new set of reasons for escalating the conflict: the political motive
of finding a scapegoat to blame for loss of life and economic distress in the USA. And China's increasingly aggressive behaviour
over Hong Kong and its reactions to criticism have poured fuel on
the fire. Biden has continued where Trump left off.

So how is the trade war going? Trump set out initially his challenge to China: to reduce the bilateral deficit of $375 billion by $100 billion. The $100 billion might appear in a greater deficit with another trade partner – and almost certainly would – but that was not his concern. In terms of such metrics, it is far too soon to tell, but there are some early indications. First, the steps he took are consistent with a central tenet of Trumponomics: that what matters in trade is bilateral deficits. Economists (and many others) would regard his objective as economic nonsense but, as Janan Ganesh pointed out in the *Financial Times*, 'say what you like about Trump's bean-counting mercantilism… it is at least a contained obsession. He is not interested in the wider clash of philosophies with China because he has no wider philosophy.'[21] To achieve this narrow objective, he started (after a round of ad hoc tariffs on steel, aluminium and other items affecting several countries) with 10 per cent tariffs on $200 billion of Chinese goods. This produced some Chinese retaliatory tariffs but initiated a bilateral negotiating process outside the WTO – where Trump wants to be. There have been further rounds of tariffs – at a higher rate (25 per cent) and covering more products – with further retaliation, leading to further negotiation. The Chinese appear to have gone a long way to meeting his concerns (perhaps understanding that Trump wants only symbolic victories) and in early 2020, bilateral negotiations were suspended, described as a truce. But as the dispute escalated over what Trump has called the 'China Virus' (Covid-19), the scene was set for deepening conflict over trade among other issues. Moreover, there was a strong bipartisan element to the aggressive conduct of the trade dispute, which continues today.

There has been widespread criticism from US business, and even from Trump's ideological allies, of raising tariffs, in particular his unwillingness to accept that tariffs are a tax on (US) consumers as well as on Chinese exports. Even the devoted Arthur Laffer told the President: 'trade protectionism is one of the four prosper-

ity killers: along with taxes, inflation, and excessive regulation…
"Tariffs are taxes".'[22] Fifty economists polled by the University of
Chicago awarded Trump A⁻ for overall economic performance
in February 2019 but an F for trade policy (before most of the
tariffs were effective). They collectively went along with economic
analysis which suggested that tariffs had largely wiped out the
benefits of earlier tax cuts (and mostly fell, regressively, on lower
income consumers). The US Chamber of Commerce warned
that Trump's trade policy (not only in relation to China) was putting 2.6 million jobs at risk as a result of retaliation, higher costs
on imported inputs feeding through to exports and reduced consumer demand. Chinese retaliation has already had an impact on
specific sectors (for example, US soya bean growers).

Apologists for Trump have said that none of this discern-
ibly affected US growth or the stock market and was already
producing some concessions from China. They argued that the
vulnerable Chinese economy – with slowing job growth and excessive leverage – was taking a bigger hit than the USA. All of
this has reinforced Trump's infamous tweet: 'Trade wars are good
and easy to win'. However, critics point to the way protectionism
is spreading across countries and sectors with the potential to do
serious damage to the world economy. And this is a world economy made more fragile after the pandemic and not in a good
position to withstand future shocks. Moreover, Trump sought to
disable the World Trade Organization, which polices the rules of
the trading system, by refusing to appoint judges to its dispute settlement panels. Where the USA has sought WTO legitimacy for
its actions it was by using a long-neglected provision – Article 21
– to restrict imports on national security grounds which could be
applied to anything and probably will be in the future as the Biden
administration also links China trade with security concerns.

What could make the battle hotter in the future would be a
currency war in which the US treats currency depreciation relative to the dollar as a hostile economic act. In relation to China,

the Chinese authorities have allowed the renminbi to appreciate
– or intervened to slow or stop devaluation – and this has facilitated the fall in the Chinese current account surplus from 10 per
cent of GDP in 2007 to under 2 per cent in recent years. But part
of the Chinese retaliatory response to Trump's tariffs has been
to allow (or engineer) a small devaluation. The accusation that
the Chinese are 'currency manipulators' once had some force
and there was a period in which (as in Japan) currency devaluation was used to achieve competitive advantage; but it has long
ceased to be an issue. Now it was being revived. There were risks
for both parties. Chinese devaluation could get out of control if
capital started to flee China, fearing further falls in value. On the
other hand, China could potentially damage the US by large-scale
offloading of some of its trillion dollars of US Treasury bonds
– though this would also cause losses on its holdings and drive
down the dollar in value and drive up the renminbi, undermining
its own competitiveness. As with trade war the likely effects are
unpredictable and would add to overall economic instability and
confidence, damaging all parties. Yet Trump threatened to unpick
this mutual financial dependency as part of the escalating conflict
with China.

One longlasting consequence of both Trump's trade war and
of Covid-19 is a decoupling of Chinese and US supply chains
where these are based on advanced technology. The US has taken
steps to stop US companies using the products of Huawei and has
threatened another Chinese telecommunications company, ZTE.
The US can reasonably claim that it is not the instigator of this
technological protectionism – Google and Facebook cannot operate in China. Companies around the world are having to make a
long-term choice between Chinese and US technologies and the
systems which stem from them.[23]

Trump, Growth and Economic Management

The core of Trumponomics was that, while the confrontational means may be unorthodox and risky, they will 'make America great again' through economic success. One of Trump's main economic advisers, Lawrence Kudlow, claimed optimistically (in 2018): 'Trump says we can get to 3, 4, or even 5 percent growth through tax reduction, deregulation, American energy production, and fairer trade deals and he is exactly right.'[24] After the first two years of the Trump presidency it was possible to make some tentative assessments. Provisionally, GDP growth was 3.1 per cent in 2018 and just over 2 per cent in 2019 (after 2.3 per cent in 2017 and annualized growth of 2.1 per cent in the previous seven years). Comparing the first two years of the Trump presidency with the last two years of Obama's, real GDP growth and nominal wage growth was – slightly – better. Unemployment continued to fall, though the rate of job creation was slightly better under Obama and both inflation and real wage growth were a little worse than under Obama. There is something of a gap between the claimed and actual performance. True to form, Trump repeatedly claimed that his performance has been 'the best in American history'. Such claims have been overtaken by the Covid-19 pandemic and the enormous economic damage which it has inflicted.

There were several specific actions to stimulate growth including tax cuts costing around $1 trillion for business and the rich and more spending ($200 billion) on infrastructure. The tax cuts involved a big cut in corporate tax rates (from 35 per cent to 20 per cent) mainly to encourage a repatriation of investment from overseas. There was also the elimination of estate duty and considerable simplification of the income tax banding with cuts in the top rate. The tax cuts did provide an economic stimulus (estimated by the Congressional Joint Committee on Tax as 0.7 per cent of GDP over a decade) but this was largely cancelled out by the tariff increases. For low income groups any gains have been more than outweighed by cutbacks in health insurance coverage. Corporate tax cuts, along with a raft of deregulatory measures, should have stimulated business investment but business investment appears to have fallen, as has labour productivity.

Trump, like other Presidents-elect, paid lip service to deficit and public debt reduction but in practice – with low inflation and low interest rates – his administration was much more relaxed.[25] The Congressional Budget Office (CBO) estimated that the tax cuts would add $2.3 trillion to public debt over ten years (contributing to a projected rise in the debt to GDP ratio from 77 per cent in 2017 to well over 100 per cent in 2028). In addition, the administration, with Congressional agreement, did on several occasions lift what are called 'sequestration caps' originally introduced to curb public spending. The CBO in its latest outlook before Covid suggested that on the then current trends budget deficits would average 4.4 per cent of GDP in the coming decade as against 2.9 per cent for the last fifty years.

All these calculations were rendered obsolete by an emergency $2.3 trillion spending and tax cutting package, from Trump and Congress, to offset the economic downturn: the equivalent of a fiscal expansion of 9 per cent of GDP and that was only the beginning. In this respect at least there was bipartisan consensus in the USA and agreement internationally that this was the correct course of action. Biden has gone even further.

Lastly, Trump's economic policy challenged one of the central features of orthodox economic policy since the 1980s: operationally independent central banks with a mandate to target low positive rates of inflation. Since the global financial crisis, monetary policy has been the dominant tool of economic policy in the developed world. Arguably, the use of Quantitative Easing via massive bond sales – cutting long-term interest rates via bond yields – in combination with very low short-term interest rates has kept Western economies from depression. But monetary policy is reaching its limits as interest rates become negative (and cannot be forced any lower – the 'liquidity trap'). And QE has generated serious side effects, such as increased inequality.

Trump had a particular set of concerns: that the Federal Reserve would seek to raise interest rates, thereby cutting growth – or fail to cut interest rates sufficiently to keep up growth. This mattered to Trump with an election to fight in 2020. He not only wanted maximum growth stimulus but to prevent relatively high US interest rates strengthening the dollar in a way that undermines the US position in the trade war (and currency war) with China. Trump didn't merely have a different view (or different interests) from the Federal Reserve – he wanted to dictate policy to the Federal Reserve. The Federal Reserve's independence is protected by law (the 1913 Federal Reserve Act) but that independence can be undermined. Trump has denounced it as 'an arm of the Democratic Party' although the Chair is a known Republican approved by him. He used Congressional allies to seek greater 'audit' powers over the Fed's decisions and to limit its discretion by imposing policy rules. In the post-Covid emergency, when monetary and fiscal policy was working flat out to counter depression, there was little prospect of the Federal Reserve slamming on the brakes but the issue has continued with recovery and as inflation risks appear.

The Legacy

The long-term consequences of Trump's approach to economics have yet to play out. But it is not too difficult to see how his economic nationalism could escalate. In a world seeking to escape from large-scale unemployment there will be a strong temptation to adopt beggar-my-neighbour measures against trade partners. Exports would stagnate and business investment would remain weak, which would further dampen the prospects of recovery.

Trump categorically rejected the idea that there is such a thing as a 'global community', as opposed to an area where nation states

– and business – compete for advantage. Encouraged by advisers like Steve Bannon, Trump saw 'globalism' as a weakness. Exposing 'globalist' views among advisers became a litmus test of unreliability and disloyalty. The repercussions go much further than trade negotiations. Lack of support for global institutions like the WTO, the World Health Organization, the United Nations, the G7 and even the Bretton Woods financial institutions, the IMF and the World Bank, makes it extremely difficult to produce a coordinated global response to the post-Covid emergency let alone maintain support for common action on shared problems like climate change.[26]

Much depends on how much of Trump's approach to economics has been assimilated by his own party and his opponents. But it is possible that Trump's unique contribution to economic policy will be to have broken beyond repair the global network of rules, standards and institutions which his predecessors, from Roosevelt on, did so much to create.

Now that Trump has been repudiated by the voters and replaced by someone committed to a more multilateral approach to international economic affairs, the key question is 'how much of Trumponomics will survive?'. The tentative answer is quite a lot. Both Biden and Democrats in Congress have endorsed Trump's approach to trade and share his approach to China. Even if the new President wants to reverse some of Trump's deregulation, he lacks the legislative majority to do much. Trumponomics might well outlast the man.

Sixteen Politicians: Sixteen Varieties of Economics

Sixteen individuals from twelve different countries, different systems of government and different episodes in over two hundred years make up a somewhat varied bunch. But they have all been immersed in the economic ideas of their time and place, and it was these ideas which informed economic policy to which they all made a distinctive and important contribution. A small number were professional economists (Erhard, Manmohan Singh and Balcerowicz) and both Roosevelt and Trump studied some economics at university (but made light of it). The rest picked up their economic ideas while serving as professional politicians, soldiers or revolutionaries.

The sixteen individual political leaders I have reviewed collectively here are very diverse, but all are consequential. There are democrats and autocrats; politicians of right and left or ideologically ambiguous; heroes and villains. What they have in common is that they changed the economic paradigm of the country in which they operated and, in some cases, more widely. We cannot be certain that some or most of the changes would not have happened anyway, and some of the leaders belonged to a party or government team which functioned collectively. But as individual politicians they all mattered.

The Slaves of Defunct Economists

I have been concerned in this book with the interaction between politics and economics. Central to that process is the question of where politicians get their economic ideas from. All of the political figures discussed here drew – consciously or unconsciously, directly or indirectly – on the ideas of economic thinkers, in the way that Keynes described. I started with Alexander Hamilton whose own ideas were massively influential in the US and elsewhere, and who became known, amongst much else, for providing the rationale for protected industrialization. But his starting point was Adam Smith and the arguments for a competitive market economy, even if they diverged on the specific issue of infant industry tariffs. Smith's liberal approach to trade was – eventually – delivered in the UK by Peel, a politician who skilfully went with the flow of opinion which had been distilled by the campaigners Richard Cobden and John Bright, who in turn had been influenced by David Ricardo – himself an economist-politician – and Smith.

Bismarck went along with the same tide of opinion, since economic liberalism was the creed of his early political allies. His epiphany – his late conversion to protectionism – occurred in part through exposure to an influential writer and lobbyist, Wilhelm von Kardorff. He had absorbed the ideas of the National School of German economists who in turn had been influenced by the American economist Henry Carey and by Friedrich List, both of whom had taken Hamilton's qualified support for protectionism a big step further. Another German philosopher and economist, Karl Marx, inspired most significantly Lenin, but also generations of political figures in the communist tradition (and, to a degree, social democrats). But in his twilight years, Lenin turned his back on doctrinaire 'leftism' and sought to fashion a hybrid of state and market which was to become the holy grail for many regimes.

Bill Clinton's observation about the economy could well have been the message of Roosevelt and the New Deal. The New Deal and Roosevelt's attempts to counter the Great Depression have often been taken to be the first manifestation of Keynesian economics. But Keynes himself had little or no influence on Roosevelt in the 1930s and his deficit-financing ideas were firmly repudiated. Roosevelt was initially influenced by the ideas of Irving Fisher, who wrote about the deflationary dangers of high levels of debt. His famous New Deal was not, however, about macroeconomics but essentially was about how to reform capitalism, drawing on the work of Adolf Berle and Gardiner Means and others who were concerned about the workings of the modern corporation. When, later in his administration, Roosevelt was more open to Keynesian ideas, they came to him through the so-called American Keynesians led by Alvin Hansen and his adviser Lauchlin Currie.

Erhard's 'social market' philosophy emerged from a German branch of the classical liberal economic tradition originating in eighteenth-century Britain and France. The German variant was led by Eugen Richter and Wilhelm Rieger who supported a strong state to impose strong market disciplines and anti-monopoly powers. They diverged from the more interventionist National Liberals who had worked with Bismarck and – ultimately – got into bed with Hitler. Erhard's views were sharpened during the war in association with German liberal economists such as Wilhelm Röpke and Walter Eucken – of the Freiberg ordoliberals – who were hostile to the 'crony capitalism' of the Nazis, to socialism in general but also to pure laissez-faire. There was also a tradition combining free market economics with Christian – specifically Catholic – ideas of social justice which Erhard firmly rejected but had to swallow as the price of becoming a leading Christian Democrat (then Chancellor). Erhard is one of the few political figures to have had a fully thought-through economic philosophy before coming to power and then systematically applying it, where politics permitted.

In parallel with Erhard, Erlander, the Swedish Social Democrat leader, was developing a different model of capitalism: social democracy. As the first graduate and intellectual to lead his party, he had been immersed in philosophical ideas: the non-revolutionary socialist tradition of Eduard Bernstein; the Keynesians of the Stockholm School of Economics led by Gunner Myrdal and Bertil Ohlin (who, confusingly, became the leader of the main, liberal, opposition); and the USA of the New Deal and wartime planning captured best in the work of J.K. Galbraith with whom Erlander strongly identified.

In much of the developing world, in Latin America and newly independent Asia and Africa, an entirely different set of economic ideas was influencing the post-war generation of political leaders. One was around the possibilities of national economic planning. Another was around industrialization and greater economic 'self-reliance' achieved by building up nascent, domestic industries through import substitution. The latter was especially important in Latin America where Raúl Prebisch, the Argentine academic and later head of UNCTAD, had a major role influencing the thinking of Juan Perón. Perón was undoubtedly more influenced by what he saw as the better side of European fascism in Italy and Spain – neither capitalist nor communist, but strongly nationalistic in economic matters. In the event, Peronism became crowd-pleasing populism with lavish spending, deficits financed by the printing presses and support for the demands of organized, or unorganized, labour as against the 'elite'. But despite repeated economic failures in office Peronism has proved remarkably durable politically, which may have a lot to do with deep-rooted ideas of social justice associated with the Catholic Church.

Especially in East Asia a different model was being developed, notably by General Park in South Korea but with variants elsewhere, such as in due course in China. Park's 'miracle on the Han River', with very rapid transformation and industrialization, had its ideological inspiration in Japan. Specifically, Park – who was immersed in Japanese culture and history – drew on the experience of the Meiji reformers who, after 1868, successfully caught up with the Western world through strong, modernizing government harnessing business and drawing on Western technology and management systems. The state capitalism of Korea was, however, intellectually indebted to more than Park's (rather idealized) interpretation of what happened in Japan almost a century earlier. Korea's military – and aid – dependence on the US ensured that Western ideas were influential too. The Kennedy administration initially produced advisers like Walt Rostow who were well disposed to Park's focus on high rates of economic growth. But Park consistently rejected Western advice to prioritize stabilization of the economy and to follow a pattern of industrialization which reflected a static view of Korea's 'comparative advantage'. There was also some evidence that Park had been (and perhaps was) a closet communist. Whatever the truth, his largely Asian hinterland of economic ideas was mostly vindicated.

The Singapore experience under Lee is very different in combining a powerful controlling state with an openness to free trade and foreign investors. Lee started out as a social democrat influenced by the British Labour Party. But when he became Prime Minister of a country which became involuntarily independent in difficult economic circumstances he relied heavily on his own judgement, not lacking intellectual self-confidence. He did, however, rely on his close colleague Goh Keng Swee, an LSE-trained development economist. Both were highly pragmatic, uninterested in economic doctrines or orthodoxies, and willing to apply useful practical ideas eclectically in the creation of a highly effective state machine alongside an open economy. Their economic advisers, the Dutch economist Winsemius and the Israeli E.J. Mayer, were of a similar disposition: doers rather than thinkers.

China, under Deng, was to replicate the hypergrowth of Korea, on a vastly bigger scale. Deng's approach to economics was pragmatic, not ideological ('it doesn't matter if a cat is black or white provided it catches mice'), and based on practical experience or trial and error ('crossing the stream by feeling for the stones'). But it is clear that he was strongly influenced by the economic pragmatism of Lenin in his New Economic Policy, which Deng saw at first hand. When the reforming Deng later started to explore ideas from outside the communist world his approach was eclectic. Some critics have suggested that he was seduced by the free market ideas of Milton Friedman whom he met and applauded,[1] but the evidence suggests that a greater source of inspiration was Japan and the success of South Korea.

Margaret Thatcher, by contrast, acknowledged an intellectual debt to Friedman and the influence of both the monetarist approach to macroeconomics and the liberal free market approach to wider economic policy. Her real inspiration came, however, from economist Friedrich Hayek whose *Road to Serfdom* she read and which validated her belief that the battle against socialist economics was not just a technical issue about economic efficiency but a moral crusade. The influence of both economic thinkers was to be felt through think tanks such as the Institute of Economic Affairs, especially, and the Adam Smith Institute which produced a generation of policy advisers and economists in the Thatcher years. Much of the pioneering academic work in economics which led to Thatcherism was attributable to Alan Peacock (a Liberal rather than a Conservative). The Chicago School of economics had a powerful influence on the Reagan administration in the 1980s, though he identified himself with this approach to policy much earlier when he endorsed the Republican presidential campaign of Barry Goldwater in 1968. During his presidency, Reagan appears to have been particularly influenced by Arthur Laffer, whose questionable message that tax cutting enhances rather than diminishes government revenue had obvious political appeal.

Poland's Balcerowicz also publicly acknowledged a debt to Friedman as he completed his intellectual journey from communist economics to a belief in liberal free market economics and stern monetary and fiscal discipline. His collaboration with Jeffrey

Sachs was especially important in clarifying the policy ideas which lay behind the 'big bang' approach to transition from communism to capitalism.

By contrast, the reforms introduced into India by Manmohan Singh were from a different ideological stable. Singh had been schooled by Keynesians of the left like Nicholas Kaldor and Joan Robinson at Cambridge and he spent much of his career as a leading economist in government seeking to make India's planned (and democratic socialist) economy work. But he absorbed, from India's interaction with the World Bank and the IMF, and from Indian economists, an openness to more economically liberal policies. This was a means to an end rather than an end in itself, however, and his first priority was poverty reduction, especially through social policy – education and health, where the ideas of Amartya Sen have been highly influential.

It cannot be said that any political leader has yet developed a comprehensive approach to the problems thrown up by the 2008 financial crisis. Rather, the monetary policies of central bankers Ben Bernanke and Mario Draghi, combined with the massive fiscal stimulus given by the Chinese authorities, kept the world from depression. A new and comprehensive approach has, however, been incorporated in Japanese Abenomics, borrowing from Abe's predecessor and Finance Minister Asō. It appears to have been influenced by officials and intellectuals urging an expansionary approach to balance sheet recession and in particular Richard Koo.

Temperamentally, Trump was less inclined than most politicians to acknowledge the influence of other people's ideas. But it is clear that, in his presidency, he has relied on economic advice, much of it an updating of the supply side approach of Reaganomics, transmitted by the likes of Moore and Laffer and his economic adviser Lawrence Kudlow. The major departure from that tradition was his embracing of economic nationalism and trade protectionism. The main source of reinforcement of his political instincts appears to have been his trade adviser, the Harvard economist Peter Navarro; but there is now a burgeoning American literature depicting trade in terms of geopolitical confrontation. Trump's unique contribution was an obsession with bilateral trade deficits which has no role in modern economic thought but was the dominant economic paradigm of the mercantilist tradition, before Adam Smith. I suspect he would not be flattered to discover that his thinking echoes the orthodoxies of seventeenth- and eighteenth-century England and France. Whether Trump's highly idiosyncratic approach outlasts his presidency remains to be seen but his economic nationalism has struck a chord in the USA and perhaps more widely, and the Biden administration has continued his protectionist approach to trade.

Good Politics, Bad Economics; Good Economics, Bad Politics

When Professor Frank Hahn made his celebrated dismissal of Mrs Thatcher's approach to economics as 'intellectually without interest', he spectacularly missed the point: that it is of interest not because of the originality or sophistication of the economics but because of the interaction between the politics and the economics. There is an extra dimension. Economic policy is not just applied economics; it is applying economics in a world where political constraints, incentives and outcomes are quite different from standard economic models of consumers and firms. In the political world there is rarely an incentive to take account of foreigners (though individuals, like Roosevelt, may have devoted part of their later years to worrying about the international system). Firms and households may have a hard budget constraint, but politicians face the constraint of losing power. Game theory has produced stylized models of how decision makers interact. But, as almost all the cases I have shown illustrate, the complex interaction between economics and politics has all manner of paradoxical and unintended consequences.

Peel is an example. The popular narrative is that a skilful and brave politician pushed through legislation (the abolition of the Corn Laws) which alleviated the hunger of the growing urban working class and established the economically optimal model of free trade with transformative economic benefits. In reality, he was a very late convert from protectionism. The politics was messy (he split his party for two decades). And an unintended economic consequence of an influx of grain was, under the Gold Standard, an outflow of gold and the contraction of money supply leading to severe recession which may have inflicted more hardship on the poor than was offset by cheaper bread. At least in the short run.

Hamilton's economic legacy was immense, and relevant to this day, but his economics helped to destroy his political standing. By creating a market for debt and establishing confidence in government bonds, he fuelled higher prices, which meant lower yields (interest rates), but also enriched the 'fat cats' who held onto their stock or speculated successfully. Worse, the rich and successful were the people with the resources then to invest in the nascent industries he was promoting. Markets and industry (and Hamilton) became associated in the public mind with 'fat cats' and 'corruption'.

A similar fate in modern times befell Manmohan Singh who – successfully – liberalized some of the stifling controls on the Indian economy, resulting in a period of rapid growth in output and living standards. However, the process of moving from controls to – partial – markets creates new opportunities for corruption. For example, introducing auctions rather than administrative allocations for a telecoms spectrum may be a great economic idea, but not if the auctioneer – the Minister – is controlling the outcome to favour his friends. In that and other ways, Manmohan Singh – who was one of the most honest men in Indian public life – became tainted with his government's wider corruption. Moreover, Indian experience of reform illustrates the more general political point that there are many firms and individuals who may be persuaded of the theoretical advantages of economic liberalization but will block it if it affects their interests. And in a democracy there are people strenuously opposed to change who may hold the keys to power. In India these conservative forces eventually overwhelmed Manmohan Singh's attempts at reform. Good economics; bad politics.

India is not the only country where leaders have run into severe unintended economic (and political) problems as a result of partial liberalization: trying to introduce markets into a controlled economy. Lenin's New Economic Policy had some major positive consequences in terms of the availability of food and other goods but also produced what was called the 'scissors crisis' as the terms of trade between town and country fluctuated wildly because of lack of stock holdings or forward markets to act as stabilizers. Deng had comparable problems when he tried to open up the Chinese economy. His attempts in 1988 to lift price controls based on conventional thinking about markets balancing supply and demand backfired badly: inflation rocketed, aggravated by speculation and panic; then, there was 'readjustment' with a slowing of growth, 20 million job losses and the abandonment of the policy. Popular anger was a major contributor to the unrest which led to the Tiananmen Square killings.

A recurrent theme, particularly in countries passing through a major transformation, is the need to manage the politics and economics of market reform while simultaneously managing the politics and economics of stabilization at a macro level. In the case of China the policy tension was expressed through the debate between 'builders' (like Deng) and 'balancers' (like Chen Yun) who supported market reform but worried that 'excessive' growth would lead to inflation and/or balance of payments problems and general instability. The same dilemma faced Park in South Korea. He repeatedly disregarded advice to scale back destabilizing growth – he was a 'builder' in the Deng mould – and in 1979 the bitter arguments about policy in his administration, including his inclination to suppress dissent, contributed to his assassination.

It was the same essential set of dilemmas which confronted European political leaders seeking to move from a highly regulated command-and-control economy: Erhard with the Nazi war economy and Balcerowicz in communist Poland. Both were faced with economies in collapse which narrowed their options. Both opted to move simultaneously and rapidly to scrap controls and introduce a market economy while maintaining control of the money supply and the government budget. In both cases the 'big bang' was successful in restoring the availability of goods and after a short, painful period of adjustment both Germany and Poland went on to achieve a long period of sustained growth. But in both cases there were casualties in the form of a sharp rise in unemployment and some groups experienced serious economic hardship. There was bitter political opposition in both. Erhard survived by subsuming his economic liberalism within a bigger entity, the Christian Democrats, whose values he did not share; and the Solidarity-led government of Balcerowicz only survived two years before being replaced by 'social democrats', ex-communists, who nonetheless allowed the reforms to survive while claiming credit for their success.

There is a special place in the heaven of economics for those leaders who achieved major economic transformation while sustaining their political popularity. There are few who did. Roosevelt was twice re-elected, as was Thatcher, and Erhard won even more elections albeit in a Christian Democratic team. Lee kept being re-elected on the back of sustained success in delivering growth though under a more controlled form of democracy. Erlander gets the prize for the political leader who presided over sustained economic success combined with repeated electoral reward for delivering popular social outcomes.

Roosevelt's popularity rested on a programme of radical reform of labour law and government activism curbing big business in the New Deal, allied to redistribution. In fact, this agenda had little to do with the problem he was primarily concerned with and has subsequently been credited with: solving mass unemployment by Keynesian means. Roosevelt's political instincts led him to oppose deficit financing and his – politically inspired – commitment to budget discipline and sound money precipitated a serious but probably unnecessary recession in his second term. Arguably, it was war as much as the New Deal which solved the unemployment problem. But, to this day, his attempts to reform capitalism, while trying to repair a damaged economy and sustain a political movement, have provided a template for leadership in crisis conditions.

Margaret Thatcher was also credited with economic achievements which were, to some extent, an unintended by-product of other policies. The early decision to remove exchange controls led to a major appreciation of the currency which broke inflation expectations (at the cost of major and long-term damage to the manufacturing sector). And on what became the defining policies of Thatcherism – privatization and deregulation – she was more cautious than her colleagues. Her significance lies in the fact that, for radical economic reform to succeed, it needs the political conviction and determination to see policies through even if, at the time, they may be unpopular and difficult (as with the confrontation with trade unions).

By contrast, as we see with populist economics, as in Argentina, an inability or unwillingness to confront the electorate with difficult choices and secure a political mandate for making them causes the economy to spin out of control. What is remarkable about Argentina and Peronism is that they have combined one of the most abject, sustained failures in economic policy with continued political popularity, evidenced by the 2019 election of a sixth Peronist President.

Simultaneously reconciling both economic and political imperatives requires a combination of political skill and luck over a long period. Roosevelt, Thatcher and Lee had both. Swedish Social Democrats under Erlander and his predecessors and successors have delivered a combination of strong economic growth, relative equality and economic security for the best part of a century and, with other Nordic social democracies, produced the most successful model yet devised. Yet even that model is now suffering politically. The fiscal discipline and market reforms required to keep the model financially sustainable have undermined the sense of idealism and social cohesion on which social democratic politics developed. The steady expansion of the demands of the welfare state required economic growth to sustain it. The growth sucked in migrant workers who have made these countries more diverse and less cohesive. Anti-immigration politics has further weakened the sense of solidarity on which the model depends.

The Japanese, in a different way, maintained impressive economic growth and cohesion with political stability but have been struggling for the last three decades to sustain growth while managing the balance sheet legacy of debt from a collapsed asset boom. Japan has now produced political leadership which has, by Japanese standards, proved remarkably innovative and durable, and has a clear plan of action in the form of Abenomics. It remains to be seen whether Abenomics will work over an extended time and whether the Japanese electorate will continue to swallow propositions – such as government borrowing to reduce debt – which may be economically necessary but strain popular comprehension. But, so far, the Japanese leadership has come closest to managing the multiple challenges of post-industrial society. It now faces the massive task of economic management after Covid-19, and has responded with remarkable economic radicalism.

It is tempting to look for a big picture and in particular a pattern of success or failure. If there is a big picture, it is probably around the attraction of hybrids. Planned socialist economies have moved towards markets, pragmatically and gradually or in a 'big bang'. State capitalism has become a distinct and seemingly successful model not just in China but in many emerging economies such as Korea's. Capitalist economies have tried to blend competitive markets and a strong state with welfare and public goods: the German model from Bismarck to post-Erhard Christian Democracy, Roosevelt's American liberalism (while it lasted) and Nordic social democracy. Lee's Singapore is perhaps an extreme example of how a powerful and effective state can coexist with an open market economy, and succeed (though there are some obvious failures like the attempts at reformed communism in Eastern Europe). Despite attempts to shift the balance, as in the Thatcher and Reagan years, such hybrids seem to have proved more durable, politically and economically, than purer models.

The Future

This book is essentially about economic history. But history is the best guide we have to the future. In the post-crisis period there has been a veritable blizzard of books and think-pieces demanding that politicians take action to revive economic growth, pay more attention to inequality, ensure that environmental challenges – especially climate change – are met and prevent the post-war rules-based international system from falling apart. But there is little sign of Western democracies throwing up political leadership comparable to, say, Roosevelt in the 1930s. At the heart of the inadequacy of the political response is the simple fact that politics is national: politicians derive their legitimacy and support from domestic electorates and parties. Western Europe has tried to create a trans-national politics but with limited success. So far.

The consequence has been a globally integrated economy with weak global governance. The instability of such a structure has been brutally exposed by the Covid-19 pandemic. Many individual governments may have responded with impressive speed and effectiveness. But others, notably the two economic superpowers, the USA and China, have not only made serious domestic errors but have opened up a new sphere of conflict. The pandemic and its economic aftermath almost certainly mark a turning point in the way both politics and economics are done. There are two major potential trends.

The first is the ongoing seductive appeal of populist economics given shape by nationalism in an approach to trade, migration and problems requiring collective action, like climate change. In the USA, Brazil, India, Russia and parts of Eastern Europe (and to a degree the UK) different elements of that kind of populist political economy are taking shape. Only recently has the lack of study and understanding of economic populism started to be addressed.[2] My two reviews of economic populism in action – Peronism and Trump – do not encourage hope of an end to populist economic policies.

The second is the belief that it is easier to achieve difficult economic and social objectives through authoritarian government. The military government of Park in Korea and the more subtle authoritarianism of Lee's Singapore provide role models. The China of Deng and his immediate successors could be said to be the most successful development model in history and with no concession to Western ideas of human rights and democracy. The model may or may not continue to work with the more controlling and nationalistic administration of Xi Jinping. The liberal orthodoxy is that sophisticated modern economies require creative and critical minds which cannot flourish in authoritarian systems. Nonetheless, we are seeing the emergence of 'strong men' with authoritarian traits in several significant countries (Russia, Turkey, Hungary, the Philippines, Egypt) and some in what were previously healthy multi-party democracies like India and Brazil. The seemingly dead and buried ideas of inter-war fascism, which Perón tried to revive without success, may be due for a resurrection.

The combination and interaction of populist economic nationalism, especially in one of the two superpowers, and authoritarian government (especially in the other) made for an unstable mix. The 1930s give a good indication of where it might lead. It doesn't have to. There is still life left in the European project. And the worlds of science and business generally tend to resist fragmentation and nationalism.

What is clear is that global economic, as well as political, outcomes will depend on a handful of individual politicians: Trump's successor; whether Xi retains and consolidates his absolute political control; whether Macron (or an extreme French nationalist) or the new generation of populist 'strong men' (Modi, Bolsonaro) succeed. The economics of politicians matters more than ever.

Acknowledgements

Thanks are due to Shona Brown for her patience and skill typing and organizing the manuscript; to Tamsin Shelton for copy-editing; to Mike Harpley for his editing and publishing; to my literary agent Georgina Capel; and to Rachel, my wife, for her support and encouragement.

Notes

Introduction

1 Ha Joon Chang, *23 Things They Don't Tell You about Capitalism*, Penguin, London (2011), p.244.

2 Douglas Irwin, *Against the Tide: An Intellectual History of Free Trade*, Princeton University Press, Princeton (1998); William Bernstein, *A Splendid Exchange: How Trade Shaped the World*, Atlantic, London (2008), pp.350–56.

3 Eric Roll, *A History of Economic Thought*, Faber & Faber, London (1953); Niall Kishtainy, *A Little History of Economics*, Yale University Press, New Haven (2018).

4 Adam Smith, *An Inquiry into the Nature and Causes of the Wealth of Nations*, edited by R.H. Campbell and A.S. Skinner, Liberty Fund, Indianapolis (1981); Adam Smith, *The Theory of Moral Sentiments*, edited by D.D. Raphael and A.L. Macfie, Liberty Fund, Indianapolis (1982).

5 Summarized in Roll, Ch. 6.

6 Charles P. Kindleberger, *Power and Money: The Economics of International Politics and the Politics of International Economics*, Macmillan, London (1970), p.15.

7 Paul A. Samuelson, *Economics: An Introductory Analysis*, McGraw-Hill, New York (1948).

8 James E. Meade, *The Intelligent Radical's Guide to Economic Policy: The Mixed Economy*, Allen & Unwin, London (1974).

9 Bernard Crick, *In Defence of Politics*, Penguin, Harmondsworth (1964), pp.160–61.

10 W.C. Sellar and R.J. Yeatman, *1066 and All That*, Methuen, London (1930).

11 E.H. Carr, *What is History?*, Macmillan, London (1961).

12 Described in Niall Ferguson, *The Ascent of Money: A Financial History of the World*, Penguin, London (2009), pp.213–20.

13 Daron Acemoglu and James Robinson, *Why Nations Fail: The Origins of Power, Prosperity and Poverty*, Crown Business, New York (2012).

1

Hamilton: The Economic Founding Father

1 Douglass North, *The Economic Growth of the United States 1790–1860*, Prentice-Hall, Englewood Cliffs (1971), p. 46.

2 Nathan Schachner, *Alexander Hamilton*, Appleton-Century, New York (1946), p.277.

3 James Conant (1901); William Culbertson (1916); Henry Jones Ford (1929); Henry Cabot Lodge (1881); David Loth (1939); John Morse (1876); Frederick Oliver (1928); Samuel Schmucker (1856); Johan Smertenko (1932); Robert Irving Warshow (1931).

4 Ron Chernow, *Alexander Hamilton*, Penguin Press, New York (2004).

5 Quoted in Schachner, p.36.

6 Ibid., p.100.

7 Quoted in Edwin G. Burrows and Mike Wallace, *Gotham: A History of New York City to 1898*, Oxford University Press, New York (1999), p.270.

8 Ibid., p.229.

9 Quoted in Schachner, p.212.

10 Gordon S. Wood, 'An Affair of Honor', *New York Review of Books*, 13 April 2000.

11 Chernow, p.403.

12 Schachner, p.275.

13 Chernow, p.377.

14 Quoted in Douglas A. Irwin, *Against the Tide: An Intellectual History of Free Trade*, Princeton University Press, Princeton (1998), p.121.

15 Ibid.

2

Peel: Free Trade

1 Harry G. Johnson, *Aspects of the Theory of Tariffs*, Harvard University Press, Cambridge, MA (1971), p.187.

2 Douglas A. Irwin, *Against the Tide: An Intellectual History of Free Trade*, Princeton University Press, Princeton (1998).

3 William Bernstein, *A Splendid Exchange: How Trade Shaped the World*, Atlantic, London (2008), p.257.

4 Dudley North, *Discourses upon Trade* (1691), discussed in Eric Roll, *A History of Economic Thought*, Faber & Faber, London (1953).

5 I draw heavily on two fine biographies among the several written: Douglas Hurd, *Robert Peel: A Biography*, Weidenfeld & Nicolson, London (2007); and Norman Gash, *Mr Secretary Peel: The Life of Sir Robert Peel to 1830*, Longman, London (1961) and the successor volume *After 1830*, Longman, London (1972).

6 Gash, p.xx.

7 Quoted in Bernstein, p.305.

8 Gash, pp.327–8.

9 Hurd, p.170.

3

Bismarck: The Economics of 'Iron and Blood'

1 Alan Krueger, *From Bismarck to Maastricht: The March to European Union and the Labor Compact*, NBER Working Paper No. 7456, Cambridge, MA (January 2000).

2 Edgar Feuchtwanger, *Bismarck*, Routledge, London (2002), pp.259–60.

3 Jonathan Steinberg, *Bismarck: A Life*, Oxford University Press, Oxford (2011), p.271.

4 Edward Crankshaw, *Bismarck*, Macmillan, London (1981), p.233.

5 In Feuchtwanger, Steinberg, Crankshaw and in A.J.P. Taylor, *Bismarck: The Man and the Statesman*, Penguin, London (1955).

6 Crankshaw, p.9.

7 Taylor, p.10.

8 Crankshaw, p.37.

9 Ibid., p.69.

10 Taylor, p.56.

11 Ibid., p.26.

12 Feuchtwanger, p.87.

13 Taylor, p.56.

14 Feuchtwanger, p.162.

15 Ibid.

16 Ibid.

17 Crankshaw, pp.141–3.

18 Ibid., p.241.

19 Gordon A. Craig, *Germany 1866–1945*, Oxford University Press, Oxford (1981), p.90.

20 Ibid., p.91.

21 Quoted in Steinberg, p.366.

22 Quoted in Craig, p.87.

23	Niall Kishtainy, *A Little History of Economics*, Yale University Press, New Haven (2018).

24	Crankshaw, p.142.

25	Steinberg, pp.202–3.

26	Crankshaw, p.341.

27	Ibid., p.359.

28	Taylor, p.162.

29	Crankshaw, p.232.

30	Taylor, p.9.

31	Werner Abelshauser, *The Dynamics of German Industry: Germany's Path Toward the New Economy and the American Challenge*, Berghahn Books, New York and Oxford (2005).

32	Steinberg, p.272.

33	Craig, pp.153–4.

34	Taylor, p.41.

4

Lenin: From War Communism to State Capitalism

1	Louis Fischer, *The Life of Lenin*, Weidenfeld & Nicolson, London (1964).

2	Ibid., p.19.

3	His arguments against the Narodnik intellectuals are set out in his book *The Development of Capitalism in Russia*, discussed in Maurice Dobb, *Soviet Economic Development Since 1917*, Routledge & Kegan Paul, London (1948), pp.62–3.

4	E.H. Carr, *The Bolshevik Revolution 1917–23*, Macmillan, London (1952).

5	The pre-revolutionary economy is best described in Alexander Gerschenkron, *Economic Backwardness in Historical Perspective*, Belknap Press of Harvard University Press, Cambridge, MA (1962), and there is a good summary in Alec Nove, *An Economic History of the USSR 1917–1991*, Penguin, Harmondsworth (1969).

6	Dobb, p.74.

7	Niall Ferguson, *The Pity of War: Explaining World War I*, Basic Books, New York (1999), p.394.

8	Dobb, p.93.

9	Nove, pp.47–50, 68.

10	Quoted in Dobb, p.123.

11	Quoted in ibid., p.130.

12	Ibid., p.145.

13	Nove, p.116.

14	Fischer, p.487.

15	Ezra Vogel, *Deng Xiaoping and the Transformation of China*, Belknap Press of Harvard University Press, Cambridge, MA (2011), p.25.

5
Roosevelt: The Keynesian Revolution Without Keynes

1 Irving Fisher, *Booms and Depressions: Some First Principles*, Adelphi, New York (1932). References to the influence of Sachs in Elliot Rosen, *The Great Depression and the Economics of Recovery*, University of Virginia Press, Charlottesville (2005).

2 Alvin Hansen, *Full Recovery or Stagnation?*, W.W. Norton, New York (1938).

3 For example, Jim Powell, *FDR's Folly: How Roosevelt and His New Deal Prolonged the Great Depression*, Crown Forum, New York (2003) and Herbert Hoover, *The Challenge to Liberty*, Scribner, New York (1934).

4 James MacGregor Burns, *Roosevelt: The Lion and the Fox*, Harcourt, Brace & Co., New York (1956), pp.18–20.

5 Quoted in William E. Leuchtenburg, *Franklin D. Roosevelt and the New Deal*, Harper & Row, New York (1963), p.11.

6 Eric Rauchway, *The Great Depression and the New Deal: A Very Short Introduction*, Oxford University Press, Oxford (2008), p.20.

7 Leuchtenburg, pp.10, 34.

8 The original article is 'The Debt-Deflation Theory of Great Depressions', *Econometrica*, 1(4), October 1933.

9 Charles P. Kindleberger and Robert Z. Aliber, *Manias, Panics, and Crashes: A History of Financial Crises*, Palgrave Macmillan, Basingstoke (2005); Hyman Minsky, *John Maynard Keynes*, Columbia University Press, New York (1976); and summarized in my book *The Storm: The World Economic Crisis and What It Means*, Atlantic, London (2009).

10 Milton Friedman and Anna Jacobson Schwartz, *The Great Contraction, 1929–1933*, Princeton University Press, Princeton (new edition 2008), p.8.

11 Leuchtenburg, p.36.

12 Ibid.

13 David M. Kennedy, *Freedom from Fear: The American People in Depression and War 1929–45*, Oxford University Press, New York (1999), p.361.

14 Robert Skidelsky, *John Maynard Keynes 1883–1946: Economist, Philosopher, Statesman*, Macmillan, London (2003), p.506.

15 Quoted in Leuchtenburg, p.44.

16 Ibid., p.45.

17 George J. Benston, *The Separation of Commercial and Investment Banking: The Glass–Steagall Act Revisited and Reconsidered*, Oxford University Press, New York (1990).

18 My own *The Storm* and also *After the Storm*, Atlantic, London (2016).

19 Leuchtenburg, p.34.

20 Ibid., p.35.

21 Adolf A. Berle and Gardiner C. Means, *The Modern Corporation and Private Property*, Macmillan, New York (1932).

22 Alistair Cooke, *A Generation on Trial: USA v Alger Hiss*, Alfred A. Knopf, New York (1950), p.18.

23 For example, J.K. Galbraith, *American Capitalism: The Concept of Countervailing Power*, Houghton Mifflin, Boston (1952).

24 Leuchtenburg, p.45.

25 Skidelsky, p.507.

26 J.M. Keynes, *Open Letter to President Roosevelt* (in Skidelsky).

27 The unemployment figures in particular have been disputed. The figures quoted are from Powell, p.226.

28 Kenneth D. Roose, *The Economics of Recession and Revival: An Interpretation of 1937–38*, Archon Books, Hamden, CT (1969), p.210.

29 Ibid. and H. Gregg Lewis, cited in Roose.

30 Joseph A. Schumpeter, *Business Cycles: A Theoretical, Historical, and Statistical Analysis of the Capitalist Process*, McGraw-Hill, New York (1939), p.419.

31 Leuchtenburg, p.244.

32 Quoted in Peter Clarke, *Keynes: The Rise, Fall, and Return of the 20th Century's Most Influential Economist*, Bloomsbury Press, New York (2009), p.165.

33 Michael Stewart, *Keynes and After*, Penguin, Harmondsworth (1967), p.132.

34 Burns, p.320.

35 Clarke, p.167.

36 Leuchtenburg, p.264.

37 Ibid., p.336.

38 Ira Katznelson, *Fear Itself: The New Deal and the Origins of Our Time*, Liveright, New York (2013).

39 Benn Steil, *The Battle for Bretton Woods: John Maynard Keynes, Harry Dexter White, and the Making of a New World Order*, Princeton University Press, Princeton (2013).

6
Erhard: The Social Market and Ordoliberalism

1 Ludwig Erhard, *Prosperity Through Competition*, Thames & Hudson, London (1958).

2 Simon Wren-Lewis, Ordoliberalism, Neoliberalism & Economics blog: https://www.socialeurope.eu/ordoliberalism-neoliberalism-economics

3 The main biographical source I have used is Alfred C. Mierzejewski, *Ludwig Erhard: A Biography*, University of North Carolina Press, Chapel Hill and London (2004). Also, and indirectly, Anthony Nicholls, *Freedom with Responsibility*, Oxford University Press, Oxford (1994) and Henry Wallich, *Mainsprings of the German Revival*, Yale University Press, New Haven (1955).

4 Alan Peacock (ed.), *Germany's Social Market Economy: Origins and Evolution*, Macmillan, London (1989).

5 Mierzejewski, pp.7–8.

6 Mierzejewski, p.xiii.

7 Frédéric Clavent, *Hjalmar Schacht: Financier and Diplomat 1930–50*, University of Strasbourg, Strasbourg (2006).

8 Edward N. Peterson, *Hjalmar Schacht: For and Against Hitler: A Political-Economic Study of Germany, 1923–1945*, Christopher Publishing House, Boston (1954).

9 Adam Tooze, *The Wages of Destruction: The Making and Breaking of the Nazi Economy*, Allen Lane, London (2006).

10 Richard J. Evans, *The Third Reich in Power, 1933–1939: How the Nazis Won Over the Hearts and Minds of a Nation*, Penguin, New York (2006), Ch.4, 'Business, Politics and War'.

11 Mierzejewski, p.23.

12 As with Alfred Müller-Armack, cited in Mierzejewski, p.25.

13 Mierzejewski, p.58.

14 Erhard, p.12.

15 Jacques Rueff and André Piettre, quoted by Erhard, p.13.

16 Quoted in Mierzejewski, p.74.

17 Paul Weymar, *Konrad Adenauer: The Authorised Biography*, Andre Deutsch, London (1957), p.250.

18 Mierzejewski, p.87.

19 Nicholls, p.3.

20 Werner Abelshauser, discussed in Mierzejewski, p.117.

7
Erlander: The Social Democratic Model Made Real

1 Andrew Heywood, *Political Ideologies: An Introduction*, Palgrave Macmillan, Basingstoke (2012).

2 Nik Brandal, Øivind Bratberg and Dag Einar Thorsen, *The Nordic Model of Social Democracy*, Palgrave Macmillan, Basingstoke (2013). There is an excellent history of the Swedish welfare state from 1945 to 1980 in Sven Olson's chapter in Peter Flora (ed.), *Growth to Limits: The Western European Welfare States Since World War 2*, De Greyter, New York and Berlin (1988).

3 Jenny Andersson, *Between Growth and Security: Swedish Social Democracy from a Strong Society to a Third Way*, Manchester University Press, Manchester (2006).

4 There is only one biography in English that I am aware of and I have used it extensively: Olof Ruin, *Tage Erlander: Serving the Welfare State 1946–1969*, University of Pittsburgh Press, Pittsburgh (1990).

5 Benny Carlson and Lars Jonung, 'Knut Wicksell, Gustav Cassel, Eli Heckscher, Bertil Ohlin and Gunnar Myrdal on the Role of the Economist in Public Debate'

in *Econ Journal Watch*, 3(3), September 2006.

6 Gunnar Myrdal, *The Political Element in the Development of Economic Theory* (1930). See William J. Barber, *Gunnar Myrdal: An Intellectual Biography*, Palgrave Macmillan, Basingstoke (2018).

7 Kjell Östberg, 'The Great Reformer': https://www.jacobinmag.com/2015/09/sweden-social-democracy-olaf-palme-assassination-reforms

8 Ruin, p.7.

9 Eduard Bernstein, *The Preconditions of Socialism*, Cambridge University Press, Cambridge (2002).

10 His memoirs were in Swedish and I have used quotations and references quoted elsewhere in English.

11 Quoted in Avner Offer and Gabriel Söderberg, *The Nobel Factor: The Prize in Economics, Social Democracy, and the Market Turn*, Princeton University Press, Princeton, p.79. The *Yellow Book* was entitled *Britain's Industrial Decline, being the Report of the Liberal Industrial Inquiry of 1928*.

12 Ibid.

13 Sheri Berman, *Understanding Social Democracy*, Minda

de Gunzberg Center for European Studies, Cambridge, MA (2008), pp.12–13.

14 Marquis Childs, *Sweden: The Middle Way*, Yale University Press, New Haven (1936), cited in Ruin, p.4. A pamphlet of the same title was written at around the same time by Harold Macmillan, the future UK Conservative Prime Minister, advocating an approach that, unlike Sweden, was highly unorthodox.

15 Ruin, p.214.

16 Ibid., p.193.

17 Wolfgang Merkel, Alexander Petring, Christian Henkes and Christoph Egle, *Social Democracy in Power: The Capacity to Reform*, Routledge, London (2008), pp.8–9.

18 Ruin, p.217.

19 Ibid., p.204.

20 Ibid., p.244.

21 Ibid., p.75.

22 Ibid., p.39.

23 Ibid., p.197.

24 Ibid., p.44.

25 Östberg.

26 Quoted from an interview with Feldt by T. Sjöberg, *Playboy Skandinavia* (5), 1999, pp.37–44.

27 Olaf Cramme and Patrick Diamond (eds), *After the Third Way: The Future of Social Democracy in Europe*, I.B. Tauris, London (2012); Ashley Lavelle, *The Death of Social Democracy: Political Consequences in the 21st Century*, Ashgate, Aldershot (2008).

28 Ruin, p.4, based on Marquis Childs.

8

Perón: Peronism and Economic Populism

1 Gerardo della Paolera and Alan M. Taylor (eds), *A New Economic History of Argentina*, Cambridge University Press, Cambridge (2013); C. Díaz Alejandro, *Essays in the Economic History of the Argentine Republic*, Yale University Press, New Haven (1970).

2 Robert D. Crassweller, *Perón and the Enigmas of Argentina*,

W.W. Norton, New York and London (1987), p.40.

3 Ibid., p.46.

4 Tom Bailey, 'A History of Economic Trouble in Argentina', *World Finance*, 10 March 2016.

5 Gerardo della Paolera and Ezequiel Gallo, *Epilogue: The Argentine Puzzle* in Paolera and Taylor, p.369.

6 Alec Ford, *The Gold Standard*,

1880–1914: Britain and Argentina, Clarendon Press, Oxford (1962), quoted in Paolera and Gallo, p.370.

7 Ibid., p.372.

8 Crassweller, p.35.

9 Kerry Bolton, *Perón and Peronism*, Black House Publishing, London (2014), p.6.

10 Crassweller, p.92.

11 Ibid., p.75.

12 Raúl Prebisch, 'Commercial Policy in the Underdeveloped Countries', *American Economic Review*, May 1959; *Towards a New Trade Policy for Development: Report by the Secretary General UNCTAD* (1964).

13 W. Arthur Lewis, *The Theory of Economic Growth*, Richard D. Irwin, Homeward, IL (1955).

14 Alan M. Taylor, *Capital Accumulation* in Paolera and Taylor, p.193.

15 Ian Malcolm, David Little, Jan Malcolm, Maurice Scott and Tibor Scitovsky, *Industry and Trade in Some Development Countries: A Comparative Study*, published for the Development Centre of the OECD by Oxford University Press, Oxford (1970).

16 Yair Mundlak and Marcelo Regúnaga, *Agriculture* in Paolera and Taylor, p.250.

17 Crassweller, pp.209–11.

18 Gerardo della Paolera, Maria Alejandra Irigoin and Carlos G. Bózzoli, *Passing the Buck: Monetary and Fiscal Policies* in Paolera and Taylor, p.73.

19 Daron Acemoglu and James Robinson, *Why Nations Fail: The Origins of Power, Prosperity and Poverty*, Crown Business, New York (2012), pp.329–32.

20 Bolton, p.182.

21 R.B. Sutcliffe, *Industry and Underdevelopment*, Addison-Wesley, London (1971), pp.229–34; K.B. Griffin, *Underdevelopment in Spanish America: An Interpretation*, Allen & Unwin, London (1969).

22 James P. Brennan and Marcelo Rougier, *The Politics of National Capitalism*, Pennsylvania State University Press, University Park, PA (2009).

23 There was a particularly vicious and widely cited biography by Mary Main, *The Woman and the Whip*, published originally in 1952 in the USA under a pseudonym (Maria Flores), then in 1980 in Argentina. The book was countered by Tomás Eloy Martínez in *Time* magazine, 20 January 1997.

24 Nicholas Fraser and Marysa Navarro, *Evita: The Real Lives of Eva Perón*, W.W. Norton, New York and London (1996); John Barnes, *Evita: First Lady*,

a *Biography of Eva Perón*, Grove Press, New York (1978).

25 Crassweller, p.288.

26 Bolton, p.349.

27 Beniamino Moro and Victor A. Beker, *Modern Financial Crises: Argentina, United States and Europe*, Springer, Cham (2016), p.30.

28 Pablo Gerchunoff, *Peronist Economic Policies, 1946–55* in Guido di Tella and Rudiger Dornbusch (eds), *The Political Economy of Argentina 1946–83*, Macmillan, Basingstoke (1987).

29 Andre Gunder Frank, *The Development of Underdevelopment*, New England Free Press, Boston (1966).

30 Reported from 1998 Annual Meeting of the IMF Board of Governors.

31 Dani Rodrik, *Goodbye Washington Consensus, Hello Washington Confusion?*, paper prepared for the *Journal of Economic Literature* (2006).

32 Joseph E. Stiglitz, *Globalization and its Discontents*, Allen Lane, London (2002).

33 Arnold Harberger, Interview with Minneapolis Federal Reserve (March 1999); Andre Gunder Frank, 'Economic Genocide in Chile: Open Letter to Milton Friedman and Arnold Harberger', *Economic and Political Weekly*, Vol. 11, No. 24, 12 June 1976.

34 Ricardo Ffrench-Davis, *Economic Reforms in Chile: From Dictatorship to Democracy*, Palgrave Macmillan, London (2010); Richard Davies, *Extreme Economies: Survival, Failure, Future – Lessons from the World's Limits*, Transworld, London (2019), pp.303–41.

35 Rafael Di Tella and Juan Dubra, *Peronist Beliefs and Interventionist Politics*, NBER Working Paper No. 16621, Washington, DC, December 2010.

36 Statement by Pope Francis on 4 June 2019. Based on earlier documents: *Evangelii Gaudium*; *Laudato Si*; and the 1965 paper *Gaudium et Spes* arising from the Second Vatican Council.

9
Park: The Development State and Hypergrowth

1 Adrian Buzo, *The Making of Modern Korea*, Routledge, London (2007); Michael Seth, *A Concise History of Korea*, Rowman & Littlefield, Maryland (2011).

2 Quote from *New York Times* in Seth, p.399.

3 Byung-Kook Kim in Introduction to Byung-Kook Kim and Ezra F. Vogel, *The Park Chung Hee Era: The Transformation of South Korea*, Harvard University Press, Cambridge, MA (2011), p.3.

4 Niall Kishtainy, *A Little History of Economics*, Yale University Press, New Haven (2017).

5 Carter J. Eckert, *Park Chung Hee and Modern Korea*, Belknap Press of Harvard University Press, Cambridge, MA (2016), pp.126–7; Chung-in Moon and Byung-joon Jun, *Modernization Strategy: Ideas and Influences* in Kim and Vogel, pp.121–2.

6 Paul Rosenstein-Rodan's theory of Big Push: the seminal article dates from 1963; W. Arthur Lewis, *The Theory of Economic Growth*, Richard D. Irwin, Homeward, IL (1955); W.W. Rostow, 'The Stages of Economic Growth', *Economic History Review*, Second Series, Vol. XII, No. 1 (1959).

7 Chung-in Moon and Byung-joon Jun, *Modernisation Strategy: Ideas and Influences* in Kim and Vogel, p.115.

8 Carter J. Eckert, *Park Chung Hee and Modern Korea*, Belknap Press of Harvard University Press, Cambridge, MA (2016), pp.185–94.

9 There is a potted history in, *inter alia*, Yushin Yoo, *The Making of Modern Korea*, Golden Pond Press, New York (1990).

10 Buzo, p.84.

11 *Inter alia*, Yong-Sup Han, *The May Sixteenth Military Coup* in Kim and Vogel, pp.36–7.

12 Don Oberdorfer, *The Two Koreas: A Contemporary History*, Addison-Wesley, Reading, MA (1997); Cho Kap-che, *Spit on My Grave*, Seoul (1998).

13 Yong-Sup Han, p.37.

14 Cho Kap-che cited in Yong-Sup Han.

15 First Communiqué broadcast on 16 May 1961.

16 Hyung-A Kim, *State Building* in Kim and Vogel, p.95.

17 Ibid.

18 The complexities of the relationship are discussed in Taehyun Kim and Chang Jae Baik, *Taming and Tamed by the United States* in Kim and Vogel, pp.59–84.

19 Ibid., p.75.

20 *Inter alia*, W.W. Rostow, *The World Economy: History and Prospect*, University of Texas Press, Austin (1978), Ch. 33.

21 The whole history of Park's relationship with the chaebols is covered in Eun Mee Kim and Gil-Sung Park, *The Chaebol* in Kim and Vogel;

also in Alice Lumsden, *Asia's Next Giant: South Korea and Late Industrialisation*, Oxford University Press, Oxford (1989) and Mark L. Clifford, *Troubled Tiger: Businessmen, Bureaucrats, and Generals in South Korea*, M.E. Sharpe, Armonk, NY (1998).

22 Kim and Park, p.272.

23 Ibid., p.271.

24 Ibid., p.270.

25 Sang-young Rhyu and Seok-jin Lew, *Pohang Iron and Steel Company* in Kim and Vogel.

26 Young Jo Lee, *The Countryside* in Kim and Vogel.

27 Byung-Kook Kim, *The Leviathan: Economic Bureaucracy under Park* in Kim and Vogel, p.219.

28 Ibid., p.221.

29 Quoted in Michael Newton, *Famous Assassinations in World History: An Encyclopedia*, Vol. 1, ABC-Clio, Santa Barbara (2014), p.404.

10

Lee: The Eclectic Economics of Lee Kuan Yew

1 Rodney King, *The Singapore Miracle: Myth and Reality*, Insight Press, Western Australia (2008), p.2.

2 Gary Roden, *Transparency and Authoritarian Rule in South East Asia*, Routledge Curzon, London (2004), p.92.

3 Lee Kuan Yew, *From Third World to First: The Singapore Story, 1965–2000*, HarperCollins, London (2000).

4 King, pp.1–3.

5 Paul Krugman, 'The Myth of Asia's Miracle', *Foreign Affairs*, Vol. 73, No. 6, November/ December 1994.

6 W.G. Huff, *The Economic Growth of Singapore: Trade and Development in the Twentieth Century*, Cambridge University Press, Cambridge (1994), p.37.

7 Lee, p.95.

8 Edgar H. Schein, *Strategic Pragmatism: The Culture of Singapore's Economic Development*, MIT Press, Cambridge, MA (1996).

9 Huff, p.359.

10 Told in his own words in his memoir, *The Singapore Story*, Prentice Hall, Singapore (1998).

11 Stan Sessor, *The Lands of Charm and Cruelty*, Vintage Books, New York (1994), p.11.

12 Arnold Toynbee, *Cities on the Move*, Oxford University Press, New York (1970), p.55.

13　John Curtis Perry, *Singapore: Unlikely Power*, Oxford University Press, Oxford (2017), p.177.

14　Ministry of Culture, *Social Transformation in Singapore*, Singapore (1964), p.105.

15　Huff, pp.1–2.

16　Lim Chong Yah and associates, *Policy Options for the Singapore Economy*, Singapore (1998), p.49.

17　Lee, p.685.

18　Tilak Abeysinghe, *Lessons of Singapore's Development for Other Developing Countries* in Linda Lim (ed.), *Singapore's Economic Development: Retrospection and Reflections*, World Scientific, Singapore (2016).

19　King, p.470.

20　Ngiam Tong Dow, *A Mandarin and the Making of Public Policy*, NUS Press, Singapore (2006), p.92.

21　Huff, p.339.

22　Linda Lim, *Fifty Years of Development in the Singapore Economy: An Introductory Review* in Lim, p.5.

23　Lee, pp.430–32.

24　Ibid., p.56.

25　Perry, p.160.

26　Quoted in Lim (ed.), p. 37.

27　Sock-Yong Phang, *Singapore's Housing Policies: Responding to the Challenges of Economic Transition* in Lim (ed.).

28　Krugman.

29　Peter Wilson, *Monetary Policy and Financial Sector Development* in Lim (ed.).

30　Tan Kim Song and Manu Bhaskaran, *The Role of the State in Singapore: Pragmatism in Pursuit of Growth* in Lim (ed.).

31　Lee, pp.104–5.

32　Irene Y.H. Ng, *Being Poor in a Rich 'Nanny State': Developments in Singapore Social Welfare* in Lim (ed.).

33　Huff, p.336.

34　Milton Friedman, 'A Welfare State Syllogism', speech to the Commonwealth Club, San Francisco (1990).

11

Thatcher: Thatcherism and Its Cousin, Reaganomics

1　Robert Skidelsky (ed.), *Thatcherism*, Chatto & Windus, London (1988).

2　Claire Berlinski, *"There is No Alternative": Why Margaret Thatcher Matters*, Basic Books, New York (2008), p.275.

3　Nigel Lawson, *The View from No 11. Memoirs of a Tory Radical*, Bantam, London, p.64.

4　Frank Hahn, *Market Economics* in Skidelsky, p.123.

5　Berlinski, p.6.

6 Enoch Powell, *Saving in a Free Society*, published by Hutchinson for Institute of Economic Affairs, London (1960).

7 Alan Peacock, *The Political Economy of Economic Freedom*, Edward Elgar, Cheltenham (1997).

8 Michael Shanks, *The Stagnant Society: A Warning*, Penguin, Harmondsworth (1961).

9 Andrew Gamble, *Britain in Decline: Economic Policy, Political Strategy and the British State*, Macmillan, London (1981).

10 James Callaghan, quoted in Andrew Marr, *A History of Modern Britain*, Macmillan, London (2007), p.364.

11 *Inter alia*, Michael Stewart, *The Jekyll and Hyde Years: Politics and Economic Policy Since 1964*, Dent, London (1977).

12 As in Stuart Holland, *The Socialist Challenge*, Quartet Books, London (1975). A contrary view is in Vincent Cable, *Import Controls: The Case Against*, Fabian Society, London (1977).

13 Marr, p.355.

14 Notably John Campbell, *Margaret Thatcher, Vol. 1: The Grocer's Daughter* and *Vol. 2: The Iron Lady*, Jonathan Cape, London (2000, 2003); Charles Moore, *Thatcher: The Authorized Biography*, Vols 1–3, Allen Lane, London (2013, 2015, 2019); Andrew Gamble, *The Free Economy and the Strong State: The Politics of Thatcherism*, Macmillan, Basingstoke (1988); Kenneth Harris, *Thatcher*, Weidenfeld & Nicolson, London (1988); Peter Jenkins, *Mrs Thatcher's Revolution: The Ending of the Socialist Era*, Jonathan Cape, London (1987); Dennis Kavanagh, *Thatcherism and British Politics: The End of Consensus*, Oxford University Press, Oxford (1987).

15 Patrick Minford, *Mrs Thatcher's Economic Reform Programme* in Skidelsky, p.96.

16 Milton Friedman and Anna Schwartz, *A Monetary History of the United States*, Princeton University Press, Princeton (1963).

17 Campbell, Vol. 2, p.79.

18 Lawson, p.199.

19 Hansard: HC Deb 10 November 1981 vol. 12 c441.

20 Lawson, p.211.

21 Macmillan quoted in *The Times*, 9 and 15 November 1985.

22 Quoted in Geoffrey Howe, *Conflict of Loyalty*, Macmillan, London (1994), p.142.

23 Friedrich Hayek, *The Road to Serfdom*, Routledge & Kegan Paul, London (1944); Milton Friedman, with the assistance of Rose D. Friedman, *Capitalism and Freedom*,

University of Chicago Press, Chicago and London (1962).

24 Mancur Olson, *The Rise and Decline of Nations: Economic Growth, Stagflation, and Social Rigidities*, Yale University Press, New Haven (1982); Samuel Brittan, *The Economic Consequences of Democracy*, Temple Smith, London (1977); Anthony King, Richard Rose *et al.*, *Why Is Britain Becoming Harder to Govern?*, BBC, London (1976).

25 Berlinski, p.115.

26 Ibid., p.8.

27 Ibid., pp.127–8.

28 Campbell, Vol. 2, p.250.

29 Minford, p.94.

30 William A. Niskanen, *Reaganomics* in David R. Henderson (ed.), *Concise Encyclopedia of Economics*, Liberty Fund, Indianapolis (2008).

31 Arthur Laffer, *The Laffer Curve: Past, Present and Future*, The Heritage Foundation (2004): https://www.heritage.org/taxes/report/the-laffer-curve-past-present-and-future

32 Quoted in Lou Cannon, *President Reagan: The Role of a Lifetime*, PublicAffairs, New York (1991), p.123.

33 'Reaganomics or Voodoo Economics', BBC News, 5 June 2004.

34 William A. Niskanen, *Reaganomics: An Insider's Account of the Politics and the People*, Oxford University Press, New York and London (1988); Michael J. Boskin, *Reagan and the US Economy: The Successes, Failures, and Unfinished Agenda*, ICS Press, San Francisco (1987); Paul Krugman, *The Conscience of a Liberal*, W.W. Norton, New York and London (2007).

35 Skidelsky, p.23.

36 Quoted in *This Week*, 22 June 2002, and Campbell, Vol. 2, p.787.

37 World Bank, *Economic Growth in the 1990s: Learning from a Decade of Reform*, Washington, DC (2005); John Williamson, *Washington Consensus*, Centre for International Development, Harvard School of Government (2003); Dan Yergin and Joseph Stanislaw, *The Commanding Heights: The Battle for the World Economy*, Simon & Schuster, New York (1998).

38 John Williamson (ed.), *Latin American Adjustment: How Much Has Happened*, Peterson Institute for International Economics, Washington, DC (1989).

39 Campbell, Vol. 2, p.797.

12
Deng: China's Economic Architect

1 There is a discussion of Deng's use of folksy, popular aphorisms to make his points in Ezra Vogel, *Deng Xiaoping and the Transformation of China*, Belknap Press of Harvard University Press, Cambridge, MA (2011).

2 Widely quoted comment attributed to Deng's son Deng Zhifang, Vogel, p.423.

3 Jonathan Spence, *The Search for Modern China*, W.W. Norton, New York and London (1990); Richard Evans, *Deng Xiaoping and the Making of Modern China*, Viking, New York (1994).

4 Jung Chang and Jon Halliday, *Mao: The Unknown Story*, Jonathan Cape, London (2005).

5 Quoted in Stuart Gelder (ed.), *The Chinese Communists*, Hyperion, Westport, CT (1946), p.201.

6 Chang and Halliday, p.471.

7 Ibid., p.497.

8 Jasper Becker, *Hungry Ghosts: Mao's Secret Famine*, Free Press, New York (1996); Frank Dikötter, *Mao's Great Famine: The History of China's Most Devastating Catastrophe 1958–1962*, Walker & Co., New York (2010).

9 Spence, p.497.

10 Vogel, pp.55–6.

11 Su Tai Ren, *The Entire Record of Deng Xiaoping's Life*, Vol. 2, p.625, quoted in Vogel, p.227.

12 Ibid.

13 There is a lot of controversy over to what extent Hua was a reformer rather than an upholder of Marxist orthodoxy in, *inter alia*, Frederick C. Teiwes and Warren Sun, *The End of the Maoist Era: Chinese Politics During the Twilight of the Cultural Revolution*, M.E. Sharpe, Armonk, NY (2007).

14 Vogel, p.247.

15 Ibid., p.262.

16 Robert S. Ross, *The Indo-China Tangle: China's Vietnam Policy 1975–79*, Columbia University Press, New York (1988).

17 Lawrence C. Reardon, 'China's Coastal Development Strategy 1979–84', *Chinese Law and Government*, 27(4), 1994.

18 Ibid.

19 Vogel, p.445.

20 Ibid., p.429.

21 Ibid., pp.428–30.

22 Edwin Lim, *Learning and Working with the Giants* in I.S. Gill and T. Pugatch (eds), *At the Frontiers of Development:*

Reflections from the World Bank, World Bank, Washington, DC (2005); Harold K. Jacobson and Michel Oksenberg, *China's Participation in the IMF, the World Bank, and GATT: Towards a Global Economic Order,* University of Michigan Press, Ann Arbor (1990).

23 Vogel, p.453.

24 Leslie T. Chang, *Factory Girls: Voices from the Heart of Modern China,* Picador, London (2009).

25 Timothy Brook, *Quelling the People: The Military Suppression of the Beijing Democracy Movement,* Stanford University Press, Stanford (1998), pp.196–7.

26 James A.R. Miles, *The Legacy of Tiananmen: China in Disarray,* University of Michigan Press, Ann Arbor (1996), p.326.

13
Manmohan Singh: The Quiet Reforme

1 Gurcharan Das, *India Grows At Night: A Liberal Case for a Strong State,* Allen Lane, New Delhi (2012).

2 Palaniappan Chidambaram (Manmohan Singh's successor as Congress Finance Minister), *One India News,* 2 May 2008, and Rediff.com Business Desk, 26 September 2005.

3 Mark Tully, *Cambridge Alumni Magazine,* Michaelmas 2005.

4 *Time,* 8 July 2012.

5 Manmohan Singh, *India's Export Trends and the Prospects for Self-Sustained Growth,* Clarendon Press, Oxford (1964).

6 W.W. Rostow, *The World Economy: History and Prospect,* University of Texas Press, Austin (1978), pp.509–10; Raymond W. Goldsmith, *The Financial Development of India, 1860–1977,* Yale University Press, New Haven (1983); Bipan Chandra, *The Colonial Legacy* in Bimal Jalan (ed.), *The Indian Economy: Problems and Prospects,* Viking, New Delhi (1992).

7 Angus Deaton, *The Great Escape: Health, Wealth and the Origins of Inequality,* Princeton University Press, Princeton and Oxford (2013), p.163.

8 Jawaharlal Nehru, *The Discovery of India,* Meridian Books, London (1946), p.15.

9 V.M. Dandekar, *Forty Years After Independence* in Jalan (ed.), p.56.

10 Nehru, pp.407–8.

11 Rakesh Mohan, *Industrial*

Policy and Controls in Jalan (ed.), p.85.

12 Bimal Jalan, Introduction in Jalan (ed.), p.xii.

13 Sukhamoy Chakravarty, *Development Planning: The Indian Experience*, Clarendon Press, Oxford (1987); Alec Cairncross, *Factors in Economic Development*, Allen & Unwin, London (1962); W. Arthur Lewis, *The Principles of Economic Planning*, Allen & Unwin, London (1949) and *Development Planning: The Essentials of Economic Policy*, Routledge, London (1966).

14 Wassily Leontief, *Input-Output Economics*, Oxford University Press, New York and Oxford (1986).

15 Martin Wolf, *India's Exports*, published by Oxford University Press for the World Bank, New York (1982); Bimal Jalan, *Balance of Payments, 1956 to 1991* in Jalan (ed.), pp.163–91.

16 J.P. Lewis, *Quiet Crisis in India*, Penguin, London, and Brookings Institution, Washington, DC (1962).

17 Gunnar Myrdal, *Asian Drama: An Inquiry into the Poverty of Nations*, Pantheon Books, New York (1968).

18 Gaurav Datt, *Poverty in India 1951–1994: Trends and Decompositions*, World Bank, Washington, DC (1997).

He explains the problems involved in measuring poverty in India with three major, and discontinuous, definitions.

19 Vijay Joshi, *India's Long Road: The Search for Prosperity*, Oxford University Press, New York (2017), p.19.

20 Jagdish N. Bhagwati and Padma Desai, *India: Planning for Industrialization: Industrialization and Trade Policies Since 1951*, Oxford University Press, New York (1970).

21 Mancur Olson, *The Rise and Decline of Nations: Economic Growth, Stagflation, and Social Rigidities*, Yale University Press, New Haven (1982).

22 Pranab K. Bardhan, *A Political-Economy Perspective on Development* in Jalan (ed.), p.323, and *The Political Economy of Development in India*, Blackwell, Oxford (1984).

23 Pulapre Balakrishnan, *Economic Growth in India: History and Prospect*, Oxford University Press, New Delhi (2010).

24 Vijay Joshi and I.M.D. Little, *India's Economic Reforms 1991– 2001*, Oxford University Press, Oxford (1996).

25 Tully Cambridge Alumni Magazine Michaelmas 2005.

26 Shankar Acharya and Rakesh Mohan (eds), *India's Economy: Performance and Challenges. Essays in Honour of Montek Singh*

Ahluwalia, Oxford University Press, New Delhi (2010).

27 Jagdish N. Bhagwati, *India in Transition: Freeing the Economy*, Clarendon Press, Oxford (1993); Bimal Jalan, *India's Economic Crisis: The Way Ahead*, Oxford University Press, Oxford and New Delhi (1991).

28 T.N. Srinivasan, *Growth, Sustainability, and India's Economic Reforms*, Oxford University Press, New Delhi (2011).

29 Joshi, p.21.

30 *Time*, 8 July 2012.

31 *The Economist*, 'Modi's Many Tasks', 23–29 May 2014.

14

Balcerowicz: Big Bang Theory and Practice

1 Timothy Garton Ash, *The Uses of Adversity: Essays on the Fate of Central Europe*, Granta, Cambridge (1989), p.315.

2 Evaluated in, *inter alia*, Olivier Blanchard, *The Economics of Post-Communist Transition*, Clarendon Press, Oxford (1997); Annual Transition Reports of the European Bank for Reconstruction and Development, 1994 and 1995; Philippe Aghion and Olivier Blanchard, *On the Speed of Transition in Central Europe*, NBER Macroeconomics Annual 1994, Vol. 9; Anders Åslund, *Post-Communist Economic Revolutions: How Big a Bang?*, Center for Strategic and International Studies, Washington, DC (1992).

3 Janice Bell, *The Political Economy of Reform in Post-Communist Poland*, Edward Elgar, Cheltenham (2001), p.6.

4 Naomi Klein, *The Shock Doctrine: The Rise of Disaster Capitalism*, Penguin Random House, London (2007).

5 Jeffrey Sachs, *Poland's Jump to the Market Economy*, MIT Press, Cambridge, MA (1993), p.42 (based on Lionel Robbins Memorial Lectures to the LSE).

6 Norman Davies, *God's Playground: A History of Poland, Vol. 2: 1795 to the Present*, Oxford University Press, Oxford (2005), p.5.

7 Sachs, p.33.

8 Bell, p.19.

9 Åslund, p.viii.

10 Ludwig Von Mises in Alec Nove and D.M. Nuti (eds), *Socialist Economics: Selected Readings*, Penguin,

Harmondsworth (1972),
pp.75–9.

11 Quoted in Klein, p.171.

12 Jeffrey Sachs, *The End of Poverty: Economic Possibilities for Our Time*, Penguin, New York (2005).

13 Klein, pp.196–7.

14 Sachs, pp.42–3.

15 Bell, p.6.

16 Leszek Balcerowicz, *Poland* in John Williamson (ed.), *The Political Economy of Policy Reform*, Institute for International Economics, Washington, DC (1994), p.177.

17 Leszek Balcerowicz, *Socialism, Capitalism, Transformation*, Central European University Press, Budapest (1995), p.309.

18 Sachs, p.46.

19 János Kornai, *The Socialist System: The Political Economy of Communism*, Clarendon Press, Oxford (1932).

20 Bell, p.13.

21 H. Kabai and T. Kawalck, 'Who is Responsible for Post-Communist Successes?'

in *East European Transitions* (World Bank), Vol. 6, July/August 1995.

22 Klein, Ch. 9.

23 Åslund, p.89.

24 Ibid., p.35.

25 Blanchard, pp.38–42.

26 David Lipton and Jeffrey Sachs, *Creating a Market Economy in Eastern Europe: The Case of Poland*, Brookings Papers on Economic Activities (1990), No. 1.

27 Richard Layard, Preface to Lionel Robbins Memorial Lecture at the LSE, 1993, pp.i–ii.

28 Interagency report quoted in Åslund, p.39.

29 Bell, p.51.

30 Simon Johnson and Gary Loveman, *Starting Over in Eastern Europe: Entrepreneurship and Economic Renewal*, Harvard Business School Press, Boston, MA (1995).

31 Bell, p.45.

32 Ibid., p.52.

33 Layard, p.xiii.

34 Sachs, p.9.

15
Abe: Japan Pioneers Abenomics

1 G.C. Allen, *A Short Economic History of Modern Japan 1867–1937*, Allen & Unwin, London (1946); Masakazu Iwata, *Ōkubo Toshimichi: The Bismarck of Japan*, University of California Press, Berkeley (1964); Henry Rosovsky, *Japan's Transition to Modern Economic Growth, 1868–1885*

in Henry Rosovksy (ed.), *Industrialisation in Two Systems*, John Wiley, New York (1965); Henry Rosovsky and Kazushi Ohkawa, *Japanese Economic Growth: Trend Acceleration in the Twentieth Century*, Stanford University Press, Stanford (1973).

2 Herman Kahn, *The Emerging Japanese Superstate*, Andre Deutsch, London (1971); Bela Balassa and Marcus Noland, *Japan in the World Economy*, Institute for International Economics, Washington, DC (1988); Allen, with supplementary chapter 1945–60; W.G. Beasley, *The Modern History of Japan*, Weidenfeld & Nicolson, London (1967); P.B. Stone, *Japan Surges Ahead: The Story of an Economic Miracle*, Weidenfeld & Nicolson, London (1969).

3 Ezra F. Vogel, *Japan as Number One: Lessons for America*, Harper Colophon, New York (1979).

4 Richard Werner, *Princes of the Yen: Japan's Central Bankers and the Transformation of the Economy*, M.E. Sharpe, New York (2003), Ch. 9.

5 Charles P. Kindleberger and Robert Z. Aliber, *Manias, Panics, and Crashes: A History of Financial Crises*, Palgrave Macmillan, New York (2011), pp.1–2 and Appendix.

6 Richard Davies, *Extreme Economics*, Bantam Press, London (2019), Ch. 7; Anne Allison, *Precarious Japan*, Duke University Press, Durham, NC (2013); Florian Coulmas, *Population Decline and Ageing in Japan: The Social Consequences*, Routledge, Abingdon (2008).

7 Nathaniel Thayer, *How the Conservatives Rule Japan*, Princeton University Press, New Jersey (1969).

8 Kahn, pp.19–85.

9 Werner, p.1.

10 Michael Pettis, *The Great Rebalancing*, Princeton University Press, Princeton and Oxford (2013).

11 Werner, p.74.

12 R. Anton Braun, Deisake Ikeda and Douglas Jones, 'The Savings Rate in Japan: Why It Has Fallen and Why It Will Remain Low' in *International Economic Review*, Vol. 50, Issue 1, February 2009.

13 Charles Mackay, *Extraordinary Public Delusions and the Madness of Crowds*; Kindleberger and Aliber; John Calverley, *Bubbles and How to Survive Them*, Nicholas Brealey, London and Boston (2004).

14 Werner, p.92.

15 Robert J. Shiller, *Irrational Exuberance*, Princeton University Press, Princeton (2000), p.92.

16 Daniela Tavasci and Jan
    Toporowski (eds), *Minsky,
    Crisis and Development*, Palgrave
    Macmillan, Basingstoke
    (2010).

17 Richard Koo, *The Escape from
    Balance Sheet Recession and the
    QE Trap*, Wiley, Singapore
    (2015).

18 Ibid., p.22.

19 Ibid., p.25.

20 Ibid., p.24.

21 Ibid., p.58.

22 Ibid., p.59.

23 Martin Wolf, *The Shifts and the
    Shocks: What We've Learned –
    and Still Have to Learn – From
    the Financial Crisis*, Allen Lane,
    London (2014).

24 Joseph Stiglitz, *The Promise of
    Abenomics*, Insight (Internet
    Archive), (2013).

25 'Krugman Warns Abe on Tax
    Increase', *Wall Street Journal*,
    19 September 2014; 'Larry
    Summers Joins Japan's
    Anti-tax Bandwagon', *Wall
    Street Journal*, 14 November
    2014.

26 Davies, Ch. 7.

27 Ibid.

28 Wolf, p.215.

29 Joseph Stiglitz, *Freefall: Free
    Markets and the Sinking of the
    Global Economy*, W.W. Norton,
    New York (2010); Paul
    Krugman, *End This Depression
    Now!*, W.W. Norton, New York
    (2012).

30 Koo, p.58.

31 Robert Harding, 'Abe's
    Stimulus brings "Bridges
    to Nowhere" Spectre Back
    to Japan', *Financial Times*,
    9 December 2019.

32 'Abenomics and the
    Japanese Economy', Council
    on Foreign Relations, 3
    November 2019, quoting
    Greg Ip in *Wall Street Journal*.

16

Trump: Trumponomics, Economic
Nationalism and Pluto-populism

1 Stephen Moore and Arthur
   B. Laffer, *Trumponomics: Inside
   the America First Plan to Revive
   Our Economy*, All Points Books,
   New York (2018); Gerald
   Epstein, 'Trumponomics:
   Should We Just Say "No"?',
   Challenge, 60:2, 2017.

2 Jan-Werner Müller, *What
   is Populism?*, University
   of Pennsylvania Press,
   Philadelphia (2018).

3 Martin Wolf, 'Donald
   Trump's Pluto-Populism Laid
   Bare', *Financial Times*, 2 May
   2017.

4 Lenka Buštiková and Petra
   Guasti, 'The State as a Firm',

East European Politics and Society, Vol. 33, No. 2, May 2019, pp.302–30.

5 *Forbes*' estimate of net wealth in 2019. Now about $1 billion less.

6 Donald J. Trump (with Tony Schwartz), *Trump: The Art of the Deal*, Arrow Books, London (1989), p.48.

7 Cited in Adam Tooze, *Crashed: How a Decade of Financial Crises Changed the World*, Penguin Random House, London (2019), p.569.

8 Bob Woodward, *Fear: Trump in the White House*, Simon & Schuster, London and New York (2018), p.56.

9 Ibid., Prologue.

10 Harry Johnson, *The New Mercantilism*, Blackwell, Oxford (1974).

11 Jagdish Bhagwati, *Regionalism and Bilateralism: Another View* in J. de Melo and A. Panagarriya (eds), *New Dimensions in Regional Integration*, Cambridge University Press, Cambridge (1993).

12 Quoted in Tooze, p.574.

13 Woodward, p.137.

14 Ibid., p.136.

15 Moore and Laffer, p.247.

16 Ibid., pp.247–9.

17 Short reports by A. Parker, P. Rucker, D. Paletta and K. Deyong, *Chicago Tribune*, 22 April 2017, and J. Mason and D. Lawler, Reuters, 26 April 2017.

18 Deepak Lal, *Resurrection of the Pauper-labour Argument*, Thames Essay 28, Trade Policy Research Centre, London (1981).

19 Kai-Fu Lee, *AI Superpowers: China, Silicon Valley, and the New World Order*, Houghton Mifflin Harcourt, Boston, MA (2018).

20 Michael Pillsbury, *The Hundred-Year Marathon: China's Secret Strategy to Replace America as the Global Superpower*, Henry Holt & Co., New York (2014); Peter Navarro and Greg Autry, *Death by China: Confronting the Dragon – A Global Call to Action*, Prentice Hall, Upper Saddle River, NJ (2011).

21 Janan Ganesh, 'Trump's Trade Obsession Keeps the Peace with China', *Financial Times*, 11 April 2019.

22 Moore and Laffer, p.248.

23 'An Iron Curtain in Tech Supply Chains is a Real Risk', *Financial Times*, 26 April 2019.

24 Lawrence Kudlow in Foreword to Moore and Laffer.

25 Sam Fleming and Chris Giles, 'Why America is Learning to Love Budget Deficits', *Financial Times*, 26 April 2019.

26 Martin Wolf, 'Donald Trump's Bad Judgment on the Paris Accord', *Financial Times*, 7 June 2017.

Conclusion

1 Naomi Klein, *The Shock Doctrine: The Rise of Disaster Capitalism*, Penguin Random House, London (2007), p.185.

2 Barry Eichengreen, *The Populist Temptation: Economic Grievance and Political Reaction in the Modern Era*, Oxford University Press, Oxford (2018); Charles Dumas, *Populism and Economics*, Profile Books, London (2018); Robert Kuttner, *Can Democracy Survive Global Capitalism?*, W.W. Norton, New York (2018).

Index

Abdul Rahman, Tunku, 184
Abe, Shinzō, 2, 16, 290–91, 302–12, 339, 345
    population decline and, 308–10; retirement (2020), 311; 'three arrows', 290, 305–8
accelerator effect, 95
Acemoglu, Daron, 19
Acharya, Shankar, 261
Adam Smith Institute, 338
Adams, John, 22, 27, 35
Adenauer, Konrad, 12, 99, 110, 112, 114
Affluent Society, The (Galbraith), 120
Agarwal, S.N., 250
Agrarian Party (Sweden), 124
agriculture
    in Argentina, 137, 142, 144, 156; in France, 32; in Germany, 11, 51, 59, 106
    in Russia, 69, 70, 73, 74, 75–6; in South Korea, 164, 166, 174; in Sweden, 106, 126; in United Kingdom, 3, 10, 34, 37, 40–41, 44–50; in United States, 33, 82
Ahluwalia, Montek Singh, 261
Alexander III, Emperor of Russia, 66
Alfonsín, Raúl, 151
Alsace Lorraine, 58
America First, 17, 83, 314, 318
Anhui, China, 233
Anti-Corn Law League, 44, 45–6, 47, 48
anti-Semitism, 63, 91, 103, 105, 142
Aquinas, Thomas, 38
Argentina, 135–58, 344
    Alfonsín presidency (1983–9), 151;
austerity, 148; corruption in, 137, 138, 140, 147, 148, 153, 155; coup d'état (1943), 141; coup d'état (1955), 149; dollar currency peg, 152; Falklands War (1982), 150, 204, 213, 218; Fernández de Kirchner presidency (2007–15), 154–5; 'gaucho banking', 138; economic nationalism, 143–5, 156; Great Rift, 137, 140; Irigoyen presidency (1916–30), 138; Kirchner presidency (2003–7), 148, 153–4; labour policies, 142; Liberal System, 136–7; Menem presidency (1989–99), 148, 151–2, 156–7; Mercosur, 146; Péron (Juan) presidency, first (1946–55), 141–9, 155–6; Péron (Juan) presidency, second (1973–4), 150; Péron (Isabel) presidency (1974–6), 150; presidential election (1946), 141; printing of money, 145, 154; Rúa presidency (1999–2001), 153; social justice in, 13, 136, 140, 141–2, 157–8; sovereign default (2001), 153; UK, relations with, 137, 138, 140, 150; Washington Consensus in, 148, 152, 153, 154, 157
Aristotle, 38
Artificial Intelligence, 242, 325
Asian financial crisis (1997), 88, 290
Åslund, Anders, 275, 282
Asō Tarō, 16, 290, 302, 303, 304, 339
Augustine, Saint, 38
austerity, 5
Australia, 7
Austria, 54, 55

Austrian School, 107
Autobahn, 104

Babiš, Andrej, 314
Bacon, Francis, 24
balance sheet recessions, 16
Balcerowicz, Leszek, 15, 269–88, 338–9, 343
    Big Bang (1990), 270, 276, 281, 283–4, 339, 343; Friedman, influence of, 277, 338; opposition to, 281
Balladur, Eduard, 189
Banc de France, 9
Banerjee, Mamata, 266
Bank of New York, 26, 28
Bank of the United States, 30, 31
Bannon, Steve, 331
Bardhan, Pranab, 258
Barre, Raymond, 189
Battle of Stalingrad (1942–3), 106
Battle of Yorktown (1781), 25
Bebel, August, 61
Berger, Samuel, 167, 172
Berle, Adolf, 88, 335
Berlin Wall, fall of (1989), 278
Berlinski, Claire, 212
Berlusconi, Silvio, 135, 314
Bernanke, Ben, 7, 305, 339
Bernstein, Eduard, 120, 336
Bharatiya Janata Party (BJP), 248, 251, 259, 262, 263, 266
big bang model, 345
    in Poland, 15, 270, 276, 281, 283–4, 339, 343; in United Kingdom, 210
Bilbo, Theodore Gilmore, 97
Birla, 250
von Bismarck, Otto, 10–11, 51–63, 100, 161, 334, 346
    anti-Semitism, 63; corporatism, 62–3; free trade, 11, 51, 55–8; 'iron and blood', 55, 62; Krupp visit (1864), 62; List, influence of, 52; militarism, 62; protectionism, 11, 51–2, 58–60, 143; revolutions (1848–9), 54, 55, 60, 61; socialism, views on, 11, 52, 60–62; welfare system, 11, 52, 60, 61–2, 114; *Wirtschaftsrat*, 63; Zollverein, 10–11, 51, 56
Blair, Anthony 'Tony', 49, 116, 132, 201
Blanchard, Olivier, 282–3
Boeing, 324
Boisguilbert, Pierre le Pesant, sieur de, 32

Bolivia, 277
Bolsheviks, 11, 67–78
Bolsonaro, Jair, 348
Boston Tea Party (1773), 24
Botswana, 7, 18
Braden, Spruille, 142
Brandt, Willy, 99
Branting, Hjalmar, 13, 117, 121
Brazil, 8, 18, 145, 146–7, 157, 347
Brest-Litovsk Treaty (1918), 70
Bretton Woods Conference (1944), 7, 97, 331
Brexit (2016–20), 50, 180, 286, 314
Brezhnev, Leonid, 227
Bright, John, 38, 46, 334
Britain in Decline (Gamble), 202
Brown, James Gordon, 132, 304
Bukharin, Nikolai, 76
Bulgaria, 282
Bürckel, Josef, 102
Burr, Aaron, 22, 35
Bush, George Herbert Walker, 216, 315
Bush, George Walker, 315, 325
Byung-joon Jun, 161

Cairncross, Alec, 252
Callaghan, Leonard James, 202, 204
Cambodia, 65, 72
Cambridge University, 118, 181, 246, 252, 261, 339
Campbell, John, 213
Canada, 7, 23, 136, 314, 321, 322
Canning, George, 37, 42
Carey, Henry, 59, 334
Carlyle, Thomas, 6, 47
Carr, Edward Hallett, 6
cartels
    in Germany, 63, 101–2, 106, 108, 111, 114, 206–7; in Japan, 292
Carter, James 'Jimmy', 214–15, 315
Cassel, Gustav, 123
Catholicism, 82, 271, 272, 287, 304
    in Argentina, 148, 151, 158; in Germany, 112; in Japan, 304; in Poland, 271, 272, 287; social justice and, 13, 112; in United Kingdom, 41, 43; in United States, 82
Cavallo, Domingo, 152
Central Intelligence Agency (CIA), 128
Cha Ji-chul, 176
Chamberlain, Joseph, 50
Chang, Jung 223, 225

Chávez, Hugo, 135, 154, 157, 314
Chen Yun, 221, 231, 234, 235, 236, 237, 238, 240, 342
Chernow, Ronald, 23
Chicago School, 18, 157, 199, 215, 277, 338
Chidambaram, Palaniappan, 261
child labour, 32, 41
child mortality, 187, 255, 263
Childs, Marquis, 122
Chile, 18, 145, 150, 157, 199
China, 3, 11, 66, 67, 72, 199, 221–43, 254, 276, 292, 323, 337–8, 342, 347
  Argentina, relations with, 153;
  'builders or balancers', 235–7;
  collectivization, 225, 233; Covid-19
  pandemic (2019–20), 243, 325, 326;
  Cultural Revolution (1966–76), 226,
  227, 228, 229, 231; decollectivization,
  233; Five Year Plans, 225, 234, 236;
  Great Leap Forward (1958–62),
  225–6, 231, 254; growth in, 160,
  234–7, 240; heavy industry in, 235;
  Hundred Flowers Campaign (1956–7),
  225; Indian War (1962), 231; Japan,
  relations with, 232, 305; Japanese War
  (1937–45), 163, 224; Korean War
  (1950–53), 162; presidential system,
  8; price controls and, 237–8, 239,
  342; Soviet Union, relations with,
  223, 226–7, 238; special economic
  zones (SEZs), 229, 232, 236, 240;
  student demonstrations (1986), 238–9;
  Tiananmen Square massacre (1989),
  14, 78, 222, 239, 276, 278, 342; Tibet
  annexation (1950–51), 225; township
  and village enterprises (TVEs), 233,
  235; United States, relations with, 232,
  243, 318, 319, 323, 324–8; Vietnam
  War (1979), 231, 235
Chirac, Jacques, 189
Christian Democratic Union (Germany),
  108, 110, 112, 113, 114, 132, 343, 346
Christian Social Union (Bavaria), 112,
  113
Chun Doo-hwan, 176
Chung-in Moon, 161
Cicero, 24
climate change, 242, 318, 332, 347
Clinton, George, 26, 29
Clinton, William 'Bill' 7–8, 88, 303, 315,
  318, 325, 334

Cobden, Richard, 38, 46, 49, 55, 334
Cohn, Gary, 317
Colbert, Jean-Baptiste, 9
communism, 4, 116, 280
  in China, 14, 184, 188, 223–9; in
  India, 249, 259, 263; in North Korea,
  159, 160; in Poland, 15, 116, 269–70,
  271–5, 277, 278, 281; in Russia, 11,
  65–78, 121; in Singapore, 184, 188,
  190, 192; in South Korea, 161, 163–4,
  167, 337; in Sweden, 121, 122, 124,
  128, 130; in United Kingdom, 183
Communist Manifesto, The (Marx and
  Engels), 11, 54, 67
Congress Party (India), 247–67
Conservative Party (Germany), 58
Conservative Party (UK)
  Heath ministry (1970–74), 207, 217;
  Peel ministry (1841–6), 3, 10, 37,
  44–50; Tamworth Manifesto (1834),
  43, 46; Thatcher ministries (1979–90),
  2, 15, 48–9, 199–214, 217–19
Cooke, Alistair, 88
Coolidge, Calvin, 81
Corbyn, Jeremy, 132, 320
Corn Laws (1804–46), 3, 10, 34, 37,
  40–41, 44–50
corporatism, 146
correlation vs causality, 6
corruption, 8
  in Argentina, 137, 138, 140, 147,
  148, 153, 155; in China, 237, 242; in
  Germany, 57; in India, 16, 247, 257,
  259, 261, 262, 264, 265; in Japan, 301;
  in Poland, 274, 283; in Scandinavia,
  133; in Singapore, 179, 188, 190; in
  South Korea, 164, 165, 166, 171; in
  United Kingdom, 41, 43; in United
  States, 81
Costa Rica, 7
Coughlin, James, 91
Covid-19 pandemic (2019–20), 79, 346
  in China, 243, 325, 326; in India,
  266; in Japan, 291, 310, 345; in
  Scandinavia, 132; in Singapore, 197–
  8; in United States, 2, 243, 313, 325,
  326, 329, 330
Craig, Gordon, 58
Crankshaw, Edward, 54, 57, 59, 61
credit cycles, 84
Crick, Bernard, 6
crony capitalism, 105, 171, 264, 335

Cuba, 78, 254
Currie, Lauchlin, 80, 95, 335
Czech Republic, 282, 283

Dachau concentration camp, 106
Deaton, Angus, 248
debt deflation, 84
declinist literature, 202
deflation, 84, 85, 89, 170, 297, 306, 335
von Delbrück, Rudolf, 52, 56, 58
Democratic Party (Germany), 101, 113
Democratic Party (US)
    Carter administration (1977–81), 214–15; Kennedy administration (1961–3), 14, 161, 167, 168, 315, 337; Obama administration (2009–17), 316, 319, 323, 325, 329; Roosevelt administration (1933–45), *see under* Roosevelt, Franklin; Truman administration (1945–53), 98
Deng Pufang, 226
Deng Xiaoping, 3, 11, 14, 66, 77–8, 221–43, 276, 337–8, 342, 347
    'builders or balancers', 235–7, 241, 342; Cultural Revolution (1966–76), 226, 227, 228, 229; decollectivization, 233; Five Year Plans, 234, 236; France visit (1975), 228, 229; Friedman, influence of, 222, 338; Great Leap Forward (1958–62), 225–6; growth and, 160, 234–7, 240; Hua Guofeng, relationship with, 230; Hundred Flowers Campaign (1956–7), 225; Japan, relations with, 232; land reform, 225; Lenin, influence of, 77, 222, 338; 'prairie fire' metaphor, 230, 240; price controls and, 237–8, 239, 342; special economic zones (SEZs), 229, 232, 236, 240; student demonstrations (1986), 238–9; Tiananmen Square massacre (1989), 14, 78, 222, 239, 276, 342; Tibet annexation (1950–51), 225; township and village enterprises (TVEs), 233, 235; 'two cats' theory, 222, 230; UN speech (1974), 227, 228; US, relations with, 232; Vietnam War (1979), 231, 235
Denmark, 7, 23, 56, 119, 132
dependency theory, 156
Desai, Morarji, 251

Development of Capitalism in Russia (Lenin), 69
dirigisme, 9, 100, 115
disaster capitalism, 281
Disraeli, Benjamin, 42, 49, 50
division of labour, 25, 38
Dobb, Maurice, 69
Dominican Republic, 149
Douglas, Lewis, 91
Douglas, Roger, 2–3, 199
Draghi, Mario, 7, 339

East India Company, 38–9
Egypt, 254, 347
Einsatzgruppen, 103
Eisenhower, Dwight, 315
employment, 5, 8
    in Argentina, 153, 154; in Germany, 111, 113, 115; in India, 264; in Japan, 293, 294, 297, 307; in Poland, 273, 281, 286; in Singapore, 185, 187; in Sweden, 120, 122, 123, 124, 130; in United Kingdom, 202, 205, 206; in United States, 80–81, 89, 216; Engels, Friedrich, 11, 52, 54, 67
Erhard, Ludwig, 3, 12, 63, 99–116, 199–200, 204, 246, 291, 333, 335, 343
    Allied occupation (1945–9), 108–13; Balcerowicz and, 276; Bundestag elections (1949), 113; cartels, break up of, 63, 101–2, 106, 108, 111, 114, 206–7; dirigisme, views on, 115; European unification, views on, 115, 116; Hahn test and, 201; Mark revaluation (1957), 115; Nazi Party, relations with, 102–6; ordoliberalism, 12, 99, 107, 116; social market, 12, 99, 113, 116, 335; welfare system, 114–15
Erlander, Tage, 13, 117–28, 130, 133, 335–6, 344–5
    education system, 125; employment and, 120, 122, 123, 124, 130; Galbraith, influence of, 120; general election (1948), 123; general election (1968), 128; housing market regulation, 125; internment camps and, 122; Keynes, influence of, 120; welfare system, 124–7, 129; World War II (1939–45), 122–3
Ethiopia, 17
Eucken, Walter, 107, 335
European Commission, 7, 103

European Economic Community, 17
European Monetary Union, 12, 30, 99
European Union (EU), 11, 29–30
    Brexit (2016–20), 50, 180, 286, 314;
    Poland in, 269, 285; Sweden in, 130,
    132; Thatcher and, 219; Turkey,
    relations with, 322; United States,
    relations with, 323–4

Facebook, 328
Factory Girls (Chang), 237
Falklands War (1982), 150, 204, 213, 218
fascism, 156
    Coughlin and, 91; Hansson and,
    122; Italian, 140, 142, 146, 156, 336;
    Nazi Party, 12, 97, 101, 102–6; Péron
    and, 140, 142, 155–6, 157; Southern
    European model, 146, 157, 336
Federal Reserve, 7, 30, 85, 93, 200, 215,
    216, 305, 330–31
Federalist Papers (1787–8), 26
Feldt, Kjell-Olof, 129–30
Fernández de Kirchner, Cristina, 148,
    154–5
Fernández, Alberto, 155
Feuchtwanger, Edgar, 56
financial crisis (2007–8), 7, 16, 88, 218–
    19, 290, 296
    in China, 241; in Greece, 202; in
    Japan, 302, 303, 305; Minsky and,
    84, 298; in Poland, 285; in United
    Kingdom, 88; in United States, 7, 316
Finland, 7, 119
Fischer, Louis, 66, 76
Fisher, Irving, 80, 84, 89, 335
Five Star Movement, 135
Ford, Gerald, 214, 315
France
    Cobden Treaty (1860), 55; Deng's visit
    (1975), 228, 229; dirigisme, 9, 115; free
    trade in, 32, 50; Front National, 315,
    320; Guadeloupe colony (1674–), 23;
    Napoleonic period (1803–15), 9, 40,
    42, 48, 53; physiocrats, 32; presidential
    system, 8; protectionism in, 189;
    Prussian War (1870–71), 56, 57;
    Revolution (1789–99), 9, 35, 41, 77;
    Revolution (1848), 54; Thirty Glorious
    Years (1945–75), 17
Franco, Francisco, 146, 149
Frank, Andre Gunder, 156
Franklin, Benjamin, 22

Frederick William IV, King of Prussia, 53
Free Democrat Party (Germany), 100,
    109, 110, 113
free trade, 4, 5, 32–3, 38–40, 60
    Bismarck and, 11, 51, 55–8; Hamilton
    and, 32–3; Peel and, 3, 10, 37, 44, 50,
    56–7; Smith and, 25, 32–3, 39
Friedman, Milton, 14, 85, 204, 211, 311
    Balcerowicz and, 277, 338; Deng and,
    222, 338; Great Depression, views on,
    85; Lee and, 197; Pinochet and, 18;
    Reagan and, 215; Thatcher and, 15,
    204, 211–12, 277, 338
From Third World to First (Lee), 179, 186
Fujimori, Alberto, 135

Gaidar, Yegor, 283
Galbraith, John Kenneth, 89, 120, 193,
    252, 336
Galtieri, Leopoldo, 218
Gamble, Andrew, 202
game theory, 340
Gandhi, Indira, 248, 251, 254, 255, 258,
    259
Gandhi, Mohandas 'Mahatma', 249–50
Gandhi, Rahul, 266
Gandhi, Rajiv, 247, 259
Gandhi, Sanjay, 254, 259
Gandhi, Sonia, 263, 265, 266
Ganesh, Janan, 326
Gang of Four, 229
Garton Ash, Timothy, 269
Gash, Norman, 42, 48
de Gaulle, Charles, 115
General Agreement on Tariffs and Trade
    (GATT), 7, 97–8, 172, 243
Genghis Khan, 4
Georgia, United States, 29
German Democratic Republic (1949–90),
    272
German Empire (1870–1918), 10–11, 51,
    52, 55, 61–3, 83, 100
German Federal Republic (1949–), 3, 12,
    99, 113–16, 132, 276
German Occupied Zones (1945–9),
    108–13
German Reich, Nazi (1933–45), 7, 12, 63,
    100–106, 122, 271, 291, 335
German Reich, Weimar (1918–33), 102,
    104
German Workers' Association, 60
Ghana, 254

Gierek, Edward, 272
Gini coefficient, 264
globalization, 4, 132, 137, 210, 319, 320
Goh Chok Tong, 179, 197
Goh Keng Swee, 181, 189, 191, 193, 337
Gold Standard, 42, 50, 89, 341
Goldman Sachs, 317
Goldwater, Barry, 215, 338
Gomułka, Władysław, 271
Google, 328
Gorbachev, Mikhail, 66, 77, 78, 223, 239, 272
Göring, Hermann, 105
government securities, 28
Great Depression (1929–39), 79–96, 335
    Argentina and, 139; debt deflation
    and, 84; Gold Standard and,
    89; money supply and, 85, 93;
    protectionism and, 83; Smoot–Hawley
    Tariff Act (1930), 83; Wall Street
    Crash (1929), 80, 82, 84, 296; World
    War I and, 83
Great Reform Act (1832), 43, 46
Greece, 4, 100
Green Party (Germany), 132
Green Party (Sweden), 131
Grey, Charles, 2nd Earl, 37
Gu Mu, 229
Guadeloupe, 23
guided capitalism, 166, 170

Hahn, Frank, 201, 340
Halliday, Jon, 223, 225
Hallstein, Walter, 103
Hamilton, Alexander, 3, 9–10, 21–36, 59,
    320, 334, 341
    child labour, views on, 32; Constitution
    (1787), 26; Continentalist essay (1781),
    25; death (1804), 22, 35; debt policies,
    29–30; Federalist Papers (1787–8),
    26–7; financial crisis (1791–2), 35;
    First Bank established (1791), 30;
    presidential election (1788–9), 27;
    populism, views on, 26, 27, 36;
    protectionism, views on, 10, 22, 25,
    31–5, 143; *Report on Manufactures*
    (1791), 31–2; slavery, views on,
    10, 22, 23, 39; Treasury Secretary
    appointment (1789–94), 27, 35; War of
    Independence (1775–81), 22, 24–5
Hammarskjöld, Dag, 118
Hansen, Alvin, 80, 90, 95, 335

Hansson, Per Albin, 13, 117, 121–2, 128
Harberger, Arnold, 18, 157
Harding, Warren, 81
Hashimoto Ryūtarō, 304
Hatoyama Ichirō, 291
Hayek, Friedrich, 15, 107, 118, 211, 212,
    338
Heath, Edward, 207, 217
Heckscher, Eli, 118, 123
Hitler, Adolf, 7, 12, 100, 102, 104
Hobbes, Thomas, 24
Hobson, John Atkinson, 11
Holocaust (1941–5), 63
Hong Kong, 14, 228, 229, 236, 238, 325
Hoover, Herbert, 80, 81, 82, 83, 86, 87,
    90
Hopkins, Harry, 91
Howe, Geoffrey, 205, 210
de Hoz, Martínez, 150
Hu Jintao, 242
Hu Yaobang, 234, 236, 239
Hua Guofeng, 221, 229, 230, 235
Huawei, 325, 328
Huff, W.G., 186, 196
Hume, David, 21
Hungary, 271, 272, 282, 347
Hurd, Douglas, 47
Huskisson, William, 42, 44
hypergrowth
    in China, 235, 263, 337; in South
    Korea, 159–60, 170, 173, 175, 177,
    263, 337
hyperinflation, 135
    in Brazil, 147; in Germany, 104; in
    Poland, 15, 270, 272, 274–6, 278; in
    Russia, 75
Hyundai, 171, 172, 173

Icke, Harold, 91
immigration, 345
    in Argentina, 137, 138; in Germany,
    115; in Japan, 309; in Singapore, 196,
    198; in Sweden, 130–31; in United
    States, 83, 314, 317, 319–20
India, 15–16, 199, 241, 242, 245–67, 339,
    341–2, 347
    Bombay Plan (1944–5), 251; British
    colonies (1612–1947), 38–9, 248;
    caste in, 247, 261, 263; Chinese War
    (1962), 231; Commonwealth Games
    (2010), 265; corruption scandals, 16,
    247, 257, 259, 261, 262, 264, 265;

Covid-19 pandemic (2019–20), 266; financial crisis (1991), 260; Gandhi, Indira assassination (1984), 248, 259; Gandhi, Rajiv assassination (1991), 247, 260; Gandhi, Indira, government, first (1966–77), 254; Gandhi, Indira, government, second (1980–84), 255, 258, 259; Gandhi, Rajiv government (1984–9), 259; Gini coefficient, 264; Green Revolution, 255; growth, 263, 266; Hindu nationalism, 248, 266; identification scheme, 264; identity politics in, 247; IMF and, 16, 247, 254, 258, 259, 260; life expectancy in, 263; literacy in, 263; monsoon, 248, 253; Muslims in, 248, 266; national indirect tax, 265; Nehru government (1947–64), 16, 247, 249, 250, 251, 253; non-performing loans, 264; Partition (1947), 247, 248; planning model, 246, 249, 251–7; quiet crisis, 254; *swadeshi*, 250; World Bank and, 247, 252, 257–8

Indonesia, 185, 192, 242, 254

Industrial Revolution (c. 1760–1840), 21, 22, 39, 46, 57

infant industry argument, 33–4, 52

inflation, 5, 8, 283
  in Argentina, 137, 144, 145, 149, 150, 151, 154, 157; in Brazil, 147; in China, 231, 235, 237–8; in Germany, 101, 104, 108, 109, 111, 114, 115; in India, 264; in Japan, 295, 297, 306, 310; in Poland, 15, 270, 272, 274–6, 278, 279, 280, 283; in Singapore, 195; in Sweden, 123, 129, 130; in Russia, 74, 75; in United Kingdom, 202, 204, 206, 212–13; in United States, 25, 85, 89, 93, 94, 216

Input–Output analysis, 252

Institute for Management, 190

Institute of Economic Affairs, 201–2, 338

interest rates, 16
  in Argentina, 137; in China, 238; in Japan, 292–5, 298–301, 306, 308, 309, 311; in South Korea, 175; in Sweden, 125; in United Kingdom, 50, 205, 206; in United States, 28, 31, 90, 93, 317, 329, 330

International Monetary Fund (IMF), 97, 191, 218, 243
  Argentina and, 148, 149, 152, 154, 155; India and, 16, 247, 254, 258, 259, 260, 339; Japan and, 300; Poland and, 270, 277, 285; Singapore and, 186; United Kingdom and, 202, 205

invisible hand, 25, 194

Ip, Greg, 311

Iran–Iraq War (1980–88), 205

Ireland, 186

Irigoyen, Hipólito, 138–9

iron and blood, 55, 62

Israel, 181, 192

Italy, 135, 140, 142, 146, 156, 336

Iwakura Mission (1871–3), 229

Jackson, Andrew, 315

Jalan, Bimal, 251

Jamaica, 199

Japan, 227–8, 254, 289–312, 339, 345
  Abenomics, 2, 8, 16, 290–91, 302–12, 339, 345; asset bubble, 293–9; bridges to nowhere, 301, 311; China, relations with, 232, 305; Chinese War (1937–45), 162, 224; corruption in, 301; Covid-19 pandemic (2019–20), 291, 310, 345; currency value, 293, 294, 295, 296, 306–8; financial crisis (1989), 289, 291, 298–300; financial crisis (2008), 302, 303, 305; Iwakura Mission (1871–3), 229; Korea occupation (1910–45), 162; Lost Decade (1991–2001), 289; Manchukuo (1932–45), 163; Matsukata Deflation (1881–5), 169–70; Meiji period (1868–1912), *see* Meiji Japan; national debt, 291, 300–301; Pearl Harbor attack (1941), 96; population decline, 290, 308–10; protectionism in, 60; Quantitative Easing, 301, 305, 306, 308; Russian War (1904–5), 169; savings rate in, 294; Singapore, relations with, 182–3, 193; South Korea, relations with, 161, 162, 173; zaibatsu model, 170, 292

Jaruzelski, Wojciech, 272

Jefferson, Thomas, 22, 23, 27, 30, 31, 35–6

Jiang Qing, 227

Jiang Zemin, 240, 241, 242

Johnson, Harry, 37

Johnson, Lyndon, 315, 316

Joseph, Keith, 203, 211

Joshi, Vijay, 256

Kádár, János, 271
Kaldor, Nicholas, 252, 261, 339
Kapital, Das (Marx), 67
von Kardorff, Wilhelm, 58, 334
Kautsky, Karl, 120
Kennedy, David, 87
Kennedy, John Fitzgerald, 14, 161, 167, 168, 315, 337
Kenya, 18
Kerensky, Alexander, 69
Keynes, John Maynard, 9, 12, 58, 118, 312, 334, 339
    Bretton Woods Conference (1944), 97; Erhard and, 102; Erlander and, 120; Hansson and, 122; Hoover and, 83; Myrdal and, 123; Roosevelt and, 79–80, 82, 87, 90, 94–5, 96, 97, 335; *Yellow Book* (1928), 120
Khama, Seretse, 18
Khrushchev, Nikita, 271
Kibaki, Mwai, 18
Kim Il-sung, 161, 162–3
Kim Jae-gyu, 176
Kim Jong-pil, 165, 166, 168
Kindleberger, Charles, 5
King, Rodney, 180, 187, 190, 195
Kirchner, Néstor, 148, 153–4
Kissinger, Henry, 177, 227, 325
Klaus, Václav, 283
Klein, Naomi, 270, 277, 281
Kohl, Helmut, 100
Koizumi Junichiro, 302
Koo, Richard, 299–300, 301, 311, 339
Korea Industry Development Corporation, 171
Korean War (1950–53), 14, 114, 159, 162, 165
Kornai, János, 280
Krishna, Raj, 245
Krugman, Paul, 180, 194, 307, 312
Krupp, 62
Ku Klux Klan, 97
Kudlow, Lawrence, 328, 339
kulaks, 71, 75
Kuomintang, 224
Kwa Geok Choo, 181, 183
Kwaśniewski, Aleksander, 286–7

Labour Party (New Zealand), 199
Labour Party (UK), 109, 131, 203
    Callaghan ministry (1976–9), 202, 204; Blair ministries (1997–2007), 49,

116, 132, 201; Lee Kuan Yew and, 180, 183, 337; Wilson ministry, first (1964–70), 187, 203
Laffer, Arthur, 15, 48, 215–16, 321, 326, 338, 339
Laski, Harold, 183
Lassalle, Ferdinand, 60–61
Latsis, Otto, 77
Lawson, Nigel, 195, 200, 206, 207, 208, 210, 211
Layard, Richard, 283, 288
Le Pen, Jean-Marie, 315
Le Pen, Marine, 315, 320
Lee Hsien Leong, 179, 181
Lee Kuan Yew, 14, 179–98, 222, 337, 344, 346, 347
    authoritarianism, 190, 197; Central Provident Fund (CPF), 194–5; communism, views on, 183, 184, 190; Economic Development Board (EDB), 181, 192, 195; *From Third World to First* (2000), 179, 186; GDP growth, 186; Housing Development Board (HDB), 193–4; Israel, relations with, 192; Japan, relations with, 193; Labour Party, support for, 180, 183; Malaya, federation with (1963–5), 184–5; miracle narrative, 185; PAP, founding of (1954), 183; social democratic politics, 180, 183, 189, 190; Sovereign Wealth Fund, 194, 195; UNDP mission (1960), 191–2; welfare, views on, 196
Left Party (Sweden), 130
Lehman Brothers, 80
Lenin, Vladimir, 11, 65–78, 121, 241, 334
    death (1924), 76; Deng, influence on, 77, 222, 224, 338; *Development of Capitalism in Russia* (1899), 69; Hanging Order (1918), 71; New Economic Policy (1921–8), 11, 65–6, 73–8, 222, 224, 338, 342; Scissors Crisis (1923), 75–6, 342; state capitalism, 74; *State and Revolution, The* (1917), 68; strokes (1921–4), 65–6, 76; War Communism, 72, 73; *What is to be Done?* (1902), 67
Leontief, Wassily, 252
Leuchtenburg, William, 85, 88, 96
Lewis, Arthur, 161, 174, 252
Liberal Democratic Party (Japan), 290, 291, 297, 299, 302–12

Liberal Party (Sweden), 118, 120, 121, 123–4, 127
Liberal Party (UK), 41, 46, 47, 90, 120, 201
Liberal People's Party (Germany), 100–101
Liebknecht, Wilhelm, 61
Lighthizer, Robert, 319
Lim, Linda, 188
Lin Biao, 227
Lincoln, Abraham, 23, 35–6
Lipton, David, 277
liquidity trap, 331
List, Friedrich, 34, 51–2, 59, 334
Little, Ian, 252, 261
Liu Shaoqi, 226
Liverpool, Robert Jenkinson, 2nd Earl, 37, 42
living standards, 1, 5, 8
    in Argentina, 136, 151, 157, 272; in Germany, 115; in Poland, 270, 272; in Russia, 77; in Singapore, 186; in South Korea, 165; in United Kingdom, 40; in United States, 83
Locke, John, 21
London School of Economics (LSE), 118, 181, 252, 304, 337
Long, Huey, 91
Louis XIV, King of France, 9
Lund University, 119
Luxembourg, 186
luxury taxes, 29

Macmillan, Harold, 209
Madison, James, 22, 23, 26, 27, 30, 31
Maduro, Nicolás, 135, 148, 314
Mahalanobis, Prasanta Chandra, 249, 252
Malaya, 183, 184–5, 192
Malthus, Thomas, 45, 49, 254
Manchukuo (1932–45), 163
Mandelson, Peter, 218
manufacturing
    in Argentina, 140, 143, 144, 153, 156; in Germany, 51, 54, 59; in India, 250, 256; in Russia, 72, 75, 76; in Singapore, 189, 192; in South Korea, 168, 173; in United Kingdom, 38, 46, 205, 210, 344; in United States, 23–4, 31–5, 84, 317, 320–21, 322
Mao Zedong, 7, 65, 67, 72, 163, 221–9
    collectivization, 233; Cultural

Revolution (1966–76), 226, 227, 228, 229, 234; Great Leap Forward (1958–62), 225–6; heavy industry and, 235; Hundred Flowers Campaign (1956–7), 225; Indian War (1962), 231; legacy, 234; 'prairie fire' metaphor, 230
Marshall Plan (1948–51), 111
Marx, Karl, 5, 334
    Bismarck and, 52, 54, 60, 61; Communist Manifesto, The, 11, 54, 67; Kapital, Das, 67; Lenin and, 11, 66, 67, 69; Park and, 161
Marxism, 120, 121, 127, 132, 183
Massachusetts, United States, 29
Matsukata Deflation (1881–5), 169–70
Mayer, E.J., 181, 192, 337
Mazowiecki, Tadeusz, 270, 276, 281, 284
Meade, James, 6
Means, Gardiner, 88, 335
Meidner Plan (1976), 129
Meidner, Rudolf Alfred, 126, 129
Meiji Japan (1868–1912), 13, 174, 289
    Deng, influence on, 222; Iwakura Mission (1871–3), 229; Park, influence on, 161, 166, 168–70, 171, 337
Melbourne, William Lamb, 2nd Viscount, 37
Menem, Carlos, 148, 151, 156–7
Mensheviks, 67, 71
mercantilism, 17, 32, 38–9, 45, 319, 321, 340
Mercosur, 146
Merkel, Angela, 99
Mexico, 8, 321, 322
Mieno Yasushi, 298
Mierzejewski, Alfred, 102, 106, 113
Mill, John Stuart, 84
Minford, Patrick, 204, 214
Minsky, Hyman, 84, 297–8, 316
Mirrlees, James, 252
Mitterrand, François, 189
Moderate Party (Sweden), 127
Modi, Narendra, 248, 251, 266, 348
Möller, Gustav, 122
Monnet, Jean, 17
monopolies
    Erhard and, 102, 106, 107, 110; Péron and, 143; Smith and, 27, 33, 34, 39
Monroe, James, 22
Montoneros, 149
Moore, Stephen, 321, 339

Morganthau, Henry, 91, 94
Mussolini, Benito, 140, 146, 156
Myrdal, Gunnar, 13, 118, 120, 123, 254, 336

Nakasone Yasuhiro, 302
Napoleon I, Emperor of the French, 9, 53
Napoleon III, Emperor of the French, 50, 55
Napoleonic Wars (1803–15), 40, 42, 48, 53
narrow money, 93
Nasser, Gamal Abdul, 254
national capitalism, 146
national debt
    Argentina, 151, 152, 153, 154; Brazil, 147; Germany, 104; Greece, 100, 202; Japan, 291, 300–301; Poland, 270, 274, 277, 285; South Korea, 175, 176; United Kingdom, 202; United States, 28–9, 31, 83, 89, 295
National Liberal Party (Germany), 56, 58, 100–101, 102, 335
National Recovery Administration (NRA), 86, 88, 90
National School (Germany), 59, 334
Navarro, Peter, 319, 340
Navigation Acts (1660–1849), 34
Nazi Party, 12, 97, 101, 102–6, 122, 291, 335
Nehru, Jawaharlal, 16, 247, 249, 250, 251, 253
neoliberalism, 7
    Erhard and, 99, 199–200; Lee and, 180, 188; Nordic model and, 118, 119, 130; Palme and, 130, 132; Thatcher and, 199, 201
Netherlands, 7, 192, 296
Nevis, 23
New Deal (1933–9), 3, 12, 79–98, 252, 335
New Economic Policy (1921–8), 11, 65–6, 73–8, 222, 224, 338, 342
New Monetary Theory, 317
New Nationalists, 83
New York Stock Exchange, 26
New Zealand, 3, 7, 199
Newly Industrialized Countries (NICs), 13–14
Nigeria, 8, 17
Nixon, Richard, 128, 177, 315, 325
Nkrumah, Kwame, 254

Nobel Prize, 118, 211, 297
Nordic model, 7, 117, 118–19, 345
North, Douglass, 21
North, Dudley, 39
North American Free Trade Agreement (NAFTA), 322
North German Confederation (1867–71), 56
North Korea, 159, 160, 161, 162–3
Norway, 7, 119, 187
Nove, Alec, 72, 75

Obama, Barack, 315, 316, 319, 323, 325, 329
Ohlendorf, Otto, 103
Ohlin, Bertil, 13, 118, 120, 123–4, 127, 336
oil shock (1973–4), 129, 175, 205, 214, 254, 260, 293
Olson, Mancur, 257
Oppenheim, Franz, 101
ordoliberalism, 12, 99, 107, 116, 213–14
Organisation for Economic Co-operation and Development (OECD), 18, 125, 157, 272, 293, 296, 300
Oxford University, 41, 246, 252, 261

Palme, Olof, 13, 117, 118, 128–30, 132
Panama Canal, 138
Park Chung-hee, 14, 159–78, 222, 235, 336–7, 342, 347
    agriculture policies, 174; assassination (1979), 176, 342; chaebol system, 170–74, 175, 177; communist links, 163–4, 167, 337; coup d'état (1961), 160, 165; debt crisis (1979), 176; Five Year Plans, 166, 168; guided capitalism, 166, 170; hypergrowth, 159–60, 173, 175, 177; KCIA and, 166, 168, 176; Marx, influence of, 161; Meiji, influence of, 161, 166, 168–70, 171, 337; SCNR, 166
Park Geun-hye, 178
Patel, Sardar, 250–51
Peacock, Alan, 202, 338
Peel, Robert, 3, 10, 37–50, 56–7, 334, 340–41
    Corn Laws repeal (1846), 3, 10, 37, 44, 49–50, 341; general election (1834), 43–4; general election (1841), 44, 48; Income Tax Act (1842), 45, 48; Metropolitan Police Act (1829),

42; Peterloo Massacre (1819), 41; Tamworth Manifesto (1834), 43

penny post, 46

People's Action Party (PAP), 179, 183, 184, 185, 188, 190, 196

People's Home, 122

Perceval, Spencer, 42

Perestroika (1985–91), 11, 66, 77, 78, 223, 272

Pérez Jiménez, Marcos, 149

Péron, Eva, 141, 142, 144–5, 147–8, 149, 150

Péron, Isabel, 149, 150

Péron, Juan, 3, 12–13, 18, 135–6, 139–58, 336, 344
  arrest (1945), 141; austerity, 148; corruption scandals, 148; coup d'état (1943), 141; coup d'état (1955), 149; death (1974), 150; economic nationalism, 143–5, 156; exile (1955–73), 149; fascism, influence of, 140, 142, 155–6, 157, 336; labour policies, 142; Latin American unity, views on, 145; Nazi Party, relations with, 142, 155; presidential election (1946), 141; Prebisch, influence of 143, 156; printing of money, 145; Rivas, relationship with, 148; social justice, views on, 13, 136, 140, 141–2, 157–8; Supreme Court, relations with, 145

Perry, John Curtis, 186, 190

Peru, 135

Peterloo Massacre (1819), 41, 42

Pettis, Michael, 292

Philippines, 347

physiocrats, 32, 33

Pinochet, Augusto, 18, 150, 199

Pitt, William, 41, 48

Plato, 38

pluto-populism, 314

Pol Pot, 65, 72

Poland, 15, 269–88, 338–9
  Big Bang (1990), 270, 276, 281, 283–4, 339, 343; emigration, 286; hyperinflation (1989–90), 15, 270, 272, 274–6, 278; IMF and, 270, 277, 285; national debt, 270, 274, 277, 285; People's Republic (1947–89), 271–2; privatization in, 274, 279, 285; shock therapy (1989), 116, 270, 273, 277–88; Sojusz Lewicy Demokratycznej (SLD), 284, 287; Solidarity, 15, 270, 271, 272,

273, 275–88, 343; Soviet War (1919–20), 70, 72; World War II (1939–45), 271

polluter pays principle, 5

Pompidou, Georges, 13

Ponzi schemes, 298, 316

populism, 135, 314, 347
  Hamilton and, 26, 27, 36; Irigoyen and, 138; Péronism, 12, 18, 135, 144, 148, 151, 153–6, 314; Roosevelt and, 91, 135; Thatcher and, 135, 200, 209, 213; Trump and, 135, 314–15

Portugal, 275

Powell, John Enoch, 201, 211

Prebisch, Raúl, 143, 146, 156, 246, 336

Preobrazhensky, Yevgeni, 76

Prescott, John, 49

presidential systems, 8, 138

printing of money, 145, 154, 274, 317

prisoner's dilemma, 257

privatization, 15
  in Argentina, 152, 157; in Chile, 150; in Germany, 105; in India, 262, 267; in Korea, 170; in Poland, 274, 279, 285; in Russia, 214; in Singapore, 195; in Sweden, 130; in United Kingdom, 15, 199, 200, 201, 207–9, 217

protectionism, 38–9, 60, 138
  Bismarck and, 11, 51–2, 58–60, 143; France and, 189; Great Depression (1929–39), 83; infant industry argument, 33–4, 52; Hamilton and, 10, 22, 25, 31–5, 143; Napoleon and, 9; Peel and, 44, 341; Péron and, 143; Trump and, 2, 10, 322–8

Prussian Kingdom (1701–1918), 10, 51–63

public services, 5, 8, 116, 120, 127, 131, 133

Quantitative Easing, 90, 301, 305, 306, 308, 331

Quesnay, François, 9, 32, 40

Radical Party (Argentina), 138, 151

Rae, John, 34

Raffles Institute, 182

Raffles, Stamford, 192

Rajan, Raghuram, 267

Rao, Pamulaparthi Venkata Narasimha, 247, 260, 265

Ravensbrück concentration camp, 106

Reagan, Ronald, 2, 15, 97, 200, 212, 214–17, 313, 315, 317, 338, 346
  Japan, relations with, 295; Laffer, influence of, 48, 215–16; NAFTA and, 322; tax cuts, 215–16; trade unions, relations with, 215
Reform Act (1832), 43, 46
Rehn–Meidner model, 126
Rehn, Lars Gösta, 126
rent seeking, 171, 283
Report on Manufactures (Hamilton), 31
Republican Party (US)
  Chicago School, influence of, 215; government intervention, views on, 80, 81; Hoover administration (1929–33), 80–81, 83, 86, 87, 90; Nixon administration (1969–74), 128, 177, 214, 325; Reagan administration (1981–9), *see under* Reagan, Ronald; Trump administration (2017–), *see under* Trump, Donald
Rhee Syngman, 164–5, 167, 171
Ricardo, David, 10, 45, 59, 161, 334
Rice, Condoleezza, 325
Richter, Eugen, 100, 335
Rieger, Wilhelm, 101, 335
Road to Serfdom (Hayek), 212, 338
Robespierre, Maximilien, 77
Robinson, James, 19
Robinson, Joan, 261, 339
Rogernomics, 2–3, 199
Romania, 101, 282
Roose, K.D., 93
Roosevelt, Eleanor, 81
Roosevelt, Franklin Delano, 3, 12, 79–98, 204, 315, 333, 335, 340, 343–4, 346
  banking reforms, 86–8, 91; deflation and, 89; Glass–Steagall Act (1933), 87–8; Gold Standard abandonment (1933), 89; Keynes and, 79–80, 82, 87, 90, 94–5, 96, 97, 335; National Recovery Administration (NRA), 86, 88, 90; presidential election (1932), 81; presidential election (1936), 91, 92; presidential election (1940), 96; Prohibition repeal (1933), 82; public works, 82, 86, 89, 90, 91, 94, 95, 104; recession (1937–8), 80, 92–6; 'soak the rich' taxation, 91–2; social insurance scheme, 91, 94; Supreme Court and, 91, 145; trade unions, policies on, 86, 91, 97; utilities regulation, 91

Roosevelt, Theodore, 36, 81, 83
Röpke, Wilhelm, 106, 335
Rosenstein-Rodan, Paul, 161, 174, 252
Ross, Wilbur, 319
Rostow, Walt, 161, 168, 337
rotten boroughs, 43
de la Rúa, Fernando, 153
Ruin, Olof, 126, 128
Russell, John, 49
Russian Empire (1721–1917), 162, 169
Russian Federation (1991–), 116, 270, 283, 347
Russian Revolution (1917), 68–9
Russian Soviet Republic (1917–91), 11, 65–78
  famine (1921–2), 73, 74, 75; Civil War (1917–23), 70–72; Hanging Order (1918), 71; New Economic Policy (1921–8), 11, 65–6, 73–8, 222, 224, 338, 342; Polish War (1919–20), 70, 72; Scissors Crisis (1923), 75–6, 342; Treaty of Brest-Litovsk (1918), 70; War Communism, 72, 73

Sachs, Alexander, 80
Sachs, Jeffrey, 15, 270, 277, 278, 279, 288, 338–9
Salazar, António de Oliveira, 146
Samsung, 173
Samuelson, Paul, 6, 193
Sanders, Bernard, 320
Satō Eisaku, 303
Scandinavian financial crisis (1990–94), 88, 290
Scandinavian model, 7, 117, 118–19, 345
Schachner, Nathan, 22
Schacht, Hjalmar, 104–6
Schmidt, Gerhard, 100
Schröder, Gerhard, 132
Schumacher, Kurt, 107, 112
Schumpeter, Joseph, 94, 107, 282
Schwartz, Anna, 85
Schwartz, Tony, 316
Scissors Crisis (1923), 75–6, 342
Seaga, Edward, 199
Sen, Amartya, 339
Shanghai, China, 240
Shanks, Michael, 202
Shastri, Lal Bahadur, 251
Shenzhen, Guangdong, 229, 240
Shiller, Robert, 297, 298
shock therapy, 15, 116, 270, 277

Singapore, 14, 19, 160, 179–98, 222, 228, 241, 337, 346, 347
  authoritarianism in, 190, 197, 347; British rule (1819–1963), 182, 183–5, 187, 192; Central Provident Fund (CPF), 194–5; child mortality in, 187; communism, 184, 188, 190, 192; Economic Development Board (EDB), 181, 192, 195; free trade in, 14, 180, 188–9; GDP growth, 186, 187–8, 191; GLCs, 195; government, role of, 14, 180, 188, 191, 193; Housing Development Board (HDB), 193–4; immigration in, 196, 198; Indonesia, relations with, 185, 192; Israel, relations with, 192; Japan, relations with, 193; Japanese occupation (1942–5), 182–3, 193; Malaya, federation with (1963–5), 184–5; miracle narrative, 185; multinational companies in, 186, 189, 192, 193, 195; social democracy in, 188, 190; Sovereign Wealth Fund, 194, 195; taxation in, 186, 189, 194; UNDP mission (1960), 191–2; welfare in, 196
Singh, Charan, 251
Singh, Manmohan, 15–16, 201, 246–67, 333, 339, 341–2
  corruption scandals, 16, 265; deregulation, 262; education policies, 264; growth, 263; Hahn test and, 201; identification scheme, 264; IMF loan (1980), 258; influences, 246, 252, 261, 339; national indirect tax, 265; Rural Employment Guarantee Scheme, 264; World Statesman Award (2010), 263
Skidelsky, Robert, 87, 90, 218
slavery, 10, 22, 23, 30
Slovakia, 282
Smiles, Samuel, 200
Smith, Adam, 5, 10, 17, 21, 32–3, 39, 59, 161, 321, 334, 340
  credit cycles and, 84; division of labour, 25, 38; Hamilton, influence on, 10, 22, 24, 25, 27, 32, 34; invisible hand, 25, 194; New Deal and, 88; Peel, influence on, 44, 334; Society for Establishing Useful Manufactures, 35; Trump administration, influence on, 34
Smith, Alfred 'Al', 82
Smoot–Hawley Tariff Act (1930), 83, 321

soak the rich taxation, 91–2
social democratic model, 13, 18, 117–33, 180, 188, 190
Social Democratic Party (Denmark), 132
Social Democratic Party (Germany), 60, 61, 62, 107, 109, 113, 116, 132
Social Democratic Party (Russia), 67
Social Democratic Party (Sweden), 117–33, 344
social justice, 13, 107, 117, 136
  in Argentina, 13, 136, 140, 141–2, 157–8; in Germany, 107, 112; in Singapore, 190; in Sweden, 117, 130
social market, 12, 99, 113, 116, 335
socialism, 13, 15
  Bismarck and, 11, 52, 60–62; Erhard and, 107; Erlander and, 123–4, 126; Lee and, 180, 183, 189; Nehru and, 16, 249, 251; Thatcher and, 201
Socialist Party (Argentina), 138
Socialist Revolutionary Party (Russia), 67, 70
Solidarity, 15, 270, 271, 272, 273, 275–88, 343
Soros, George, 277
South Africa, 8
South Korea, 14, 159–78, 197, 222, 235, 241, 242, 254, 292, 336–7, 342
  agriculture in, 174; chaebol system, 170–74, 175, 177; coup d'état (1961), 160, 165; debt crisis (1979–80), 176; Five Year Plans, 166, 168; guided capitalism, 166, 170; hypergrowth, 159–60, 173, 175, 177, 263, 337; Japan, relations with, 161, 162, 173; KCIA, 166, 168, 176; presidential election (1960), 164–5; Rhee presidency (1948–60), 164, 167, 171; SCNR, 166; United States, relations with, 161, 162, 177
South Sea Bubble (1720), 296
South Vietnam (1955–75), 167
Soviet Union (1922–91), 11, 65, 174
  China, relations with, 223, 226–7, 238; dissolution (1991), 242; Five Year Plans, 159, 249, 252; New Economic Policy (1922–8), 11, 65–6, 73–8, 222, 224, 338, 342; Perestroika/Glasnost (1985–91), 11, 66, 77, 78, 223, 272; Scissors Crisis (1923), 75–6, 342
Spain, 146, 149, 275, 336
Speer, Albert, 291

St Croix, 23
Stagnant Society (Shanks), 202
Stalin, Joseph, 7, 11, 65, 72, 77, 174, 194,
    271
    Five Year Plans, 159, 249; New
        Economic Policy (1922–8), 76, 224
Standard Oil, 148
State and Revolution, The (Lenin), 68
state capitalism, 4, 65, 74, 78, 171, 172,
    241, 319, 337, 345
Steuart, James, 34
Stewart, Michael, 95
Stiglitz, Joseph, 157, 307, 312
Stockholm School of Economics, 13, 118,
    119, 123, 336
Stoecker, Adolf, 63
Stolypin, Pyotr, 68
Stöpel, Friedrich, 58
Stroessner, Alfredo, 149
strong men' leaders, 8
Sukarno, 254
Summers, Larry, 307
supply side economics, 93, 206–11, 217,
    318, 339
Supreme Council for National
    Reconstruction (SCNR), 166
Sweden, 7, 13, 117–33
    communism in, 121, 122, 124,
        128, 130; education system, 125;
        employment in, 120, 122, 123, 124,
        129, 130; Galbraith, influence of,
        120; general election (1948), 123;
        general election (1968), 128; general
        election (1988), 130; housing market
        regulation, 125; immigration in,
        130–31; internment camps and, 122;
        Keynes, influence of, 120; Meidner
        Plan (1976), 129; 'new left' movement,
        127; Rehn–Meidner model, 126,
        129; welfare system, 124–7, 129, 131;
        World War II (1939–45), 122–3
Switzerland, 7
syndicalism, 142–3

Taiwan, 14, 160, 197, 232, 238, 242, 292
take-off theory, 168, 252–3
Tamworth Manifesto (1834), 43
Tata, 250
taxation, 5
    Abe and, 307, 311; Deng and, 224;
        Erlander and, 123, 124, 125, 126;
        Hamilton and, 25, 29; Park and,

167, 174; Peel and, 45, 48; Reagan
    and, 215; Roosevelt and, 91, 93, 94;
    Singapore and, 186, 189, 194; Singh
    and, 265; Thatcher and, 210–11;
    Trump and, 317, 329–30
Taylor, Alan John Percivale, 56, 62, 63
Taylor, Alan M., 144
Temasek, 194, 195
Temin, Peter, 85
Tennessee Valley Authority (TVA), 86
Thatcher, Margaret, 2, 15, 199–214,
    217–19, 338, 340, 343, 344, 346
    Big Bang (1986), 210; deregulation,
        206, 209–10, 214; EU, views on, 219;
        exchange rate mechanism and, 195,
        206; exchange controls abolition,
        205, 210, 213; Falklands War (1982),
        204, 213, 218; inflation and, 204,
        206, 212–13; monetarism, 204–6;
        nationalism, 200, 209, 219; populism,
        135, 200, 209, 213; privatization, 207–
        9, 214; right to buy policy, 208; social
        market and, 116; socialism, views
        on, 201, 212; supply side economics,
        206–11, 217; taxation, 210–11; trade
        unions, relations with, 204, 207,
        213; unemployment and, 202, 205,
        206; video market regulation, 210;
        Whitelaw, relationship with, 49
Thucydides Trap, 325
Thunberg, Greta, 132
TINA (There is No Alternative), 281
Tito, Josip Broz, 254
Tobin, James, 237
Tories, 37–46
Toynbee, Arnold, 185
trade unions, 9
    in Argentina, 141, 142, 147, 149, 150;
        in Germany, 109, 112; in Russia, 70; in
        Sweden, 126, 129, 131, 133; in United
        Kingdom, 204, 207, 213; in United
        States, 86, 91, 97, 215
Trans-Pacific Partnership (TPP), 308,
    323, 325
Transatlantic Trade and Investment
    Partnership (TTIP), 323
transfer problem, 83
Transparency International, 190
Treaty of Brest-Litovsk (1918), 70
Trotsky, Leon, 11, 76
Trujillo, Rafael, 149
Truman, Harry, 98, 315

Trump, Donald, 2, 10, 16–17, 34, 308, 313–32, 333, 339–40, 348
  Apprentice, The, 316; *Art of the Deal, The,* 316; business career, 315–16; China, relations with, 243, 318, 319, 323, 324–8; Covid-19 pandemic (2019–20), 243, 313, 318, 325, 326, 329, 330; growth strategy, 318, 329–31; Hamilton, influence of, 34, 36; immigration policies, 314, 316, 317, 319–20, 322; Laffer, influence of, 48; populism, 135, 314–15; printing money, views on, 317; Smith, influence of, 34; South Korea, relations with, 319; Supreme Court and, 145; tax cuts, 317, 329–30; trade policy, 318–28
Tully, Mark, 246, 261
Turkey, 8, 156, 314, 322, 347

United Kingdom
  Argentina, investment in, 137, 138, 140; Big Bang (1986), 210; Blair ministries (1997–2007), 49, 116, 132, 201; Brexit (2016–20), 50, 180, 286, 314; Callaghan ministry (1976–9), 202, 204; Chartist movement (1838–57), 47; Corn Laws (1804–46), 3, 10, 34, 37, 40–41, 44–50; declinist literature, 202; devaluation (1967), 202; exchange rate mechanism and, 195, 206; Falklands War (1982), 150, 204, 213, 218; general election (1834), 43–4; general election (1841), 44, 48; Gold Standard abandonment (1931), 89; Great Reform Act (1832), 43, 46; Heath ministry (1970–74), 207, 217; IMF loan (1976), 202, 205; Income Tax Act (1842), 45, 48; Indian colonies (1612–1947), 38–9, 248; Irish famine (1845–9), 49; Malaya colony (1826–1957), 183, 184–5; Metropolitan Police Act (1829), 42; Napoleonic Wars (1803–15), 40, 42, 48, 53; Navigation Acts (1660–1849), 34; North Sea oil, 205; Peel ministry (1841–6), 3, 10, 37, 44–50, 334, 340–41; Peterloo Massacre (1819), 41, 42; recession (1973–5), 202; Singapore colony (1819–1963), 182, 183–5, 187, 192; slavery in, 41; South Sea Bubble (1720), 296; Thatcher ministries (1979–90), *see under* Thatcher,

Margaret; Vickers Report (2011), 88; Wilson ministry, first (1964–70), 187, 203; Winter of Discontent (1978–9), 202, 207
United Nations, 118, 123, 143, 191, 227, 228, 246, 331
United States
  Boston Tea Party (1773), 24; Bretton Woods Conference (1944), 7, 97, 331; Bush administration (2001–9), 325; Carter administration (1977–81), 214–15; China, relations with, 232, 243, 318, 319, 323, 324–8; Civil War (1861–5), 23, 35; Clinton administration (1993–2001), 7–8, 88, 303, 315, 318, 325, 334; Constitution (1787), 22, 26; Covid-19 pandemic (2019–20), 2, 243, 313, 325, 326, 329, 330; Federal Reserve, 7, 30, 85, 93, 200, 215, 216, 305, 330–31; Federalist Papers (1787–8), 26–7; financial crisis (1791–2), 35; financial crisis (2007–8), 7, 316; First Bank established (1791), 30; Ford administration (1974–7), 214; Glass–Steagall Act (1933), 87–8; Gold Standard abandonment (1933), 89; Great Depression (1929–39), 79–96, 335; Hamiltonian economics, 3, 9–10, 21–36, 50, 320, 341; Hoover administration (1929–33), 80–81, 83, 86, 87, 90; Kennedy administration (1961–3), 14, 161, 167, 168, 315, 337; Korean War (1950–53), 162; Ku Klux Klan, 97; Marshall Plan (1948–51), 111; national debt, 28–9, 31; National Recovery Administration (NRA), 86, 88, 90; New Deal (1933–9), 3, 12, 79–98, 252, 335; Nixon administration (1969–74), 128, 177, 214, 325; Obama administration (2009–17), 316, 319, 323, 325, 329; presidential election (1788–9), 27, 34; presidential election (1932), 81; presidential election (1936), 91, 92; presidential election (1940), 96; presidential system, 8; Prohibition (1920–33), 82; Reagan administration (1981–9), *see under* Reagan, Ronald; recession (1937–8), 80, 92–6; Roosevelt administration (1933–45), *see under* Roosevelt, Franklin; slavery in, 10, 22, 23, 30, 39; Smoot–Hawley Tariff Act (1930), 83, 321; South

Korea, relations with, 161, 167, 177, 319; Supreme Court, 91, 145; Tennessee Valley Authority (TVA), 86, 89; Truman administration (1945–53), 98; Trump administration (2017–), *see under* Trump, Donald; Vietnam War (1955–75), 127, 128, 167; Wall Street Crash (1929), 80, 82, 84, 296; War of Independence (1775–83), 22, 24–5
United Progressive Alliance (UPA), 263, 264, 265

Vargas, Getúlio, 18, 146–7, 157
Värmland, Sweden, 119
Venezuela, 18, 19, 135, 148, 149, 154, 157, 314
Vernon, Ray, 193
Vershofen Institute, 102
Vershofen, Wilhelm, 101–2, 103
Vickers Report (2011), 88
Vietnam, 78
    American War (1955–75), 127, 128, 167; Chinese War (1979), 231, 235
Visvesvaraya, Mokshagundam, 249
Vogel, Ezra, 223
Volcker, Paul, 215
VSNKh, 72

Wałęsa, Lech, 281, 286
Wall Street Crash (1929), 80, 82, 84, 296
Walters, Alan, 206
Washington Consensus, 148, 152, 153, 154, 157, 199, 218, 236, 258
Washington, George, 21, 22, 24, 26, 27, 31, 34
welfare systems
    Bismarck and, 11, 52, 60, 61–2, 114; Branting and, 121; Erhard, 114–15; Erlander, 124–7; Lee and, 196; Palme and, 129; Péron and, 144; Roosevelt and, 91
Wellington, Arthur Wellesley, 1st Duke, 43, 48–9
What is to be Done? (Lenin), 67
Whigs, 41, 43, 44, 47, 48, 49
White, Harry Dexter, 97
Whitelaw, William, 49
Why Nations Fail (Acemoglu and Robinson), 19

Wicksell, Knut, 118
Wigforss, Ernst, 123
Wilhelm I, German Emperor, 55
Wilhelm II, German Emperor, 62
Wilson, Harold, 187, 203
Wilson, Woodrow, 81, 86
Winsemius, Albert, 181, 191, 337
Winter of Discontent (1978–9), 202
Wirtschaftsrat, 63
Wirtschaftswunder, 3, 100, 114, 291
Witte, Sergei, 68
Wolf, Martin, 306–7, 311, 314
Woodward, Robert 'Bob', 317, 319, 321
World Bank, 16, 97, 191, 222, 331
    Argentina and, 149, 152; China and, 235, 237, 243; India and, 247, 252, 257–8, 339; Poland and, 285; South Korea and, 175; Washington Consensus, 218
World Economic Forum, 190
World Happiness Index, 119
World Health Organization (WHO), 331
World Statesman Award, 263
World Trade Organization (WTO), 7, 98, 243, 318, 319, 322, 324, 326, 327, 331
World War I (1914–18), 62, 68, 69, 83, 100, 101, 138
World War II (1939–45), 12, 96, 103, 106, 122–3, 271

Xi Jinping, 242–3, 323, 347, 348

Yakovlev, Alexander, 77
year of revolutions (1848), 54, 55, 60, 61
Yellow Book (Keynes), 120
Yeltsin, Boris, 270, 283
Young Turks, 161
Yugoslavia (1945–92), 229, 242

zaibatsu model, 170, 292
Zhao Ziyang, 234, 236, 238, 239
Zhou Enlai, 223–4, 227, 228
Zhu Rongji, 240
Zhuhai, Guangdong, 240
Zimbabwe, 18, 19
Zollverein (1834–1919), 10–11, 51, 54–5, 56, 59
ZTE, 328